CREATIVE STRATEGY IN DIRECT MARKETING

Susan K. Jones

NTC Business Books
a division of *NTC Publishing Group* • Lincolnwood, Illinois USA

5-12-93

Library of Congress Cataloging-in-Publication Data

Jones, Susan K.
   Creative strategy in direct marketing / Susan K. Jones
      p.   cm.
   Includes bibliographical references and index.
   ISBN 0-8442-3179-7
   1. Direct marketing.   I. Title.
HF5415.126.J66   1990
658.8'4—dc20   90-41587

Published by NTC Business Books, a division of NTC Publishing Group,
4255 West Touhy Avenue,
Lincolnwood (Chicago), Illinois 60646-1975 U.S.A.
© 1991 by NTC Publishing Group. All rights reserved.
No part of this book may be reproduced, stored in a retrieval system,
or transmitted in any form or by any means,
electronic, mechanical, photocopying, recording or otherwise,
without the prior permission of NTC Publishing Group.
Manufactured in the United States of America.

1 2 3 4 5 6 7 8 9 AG 9 8 7 6 5 4 3 2 1

For Billy, Shannon and Scott

CONTENTS

FOREWORD

Reflecting upon a direct marketing career that spans 50 glorious years, I have come to one conclusion—I am the luckiest person I know.

Few have had the privilege of sitting at the knees of a Bob Collier, a John Caples. I have. Few have had the privilege of dialogues with creative superstars like Bill Jayme, Hank Burnett, Tom Collins, Joan Throckmorton, Max Sackheim, and Bill Gregory. I have.

And now I would like to add Susan K. Jones to this elite group. For not only is she an outstanding creative person in her own right, but she possesses the rarest of talents: she has the innate ability to teach creativity to others.

My feelings about Susan are much deeper than surface observations: my feelings are based upon firsthand experience. At Northwestern University, where I teach the fundamentals of direct marketing to degree students, Susan follows with a course in creativity. The feedback I get is consistent. The joys of discovery. Excitement. Enthusiasm. The will to be creative. A transformation. And now this book which I have read in its entirety, for all who would be creative.

With the luxury of looking back on the history of great direct marketing creatives, I have asked myself the question, "What is it that all great creative people have in common?" And I have no doubt whatever as to what the common thread is: *great creative people are astute students of human behavior.*

Great creatives ask probing questions of themselves. Why will more people say *Yes* if you give them the opportunity to say *Yes* or *No*? Why will more people respond favorably if you give them the opportunity to win in a sweepstakes? Why will more people respond affirmatively if you give them an opportunity to become involved, using stamps, or tokens as the device? Great creatives know why. They understand human behavior.

In this book Susan Jones wisely spells out all the techniques that are the tools at the disposal of the creative person. Knowing the tools is essential. But my caveat is: knowing the tools—the gimmicks—is tactical. Nothing more. Creativity is far more: it's *strategic*.

The professional creative person, understanding human behavior, knows how, when, and where to use gimmicks. Indeed, when to use no gimmicks at all. The pro creates nothing until the process of research is completed. Research involving the product, or service. Research into the types of people most likely to respond. Their lifestyles. Hopes. Dreams. Motivations. Then, and only then, do the professionals create a strategic creative plan.

If you would read but one passage from this great book, I would recommend Susan K. Jones' "Ten Steps to Personal Creativity." And I would underscore Step 9, "Let your work rest before evaluation." Every great creative person I have ever known has had the wisdom to put his or her work through an incubation period. My admonition is, go forth and do likewise.

So, if you are truly serious about your creative goals, don't short-change yourself. Read not only passages, but the entire book, cover-to-cover more than once. It will change your creative work. Forever. I guarantee it!

Bob Stone
Chairman Emeritus, Stone & Adler
President, World Book Direct Marketing
Professor, Northwestern University

PREFACE

I was thrilled to be asked to write the Preface for Susan K. Jones' new book on the development and application of creative strategy to direct response marketing. For as long as I've been in the direct marketing business, Susan Jones has been successfully applying the principles she outlines in this book. She has helped refine The Hamilton Collection's product positioning strategies, written scores of our direct mail packages, space ads, and collateral pieces, and served as a key player in many of our marketing success stories.

Now the good news for you is that Susan has beautifully organized and thoroughly presented her special insights and practical experiences in this book.

Creative Strategy in Direct Marketing is for writers, managers and directors, public relations specialists, product development strategists, and advertising managers. Comprehensive in scope, Susan's treatise offers equally comprehensive vertical coverage on each subject. From the definition of marketing issues and how to address them from a creative and promotional perspective, through methods for formal and informal research to refine the creative message to the initialization and management of "intangible" aspects of the creative process, Susan prescribes the formulas you need to make creative strategy work for consistent, superior results.

This book is fresh, practical and eye-opening for anyone who is already in the direct marketing industry, and for those who are just now planning a direct marketing career or business venture.

Without question, there is always lots of room for all of us to learn as we consolidate lessons of the past, and apply them to new opportunities in this fast-changing business and consumer environment. This is one of the books you will find on my shelf of direct marketing "bibles."

I'm looking forward to distributing copies of *Creative Strategy in Direct Marketing* to my creative, marketing, and product groups as "must" reading and I think you will see why in the pages that follow. This is your chance to gain access to the inner workings of one of the wonderful creative and marketing minds of our business. Needless to say, I think you've chosen your reading material well.

James P. Smith, Jr.
Chairman, The Hamilton Group

LAYING THE GROUNDWORK

I

A PROFITABLE BLEND OF ART AND SCIENCE

1

Direct marketers enjoy the best of both worlds: the freedom to express creativity balanced by the discipline of measured response . . . the excitement of striving for breakthrough ideas and the satisfaction of proving those ideas' worth in absolute dollar terms.

To become a good direct marketer, it is essential to fuel and tend one's creative fires: to move beyond the predictable formula and format toward fresh words and pictures that incite prospects to action. Yet even direct marketers who call themselves "creatives"—copywriters and art directors—need to become firmly grounded in the scientific side of the business.

Ever since Claude Hopkins coined the term *Scientific Advertising* in his 1923 book by that name, direct marketers have striven to reach a profitable balance between creativity and technique. This chapter offers a historical review showing how direct marketing blends art (the spark of creativity and talent) with science (research, market testing, segmentation, and measurable results). But first: a brief discussion of direct marketing and database management.

What is direct marketing?

Henry R. "Pete" Hoke, Jr., publisher of *Direct Marketing* magazine, defines direct marketing as

> An interactive system of marketing that uses one or more advertising media to effect a measurable response and/or transaction at any location.

This definition touches on several important points.

1. Direct marketing is a *system of marketing*. That means that it hinges on the marketing concept: creating and promoting products that fill specific consumer and business needs.
2. Direct marketing is *interactive*. It attempts to set up a cause-and-effect relationship with the prospect, asking for a certain response to a call to action.
3. Direct marketing uses *one or more advertising media*. In previous generations, direct marketers delivered most of their messages via space advertising, direct mail and catalogs. Today, additional media such as telephone, television, radio, and even home computers may serve as a direct marketer's conduit to customers.
4. Direct marketing produces a *measurable response*. To achieve this, the direct marketing message includes a response device such as a coupon, toll-free telephone number, FAX number, order form, or address. The direct marketer's call to action is met with an exact number of sales or leads which then can be measured against objectives.
5. Direct marketing may involve a *transaction at any location*. Thus direct marketers may receive their responses when customers bring mail-sent coupons to a retail outlet, show up for an advertised sale, or contact a local dealer mentioned in a national ad campaign.

These points put forth the academic theory behind direct marketing. An exploration of the database concept helps explain the dynamic force that makes direct marketing a very effective form of one-to-one salesmanship.

The importance of the database

All direct marketing involves the use or creation of a database, or list. Some direct marketing media, such as direct mail and outbound telephone marketing, require a database of customers and/or prospects to receive mail or phone calls. Other media, such as magazines, newspapers, radio, and television, rely upon prospects to identify themselves when they see ads that appeal to them. Once these prospects have "raised their hands" by inquiring or making a purchase, their names, addresses and other vital information are added to the database.

Ashleigh Groce, Vice President of Leo Burnett USA Advertising, defines database marketing as

> An automated system to be used to identify people—both customers and prospects—by name, and to use quantifiable information about these people to define the best possible purchasers and prospects for a given offer at a given point in time.

Delete the word "automated" from this definition, and such a system could apply to some of the oldest marketing concepts in the world: what went on at the corner grocer, the old-fashioned hardware store or even the general store of America's pioneer days.

Herein lies a fascinating paradox for direct marketers: the more sophisticated our futuristic database technology becomes, the more it allows us to treat customers just as individually as the corner merchant did generations ago.

The corner merchant's selling method

Once upon a time, the local grocer knew the name of every member of his customers' families. He could even tell you their birthdays: after all, he helped Mother pick out the makings for each birthday cake! The butcher could tell you which families ate pork chops every Wednesday—and he'd put the choice chops aside for them. The neighborhood druggist sympathized with folks who had asthma attacks, and he could tell you just by the way the wind was blowing when Mr. Smith would be in for his hay fever medicine.

Let's say you are a 10-year-old who has been sent to the grocer's for a quart of milk. If Mr. Jones, the proprietor, has just received the spring's first shipment of strawberries, he'll be likely to give you a sample and send a few berries home with you along with a note to your Mom saying "berries are in."

And say Mr. Jones knows it's your parents' anniversary tomorrow. Since your family has shopped with him for years, he'll probably provide an extra-fancy gift box of cookies with his best wishes for the happy couple.

Back then, Jones the grocer made it his business to know your likes and dislikes—what you could afford to buy, the types of things you splurged on, and places where you economized. He found ways to say "thank you," and "I value your business."

But eventually, Jones' family grocery store faced a formidable competitor: a shiny new supermarket with greater selection and lower prices. Many families stayed with their friend Mr. Jones until the bitter end, but eventually they watched him go out of business, a victim of the supermarket's volume buying power.

There are still a number of retailers who pride themselves on the personal touch. But today's largest firms—the K-Marts and Wal-Marts of the world—are more likely to offer unmanned self-service aisles than the personal attention style of yesteryear.

How database marketing helps direct marketers sell one-to-one

More than ever in today's world, consumers wish to assert their individual identities. There's not much satisfaction—other than saving money—in being another one of the nameless, faceless customers at K-Mart. It's even more disheartening to pay large mark-ups in major department stores and still find yourself being waited on by transient clerks who don't know their merchandise—or you.

That's where direct marketing comes in. It provides that personal, "I know you" feeling we used to get at the corner store. And it fits in with today's busy lifestyles, since few people have time to chat with a storekeeper anyway.

Direct marketing allows firms to talk one-on-one with customers, keying in to all known factors about them: age, income range, family size, interests, hobbies, travel preferences, and much more. Yet these communications are going on thousands or even millions at a time—making this form of personalized selling very cost effective.

Characteristics of direct marketing

Direct marketing is more than just general advertising with coupons and toll-free telephone numbers thrown in. The essential character of direct marketing lies in its *action orientation*. Direct marketers *sell*—they don't just put the product before the public. As Tom Brady of Kobs & Draft Advertising explained in Jim Kobs' book, *Profitable Direct Marketing,*

> Basically, the general advertiser attempts to build brand or name awareness—*image*, if you will—so that when a customer is ready to buy, he or she will be favorably inclined toward the advertiser's product. Thus, the general advertiser may have to wait months or even years before the full effects of today's ad dollars are realized.
>
> The direct response advertiser, on the other hand, wants to sell his product *right now*! And he uses all the salesmanship techniques at his command to persuade the reader to act immediately.

In addition to action orientation, direct marketing has several other important characteristics.

Direct marketing is targeted

Successful direct marketers develop products and services that will appeal to specific groups of consumers—groups that are *measurable, reachable* and *sizeable* enough to ensure meaningful sales volume. Direct marketers' ability to tailor a list of prospect names combining several characteristics—for instance, proven mail order buyers who own VCR machines and take at least two ski vacations a year—allows them to carve out new market segments with profit potential.

Direct marketing is personal

Because direct marketers can find out so much about their customers and prospects, they are able to address these people in very specific terms—as ski enthusiasts, old movie buffs, or what-

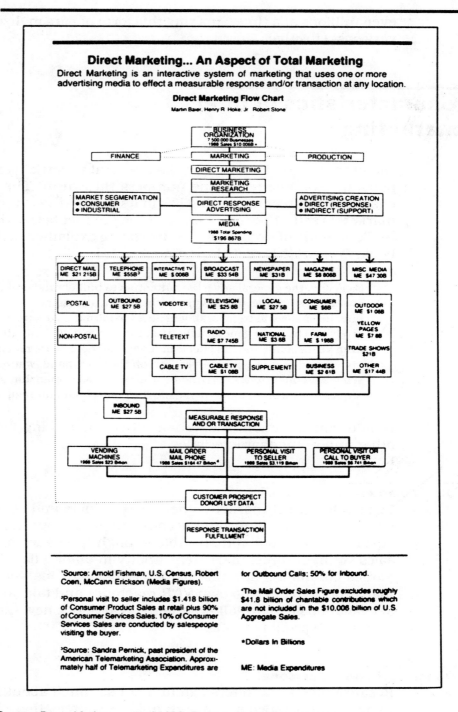

Direct Marketing... An Aspect of Total Marketing

Direct Marketing is an interactive system of marketing that uses one or more advertising media to effect a measurable response and/or transaction at any location.

Direct Marketing Flow Chart

Martin Baier, Henry R Hoke Jr   Robert Stone

Source: *Direct Marketing*, April 1990. Reprinted with permission.

ever. What's more, today's computer and printing applications make possible a broad range of personalization techniques.

Direct marketing is measurable

Because each direct marketing message carries a call to action, the advertiser is able to measure the effectiveness of mailings, calls and ads by tracking the sales, leads or other responses received. This makes direct marketers *accountable* for every dollar they spend.

Direct marketing is testable

Because direct marketers can generate firm numbers that measure the effectiveness of their efforts, it is possible for them to devise accurate head-to-head tests of offers, formats, price, payment terms, creative approach, and much more—all in relatively small and affordable quantities.

Direct marketing is flexible

This is especially true in direct mail, where there are few constraints on size, color, timing and format. Other than conformance to U.S. Postal standards, a direct mail marketer can sell with formats ranging from a post card to a 9″ × 12″ envelope to a three-dimensional package. The mailing date is set by the marketer—not by a publication.

Direct marketing: A brief history

Social changes and technological advances have fueled major development and growth of direct marketing since the late 19th century. Yet even 500 years ago, publishers in Europe used catalogs to attract customers for the new wealth of books available after Johann Gutenberg invented moveable type around 1450. And nurserymen let gardeners know of their wares with seed and plant catalogs issued regularly in England by the late 1700s.

Meanwhile in the American colonies, Benjamin Franklin formed what might be called the first continuity-style book club. Each member paid an entrance fee and dues for the privilege of reading books they selected by catalog. Franklin also published his own bookselling catalog in 1744, boasting nearly 600 titles. In it he pioneered the basic idea of "satisfaction guaranteed or your money back."

During this same period, another major influence of direct marketers came into play: the peddler who sold soaps and patent medicines by means of demonstration, traveling door to door or gathering crowds in village squares. Direct marketing masters from Claude Hopkins to Alvin Eicoff have attributed much of their success to techniques learned from these eloquent stand-up salesmen.

Ward and Sears herald modern direct marketing

Although such enduring American direct marketing firms as Orvis, L. L. Bean and Tiffany were already well established with catalogs in the early 1800s, the innovations of Montgomery Ward and Sears, Roebuck & Co. are generally considered the beginnings of modern direct marketing in the United States.

As a peddler traveling across the Midwest, Aaron Montgomery Ward developed a unique business strategy idea. It hinged upon the slogan of the powerful farmer's group called the Grange: "Eliminate the Middleman." Ward would sell directly to the consumer and save his customers the money they perceived as going to undeserving intermediaries. Ward started his direct mail business in America's transportation center, Chicago, in 1872. By 1884 his catalog grew to 240 pages.

Many of Ward's brilliant innovations still are used today to good effect by direct marketers. He guaranteed all products unconditionally, and showed pictures of his employees throughout the catalog to prove that this was indeed a person-to-person operation. His folksy customer service letters matched the tone of friendship in those he received from his isolated rural customers.

Richard Warren Sears first learned the power of direct selling when he peddled a package of watches to his fellow railroad agents in Minnesota. Ads in newspapers followed, and by 1887, young Sears was ready to team with Alvah Curtis Roebuck, a watchmaker and printer.

Like Ward, Richard Sears and his partner offered money-back guarantees on all products. Hard work and a natural instinct for direct marketing helped Sears, Roebuck & Company grow to an annual mailing volume of 75,000,000 pieces by 1927.

Besides the family Bible, Wards and Sears catalogs were often the only books in the house for America's turn-of-the-century rural families. Some social historians argue that the electric refrigerators and other appliances offered in these wish books provided the concrete evidence farmers needed to understand and support the drive for rural electrification.

Business for both Ward and Sears grew even more once the U.S. Postal Service began Rural Free Delivery in the 1890s and Parcel Post in 1913, making shipping to even remote areas a simple and timely proposition.

Salesmanship in print

The next generation of advertisers built upon the principles established by Montgomery Ward and Sears, Roebuck & Co. to expand the applications of direct marketing in space advertising and direct mail.

Albert Lasker, a fledgling newspaper man who fell in love with advertising and never returned to journalism, learned two key direct marketing ideas from his enigmatic mentor, John E. Kennedy. In his reminiscenses, first published years ago in *Advertising Age,* Lasker recalled how Kennedy's definition of advertising changed his life and the course of his career.

In those turn-of-the-century days, the main function of an advertising agency was to act as a space ad placement broker for clients. To make their services more attractive, some of these advertising agents offered to create the advertising for their clients. In most cases, their main objective was simply to keep the client's name before the public.

But Kennedy told Lasker that advertising should be much more than that. Effective advertising was *salesmanship in print.* He went on to explain that the key to this salesmanship was "reasons why" copy—writing that convinced the reader that the product was worthy because of its *features* and *benefits.*

Other advertising men of Lasker's and Claude Hopkins' generation were discovering and amplifying the same principles in agencies and companies throughout the East and Midwest. Notable among these were Harry Schermann and Maxwell Sackheim, who launched their "Little Leather Library" in 1916.

Unimpressed by the volume of sales they could obtain through retail outlets, the two men began offering their books by mail. At that time, there were few bookstores outside major cities. Availability of the Library by mail enabled thousands of striving Americans—many of them immigrants—to obtain the books they desired for themselves and their children. The Library's success led Schermann and Sackheim to develop the Book-of-the-Month Club in 1926, paving the way for today's plethora of continuity programs selling books, records, collectibles and food on by-the-month plans.

The Direct Mail Advertising Association (now the Direct Marketing Association) was founded in 1917, and the U.S. Postal Service inaugurated third class bulk mail in 1928. In those days, the first major business-to-business direct marketers emerged, seeking qualified leads for their sales forces. Principal among these were National Cash Register Co. and Burroughs Adding Machine Co.

After World War II, the parents of the "baby boom" generation sought all manner of goods, but often found them in short supply in neighborhood stores. New catalog and direct marketing firms filled the void, including Miles Kimball, Hanover House and Fingerhut. The 1950s saw the growth of Time-Life, perhaps the first firm to fully understand the potential of a database, recording demographic and psychographic information about customers.

The growth of direct marketing: Social and technological change

The 1960s was a decade of profound social change in the United States, as well as a time of many technological advances that spurred the growth of direct marketing. It was during this time period that most of the forces that drive the direct marketing boom first emerged.

Advances in computer technology

Recording and manipulating a database became feasible when fast and affordable computers penetrated the American business market. The new technology also has allowed for useful innovations in printing and production such as laser and ink-jet personalization techniques and computerized typesetting. Even more recent are the efforts of several firms to offer products and services to consumers via personal computer/telephone modem hook-up, right in the home.

Targeted media opportunities

Just as the Sears general catalog has given way to myriad smaller and more specialized books, the old mass magazines such as *Life* and *Look* have been supplanted by books that define their audiences: *Working Mother, New Age,* and *Tennis,* just to name a few among hundreds of targeted titles. And the three old-line television networks, with their "all things to all people" programming, lose ground year by year to specialized outlets like Cable News Network, ESPN (all sports), and a wide range of home shopping channels. At the same time, marketers have learned to use radio stations geared toward news, talk, classical music and other defined audiences for direct response offers.

Growth of consumer credit

Diners Club, American Express, MasterCard, Visa, Discover and other widely distributed credit cards offer consumers the opportunity to make impulse buying decisions, a boon for direct marketers. Consumer credit works hand-in-hand with telemarketing to streamline the buying process: customers can call a toll-free telephone number, provide their card numbers, and order products from the comfort of home. Credit cards also increase the opportunity for trust on both sides of the buying transaction. The marketer is protected against much of the risk of bad credit, and the buyer can call on the credit card firm to help if there is a customer service problem.

Decline in personal service

Americans believe that they got better service from retailers in the "good old days." They remember when career salespeople who knew their merchandise well would provide individual service, calling customers by name and showing them deference and respect. Contrast this with today's gum-popping retail sales clerk, paid a minimum wage and no commission. Add the time-wasting prospect of standing in line only to find that the desired item is out of stock, and it is no wonder that consumers are ripe for the convenience of shopping at home.

Changing lifestyles

The classic American family, with Dad employed outside the home and Mom staying at home with two or more children, now accounts for less than one-fourth of American family units. There are more single-parent families and dual-career families than ever before. In fact, women now account for more than half of the work force.

With these changes has come an important alteration in family buying patterns. Today's working woman often has more money than time to invest in shopping. Thus she prefers to complete her buying transactions as quickly and painlessly as possible. Direct marketers offer ways to do this: catalog shopping at any hour of day or night, toll-free, 24-hour phone lines for ordering, home or office delivery, liberal guarantees, free-trial privileges, and much more.

In addition, the higher incomes of dual-career families allow them to indulge in hobbies and leisure activities. Special-interest groups like white-water rafters, figurine collectors, movie buffs and many more offer direct marketers a fertile field for development of targeted product lines.

Higher education allows for a longer story

Although illiteracy is a major problem in America today, the up-scale target prospects of most direct marketers are better educated than ever before. Thus they are ready and able to read the long, meaty, "reasons why" copy that helps direct marketers sell thoroughly and effectively in print media.

Prospects for creative people in direct marketing

With all of these factors in its favor, direct marketing has shown phenomenal growth over the past three decades. What's more, Fortune 500 companies and their advertising agencies have come to understand the wisdom of integrating direct response techniques into a great percentage of their marketing plans.

This growth gives rise to a continuing need for more and better direct marketing copywriters and art directors. Experienced direct marketing creative people with successful track records often command six-figure salaries and lucrative free-lance opportunities. But they reach that exalted level only through years of study and practice—usually beginning at subsistence-level salaries.

Time was, direct marketers learned strictly through a mentor system. Their craft was handed down from generation to generation. Albert Lasker, for example, staffed about a dozen cubicles at Lord and Thomas with fledgling writers whom he schooled in the concepts of "salesmanship in print" and "reasons why" copy. When these men left Lord and Thomas, many of them went on to head some of the most successful advertising agencies of the 20th century.

Today, direct marketing has become an academic subject, with at least one course of study available at many colleges and universities across the United States. There are centers for direct marketing at the University of Missouri–Kansas City, Chicago's DePaul University, and New York University. Northwestern University offers a Master of Science degree with a number of available elective courses in direct marketing. The Direct Marketing Association and a number of regional direct marketing clubs host frequent how-to seminars staffed by seasoned practitioners.

This book will provide the key information a direct marketing creative person needs to understand: how to unlock direct marketing creativity, and discipline it to develop selling propositions that maximize profit potential. This material will help copywriters and art directors approach their jobs well grounded in the hard-won knowledge of their predecessors. What's more, it will enable those who supervise and manage creative people to draw out the best possible work from their writers, artists and production staff.

THE DISCIPLINE OF DIRECT MARKETING CREATIVITY

2

Creativity in direct marketing requires four major ingredients: knowledge of proven direct marketing techniques, specific research, the patience to work through a time-consuming process of discovery, and the courage to put your ideas to the test. This formula may come as a surprise to those who think of creativity as a God-given talent rather than a hard-won accomplishment. But successful direct marketing creative strategy relies as much upon proven techniques as it does upon a unique approach to a given situation. And thus most any reader of this book can become a good direct marketing creative strategist—not just those born with a talent for language or art.

This chapter will discuss the disciplined form of creativity that successful direct marketers must develop. It will explain how historical perspective can save creative people from reinventing the wheel by considering the many "dos and don'ts" established at great cost by direct marketers of the past. It will explore ways in which direct marketers can prime themselves to become more creative. Then it will offer several proven, step-by-step methods of idea generation and applied creativity. By these means anyone can increase his or her potential for creativity in direct marketing.

Study the techniques of the masters

Historians often comment that those who do not learn from the mistakes of the past are destined to repeat them. As direct-marketing creative people, we can gain as much by studying the successes of our predecessors as we can from their failures. Indeed, their successes are much more likely to be discussed in detail in their "how-to" volumes for direct marketers!

Books like Claude C. Hopkins' *My Life in Advertising,* David Ogilvy's *Confessions of an Advertising Man* and *Ogilvy on Advertising,* Richard V. Benson's *Secrets of Successful Direct Mail* and Gordon White's *John Caples: Adman* offer narratives that are richly laced with information creative people should keep at their fingertips. Other top direct marketers have presented their knowledge in textbook form, enabling fledgling writers and art directors to learn from the experience of Bob Stone, Richard Hodgson, Jim Kobs, Ed Nash, Joan Throckmorton and scores more.

Those who aspire to new heights of direct marketing creativity should first climb onto the shoulders of the great practitioners of the past and present. At $20 to $100 per volume, these books are the greatest bargains a direct marketer ever will find. One "big idea" from each book you read could make or save your firm millions of dollars. Learn all that books can teach before you begin investing your company's money in mail, space, telephone and TV. Trade publications, classes, conventions and seminars can also be very beneficial for direct marketing creative people seeking to increase their knowledge base.

Examples of proven direct marketing formulas and checklists

In past generations, direct marketers learned their craft by doing. Drawing upon their knowledge of human nature and the techniques of successful one-on-one salespeople, they created and tested direct mail packages and space ads. In this way, they built upon their successes and eliminated their failures. And after some years in the business, they developed formulas and checklists—

both as benchmarks for themselves and to use in training new writers and art directors.

To make these formulas and checklists a part of your professional bag of tricks, read them over and then gather some samples of direct response space ads and direct mail packages. Try to apply one or more of the formulas to each ad or package. Determine for yourself where they measure up and where they are lacking. Sometimes an ad or package will not fit any formula, yet still be exceptionally fresh and effective. Take a crack at analyzing why these renegade ads and packages work, and you may be on your way to developing some new "dos and don'ts" of your own.

Once you have practiced applying the formulas and checklists on other peoples' work, try using them to develop and critique your own ads and packages. Eventually, the principles expressed in these lists will become second nature to a seasoned direct marketing creative person. But a refresher course from time to time will help to keep your work on target.

Famous direct marketing formulas

Perhaps the best-known of the direct marketing formulas is **A-I-D-A.** It describes the consumer adoption process:

A = Awareness/attention
I = Interest
D = Desire
A = Action

These are the stages a good ad or selling letter will move the consumer through, leading to a positive purchase decision. It is important to remember that the process can end at any point if the marketer's pitch fails to move the consumer along. For direct marketers, the result of this failure is all too poignant: packages that fail to generate awareness or attention land immediately in the wastebasket.

Henry Hoke, Sr. is credited with another oft-quoted formula which centers on the same process of moving the consumer toward the sale. His "Four Ps" are:

Picture
Promise
Prove
Push

Hoke suggests beginning with a sizzling word picture, followed by a promise, or success story. Then these claims are backed up by proof in the form of testimonials, endorsements, and feature/benefit copy. Finally, the "push" comes with the call to action.

Another description of the consumer adoption process comes from Frank Dignan. He called it:

Star-Chain-Hook

Dignan suggested "hitching your wagon to a star" with an attention-getting opening, then coming back down to earth with a chain of convincing facts assembled link by link. Finally, the hook is the call to action, moving the consumer toward a buying decision.

While these three formulas are somewhat theoretical, both Bob Stone and Joan Throckmorton offer more specific step-by-step lists. Stone's appears in his excellent book, *Successful Direct Marketing Methods,* while Throckmorton's is taken from her readable and entertaining volume, *Winning Direct Response Advertising.*

Bob Stone's seven-step formula for good letters

1. Promise a benefit in your headline or first paragraph, your most important benefit.
2. Immediately enlarge on your most important benefit.
3. Tell the reader specifically what he or she is going to get.
4. Back up your statements with proofs and endorsements.
5. Tell the reader what will be lost by not acting.
6. Rephrase your prominent benefits in the closing offer.
7. Incite action now.

Joan Throckmorton's five big rules

1. *Establish credibility.* Who is the seller and why is he or she qualified to make this offer?
2. *Get involvement.* This means use the "you" and sing the benefits.
3. *Motivate your prospect.* Why now, not later?
4. *Structure a strong offer.* Unless your product is unique, you'll need all the competitive ammunition you can muster.

5. *Common sense.* Ask yourself, "does all this make sense to the prospect?"

Tom Collins' checklist

One of the most famous checklists for direct marketers is Tom Collins' 28 rules for good direct mail packages, which appears in Bob Stone's *Successful Direct Marketing Methods.*

28 Rules from Tom Collins
(Chairman of Rapp & Collins)

1. Do you have a good proposition?
2. Do you have a good offer?
3. Does your outside envelope select your prospect?
4. Does your outside envelope put your best foot forward?
5. Does your outside envelope provide reading motivation?
6. Does your copy provide instant orientation?
7. Does your mailing visually reinforce the message?
8. Does it employ readable typography?
9. Is it written in readable, concrete language?
10. Is it personal?
11. Does it strike a responsive chord?
12. Is it dramatic?
13. Does it talk in the language of life, not "advertise at"?
14. Is it credible?
15. Is it structured?
16. Does it leave no stone unturned?
17. Does it present an ultimate benefit?
18. Are details presented as advantages?
19. Does it use, if possible, the power of disinterestedness?
20. Does it use, if possible, the power of negative selling?
21. Does it touch on the reader's deepest relevant daydreams?
22. Does it use subtle flattery?
23. Does it prove and dramatize the value?
24. Does it provide strong assurances of satisfaction?
25. Does it repeat key points?
26. Is it backed by authority?
27. Does it give a reason for immediate response?
28. Do you make it easy to order?

Can technique take the place of creativity?

Many a misguided direct marketer looks askance at those who invest time and money in an involved process of creative discovery. Alas, more than one direct mail creative challenge has been "solved" by copying a competitor's positioning and package right out the window. Some direct marketers confine their creative process to a matter of sorting through the swipe file looking for a likely format to emulate.

On the other hand, even in a strong creative environment, no "high art" mentality will survive in a direct marketing creative shop. No matter how clever an idea for art or copy, it must advance the selling proposition or be killed. Thus, the pressure to sell with each photo and every line of copy may lead creative types back to the tried and true. In their own minds, direct marketing creative people often walk a fine line between taking the easy way out and striving for a unique, fresh, and possibly untried approach.

As David Ogilvy says, direct marketers "sell, or else." We need to persuade the reader any way we can. Sometimes the best method is brilliant copy or a striking design. Other times, the very best creative solution is one of those tried and true techniques, applied smartly to the current situation.

Scratch-offs, yes-no stickers, fake Federal Express packages, personalized letters and other format techniques may raise response rates far more than subtleties of copy and style. But deciding which techniques to use—and how to apply them—requires more time and effort than simply "knocking off" other peoples' work.

The truth, then, is that technique cannot and should not take the place of creativity. Formulas, checklists, offers and formats should be studied carefully so that they can be applied where they fill the bill. But technique alone is not enough: copywriters and art directors need to dig deep into their own experiences . . . research the specific product and marketing opportunity at hand . . . and then allow themselves time to develop the best possible solution to each new creative challenge.

What it takes to be creative
in direct marketing

Over the past few decades, academicians have devoted considerable time to the study of "how to be creative," and "what makes a
person creative." Their lists of creative characteristics sound like
every mother's dream profile of her beloved child. Drawn from
various sources, these creativity traits include:

Curious	Good imagination
Sense of humor	Energetic
Independent	Hard-working
Observant	Ambitious
Persistent	Visual thinker
Motivated	Original
Eclectic taste	Self-confident
Voracious reader	Sees the "big picture"

If you have decided to make copywriting or art direction your life's
work, it's a good bet that many of these traits describe you
already—at least on your best days. People who do not enjoy reading, imagining things, and thinking visually would be ill-suited to
a career in which the main repetitive tasks are studying subjects
and then writing and illustrating selling messages about them.
Those who are not hard-working and ambitious would become
frustrated quickly with a career that involves little maintenance
work: direct marketing creatives are faced with new challenges,
new products, and new clients almost daily. Those who are not
self-confident and independent would suffer greatly in a career
where their work is scrutinized and critiqued constantly.

There are ways to enhance your creativity characteristics so
that you can draw upon them as a direct marketer. The best
method is to groom yourself for greatness, just as an ambitious
and indulgent parent might groom the proverbial child "born
with a silver spoon in his mouth."

Studies of highly creative people show that they often enjoy
childhoods of great diversity. They travel, experience different
cultures, see plays and movies, visit the ballet and the opera, and
enjoy intellectual freedom and stimulation. Their parents ask
them questions and give them decisions to make from the time
they are toddlers. Yet creative people seldom have lives free from

strife: the process of overcoming adversity helps them to develop skills they can bring to bear on creative problem solving.

To remain in top form as a creative person, you must experience the world with a child's innocence and wonder. Make every day a process of discovery. Be the kind of person who reads everything from ketchup bottle labels to *People* magazine to Plato. Listen to music: everything from Top 40 Hits to Bach to classic Beatles. Frequent the theater. Join a Great Books group. Sit on a park bench and make up stories about passersby. Make chance encounters into market research adventures: ask people questions about their lives and opinions and store their answers away in your memory file.

Avoid isolation like the plague. The folly of many direct marketers is that as soon as they become successful, they move out of the old neighborhood and forget their roots. Market research expert Howard Gordon calls this ''confusing yourself with America''—coming to the delusion that everybody thinks and acts just like you. The best way to overcome this problem is to develop your empathy quotient. Plunge into situations with people whose socioeconomic status and world view are very different from your own. Strive to understand their motivations, feelings, hopes and dreams.

To stay in touch with America, attend church socials in small towns. Accept invitations to wedding receptions in VFW halls. Nurse a soft drink in a booth at a Truck Stop coffee shop and listen to the drivers as they shoot the breeze. Visit your cousin in rural Tennessee or your great aunt who lives in a Florida mobile home park. Volunteer in a nursing home. Get a part-time job at Christmas, selling toys in a department store. Go to the supermarket at least once a week—all the more important once you're so rich and successful you have a housekeeper to do the shopping.

Watch the Nashville Network and MTV on cable television. Use your TV remote control device to sample all the cable channels and see what's being advertised by direct response. Tune in to network TV and check the latest trends in situation comedies, dramas, and game shows. Listen to all the radio stations on the dial, not just your favorite. Watch and listen to talk shows. Read magazines and newspapers—even the *National Enquirer*—to keep current with the interests of different target markets.

Don't confine your creative grooming to these everyday activities: find the time and the means to travel as well. Visit the world's great museums and fabled cities. Look at America through the eyes of Italy or France or Canada. Even as you keep up-to-date with best sellers and hot magazines and music, discipline yourself to read history, classic novels, philosophers and poets. Take a tip from direct marketer Eugene B. Colin and increase your word power: every time you look up a word in the dictionary, read and consider the definitions of the five words above and below the one you originally sought.

Develop an environment for creativity, too. Equip yourself with reference books and computer databases. Familiarize yourself with the best library in your area, and cultivate the librarian so he or she will help you borrow needed research materials from other libraries as well. Attend direct-marketing seminars and luncheons—as much to network with other creative people as to hear the speakers.

Practice various ways of attacking problems, drawing on both qualitative and quantitative skills. Use analytical thinking to take a problem apart and examine its distinct ingredients. Try synthesis to identify related elements and put the parts back together in a useable whole. Use deductive reasoning to move from general theories to specific applications. Call upon inductive reasoning to draw general conclusions from specific examples and anecdotes.

If all of this seems like too much work, you may be aspiring to the wrong field of endeavor. To the best creative people, these personal development activities come as naturally as breathing. They can't imagine why anyone wouldn't prefer a trip to Europe over a new living room suite. They feel somehow compelled to keep up with the latest rock group and the hottest plays and restaurants, just because they want to be "in the know." Instead of shying away from people and situations that are different, they seek them eagerly. Instead of defending their own opinions, they prefer to play devil's advocate, hoping to draw out lots of ideas from people around them. And they enjoy mulling over all that they have learned, drawing connections and conclusions that will serve them well in appealing to various target markets.

What it takes to generate and apply new ideas for creative strategy

The Italian sociologist Vilfredo Pareto said that an idea is merely a new combination of old elements. Take a kaleidoscope, for example. It contains myriad bits of color, forming into many different

A silken vision of one of nature's miracles...
a Bradford Exchange recommendation

This collector plate offering from The Bradford Exchange continues the tradition established in the early 1970s by J. Roderick MacArthur. Bradford offers handsome works of art on porcelain plates with the added enticement of possible price appreciation. Reprinted with permission of The Bradford Exchange.

patterns as the kaleidoscope turns. The pattern is never the same twice, yet it combines all the same ingredients. The Bible says that "there is no new thing under the sun"—only unique ways of relating old elements. Creating an idea, then, is the result of a step-by-step process designed to identify relevant elements and arrange them in new and effective patterns.

When the late Rod MacArthur founded the Bradford Exchange in the early 1970s, he combined existing elements in an unexpected way—thereby developing a direct marketing business that now spans the globe, grossing tens of millions of dollars each year. MacArthur was offered the opportunity to sell limited-edition collector plates from France in the United States. He recognized the fact that the product would need a certain mystique to command $15.00 and up for a simple, decorated porcelain plate. Through extensive research, he learned that there was already a secondary market—albeit fragmented and inefficient—for limited-edition collector plates. He founded The Bradford Exchange as a sort of stock market for plates, providing a central source for buying and selling.

In developing this combination of elements, MacArthur produced an appealing opportunity for consumers. He could now sell plates with an extra "hook" in addition to their beauty and decor value: the possibility of price appreciation. Once a limited edition of plates was sold out, it would become available only on the secondary market. The Bradford Exchange made buying and selling these scarce plates efficient and accessible. When some plates became so popular that they rose as much as 10 times in value over a few years' time, the resulting excitement helped stimulate the boom in plate collecting. Today there are several million plate collectors, a good percentage of whom buy by mail from The Bradford Exchange.

Rod MacArthur may not have used a written, step-by-step idea generation plan to develop his concept for the Bradford Exchange, but his story exemplifies the process of identifying and implementing new ideas that makes for effective direct marketing. MacArthur worked for years in the family-owned direct marketing business anchored by Bankers Life & Casualty Co. and founded by his father, John D. MacArthur. He honed his direct marketing creative skills by selling everything from insurance to banking products to travel clubs and stereo systems by mail. Widely traveled, Rod MacArthur was a former journalist and war correspondent with a French-both wife and an eclectic education. In fact, the reason he was offered the chance to sell Limoges collector plates was because of his fluency in French.

When the collector plate opportunity presented itself, MacArthur did not content himself with writing an ad or two to see if the product would fly. He immersed himself in the world of collector plates, making friends with plate dealers and asking them endless questions about why people collect plates, what makes a plate collectible, how the secondary market works, and much more. Only after many weeks of fact-finding did his mission become clear: the creation of the Bradford Exchange as the centerpiece for a direct mail business selling limited-edition plates.

Creating new ideas step by step

There are as many written creativity formulas for direct marketers as there are technique checklists for copy and art. Some of these step-by-step processes come from direct marketing practitioners, while others are advanced by academicians studying the history of ideas. Here are capsulized versions of several helpful creativity formulas.

A technique for producing ideas

In this slim volume which has been printed and reprinted for half a century, James Webb Young advances a five-step process for creative thinking.

1. *Gather raw materials.* Webb suggests studying both general information about life and events, and specific facts about the product and the target market. He advocates the use of 3″ × 5″ cards, each containing single facts.
2. *Mental digestion.* Webb likens this process to putting together a jigsaw puzzle. Using the 3″ × 5″ cards, he suggests arranging and rearranging them to find patterns, contradictions and relationships among the facts.
3. *Incubation.* Once the digestion period is over, Webb says to drop the subject and forget it—go on to another activity such as music, the movies, exercise, making dinner or sleeping.
4. *Eureka!* At some point, out of nowhere, an idea will appear, thanks to the work of the subconscious mind.
5. *Testing.* Submit the idea to your own criticism and that of your peers, then refine or reject it.

Eugene B. Colin's how to create new ideas

Gene Colin, who has practiced direct marketing and advertising creativity for over 40 years, offers nine guideposts "to lead you from a blank sheet of paper to a rousing success."

1. *Pick a problem.* Define your problem, in writing. State what's wrong, what needs fixing. State your objective, the end result you seek.
2. *Get knowledge.* Get known facts and new knowledge. Study written references. Experiment. Explore. Research deeply and broadly. Talk with informed people. Check your findings. Put them in writing.
3. *Organize knowledge.* Put your information into understandable form; sort it, organize it, write it.
4. *Refine knowledge.* Screen knowledge for relationships and principles. Match fact against fact. Look for similarities. Differences. Analogies. Cause and effect. Combinations. Patterns.

5. *Digest.* Let the conscious mind get its second wind. Put the subconscious mind to work. Relax, take up another problem, work at a hobby or enjoy some mild diversion until refreshed.

6. *Produce ideas* with total freedom and speed, or concentrate anew on your problem until ideas begin to emerge. As they occur, write them down. Don't stop to judge them. Produce and write and build up as many as you can.

7. *Rework ideas.* Check your new ideas for flaws. Examine each new idea objectively. Question it, challenge it, test it, rework it, improve it, follow it through.

8. *Put ideas to work.* If the approval and acceptance of others are required, sell your ideas. Plan each sale. Allow enough time. Get participation. Use samples.

9. *Repeat the process* until it becomes a natural habit.

Ten Steps to Personal Creativity from Susan K. Jones

Your author has developed this creativity process over the course of a 20-year writing career.

1. *Block out the time.* Don't try to create a breakthrough layout or copy outline in a half-hour between meetings. Carve out a period of an hour or more—preferably much more—in which you can devote yourself totally to the question at hand. For those who work in distracting surroundings, this may well call for early-morning, late-night or at-home work sessions.

2. *Get comfortable.* My favorite outfit for creative work is a sweatsuit in winter, shorts and T-shirt in summer. Your corporate environment may not allow for this, but make sure that your waistband doesn't bind and your shoes don't hurt. Such distractions keep you from concentrating.

3. *Eat something healthy.* To be creative, you need to have your energy level at a peak. Have a few cheese crackers or your own equivalent of a healthy snack. No candy bars: they produce a shaky high followed by a no-energy crash.

4. *Soak up lots of background—then do something else.* Quiz the client like a journalist writing a story about the product— who, what, where, when, why, how. Read every bit of background you can get your hands on, and use or at least go and see the product if at all possible. Check the competitive files. Then give it a rest—do something else or call it a day. Let what you've learned roll around in your subconscious. Don't try to work with it right away.

5. *Experience the world.* When you are looking for a break-through, let the world around you serve as inspiration. Signs over storefronts, packaging in the supermarket, TV ads, school classrooms, popular music, and many other seemingly unrelated sights and sounds can provide a spark that leads you to a fresh layout or piece of copy. Get away from the desk and soak things up if you're running dry.

6. *Be ready when the ideas strike.* Some of my best ideas have come to me in the shower, driving alone in the car, or walking around the neighborhood. Thus I keep a pencil and paper handy at all times—by the bedside, too. That idea you thought of in the middle of the night is guaranteed to be gone in the morning unless you write it down.

7. *Have a dancing hat.* The "dancing hat" is a leftover from my college days. Living in a sorority house, each of us had one article of clothing that we would wear as a signal when we needed to be left alone to study. Yours doesn't have to be a hat—just something you put on to tell yourself and others that you're working in an intense manner and shouldn't be disturbed for mundane matters. Putting it on sends signals to others—and will begin to have a "Pavlov's Dogs" effect on you, too.

8. *For blue-sky projects, have a glass of wine.* After reading all the background material and taking a break, pour yourself a glass of wine and start sketching or writing down ideas. Some of the ideas may not pass muster the next day, but by lowering your inhibitions you just may come up with a germ of a breakthrough idea.

9. *Let your work rest before evaluation.* Once you've done a rough layout or copy draft, let it sit at least overnight before you begin to touch it up. Looking at it fresh will help you see where it can be improved. More important, the next day you'll have the energy to pull it apart and start over if necessary—not just do a patch job.

10. *Enjoy the process.* Remember that we creative types are lucky. People pay us to learn about things and then share what we have learned with others to stimulate a sale. What we do for a living keeps our minds alive—and there is always a new challenge. So enjoy it: many people envy our freedom to create!

A quick read through these idea-generating formulas shows that the basic process follows a predictable pattern: outlining the problem, gathering information, evaluating information, walking away from the problem to let the mind do its work, enjoying one moment when ideas strike, weighing the pros and cons of various ideas, and then implementing the best idea.

The process begins with ambiguity and generality and proceeds to a concrete and specific plan of action. When set forth in these terms, creativity no longer seems a mysterious concept. Yet few of us reach our full creative potential because of stumbling blocks imposed by our upbringing, ourselves, and our society.

Roger von Oech, writer of the popular books *A Whack on the Side of the Head* and *A Kick in the Seat of the Pants* is noted for his humor. He pokes fun at the "shoulds" and "givens" in our lives, and challenges us to overcome them. He suggests that the American educational system is more concerned with putting youngsters into pigeonholes than nurturing their individual creative powers. As von Oech says, "children enter school as question marks and leave as periods."

The result is that American adults live by guidelines that serve as roadblocks to creativity: rules such as "there's only one right answer," "be practical," "be logical," "don't be ambiguous," and "don't be foolish." Direct marketers who find that such ingrained rules are inhibiting their ability to create may find new freedom by reading Von Oech's books.

Other factors that keep us from achieving our maximum creativity include poor health, lack of encouragement, narrow mindedness, fear of failure, and plain old-fashioned laziness. Indeed, in his book *The Care and Feeding of Ideas*, James L. Adams asserts that "the most common reason for lack of individual creative accomplishment is simply unwillingness to allocate the resources."

Becoming a "creative person" requires a major investment of time, dedication, and diligence. Yet the rewards are well worth the effort: indeed, the exhilaration of the "ah-ha" or "Eureka" moment is all the greater because it follows a long period of careful and disciplined work.

RESEARCH IN DIRECT MARKETING

3

One of the greatest strengths of direct marketing is the ability to test different creative concepts against each other, and obtain a readable, actionable result. Yet because direct marketers are such sophisticated database managers, they often focus much more attention on *how* to test than on *what* to test.

While our general advertising counterparts invest millions on focus group interviews, creative pre-testing and other costly research methods, many direct marketers hammer out their creative concepts in a vacuum. Then they place their ideas head-to-head in space ads, direct mail or television, and wait to see whether Concept A or Concept B sells best. But the nagging question remains: might there be a Concept C, yet to be discovered, that would sell even better?

Howard Gordon, of the Chicago-based market research firm George R. Frierichs Inc., points out a paradox in the way general advertisers and direct marketers treat marketing research. General advertisers, he says, spend considerable time, effort and money in discovering and pre-testing creative ideas. Then they dilute the effectiveness of their work by broadcasting these creative ideas via mass marketing—network television, general-interest magazines and the like. They seldom customize their space ads, for instance, to acknowledge the subtle difference between readers of *Time* and *Newsweek,* or even the vast difference between readers of *Architectural Digest* and *1001 Home Ideas.*

With more and more segmentation possibilities available via cable television and specialized publications, it is all the more important that general advertisers recognize the extra impact they may obtain through target marketing.

On the other hand, direct marketers are experts at targeting messages. They are able to segment lists they mail to and call individuals out by name as "owner of a 1989 Volvo station wagon," "parent of a Sesame Street fan" and so on. Yet they may be reluctant to take advantage of even the least costly and time-consuming research methods that could ensure the messages they send these people are as effective as they could be.

Careful market research will help you strengthen and improve your creative strategy. This chapter will discuss the most useful methods of research for direct marketers and how they impact creative strategy decisions. It will focus first on general topics such as consumer behavior, lifestyle trends and popular culture, and then on means of standard or customized research to develop a creative concept for a particular product or service.

What research can do for direct marketers

Although the term "marketing research" may conjure up visions of complex and costly programs that only Ph.D.s can understand, its real purpose is simple and straightforward. Marketing research offers a way to find out how people think about products and services, and how they go about buying them. It allows direct marketers to gain direction on basic questions such as

- Who is our market for this product or service?
- What are some possible, undiscovered additional market segments?
- What are the characteristics of our prospects?
- What should we tell the prospects in each market segment about this product or service? Which benefits do they consider the most important and unique?
- How should we tell them about the product? What words, what tone, what format and graphic style, what medium should we use? Which offer (price, payment terms, add-on features, etc.) will work best?

Research cannot answer these questions conclusively, but it can point direct marketers in the most promising directions for testing. It may not be able to predict creative winners, but it can save a great deal of time, effort and cost by weeding out creative losers.

Barriers direct marketers erect against research

Today, many of the largest and most sophisticated direct marketing firms have recognized the cost effectiveness of marketing research. In addition, packaged goods companies with vast experience in general advertising and marketing research are using direct marketing in greater numbers. Yet creative people may still find barriers to marketing research in a number of direct marketing firms.

First, some old-school direct marketers consider direct mail, space or television testing a perfectly effective research tool. Indeed, once the test is complete, they will know which test cell won. But will they know why it won? Research could help them find out. What's more, even the most ambitious testing programs are limited as to how many concepts can be tried. Marketing research allows actual prospects to help select the top three or top five creative ideas for testing.

Another barrier is financial. A single focus group costs $2000 or more, and a full-scale program of quantitative and qualitative research can easily run $50,000. Some direct marketers consider the expenditure frivolous. They are used to receiving orders when they test, so they're making money even as they discover the best way to sell. But with the average direct-mail package costing $400 per thousand or more, it makes good sense to refine the selling message as much as possible to maximize sales, even at the testing stage.

A third barrier is lack of understanding. Many direct marketers understand testing, but they don't understand research. They consider it mumbo-jumbo, and they don't trust it. Howard Gordon recommends that direct marketers approach these decision-makers without ever using the term "marketing research." He says they take much more kindly to this request: "We want to go out and ask some people what they think about X."

Types of direct marketing research

Direct marketing creative people should ground their research work with a general understanding of *consumer behavior:* how people think, make decisions, and react to the world around them. Then when faced with specific selling propositions to perfect, direct marketers may engage in *secondary* research, which comes from standard reference sources or other organizations' findings; or *primary* research, which is customized to answer certain questions about a specific topic. They may choose to do *quantitative* research, which provides numerical information reflecting the prevalence of various characteristics, attitudes and behavior; or *qualitative* research, which provides concepts and ideas but cannot be projected statistically. Direct marketers may develop *pretests* which help them determine exactly who they should address and what they should say, or *post-tests,* which help ascertain why buyers bought and nonbuyers did not.

Consumer behavior

The study of consumer behavior in the United States is largely a 20th-century phenomenon, although Alexis de Tocqueville did a skillful job of analyzing the emerging American character in *Democracy in America,* about 150 years ago. There he pointed out how Americans lack the sense of belonging that strict class systems traditionally provide to Europeans. Thus, Americans seek out other means of affiliation by joining groups. Some of these groups are organized and structured, such as unions, fraternities, clubs and societies. Other groups are completely unstructured— they are simply labels applied to people who appear to exemplify certain traits. Examples would include the social "in crowd," the "preppies," "yuppies," "hippies," or "highbrows."

To enhance their sense of belonging to either the structured or unstructured groups, Americans may make buying decisions that echo these groups' values. Some such decisions are blatant: purchasing a hat or jacket with a union logo, for example, or proudly swinging a keychain decorated with the logo of a BMW automobile. Others are more subtle or even unconscious: for instance, a consumer might choose to purchase the same pair of shoes she saw worn by a leader of a neighborhood social enclave she wishes to join.

Of course, not all consumers are sufficiently safe and secure to invest their time and money feeding the desire for affiliation. From Abraham Maslow's classic Hierarchy of Needs, we learn that humans move along a continuum of concerns, ranging from food, clothes, shelter and safety at the lower levels to affiliation, self-esteem, and finally self-actualization. Once a need is met, an individual is free to move up to the next level of concern. If a problem occurs, he or she may slide back down to a lower level. Direct marketers who can pinpoint the psychological "need level" of their target markets will be in a better position to tailor products, services and selling messages to fulfill the desires of their prospects.

At the turn of the century, Thorstein Veblen advanced the concept of conspicuous consumption, whereby consumers make many of their purchase decisions based on what they see others doing around them—also known as "keeping up with the Joneses." Some years later, John Kenneth Galbraith decried materialism, a term that describes American consumers' interest in more and better houses, cars, clothes and personal playthings at the expense of cultural and social values. To help explain why consumers do what they do, Ernest Dichter developed motivational research. By means of long and intensive interviews, Dichter was able to discover hidden reasons for certain buying behaviors.

In 1966, Dr. Steuart Henderson Britt of Northwestern University introduced a book entitled *Consumer Behavior and the Behavioral Sciences—Theories and Applications.* His goal was to bridge the gap between the behavioral sciences and marketing—to help marketers apply what they learned about consumers to develop products and selling messages that touch consumers where they live.

How consumers make buying decisions

Over the past few decades, many advertising agencies and research firms have built upon Dr. Britt's concept, conducting rigorous scientific testing and then applying the results to advertising and direct marketing. Knowing how individuals make decisions, for instance, allows marketers to facilitate this decision-making process via their selling messages.

As a professor at Northwestern University, Dr. John Maloney introduced this step-by-step process of decision-making based upon the classic stimulus/response model:

1. New information enters the consumer's field of vision.
2. Interest/curiosity level determine whether—and to what extent—the consumer pays attention.
3. Socialization, prior learning and memory combine to help determine the consumer's attitude toward the information.
4. The consumer reaches a decision regarding the information.
5. The consumer either stores the decision for later reference, or acts upon the decision.

This process corresponds to the classic advertising decision-making model of Awareness-Interest-Desire-Action. The decision can be short-circuited at any point if the consumer does not proceed to the next level. Curiosity and prior positive associations with similar information are helpful to the process. Boredom, distractions, or negative associations can end the process.

There are ways that direct marketers can enhance positive decision-making in their selling messages. According to decision researchers, they may:

■ *Associate the product offer with something/someone consumers know and trust.* Your offer may be foreign to the person's experience, but if you relate it to a comfortable person or idea, the consumer may well make the "mental leap" along with you. For example, a senior citizen may find the idea of buying insurance by mail intimidating. But when a known and trusted spokesperson, Ed McMahon, suggests such a purchase, the transaction becomes less threatening.

■ *Make positive statements.* Decisions are hampered by mental negativism. Remember the old question about whether the cup is half-full or half-empty? Be optimistic in copy. Say that "90% of those who used this product lost weight," not "our failure rate is only 10%."

■ *Set up a flattering comparison.* A direct marketer of figurines planned to sell a new product for $19.95. Then a focus group of experienced dealers told the firm that the price was too low for the market—the product was worth $29.95. The firm positioned the figurines as "a $29.95 value, available to preferred customers at only $24.95," and tested that concept head-to-head with the $19.95 price point. The $24.95 price point won—probably because it had been compared with a higher number and thus was perceived as a bargain.

- *Overcome disbelief.* Consumers must trust the seller in order to make a purchase by mail. A solid guarantee, testimonials, and discussion of the firm's long and solid track record for customer satisfaction are some of the ways to cultivate consumers' trust and help move them toward a buying decision.

Lifestyles and social classes in America

Two books introduced during the 1980s offered ways of classifying American consumers based on their lifestyles and values systems. These are *The Nine American Lifestyles* by Arnold Mitchell, and *Class* by Paul Fussell.

The Nine American Lifestyles reports upon a quantitative mail survey which took place in 1980. The survey asked over 800 specific questions of more than 1,600 randomly chosen adult respondents. As a result of this work, which is known as "Vals" research, Mitchell was able to classify Americans in three main lifestyle groups: Need-Driven, Outer-Directed, and Inner-Directed.

Need-Driven groups are characterized by poverty, and they include two sub-groups: the survivors, who have little hope of upward mobility, and the sustainers, who still have hope of bettering their lot in life. Outer-Directed groups include more than two-thirds of American adults. Influenced by the beliefs and values of those around them, the Outer-Directed include three subsets: belongers, whose goal in life is to fit in; emulators, who strive to get ahead; and achievers, who exemplify the American dream of visible success and material well being. A smaller but growing segment of Americans are the Inner-Directed groups. Mitchell sees these not as selfish people, but as folks who hear and act upon internal driving forces. They include the young and rebellious I-am-me personalities; the experientials, who are independent and want to experience everything vividly for themselves; and the societally conscious, who are concerned with conservation, environmental issues, and political action.

Direct-marketing creative people may wish to study the lifestyle groups outlined by Mitchell, as well as the updated "Vals" groups published in the late 1980s, and to consider which group they may be addressing with each solicitation they create. Since Mitchell offers a detailed profile of each group—including average age, income, race, educational attainment, occupation, political affiliation, self-perceived social class, and geographic location—it is very possible to compare characteristics with well-defined mailing lists or magazine reader profiles of target groups you plan to solicit.

For example, sustainers might well be an excellent market to tap when selling multi-volume book sets on how to repair and remodel one's own home. In their attempt to better themselves and their families, sustainers often are quite thrifty and resourceful. Playing up these traits—and offering a split-payment plan even those with low income can afford—could make the book set all the more attractive to this group of people.

On the other hand, hard-driving achievers are unlikely to have the free time or interest to purchase such a book set. They would be a better target for the trappings of upper-middle-class success: a second or third set of dinnerware, for example, or executive playthings such as those sold in a catalog called "The Price of His Toys." The selling pitch might acknowledge the reader's status as one who has made it, and explain how this product or service befits such a person.

Belongers will spark to products that stress group identity such as family crests, statues that indicate a certain occupation or avocation, or sweatshirts reading, " 'Tis a Blessing to be Irish." Copy could emphasize the warmth and comfort of being part of an admirable and highly acceptable group.

Emulators are the perfect market for limited-edition collectibles, which allow them to own the works of artists they admire—Norman Rockwell, for example—at prices that fit their still-modest pocketbooks. They will be impressed by copy that favorably compares the item they are purchasing with more costly prints and oil paintings by the same artist. Emulators also offer a fertile field for those who sell products aimed at helping people get ahead in business, dress for success, or become more socially adept.

The Inner-Directed groups are also approachable via direct marketing, as counter-culture publications such as *Mother Jones* and *New Age* have discovered. These magazines include numerous ads for travel opportunities, seminars, and products that cater to people outside the mainstream in thought and interests. For the societally conscious, they also offer a number of opportunities to donate money to environmental causes or to help end suffering of laboratory animals. There are even mutual funds and other financial services that cater to those who wish to invest only in socially responsible firms.

In *Class*, Paul Fussell makes fun of the American social class system. In so doing, the curmudgeonly author points out a number of telling characteristics which direct marketers should remember when writing copy and designing ads.

Fussell divides Americans into nine social classes: top-out-of-sight, upper, upper-middle, middle, high-proletarian, mid-proletarian, low-proletarian, destitute, and bottom-out-of-sight. He discusses class differences based upon patterns of speech, manner of dress, home decor, occupation, social life, and intellectual life.

Patterns of speech are especially telling for direct marketing copywriters, who often find themselves pitching to upper-middle-class executives one day and blue-collar workers the next. For instance, Fussell's research indicates the following class differences in announcing a family tragedy:

Upper class: ''Grandfather died''
Middle class: ''Grandfather passed away''
Lower class: ''Grandfather was taken to Jesus''

A warning: some readers find Fussell's work offensive because he spares nothing in his description of class quirks and inanities. However, he is just as scathing in his discussion of every class—except for the exalted X-class, people who have risen above all class stereotypes and are unashamedly and uniquely themselves.

Your author, however, finds frequent re-readings of *Class* an indispensable aid to switching class mindsets. For instance, intensive study of Fussell's writings on the upper-middle group is helpful in writing upscale giftware catalog copy. On the other hand, for an assignment selling accidental death and dismemberment insurance by mail, a quick review of proletarian characteristics and speech patterns is vital.

The direct mail buyer

Until recently, direct marketers have taken a less-than-academic approach toward the study of consumer behavior, relying on their own observations borne out through head-to-head testing of concepts. In the past, direct marketers concentrated on learning why people choose to buy by mail. But today, much time and effort is channeled into finding out why certain people choose *not* to buy by mail—and how they can be convinced to enter the ranks of mail-order buyers.

Studies commissioned through Simmons for the Direct Marketing Association's Consumer Acceptance Program showed that of the 169,000,000 adults in the United States, 45% ordered by mail within a recent 12-month period. This leaves 55%, or a staggering 93,000,000 American adults, who do not currently buy by mail. If the field of direct marketing in general—and individual firms in specific—are to continue to grow during the 21st century, it is essential that they find ways of serving the 45% of mail order buyers more effectively—and cultivating the 55% of nonbuyers as well.

Three reasons why people buy by mail are cited most often.

- *Convenience.* Busy dual-career and single-parent families have little time to brave crowded shopping malls, especially during typical business hours. They have little patience with the ill-trained, transient salesclerks who hold forth in today's department stores. They prefer to shop from home, and enjoy direct marketers' 24-hour-a-day service, toll-free telephone numbers, home delivery, liberal guarantees, and free-trial privileges.
- *Target marketing.* Few can resist the lure of slick offers targeted directly to them: the fly-fisherman, the career woman in need of a wardrobe, the amateur interior decorator, the concerned money manager, etc. As the world expands and retail stores become more and more impersonal, consumers delight in the cozy, me-to-you friendliness of custom-tailored direct-marketing pitches.
- *Uniqueness and selection.* When every chain store carries the same narrow range of merchandise, consumers enjoy shopping in direct-mail channels that offer products not available on local store shelves. The items they select by mail may be unique, or simply available in more depth: for instance, Martex towels in all 22 colors and four quality levels Martex manufactures rather than the 10 colors and two quality levels offered by a department store.
- *Lack of credibility.* The most often-quoted reason why people choose not to buy by mail is lack of credibility. Since direct marketing began as a mail-order version of the patent medicine "pitch men," many direct-mail, space and television offers still rely on "such a deal" techniques. Exaggerated

claims and starbursts do sell products to many Americans, but they are one of the top complaints of the 55% who do not currently buy by mail. These nonbuyers find such low-class selling methods less than credible. In addition, credibility suffers at the hands of some direct marketers whose customer service records are less than pristine. Indeed, the DMA's Simmons study showed that 37% of those who had bought by mail in a 12-month period had customer service problems or complaints about the buying process.

Secondary research

The preparation for a particular creative assignment often includes some secondary research. Here are some typical sources for secondary research material.

- *Federal, State and Local Governments*—census data, labor statistics, health statistics, etc.
- *Competitive Information*—gathered via observation, decoying, trade groups, etc.
- *Associations and Groups*—surveys, statistical data, staff library resources.
- *Direct Marketing Database Firms*—information compiled from telephone directories, census figures, auto and boat registrations, real estate records, purchase histories, Nielsen data, surveys, etc.
- *Libraries*—public, private, university sources.
- *Trade publications*—case histories, articles and surveys.

Primary research

Although direct marketers may do some of their primary research directly, many times they call upon specialized market research firms for this work. Joseph Castelli of Ogilvy & Mather Direct in New York pointed out several criteria for the selection of a market research firm in his article on research methods for McGraw-Hill's 1984 book edited by Ed Nash, *The Direct Marketing Handbook*. Castelli suggested that direct marketers should select a firm that:

- Has a broad range of experience and a proven track record of helping other companies.
- Is problem-oriented rather than technique-oriented. Good researchers will be sure they understand the problem before they offer a solution. They have no vested interest in using a particular research technique.
- Has a staff that can communicate well. The most brilliant research study will be of little value unless the results and implications can be clearly communicated.
- Is concerned with quality control. Choose a firm that pretests the questionnaire as a standard practice and provides a series of controls throughout the research process.
- Is marketing-oriented. Their conclusions and recommendations should be specific and practical.

Castelli goes on to advise direct marketers how to get the best work from their research firms:

- Confide in them. Tell them what your problems are. Give them all the background they need to fully understand the situation.
- Trust them. Rely on them to determine whether research can be helpful, and if so, how the research should be done.
- Don't be penny wise and pound foolish. If they recommend research that you regard to be too expensive, consider the value of the information. It may well be worth the cost.

What market research firms can do for direct marketers

Research firms can conduct both quantitative and qualitative tests for direct marketers. Here are several examples of the type of work they may be engaged to do.

Interviews and surveys

Whether conducted person-to-person, by telephone or by mail, these methods may be useful in determining information about a particular group such as:

- Demographics—age, sex, income, residence, point in the family life cycle.

- Psychographics—lifestyle and attitudes.
- Buying behavior—decision process and action.

Physiological/emotional tests

Although only the most sophisticated direct marketers use these tests today, general advertisers find them especially meaningful because they are free from the self-censorship imposed by consumers when they answer verbally. Brain-wave tests, pupil dilation, voice pitch, and other measures show whether a consumer reacts to a given selling message. A strong reaction may mean repulsion or attraction—and therefore is not conclusive without further testing. No reaction to a particular selling message means it has no impact, however, and thus can be discarded.

Focus groups

A focus group includes between six and twelve consumers interacting under the leadership of a trained moderator who uses a prepared discussion outline. For maximum effectiveness, direct marketing focus groups should include only proven mail-order buyers. Other qualifying factors will depend on the subject of the focus group. For example, a focus group sponsored by a book club might require that each attendee had bought at least 12 nonfiction books during the previous year, and be a current or former member of at least two mail-order book clubs.

Ideally, the focus group's sponsor observes the group from behind a two-way mirror. In addition, the group should be videotaped or tape recorded for future reference. After completion, in most cases the moderator will prepare a written interpretation of each focus group's findings.

The best focus groups are those in which consumers are allowed to function as consumers—making choices and evaluations just as they would in the marketplace. Focus group participants should not be allowed to act as amateur marketing consultants. For example, they should not be shown a creative concept and asked, "what do you think of this copy and layout?" Rather, they might be shown an ad and asked, "what kind of person would buy the product presented here?"

Focus groups may be used to help direct marketers find the right words to use in communicating with a target market of consumers. They may help marketers discover how certain types of consumers think, and how they become motivated to buy particular products. Some direct marketers use a series of focus groups in a step-by-step process. First they show a group a number of rough creative concepts, eliminating those that draw indifferent or negative responses. Then they proceed to copy and layout on the most promising concepts, and show these to focus groups at various points in the creation process, seeking more and more refinement.

Market research experts caution direct marketers not to expect direction from a single focus group. Two, four or even more sessions may be necessary to cover a particular topic adequately. Cost per session may range from $2000 to $3500, which may or may not include the cost of the written report.

Benefit tests

Perhaps the most immediately useful and cost-effective marketing research tool for direct marketers is the benefit test. To develop a benefit test, a direct marketing copywriter prepares a list of possible benefit statements pertaining to a product or service. These statements may be drawn from comments at focus groups, consumer interviews, or brainstorming sessions. Each benefit should be stated individually, in sentence form, on a card. In private interviews, qualified prospects should be shown the cards, one after the other, and asked to rate the importance of each in the product purchase decision on a scale of 1 to 10. Then the consumer should look at each card again, this time rating the same benefits as to their uniqueness.

To evaluate a benefit test, determine which benefits are considered both important and unique by prospects. These are the most promising benefits to use in developing creative concepts.

Buyer/nonbuyer surveys

Post-testing often takes the form of a buyer/nonbuyer survey. The objective is to learn the differences between prospects who responded to an offer, and those who did not. Such a survey should focus on demographic information, general attitudes, and specific reactions to the selling message received. A well-done buyer/nonbuyer survey may point the way toward new creative approaches that reinforce buyers' positive attitudes and find new ways to increase appeal and believability to those who failed to respond in the past.

The future of research in direct marketing creative strategy

In the summer of 1987, a Research Symposium was sponsored by the faculty of the Graduate Program in Direct Marketing at Northwestern University's Medill School of Journalism. The full-day program resulted in the development of a list of important topics for academic research, as identified by a panel of 32 experienced direct marketing practitioners.

The group awarded top priority to the development of more effective means of pretesting direct marketing creative concepts. Several of the other topics which were identified have much to do with the creative process: customer care, image correlation, and literacy.

Thus an agenda has been set for direct marketing research, and dialogue has been initiated between academics and practitioners. As more students earn graduate degrees in direct marketing and set their sights on academic advancement for the field, there is growing potential for creative strategy research breakthroughs in the years to come.

HOW CREATIVE STRATEGY FITS INTO THE DIRECT MARKETING PLAN

4

Direct marketing is a complex selling method that requires careful orchestration of market evaluation, product development, marketing strategy, execution and research. As much as direct marketing creative people would like to consider their work the central focus, the fact is that creative strategy and execution represent only part of the overall marketing plan.

This is not to say that creative involvement in direct marketing programs has a finite beginning and end. On the contrary, the best way to develop successful creative campaigns is to become involved in each marketing venture as early as possible, and see it through to the post mortem.

This chapter will provide a general outline for a comprehensive direct marketing plan. It will show how the creative function fits in as part of the overall plan. In addition, it will focus on the important role of the direct marketing creative person at all stages of the marketing plan.

The direct marketing plan

The function of a direct marketing plan is to lay groundwork, set a step-by-step course for timely action, and provide a control document to measure and evaluate results. Such a plan helps everyone involved to retain their marketing orientation, and to orchestrate their actions to bring about a desired result.

The basic format illustrated in Exhibit 4.1 may serve as a guide in the preparation of a direct marketing plan.

EXHIBIT 4.1   The Direct Marketing Plan

I. *Direct Marketing Review*—Provides the groundwork that is necessary before new plans can be initiated.
- A. Description of Your Product or Service
  1. Features
  2. Benefits
  3. Positioning Statement
  4. Possible Alternates/Variables
- B. Description of the Market for Your Product or Service
  1. Size and Scope
  2. Market Trends
  3. Evidence of Demand
  4. Distribution Patterns
     - a. Direct Marketing Channels
     - b. Other Distribution Channels
- C. Description of Competitive Facts
  1. Share of Market—Yours and Competitors'
  2. Competitors' Product/Service Descriptions—Quality, Price, Features/Benefits
     - a. Your Product's Advantages
     - b. Your Product's Disadvantages
     - c. Competitors' Advantages
     - d. Competitors' Disadvantages
  3. Competitors' Marketing Efforts
     - a. Media
     - b. Creative
     - c. Offer(s) Including Pricing, Premiums, etc.
- D. Problems and Opportunities—Using knowledge of product, market and competition to develop a target market segment or segments that fit your product's strengths and weaknesses and maximize chances for success considering competitors' known strategies.

II. *Marketing Objectives*—Make these as specific and measurable as possible.
- A. Total Sales Volume
- B. Share of Market
- C. Number of and Projected Lifetime Value of New Customers

(continued)

EXHIBIT 4.1 *continued*

III. *Marketing Strategies*
  A. Media Objectives by Medium—Direct Mail, Space, etc.
    1. Overall Projected Results (Leads, Sales)
    2. Projected Response Levels by Vehicle (List, Magazine Insertion, etc.)
  B. Media Strategies
    1. Direct Mail Testing Plan—i.e. begin with eight lists of 5,000 names each to be followed by validations and mass mailing.
    2. Testing Plan for Each Medium—Similar projections for space ads, telephone marketing, other media selected.
  C. Creative Objectives—Typical objectives could be:
    1. Sales or Leads at Specific Volume Levels
    2. Heightened Awareness of Company Image
  D. Preliminary Creative Strategies
    1. Features and Benefits in Order of Importance
    2. Changes of Emphasis for Various Market Segments
    3. Creative Plan
      a. Assignments—Creation of direct mail package, ad(s), etc.
      b. Preliminary Guidelines for Graphics and Copy
      c. Needed Collateral Materials for Back End—Acknowledgements, package inserts, etc.

IV. *Operations Guidelines*
  A. Program-Specific Instructions for Departments
    1. Order-Processing
    2. Data-Processing
    3. Fulfillment
    4. Customer Service
  B. Master Timetable—Beginning with mail date or day materials are due and working back

V. *Budget Summary*—A chart listing projected expenditures for media, list rentals, production, postage, etc.—every cost that is not considered a part of the firm's overhead.

VI. *Special Activities*—Research, public relations, sales promotion, special events or other related activities that will impact this marketing plan.

VII. *Evaluation*—Each marketing plan should include a mechanism for evaluating results and using what has been learned as input for the next plan's Direct Marketing Review.

The creative person's role in marketing planning and execution

In the marketing plan above, creative objectives and strategies are listed specifically under Marketing Strategies. Chapter 10 of this book will provide more in-depth information on creative strategies. However, before copywriters and art directors begin deciding the finer points of how to motivate prospects to buy, they must develop, understand and implement other parts of the marketing plan.

Direct marketing review

As part of their overall research efforts, creative people should make sure they have access to all materials used in writing the review section of the marketing plan. Creatives should study competitors' products and marketing techniques, get on competitors' mailing lists, and decoy their products to receive at home. Competitive ad samples look one way in a stack with other samples, and another way altogether when juxtaposed with one's own electric bill and personal letters in the family mail box. There is a world of difference between looking over the limp and incomplete contents of a competitor's product package that many others have already pondered, and receiving that same package at home via U.P.S. or U.S. Mail.

Once creative people have considered competitive promotions and products in light of the challenge at hand, they should share their insights with general marketing types. Indeed, the creative perspective may be invaluable to the marketer who is struggling with issues regarding the offer—pricing, premiums, guarantees, etc. In addition, creative people may turn up unique product advantages—or ways to turn possible disadvantages into selling plusses.

Marketing objectives

Creative people need to understand the scope of the challenge they are involved with. If the marketing plan calls for an ultimate sales volume of $50,000,000, and the generation of a million new customer names, the perspective is quite different than if the strategy outlines an initial test of three or four small-space ads to determine the product's initial viability. Sadly, some creative people fail to gain this kind of perspective. When this occurs, they may find themselves suggesting a full-scale jumbo spectacular package costing $700 per thousand in quantities of a million or more to an entrepreneur with an initial testing budget of less than $50,000.

Marketing strategies

The copywriter or art director who shows active interest at this stage of the game is much less likely to be "force-fed" a formula plan. Do you believe that a self-mailer is a better alternative than an envelope mailing for this proposition? Do you think this marketing plan should include telephone marketing or broadcast advertising, even though use of these media would be considered unorthodox? It is essential that you state your views and back them up with precedents, projections and creative scenarios at this level, before plans are approved and budgets are set.

Operations guidelines

On the surface, it might seem that the creative person has little to do with the nuts and bolts of order processing and fulfillment. But unfortunately, many a "front-end" program is allowed to lose its vital marketing orientation when it reaches the "back end." For best results, creative people should dig in and find out every detail about how each order or lead will be handled when it reaches the firm. What kind of order acknowledgments will be sent? Who will write them? Who is in charge of creating the 30-day notices that will be sent to customers in case their product shipments are delayed? How will the product be packaged? What kind of collateral materials will accompany the shipment? Does the customer service department have a good, marketing-oriented set of standard letters to use in responding to customer complaints and requests? If you do not have sufficient clout to find out the answers to these questions from inside your firm, do a little investigation on your own. Order from your own firm, and have several friends or relatives do the same. Find out how you are treated as a customer, and document the results. Handled with tact and care, such information can provide the ammunition you need to improve the marketing orientation of the firm's operations. Such care is needed because many firms routinely send out letters and notices to hard-won customers that read as if computers had written them.

And many a customer service department comes across instead as a group of customer discipline specialists, because their letters are production oriented—aimed at internal goals rather than customer satisfaction. The need for such vigilance in customer care is obvious, considering this catalog industry statistic from consultant and author Richard Hodgson: on average, only 50% of new catalog customers ever order from that same company again!

Budget summary

The creative person's concern here is similar to that expressed under objectives: an understanding of available dollars helps creatives keep their plans and ideas in proportion with budget reality.

Special activities

Based on their research and analysis of competitors, creative people may well be able to suggest public relations ventures, sales promotion ideas, or events that would amplify the impact of direct marketing programs. Preparing their proposals at the marketing plan stage ensures that the necessary time and budget can be allocated if these ideas are approved.

Evaluation

The creative person who spends the necessary time to study campaign evaluations in depth can become an invaluable resource to the firm. Analysis of individual list and media results, creative testing, formats and offers is important—but even more vital is the ability to develop logical hypotheses for future testing based on market research and the synthesis of various prior results.

A CREATIVE PERSON'S VIEW OF DIRECT MARKETING MEDIA

5

Every good Direct Marketing Plan calls for an outline of media objectives and strategy. Creative people can be of great help in determining appropriate media for a given marketing plan, based upon the creative advantages, disadvantages and budgetary impact of various media alternatives. This chapter discusses the pros, cons and costs of entry for the most frequently used direct marketing media.

Direct marketing media may include any channel of communication that invites a direct response. Even skywriting can be considered direct marketing if it includes a call to action and a telephone number or address. Most direct marketers, however, begin their campaigns with the tried and true: various forms of direct mail, print advertising, telephone and broadcast.

Direct mail

Creative advantages

- Almost unlimited format opportunities—size, looks, colors, paper, use of gimmicks, extent of copy, three-dimensional packages, pop-ups, etc.
- Extremely well targeted if list selections are done correctly.
- Allows for personalization.

- Utilizes all technological advances as they hit the market—you needn't wait for the medium to catch up, as you often do in dealing with print media.
- Ability to take advantage of database management and computer applications.
- Helps you learn in a controlled environment. You can develop test cells you want, not be at the mercy of a publication, or limited by their ability to do A/B splits, geographic and life-style splits, etc.
- Highly responsive—only telephone marketing has higher response rates.

Creative disadvantages

- Expense may bar entry—space ads can be placed much more cheaply to test viability of a concept. Direct mail costs $400 per thousand to $1000 per thousand or more, even in large quantities.
- May be difficult to discover and reach a wide enough audience to meet volume goals, given limited universes and "list burn-out," a phenomenon in which good lists are barraged with so many offers that their value declines rapidly—especially if not replenished constantly with fresh names.
- Post office restrictions must be followed to the letter. Risks include paying extra postage and producing packages that cannot be mailed.
- Post office is less reliable on timing of delivery than broadcast and most print media. In addition, horror stories persist about nondelivery of significant amounts of third class mail.
- Direct mail is very complex—requires coordination of lists, creative production and mailing. Other media are much easier to prepare for.

Magazines

- Ability to reach mass markets with magazines like *People* and *Reader's Digest,* or very carefully segmented markets with magazines like *Walking, Skiing, New Age, Country Living, Working Mother,* etc.
- Rising costs of direct mail and dearth of good lists in many market segments make magazine advertising cost effective where it wasn't a decade ago.

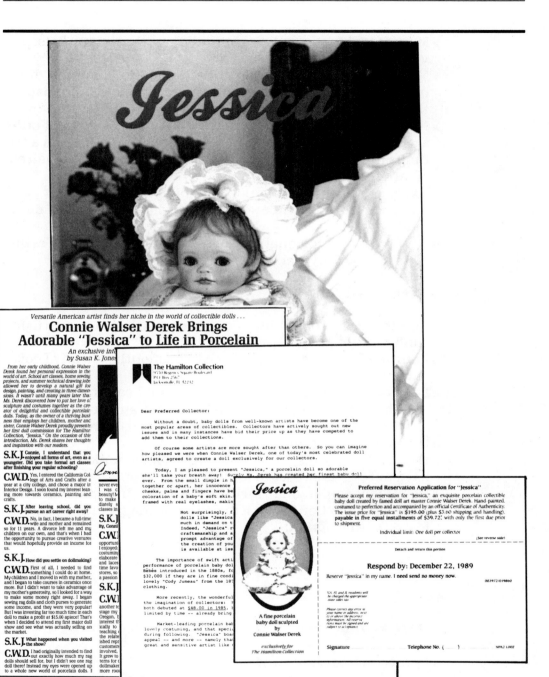

Direct marketers may capitalize on the creative advantages of various media to sell the same product. The Hamilton Collection used both a one-page space ad and a direct mail package to present the same selling message for the "Jessica" doll. © The Hamilton Collection. Reprinted with permission.

- Mass magazines offer larger circulations than many lists, providing more exposure.
- Magazines come invited into the home, unlike much direct mail. This facilitates trust among readers, and a predisposition to feel positive about advertised products.
- No barrier to entry: $1/6$ page black-and-white ads in mail-order sections of mass publications can be had for as little as a few thousand dollars in highly targeted magazines with small circulation.
- Excellent color reproduction capability.
- Much easier to produce—less to coordinate than with direct mail.
- A/B splits and regional editions are often available. Testing can be done fairly inexpensively.

Creative disadvantages

- Limited format possibilities due to page sizes and advertising configurations.
- Long lead time—closing dates can be months ahead of cover dates.
- Lack of control over position—some publications bunch ads together, creating ad "ghettos" without surrounding editorial. Response may vary a great deal between far-forward and far-back ad position.
- Relatively slow response and long shelf life make magazines hard to read and react to for further testing.
- Relatively impersonal medium. Although personalization and customization are possible in some magazines, relatively few offer this option.

Newspapers

Creative advantages

- Immediate, authoritative and newsy.
- A good medium for quick testing. Late closing dates and quick response, so results are available fast.
- Broad local coverage.
- National newspapers like *Wall Street Journal* and *Christian Science Monitor* offer broad reach; excellent regional testing possibilities at affordable cost.

DAMARK International, Inc. attracts new customers with a full-page coupon ad in *USA Today*. This four-color ad is an example of the improved color reproduction available today from some newspapers. *Source: USA Today,* July 13, 1990. Reprinted with permission of DAMARK International, Inc.

- Comes invited into the home by subscribers.
- Editorial-style ads let you trade on the publication's franchise as a respected source of news.
- Inexpensive to test—many publications will even provide layout and typesetting so a concept can be tested in small papers for a few thousand dollars, then expanded as warranted.
- A/B split testing available in some local papers.

Creative disadvantages

- Poor color reproduction in many cases; poor photo fidelity.
- Impersonal medium.
- Position and format problems abound.
- A mass medium—little selectivity except by city and suburban zones in medium to large cities.
- Can be a complex media procedure to create a national campaign using local newspapers.
- Local events and conditions can affect ad response, jeopardizing projectability of results.

Free-standing newspaper inserts and weekend magazines

Creative advantages

- Many of the same advantages as direct mail—format flexibility, good color reproduction, control of production.
- A plus over direct mail: exact timing, since your Free-Standing Insert arrives in a specific day's paper rather than whenever the third class mail happens to be delivered.
- Huge potential reach—as many as 60,000,000 American homes.
- Co-op Inserts like those of Vallasis and Quad allow for cost-effective testing in a small number of markets before roll-out.
- Advertising in newspaper-circulated magazines such as *Parade* and *Family Weekly* provide good testing possibilities and mass roll-out quantities.

Creative disadvantages

- In some markets there is a great deal of clutter among Free-Standing Inserts. In addition, studies show that certain market segments almost never read FSIs.

- A mass medium with little opportunity to target prospects. May be effective only for relatively low-end, mass-appeal products and services.
- Individual FSIs can be very costly: $50 per thousand or more. Response is considerably less than direct mail.

Billing inserts / package inserts / co-ops / card decks

Creative advantages

- Extends reach for direct-marketing programs that have been proven effective in mail and/or space.
- Affordable: may cost only $1/10$th as much as direct mail, but results are proportionately lower.
- Ability to control your own color quality and production within the confines of size and format restrictions.

Creative disadvantages

- Format and size constraints, especially in card decks and co-ops.
- Usually not considered a stand-alone medium—most often used to extend the reach of successful, proven programs.
- Must be controlled to ensure your offer is being promoted in a compatible medium. Co-ops range from the mass-market Carol Wright coupon envelope to the exclusive ranks of executive card decks. Some products that could pull well as Horchow package inserts might be out of the league of Lillian Vernon buyers.

Telephone

Creative advantages

- Immediate, personal, selective and very flexible. Allows for spur-of-the-moment up-selling and cross-selling.
- Allows you to ask specific questions to gain market research information while selling or reinforcing sales.
- Highest response medium; also most costly per prospect contact.
- May be used as a primary selling medium or a follow-up for continuity sales.

- Works best with established customers, for business-to-business pitches, or when you have specific questions to ask.

Creative disadvantages

- More consumers consider outbound telemarketing an invasion of privacy than any other main direct marketing medium.
- Does not allow for visuals.
- Expensive on a per-call basis, although a small test may be designed to test viability at a reasonable rate.
- Many consumers are virtually unreachable by phone because of long work hours, unlisted numbers, screening calls on phone answering machines, etc.

Television

Creative advantages

- Best medium for demonstration.
- Endless possibilities for formats and forms: drama, slice of life, pitchman, some combination—in studio or on location.
- More and more targeting is possible with cable and networks' reactions to the growth of cable.
- Versatile medium—may be used for sales, lead generation or support of other media.
- Quick responses: you can get a read on a commercial in minutes as customers call the toll-free number.
- By their very length, many direct marketing commercials eliminate clutter. At 90 to 120 seconds, they may consume all the time allotted to a commercial break period.
- Infomercials—entire 30-minute shows with an advertising message—offer the luxury of time to explain, demonstrate, and sell a product or service.

Creative disadvantages

- Very expensive: usually takes $100,000 or more for even a simple test. High production and time costs make this the realm of large and sophisticated direct-marketing firms.
- Finite amount of television time available. Time is especially scarce in the year's second and fourth quarters, when general advertisers beef up their broadcast buys.

- The woes of general advertisers on television hold for direct marketers: more consumers are "zapping" commercials of all kinds, eliminating them from videotapes and using remote control devices to sample other shows while commercials are on the air.
- A fleeting medium: unless you can move the consumer to action in 120 seconds or less (or 30 minutes in the case of an infomercial), you have lost your opportunity since nothing is written down.

Radio

Creative advantages

- Stations with specific formats allow for considerable targeting to business people, country-western fans, classical music buffs, etc.
- Inexpensive to test on a local basis; most rates are open for bargaining.
- Radio networks allow for considerable nationwide reach.
- Timely and newsy.
- A good medium for fantasy and humor.
- Ability to go on the air almost immediately—copy can be written one minute and read by an announcer the next. Even studio-produced spots take little time to prepare.

Creative disadvantages

- Much the same as television: a fleeting medium with nothing written down; listeners may switch stations when commercials are heard.
- Except for a few networks, it is a difficult and complex job to obtain national reach via radio.
- No visuals; no response device.
- Reports of listening audience may be exaggerated since many use radio as background noise.
- Number of people who do most of their listening in cars cuts down potential response, since they may not have access to phone or paper and pencil. Increased penetration of car phones may cut down this problem, especially for drive-time pitches to business people.

How to choose the media mix

For best results, start testing a new direct marketing concept in the medium where you have had the most previous success. If the firm is new, track the media buys of competitors for clues as to where the most fertile customer base might be. In most cases, direct mail and space advertising will be your best bets for initial testing. If tests prove successful, then consider expanding to additional media such as television, radio, or co-ops and package inserts. One exception: in some cases, firms will choose to begin with telephone marketing since they can obtain direct feedback from customers—not only on whether they will buy, but also on why or why not.

In evaluating any media selection, be sure that results are tracked not only on initial responsiveness, but also on continued performance levels. In most cases, your ultimate goal is to obtain customers with maximum lifetime value—not just individuals who have a high front-end response rate.

WHO SHOULD DO THE CREATIVE WORK AND WHAT DO THEY NEED TO KNOW

6

In recent years, management experts have made much of the "corporate culture" concept, pointing out how each of our most successful firms is run according to a distinct combination of written and unwritten norms.

Yet as Thomas J. Peters and Robert H. Waterman, Jr. pointed out in their landmark book, *In Search of Excellence*, there are several traits which first-rate firms have in common. Most essential of these for direct marketing managers is "productivity through people"—the company's genuine respect for its employees as partners in producing sales and profits.

If you visit the direct marketing agencies and companies with the best track records for bottom-line performance, you will sense a special energy in the air. That energy springs from a staff that works in a healthy, creative environment. In this chapter, both managers and creative practitioners will learn ways to develop such an environment in their own firms and agencies.

Once the atmosphere for creative thinking is established, direct marketers must develop a system for gathering and sharing background information for creative assignments. This chapter provides a guide for managers on what the creative team needs to know, and some hints to creatives on how to draw out this essential material from clients.

This discussion of the human element in direct marketing concludes with some pros and cons for managers deciding whether to have creative work produced by an outside agency, in-house staff, or a team of freelancers. There are also some pointers for creative people considering whether to work for an agency or company, or to hang out a freelancer's shingle.

How managers can nurture the creative person in direct marketing

During the 1960s, the prevailing image of the advertising creative person was wild, undisciplined and free spirited. "Dress for success" as a creative person was supposed to mean "dress crazy." Creative offices were decorated in bold colors, with accessories ranging from slinky toys to sofas in the shape of huge red lips. People envisioned copywriters and art directors roller skating down the halls and standing on their heads—ostensibly in search of that breakthrough idea.

Some of this was true, but it was mostly a myth. In the direct marketing field, very little of this creativity window dressing ever occurred.

The main reason direct marketing creative people have always appeared and acted more businesslike than their general advertising counterparts is rooted in the quantitative measurement of direct marketing success. Few direct marketers consider an ad or direct mail kit creative if it does not generate leads or sales at acceptable levels.

General advertising creative people often fill their résumés with the lists of creative awards they have won. But in direct marketing, even the creative awards competitions ask very specific questions about a campaign's performance against quantitative objectives.

Even so, it is important not to envision the direct marketing creative person as a nuts-and-bolts numbers cruncher. Some look just like account executives or marketing managers, right down to their gabardine suits and leather attachés. Indeed, some of the most successful heads of direct-marketing agencies and companies are also excellent writers or artists: David Ogilvy, Bob Stone, Joe Sugarman and the late Rod MacArthur, just to name a few. Other creative types wear Mickey Mouse sweatshirts or comfortable old golf sweaters to work, but they may well have a sharper bottom-line business sense than their appearances would indicate.

> Thus the first lesson about direct
> marketing creative people is this:
> you do yourself and them a disservice
> if you judge them by appearances alone.

There are, however, several truisms about copywriters and art directors that should be kept in mind. These traits may make creative types exasperating to deal with at times. But the manager who understands the creative mindset and handles creative people accordingly can look forward to top performance from them—and in many cases a resulting boost to the bottom line. Here, then, are some essentials about direct marketing creative people.

1. What the creative person loves is to write or to create art.

The first quirk of the creative person is that he or she probably doesn't really love business. In fact, he or she may be one of business's harshest critics. But working in advertising or direct marketing allows the creative person to write or create art for a living, with some job security and a fairly predictable income.

Get to know copywriters and art directors, and you will learn that most of them have some less commercial ambition for their talent. Many of them do these things part-time already: creating novels, poems or short stories, fine art canvases, plays or movies that may or may not ever be produced.

Others keep this higher ambition on the back burner for years. Believing that some day they will make movies or write novels or poetry—or paint landscapes instead of layouts—keeps these people relatively content in the work-a-day world of advertising.

The point behind this discussion is a simple matter of motivation. You won't motivate most creative people by rhapsodizing about business and how their latest ad is going to improve the bottom line. You will reap much greater rewards by focusing on the creative product and how to make it the best it can be—while still fulfilling marketing objectives.

Many managers become impatient with discussions involving subtle nuances of photographic lighting, choice of one adjective over another or the difference between PMS color 403 and

404. But if you show a creative person that you care about her craft, and that you're willing to take the extra time to make the ad a source of pride for her and for you—you will win her everlasting loyalty.

    2. Creative people are sensitive, and they always take their work personally.

Good copywriters and art directors nurture their projects like children. In fact, Joan Throckmorton actually refers to her hypothetical direct mail package as "Baby" and "the kid" in her fine book, *Winning Direct Response Advertising.*

With this level of care invested, the creative person is extraordinarily sensitive to criticism—just as parents are when relatives or teachers start picking on their beloved offspring. Yet toning down the creative person's emotional involvement might well lead to a less effective product.

Thus the smart direct-marketing manager keeps the creative person's point of view firmly in mind when critiquing copy and layout. Doing so is not only a good investment in human relations, it's also a guaranteed way to save money, time and aggravation.

Most every creative person can tell a horror story or two about insensitive clients and account executives whose ideas of constructive criticism include marginal notes such as "yuck," "ugh," or "this stinks—fix it by Friday *or else!*"

Obviously, such statements are counter-productive because they give no specific direction for improvement. But more destructive is the fact that pejorative terms are interpreted as personal attacks on the creative person. The resulting anger and insecurity lead inevitably to lower productivity.

In his book *The Inner Game of Tennis*, Tim Gallwey explains that "the safer you make a situation, the higher you can raise the challenge." At Apple Computer, John Sculley and his team of creative impresarios have learned that by making their staff feel supported and worthy, they can raise the creativity stakes higher and higher. When worry or lack of trust are part of the prevailing atmosphere, creativity plummets.

    3. Creative people need time to think—they can't always be doing what looks like work to you.

According to legend, Wolfgang Amadeus Mozart wrote some of his most brilliant musical pieces as fast as he could place the notes on paper. Samuel Taylor Coleridge's famous poem *Kubla Khan* is said to have come to him word for word in a dream. Nashville's country music museums display the originals of some of today's most popular songs scribbled longhand on envelopes or other paper scraps.

Yet for every piece of creative work that seizes its author or artist all at once, there are hundreds that develop only by means of painstaking effort, word by word and image by image.

Business people who are used to assigning specific time limits for jobs may be appalled to find that it is impossible to stop-watch creative work. A faster writer is not necessarily a better writer. An art director who always delivers on time may be following predictable patterns to meet deadlines rather than striving for a creative breakthrough.

Schedules are a fact of life in direct marketing, and successful creative people learn to keep them firmly in mind. But it is essential to build enough time into the schedule to allow the creative process to work. Research, time to digest background material, freedom to make false starts and to reach for the best possible approach will yield a much better product. What's more, your creative people will appreciate your respect for the intricacies of their craft.

4. Creative people thrive on recognition and opportunities for growth.

It costs the manager very little in time or effort to reward good ideas with recognition. Team spirit is healthy and constructive, but if one person's germ of an idea becomes the centerpiece of a winning campaign, make sure that person is recognized and publicly congratulated.

Creative people greatly appreciate memos of commendation, especially those which the boss and the rest of the staff see as well. Encouraging copywriters and art directors to enter creative awards competitions is another positive step. Even though direct marketing results are ultimately measured on the bottom line, the recognition of peers provides a powerful tonic to most creative people.

Make sure copywriters and art directors are not cloistered away from clients and the direct marketing world at large. Encourage them to attend client meetings, both to soak up background information and to receive face-to-face recognition for their work. Trips to direct marketing workshops, seminars and conventions help provide the outside stimulation that keeps creative people sharp and open to new concepts.

How creatives can help develop an environment where ideas flourish

Direct marketing managers and account executives can do a great deal to help foster a positive atmosphere for creativity. But copywriters and art directors must do their part as well, harnessing their creative powers to conquer specific marketing problems.

Here are several tips for creative people on how to work better with business people.

1. Remember that in direct marketing, creativity is a means to an end.

If your business associates are smart, they will value you for your creative flair—your ability to develop unique ways of highlighting product features and benefits and motivating prospects to buy. But as a copywriter or art director you must remember that *all* of your talents must be aimed at meeting marketing goals, not satisfying your personal creative Muse.

Many direct-marketing creative people complain about having to produce the same old stuff over and over. They lobby for the opportunity to do four-color work when test results have proved conclusively that two-color pieces are more cost effective for the offer at hand. They yearn for the chance to start from scratch and create a package or ad that ignores hard-won direct marketing principles.

Yet most breakthrough ideas in direct marketing are built upon principles, dos and don'ts developed through decades of careful testing. Remember that before Pablo Picasso broke new ground with his unique artistic vision, he spent years studying the Old Masters. Direct marketing creative types should do the same.

Read the works of creative giants like John Caples and Dick Hodgson. Study direct mail and ad samples diligently and learn all you can about their results. Do your homework on each product or service, investing the time you need to fully understand its attributes and drawbacks. Become as much of a direct *marketer* as you are a creative person, so that you can understand the numbers side of the business. And above all, remember that in direct marketing, the ultimate creativity of a campaign is in direct proportion to its sales and bottom-line performance.

2. Understand and accept the marketing concept of "sunk costs."

Business people often warn of "throwing good money after bad." They advise others to cut their losses and abandon a floundering product line or sell a stock that's falling in price rather than follow it to the bitter end.

Their business training makes it easier for marketers to abandon impractical advertising campaigns than it is for the creative types who developed them. Business people are interested in the *commercial* value of any given idea. If its commercial value plummets, the idea is no longer any good to them. Money that has been invested in such an idea is considered "sunk costs" to be written off and forgotten as soon as possible.

As a creative person, ideas are your stock in trade. Even though an idea no longer fits strategy, you may have a hard time abandoning it. But don't fight for it just because you have time, blood, sweat and tears tied up in it. Remember that it's just the *idea* that's being abandoned, not the talent that developed it. Keep your eye on the marketing plan and the bottom line.

3. Park your creative ego at the door and watch the gamesmanship stop.

Many times when a creative person and a business person try to work together, their value systems, personality traits and conflicts take over the conversation. The project they're trying to complete languishes while the two egos fight head to head.

Creative types often fan such a fire by becoming defensive about their work, accusing the manager or account executive of insensitivity or lack of discernment. Yet they can easily turn the conversation into a productive dialogue with a simple change of attitude.

Instead of setting up an adversarial, head-to-head encounter, try standing side-by-side with the person you're working with. Figuratively, you're placing yourself on the same team with that person, looking out toward the project and its possible solutions from the same vantage point. You're a partnership ganging up on the project, not on each other. In this way, you'll place the emphasis where it should be: on the job itself, not the power struggle within the relationship.

4. Strive to work well with your creative counterparts.

Even direct marketers who claim that copy is king must admit that there is considerable difference in reader perception between an ill-designed direct mail piece and a masterful job by an art director. Better to proclaim that the *product* is king, and that both copywriters and art directors should work to enhance it, forsaking "art for art's sake."

Unfortunately, in many cases copywriters and art directors may seem to be natural adversaries, like cats and dogs. The copywriter fights for another paragraph of copy space and complains that the art director really didn't try to arrange the location shots that would have been perfect for a particular brochure. The art director complains about long copy—in his mind, anything over 30 words—and insists on breaking up a block of type that needs to be read in sequence because it looks better his way.

But if the copywriter and art director respect each other's work and understand how much each can do to make the other look good, their cooperative efforts can be a joy to behold.

In practice, you will find many situations where the copywriter receives completed layouts to write from, and never even sees the art director face to face. Or the writer may prepare rough layouts and send them off into a void for production. But having the writer and artist work together from start to finish is the ideal that creative people should strive for.

What the creative team needs to know

Everyone has heard the old saw about computers, "garbage in, garbage out." The same holds true in the relationship between direct marketing client and creative person: the better (or worse) the input, the better (or worse) the finished product. This refers less to grammar, sentence structure and flow than to the selling message and thrust of a direct marketing piece.

As a manager, you must do your homework before meeting with the copywriter and art director. You will either have to provide the type of information described below, or point your creative people in the direction in which to obtain it. Keep in mind that the more digging you expect them to do, the more the assignment is likely to cost in time and money.

If the creative team has worked with you before, they may already know about the company, product, and market. But even so, you will need to talk specifically about objectives, copy points, and the plans that have been made for this particular promotion.

Here, then, is a checklist of information creative people should have to begin a direct marketing project. Both managers and creatives can use this list to ensure they have compiled and shared all necessary material.

What is the company behind your product?

- Has your firm been involved in direct marketing before?
- How long has it been in business?
- What is its reputation?
- What kind of people and businesses form its present customer base?

What is the competitive environment for this product?

- Who are your competitors?
- How do their products differ from yours?
- What features of your product, if any, excel theirs?
- Do you have a lower price or better overall benefit package?
- How have the competitors been promoting their products as compared to your efforts?

What is the product?

- Provide a product sample for the copywriter and artist.
- If you are selling a service, allow the creative team to participate in the service.
- Provide all collateral materials that come with your product or service.
- Put the writer in touch with the buyer or developer of the product, if someone other than yourself.

- Answer the creative people's questions about how the product works and what it can do for the customer.
- Provide library research, articles, books, or anything else that will help the creative people understand the product and its benefits.

Who is the customer?

- Describe the likely buyer of your product.
- Include known demographics such as age, sex, income level, family size, region in which he or she lives.
- Include known psychographics such as lifestyle factors, buying patterns, etc.
- For new products, share plans for list or media testing to provide ideas about likely buyers.
- Include testimonials from users of this or similar products.

How will we sell this product?

- Share media plan—direct mail, space, broadcast, telemarketing, etc.
- Explain reasons for using these media and share ideas with creatives for more media concepts.
- Explain budgetary restrictions.

How have we sold the product in the past?

- One of the best sources of research for creatives is studying past efforts for a product.
- Don't mention only the winners. As much can be learned from what did not work as from what did.
- If the product is new, provide samples of past efforts on your other products. This can be supplemented by competitors' advertising samples.

What are the objectives for this project?

- Lead generation or sales campaign?
- Specific numbers: percentage response, orders per thousand, etc.

■ Are you looking for loose leads (people who are interested but not committed) or tight leads (people who are already somewhat prequalified)?

■ For retail campaigns: are you looking to generate traffic, direct mail and phone sales, or both?

What are the copy points for this product?

■ Work with copywriter to develop this set of points.

■ Make a list of what you want the advertising to get across starting with chief product benefit and working down.

■ Include important specifications such as price, size, shipping information, guarantee, etc.

What other creative work has been done so far for the product?

■ If rough or comprehensive layouts are done, share them with the copywriter and provide the layouts themselves or photocopies.

■ If you have rough copy, share it with the art director.

■ Get copywriter and art director together as a team if at all possible.

What are your preferences as to creative tone and look?

■ Share information about the overall impression you wish to make: friendly, upscale, snobby, down-to-earth, sporty, etc.

■ Provide samples of direct marketing you admire, and explain what you like about it.

What is the immediate assignment?

■ Outline and thumbnail sketches?

■ Rough layouts with headings and a concept piece attached?

■ Full-copy treatment plus comprehensive layouts?

■ Deadline information and overall timetable.

Few clients are organized and experienced enough to provide all—or even part—of this information on their own. Creative people must learn to dig for it by asking these questions themselves, sometimes over a period of days or weeks to avoid overwhelming the client.

In the meantime, they can prepare for assignments to come by doing general research on the client's product category, visiting retail outlets where such products are sold, visiting the factory where the product is made, accompanying field salespeople, and any number of other background activities. Marketers who encourage such detailed research on the part of their creative staff will reap extraordinary benefits in the resulting copy and layouts.

This next step is the topic for Chapter 10 which details the step-by-step process of copywriting and art direction. There you will see how background research leads to a finished direct marketing creative piece. You will also learn specifics on how to evaluate copy and layouts.

Who should do the creative work: An agency, in-house staff, or freelancers?

The array of direct marketing creative service options can be confusing to the novice. Should you hire a full-service agency, or develop an in-house creative staff? Is freelance help the best option for you due to seasonal ups and downs in your creative needs? Or should you invest the time to learn the ropes of direct marketing creative work yourself, and go it alone? Here are some of the basic pros and cons of each option.

The benefits of working with a direct marketing agency

- *A full staff of personnel to meet your needs.* You can assume the role of manager and supervisor of your campaigns, meanwhile delegating a great deal of the creative and production work without giving up the decision-making function.

- *Direct marketing experience.* Even if you are somewhat seasoned in direct marketing, you probably don't have the broad background that the staff of an agency can offer you, including knowledge about what works and what doesn't, and experience in getting mailings, ads and other promotions done on time and effectively.
- *Unbiased feedback.* The agency is an outsider, with the ability to give you a fresh view of your objectives, your product, your promotions, and your results. You don't have to work in a vacuum or rely strictly on the opinions of your own staff.
- *A constant idea supply.* Assuming you have found a good agency, you won't be stuck in a rut in terms of your product or promotions. The stimulation of seeing what works and what "bombs" for other clients will keep your agency alive to new creative possibilities for you.

Why some direct marketers don't like agencies

Here are some of the negative aspects of working with a direct marketing agency.

- *Expense.* The bigger the agency, the bigger its overhead. Whether you use them or not, you'll be helping to support the agency's media department, production staff and other facilities right along with the creative department whose help you really need. So think hard about going with a full-service agency unless you need all or most of its services.
- *Ongoing costs.* Most direct marketing agencies want to work on a retainer basis only; very few will do more than a single introductory job on a project basis. This makes sense from the agencies' viewpoint, since the time and energy they must invest to win a new client and learn the business is quite large. But you must ask yourself if your business is year-round and constant enough to justify the payment of a monthly retainer. Perhaps you'd be better off calling in a consultant or one-person agency when you need help, with no strings attached.
- *The education process.* If your product, proposition or way of doing business is quite complex, you may be better off training people to do your direct marketing work for you—at least the marketing planning and creative work—on an in-house

basis. With an agency you run the risk of getting the agency copywriter "where you want him" in terms of product knowledge, and suddenly having him transferred to another client or account group.

- *Your size/their size.* Perhaps you've read about some of the agency giants of the direct marketing field and would like to have one of them work for you. If you're a division of a *Fortune* 500 company with a sizeable budget, you may have no problem getting this. But if you're beginning with more enthusiasm than money, you may have a problem finding even a small agency that's willing to gamble the time it will take to get your fledgling program off the ground.

The in-house creative staff: Pros and cons

A number of direct marketers, large and small, prefer to develop an in-house staff to handle all or most of their promotional needs. There are three main plusses of such an arrangement.

- *The in-house agency can develop experts and keep them.* If the product is complex or the method of selling unique, it may be easier for a firm to develop its own creative talent than to teach its business over and over again to outsiders.
- *Work can be turned around quickly.* Since the in-house writers and artists seldom have clients other than the parent firm and its divisions, they can meet the firm's creative priorities on a daily basis. Often an outside agency can get away with longer lead times simply because the advertiser is not fully aware of the mechanics of getting a job done. With the in-house staff, these mechanics are much more open to scrutiny, and built-in contingency time is therefore harder to obtain.
- *The advertiser has more control.* For an in-house creative staff, company philosophies are easier to get across and keep in mind. There is more day-to-day supervision of the creative work, and more give and take between creative people and the firm's other personnel.

There are, however, some harsh critics of the in-house creative shop. Here are a few of the negative comments.

- *Work from an in-house agency tends to lose freshness.* Agency people benefit from the stimulation of working on a variety of accounts, and seeing different marketing strategies succeed. The in-house writers and artists may turn out less innovative work than outsiders would.
- *The firm with an in-house staff takes on a good deal of overhead.* Rather than treating creative help as an expense, the in-house agency owner must pay advertising support costs as a part of the regular corporate payroll. This continuing cost of doing business must be warranted by the results.
- *Bureaucracy or inner-directed thinking.* In-house creative people are often less sales oriented than their outside agency counterparts. They consider themselves a service department in the same mode as data processing or accounting. Thus these creatives tend to become more inner directed, concerned with office politics and corporate problems rather than finding the best way to intrigue consumers.

Working with freelancers

If you do not hire a direct marketing agency or develop your own in-house staff, you will have to find your own copywriter and art director. If you already have a list broker or other consultant whom you trust, you can ask them to refer you to creative people. You might also discuss your requirements with colleagues who do direct marketing, to see if they know a freelancer who may suit your needs. Checking the classified ads in publications like *Direct Marketing* or *DM News* is a third option. And if you are a member of a local or regional direct-marketing organization, its roster should provide you with a list of the creative services in your area.

Once you've located a likely candidate, call him or her on the phone and introduce yourself. Explain the kinds of products you're going to be marketing and any ideas you have about media or themes for your campaign. If the information is confidential, say so right away. Direct marketing freelancers who expect to stay in business know that confidentiality is nearly as important in their profession as it is for the clergy and for doctors.

Listen carefully for the reactions of the copywriter or art director to your product and your ideas. Does the person sound enthusiastic about your proposition? Does he or she know what you're talking about, or does your field seem foreign to that person's experience? If a freelancer has heard of your firm and starts mentioning your previous efforts and those of your competitors in a knowledgeable way, you may have found yourself a gem. But you might also ask for verification of experience in your own or a related area. Some direct marketers have sufficiently broad backgrounds and interests to sell almost any type of product if they get complete input, while others choose to specialize in consumer or industrial goods, retail clients, or even something as specific as collectibles or financial services.

Don't talk only about the product. Make sure the creative person knows whether you are considering a mail program or space advertising, television, business-to-business, or telephone marketing. It's a rare creative who is equally proficient in all of these areas, and an honest one will tell you where his or her specialties lie. A well-connected writer or art director may be able to help you find a colleague who can do television scripting or collateral design for you, while handling your direct mail kits, space ads and catalog work personally.

If the phone contact goes well, invite the creative to send you some work samples. The promptness of the response and presentation of the materials will be good indicators of the way in which this person will handle your account. Are the samples keyed in to your expressed interests in terms of product and media? Or do they look like a canned package of samples that would be sent to any prospective client? Does the style of writing and art please you? Is the copy meaty and specific, or vague and general? Is the layout clear and easy to follow? Do your best to separate the graphics presentation from the copy itself, since the writer often has no say about the work of the art director, and vice versa, especially as a freelancer.

Once you have evaluated the samples, a face-to-face meeting is the next step. Make sure you have an advance understanding of whether the meeting will be held on a speculative basis or whether you will be charged for this consultation time. A good way to get started is to give the creative person a straightforward, simple assignment like a one-column space ad or a direct mail flyer. But to indoctrinate the person, you will have to provide plenty of the background information discussed earlier.

Before giving the creative person an initial assignment, keep in mind that you are asking him or her to do research on your firm and its products that will continue to pay off if you give that person more work to do in the future. A flat fee is probably safer than an hourly rate at this point, because creative people work at greatly varying speeds. But do inquire about the person's usual rates and payment terms.

To establish trust from the beginning, you should provide the writer or art director with a purchase order (P.O.) number. Also state your policy about payment (net within 30 days, payment on receipt, payment when your material appears in print, or whatever). Clients who are candid about their payment arrangements and keep their word are rewarded with loyal and swift service by grateful freelancers.

If you decide to create your own direct marketing promotions

Most firms and individuals who hope to grow smoothly and quickly in the direct marketing field feel more confident with expert creative help right from the beginning. But teaching yourself the ropes is not an impossible task, assuming you have a measure of talent for writing and design and an ability to soak up knowledge and put it to work. This book and those listed in the Appendix should be your first sources of information. You'll learn hard-won facts about what works in direct response marketing and what doesn't.

Attending seminars, trading experiences with direct marketing professionals, and reading trade publications as well as books may help you—if you are also smart and lucky—to build a lucrative and successful business on the basis of your own creative skills.

Decisions for creatives: Agency, in-house or freelance?

For direct marketing creative people, the grass always seems to be greener on the other side of the business. Agency creatives believe that a position on the client side would be less pressured. They imagine working 9 to 5 and concentrating on just one product line instead of the ever-changing array of assignments that is part of agency life.

In-house creative people imagine work in an agency as more glamorous. They dream of building their portfolios with a wide variety of projects in consumer markets, business-to-business, catalog and broadcast. They wonder if agency people make more money than they do, and fantasize about living in Chicago or New York instead of less cosmopolitan towns like Freeport, Maine and Emmaus, Pennsylvania.

Both agency and in-house people have been known to consider the freelance route, envying the independent writer or artist his ability to make his own hours, demand high fees and travel at will. On the other hand, freelancers may well covet the employed person's regular paycheck, benefits package and team identity. They sometimes find being on their own unsettling and lonely.

If you are a creative person considering these various employment options, consider these pros and cons carefully. If you are wise, your decision will combine factors of personal temperament, your age and the stage of your career, areas of expertise, supervisory ability and aspirations, and much more.

In general, *agency creatives* need to thrive on pressure. They must be able to juggle several clients' needs at one time, and to express their ideas well in meetings. As their careers progress, agency creatives often move into supervisory roles, watching over other creative people's work. Necessarily, they do less and less writing or art direction on their own as they move up this supervisory ladder.

On the other hand, *in-house creatives* must be able to sustain curiosity about and interest in the same product or service for months or even years at a time. They must be willing and able to become experts in their company's product line, actually considering themselves as much insurance people or collectibles people or office products people as they are direct marketers. They must strive for fresh ways of looking at the same old thing, and inspire this attitude in those they work with. In general, their jobs may be less stressful than those of agency creatives, but some in-house agencies are more pressured than New York or Chicago's hottest direct marketing shops.

Freelance creatives must combine their talents for writing or art with salesmanship. They must be accomplished enough to convince companies and agencies to use their services, and to pay them hefty rates for the privilege. Even more than those who are employed, they must be deadline oriented and disciplined. Since many of them work at home, they must be able to separate their work lives from their personal lives. On the plus side, the best freelancers enjoy a great deal of flexibility in timing their work and selecting their clients.

As creative people consider these options, they should keep in mind that in a career spanning 40 years or more, many writers and artists sample each of these options: agency, in-house and freelance. Each opportunity provides some of the ingredients for a well-rounded career in the creative arena of direct response marketing.

THE ART AND SCIENCE OF CREATIVE DIRECT MAIL

II

THE OFFER IN DIRECT MARKETING

7

Before a single word goes on paper or a line is sketched on the layout pad, the direct marketing creative team must focus on the *offer* they plan to make in their promotion. Creative types who work with established, well-organized firms or agencies may be lucky enough to receive a succinct statement of the offer at the outset of any project. Better yet, the copywriter and art director will be invited to help hammer out the details of product, price, place and promotion. If such an offer statement is not forthcoming, it may be up to the writer and artist to work with the company or client to establish one, using the structure outlined in this chapter.

The marketing mix—product/price/place/promotion—must be addressed fully to ensure that your prospective customer receives a clear picture of the proposition at hand in your direct mail package, ad, or other communication. What's more, even a slight adjustment in one or more of these factors has been known to affect response quite dramatically. For instance, some careful testing to determine the maximum acceptable price for an item may greatly increase profitability at roll-out time. The introduction of a premium, strengthening of a guarantee, offer of a free trial period, or addition of a split-payment option may all have significant impact on response as well.

Designing a package of product/price/place/promotion cannot be done in a vacuum. Before the terms of the offer are set, it is essential for direct marketers to analyze the target market carefully. It is also important to focus on the long-term goals of the promotion at hand—obtaining a house list for future promotions, for example, and maximizing the lifetime value of each customer—not just making an initial sale.

As Bob Stone says in *Successful Direct Marketing Methods,* the most important objective in designing any offer is to overcome inertia on the part of the prospect. Every detail of the offer and its presentation must be considered from the point of view of the prospect. What will spur him on to mail or call in an order? What will deter her from completing the order form or making a decision?

The financial services industry offers many examples of marketers keying in very specifically to the target market's wants and needs. The proliferation of credit cards and the elimination of the consumer-interest tax deduction are just two reasons why banks and other financial firms have had to compete harder than ever for customer loyalty. To fine-tune their offers, they find out from the customers themselves what would make a good credit offer: no yearly fee, a more favorable interest rate, or a longer grace period before interest is charged.

These three examples represent a simple manipulation of standard parts of the offer, but financial service marketers have become much more creative in recent years. They have learned that consumers resist filling out long applications, so they offer preapproved credit, requiring only a few pieces of information to apply. To differentiate one Visa or MasterCard from hundreds of others, marketers have developed affinity programs whereby individuals can carry credit cards that indicate their affiliation with an institution or charitable group—and each purchase nets a small donation to that group. Discover Card offers cash back to the card holder on every charge. American Express now gives customers the chance to invest money each month by being billed for it right along with their purchases—and to have that money grow in a tax-deferred, interest-bearing account.

Whatever your product or service may be, the example of the financial service marketers provides an excellent guide. In structuring an offer, consider first the usual possibilities for manipulation: modifying the product, testing the price, establishing a stronger guarantee, etc. But also spend the time and effort necessary to talk with customers—informally or in focus groups—to get ideas for creative enhancements that would strongly entice them to buy.

**The Discover Card attracts credit card members by offering them a "Cashback Bonus" ©
for purchases. Each year, card members receive an elaborate "Cashback Bonus Report"
including a check for the Cashback Bonus amount and an update on Discover Card services.** Reprinted with permission of Discover Card Services, Inc.

This chapter presents the specifics on how to build an offer based upon the four "Ps" of the marketing mix: product, price, place and promotion. The following pages contain idea-starters on how to structure each aspect for maximum customer interest value, short-term sales gains, and long-term customer loyalty. There is also information on how to develop direct marketing offers for the generation of qualified sales leads.

The product

The product or service you sell via direct marketing must be differentiated in some way from items consumers can pick up at any store near home. You must make prospects perceive that your product is different . . . more exclusive . . . easier to buy . . . or more economical. Remember also that in any sales proposition, it is important to focus on results, not just the product itself; on benefits, not simply product features. Products most likely to succeed in direct mail are those that can be demonstrated or dramatized by means of illustrations, descriptions, and well-written selling copy. To overcome inertia, and to combat the prospect's natural resistance to buying "here and now," you must convince him or her that you have the best item or service of this type, and that buying it directly from you is the best available option. Here are some techniques to help you develop and present your product in the most effective way.

Market segmentation

You may segment a market by region or state, by psychographics and personality elements, or by statistical measures like gender, income or age. Study packaged goods marketers for excellent examples of effective market segmentation. There are cigarettes aimed at outdoorsmen, sophisticates, and liberated women. There are cereals targeted at health-conscious adults, nutrition-conscious parents, and at children seeking out the latest breakfast fad.

Among direct marketers, those who sell clothing offer excellent examples of segmentation. The same basic garments are modified and marketed with subtle differences in color, construction and presentation by old-line sporting goods firms like Orvis and L. L. Bean, and by sportswear firms exhibiting a more timely fashion flair, like J. Crew and Tweeds. Direct marketers of books and records also do a superb job with segmentation: pick up *Rolling Stone* for an offer of a record club based on rock music, or *Smithsonian* to read an ad for a classical record club. Readers of *British Heritage* are invited to join a history book club, while women's service magazines offer clubs with books for children of various ages. As you can see from these examples, your choice of mailing lists or space ad media will help you reach the prospects who feel most at home with your clearly defined product concept.

Product differentiation

Marketing textbooks often tell the stories of Lucky Strike and Wonder Bread to illustrate product differentiation. Decades ago a classic Lucky Strike cigarette ad carried the two-word slogan, "It's toasted," winning converts from among smokers who liked the idea of smoking toasted tobacco. The fact is that all cigarette tobacco is toasted in its processing, but it took a smart marketer to visit the Lucky Strike factory and discover this intriguing point. The same concept holds true for Wonder Bread's classic slogan, "It builds strong bodies 12 ways." The twelve nutritional points apply equally to all enriched breads, but since Wonder Bread pointed them out, consumers perceived that this brand was unique.

If your product does not carry inherent differences from the competition that you can point out to win favor, consider how you could differentiate it enough to make ordering from you an attractive alternative. Perhaps you could negotiate with manufacturers for exclusive items, or items emblazoned with your company name or a designer's name. Or, say that a number of firms offer a popular handbag designed with special pouches for wallet, make-up, keys, etc.—but it is available only in vinyl. If you can offer the same design in leather, customers may perceive this as a positive differentiation worthy of special attention.

Brand name

At holiday time, dozens of firms sell popcorn and pretzels in gift tins—but only Neiman-Marcus can sell these snack items in a tin emblazoned with the famous N-M logo. Scores of companies sell cotton turtlenecks, but only Land's End can trade upon its hard-won reputation for the utmost value for money, emphasized by double-page catalog spreads that have explained the turtleneck's attributes and improvements over the years.

Promoting a strong brand name is a tried-and-true way to overcome inertia on the part of a prospect—especially if the branded item is available only by mail, and only through you. Direct marketers with strong brand names may find that they are able to sell otherwise parity products successfully—perhaps even at a premium price—by emphasizing that this is a Lord & Taylor night shirt or a Hormel food gift box, not just a generic product.

Capitalize on demonstration

Some products require little or no demonstration to sell, but the interest value of most products can be enhanced by carefully crafted copy and appropriate illustrations. Your competition selling stereo equipment or down comforters in a retail store has a sales person available to point out the item's features and benefits. In direct marketing, it is up to the writer and artist to grab the prospect's attention and maintain interest by explaining the product's attributes and what it could do to enhance its owner's life.

Brochures provide the perfect opportunity to introduce cross-sections, large illustrations with call-outs describing product benefits, testimonials discussing the product's attributes in use, etc. If possible, send along a sample of the product to enhance demonstration: a sample cassette to exhibit the quality of a set of teaching tapes, for instance, or perhaps a computer disk or fabric sample, just to mention a few possibilities.

Enhance product presentation

Order the same type of product from an assortment of direct marketing companies, and you will be fascinated by the range of ways in which products are presented at the time of shipment. Some direct marketers merely shove the product into the proverbial plain brown wrapper and ship it off as is. At the other end of the spectrum is Eximious, a marketer of fine English and European products that presents most every item in a striking gold-and-navy gift box or wrapping at no additional charge.

Naturally, the care and money which you invest in packaging your product will depend upon its price tag. But no matter what price level of product you are selling, it pays to keep the recipient's probable reaction in mind. When your package arrives via mail or U.P.S., there is no salesperson on hand to thank the customer or reinforce the wisdom of this buying decision. At the very least, your product presentation should handle this function with a "thank you" communiqué of some sort, and a tasteful and protective product wrapper.

Product assortment

You may be able to increase your average order size and do your customer a favor at the same time if you offer helpful advice about the proper assortment that should be purchased for a given family situation, occasion, or gift. Study direct marketers of food for some excellent examples of how this is done. Many food marketers offer "fruit-of-the-month" plans, or similar selections that feature monthly gifts of nuts, coffees, desserts, or even English muffins. Firms selling steaks and other fine meats put together "executive assortments" and "surf and turf dinners," while some food catalogs provide holiday gifts in typical price ranges such as $20.00, $30.00, $50.00, and up.

You can do this with other product lines and even with intangible products and services. Life insurance marketers, for instance, often offer the customer a chance to choose coverage in the $20,000, $50,000 or $100,000 range, and within these ranges, to select a program for the individual, or for the entire family. Consider a wardrobe assortment—a week's worth of men's dress shirts at a special price, for instance—or groupings of toys selected especially for two-year-olds, four-year-olds, etc. Whatever your product or service, brainstorm ways to combine it into a package deal that prospects will find appealing.

Preselected kits

Just as customers enjoy an expert's advice on how many shirts to buy or how to select the right amount of insurance, prospects also find it helpful to be offered a preassembled package that accomplishes a goal of theirs. Examples might include an all-in-one home entertainment center, or a prechosen baby nursery decor including bedding, accessories and wallpaper. This is especially true in today's climate of serve-yourself retailing, when very little expert help may be forthcoming for the customer in a store.

Copy for such a presentation should explain why this particular kit or outfit was selected, and point out the features and benefits that set it apart from alternative products or packages. Illustrations and call-outs can help explain how the elements of the kit work together, and help the prospect visualize the package as it would appear and function in the home.

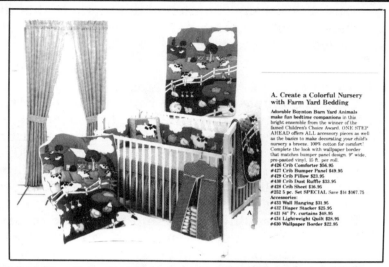

A. Create a Colorful Nursery with Farm Yard Bedding

Adorable Boynton Barn Yard Animals make fun bedtime companions in this bright ensemble from the winner of the famed Children's Choice Award. ONE STEP AHEAD offers ALL accessory pieces as well as the basics to make decorating your child's nursery a breeze. 100% cotton for comfort! Complete the look with wallpaper border that matches bumper panel design. 9" wide, pre-pasted vinyl, 15 ft. per roll.
#426 Crib Comforter $56.95
#427 Crib Bumper Panel $49.95
#429 Crib Pillow $23.95
#430 Crib Dust Ruffle $33.95
#428 Crib Sheet $16.95
#252 5 pc. Set SPECIAL Save $14 $167.75
Accessories:
#433 Wall Hanging $31.95
#432 Diaper Stacker $25.95
#431 84" Pr. curtains $48.95
#434 Lightweight Quilt $28.95
#630 Wallpaper Border $22.95

The "One Step Ahead" catalog offers new parents several fully merchandised sets of crib bedding, such as this "Barn Yard Animals" ensemble. A number of accessories are included as well as standard pieces. Such a wide range of coordinated items is seldom available at a retail store, which gives the catalog a competitive advantage. Reprinted with permission of Chelsea & Scott.

Customer involvement in product parameters

Consider letting the customer choose the unit of sale or help in the design of the product. Magazine publishers increase customer involvement by allowing prospects to select the exact number of issues of a publication they would like to receive, at a certain per-copy price. This lets the prospect choose his or her own comfort level as to length of subscription term and dollars spent. As for product design, personalization is one form of this phenomenon. Also, some clothiers show outfits made up in various materials and colors and then offer many other color and fabric options. This is especially appealing today, when very few stores offer custom tailoring. Direct marketers of furniture and home accessories may offer options for fabric, wood finish, brass or chrome accents, etc.

Timing of product delivery

Try to find a way in which you can serve the customer with timely delivery and increase your own volume and revenue at the same time. Perhaps you could arrange to send a woman a half-dozen new pairs of pantyhose monthly, or a month's supply of a special pet food to a dog owner or cat fancier. Or maybe you could offer to fulfill all of a customer's gift-giving needs throughout the year—sending preselected products on the appropriate dates.

Good, better, best

In the days when Chicago-based catalog firms like Alden's, Spiegel, Montgomery Ward and Sears dominated the direct marketing scene, many merchandising departments were structured around the trade-up concept, or "good, better, best." Direct marketing is an ideal medium for this type of comparison shopping, since similar products can be shown together on a brochure or catalog page, and their features and benefits can be displayed head to head.

The classic catalog trade-up begins with a picture and selling description of the basic model. Then the more expensive items are discussed one by one, balancing their additional features and benefits with their higher prices. In this way, the customer gets the positive feeling of being involved in an informed decision-making process.

The club concept

People enjoy affiliating with clubs that bring them benefits such as savings, special opportunities, information on favorite topics, or strength to fight for a cause. Book and record clubs provide the savings concept with many variations of an offer like this: "choose six books now for just $1.00 and buy six more over the next year at below-publisher's rates." Collectibles clubs offer members the chance for affiliation with others who collect Lladro, Hummel, or Swarovski products, and also the opportunity to purchase special, "members-only" figurines and participate in "members-only" tours to Europe.

Groups like the American Association of Retired Persons (AARP) may begin as a springboard for the sale of products or services, but when millions of like-minded individuals band together, such organizations may become powerful lobbyists or even activists for the rights of elderly people, environmental causes, etc. When structured with the consumer's interests in mind, such clubs may provide substantial services to their members—while still offering an ideal opportunity for selling merchandise, trips, insurance, and other services. Auto clubs spon-

Now you can own what may well be the next collectibles legend.

In 1985, members of the Lladró Collectors Society had the opportunity to buy the first annual Collectors Society figurine, "Little Pals." Available only to Society members, it sold for $95.00. In 1989, this same figurine sold at auction for $3,750.00.

"Little Pals" became a collectibles legend. And it started something. Every members-only figurine since "Little Pals" has increased in value once its redemption period has closed.

For 1990, you can own what could be the next "Little Pals."* This year's Lladró Collectors Society figurine, "Can I Play?," will be available to those who join the Society by December 31, 1990. Once "Can I Play?" is retired, the only way you'll be able to purchase it will be on the secondary market.

The yearly members only figurine is just one of the benefits of Society membership. For joining you'll also receive:
• A members-only porcelain plaque bearing the signatures of the three Lladró brothers

Shown above, "Can I Play?", 8½", $150. Available only to those who join the Lladró Collectors Society by Dec. 31, 1990.

*Lladró figurines should always be purchased for their inherent handcrafted and handpainted beauty, as future value cannot be guaranteed.

• A full years subscription to *Expressions* Magazine
• A leatherette binder in which to store your magazines
• A personalized membership card

All told, your Society membership, which includes a "Can I Play?" Redemption Certificate, your free gifts and other Lladró Collectors Society benefits, adds up to an offer worth $71.50—for a modest $25.00 membership fee.

Enroll today and join with others—from experienced collectors to enthusiastic beginners—in the world's foremost collectors society. Simply fill out and return the attached application today!

Or, for even faster enrollment, you may call us toll-free at: 1-800-345-5433, Ext. 1219. In Illinois, please call: 1-800-972-5855, Ext.1219.

Circle FREE Reader Information Number 20, on Card at Page 46.

The Lladro Collectors Society stimulates "loyalty, caring and sharing" among collectors of these fine porcelain figurines through publications and other membership benefits offered via direct mail. One of the most popular benefits is the opportunity to purchase a yearly "members only" figurine, such as the "Can I Play?" piece featured in this ad. Reprinted with permission of Lladro Collectors Society.

sored by oil companies and by diversified retailers like Sears and Ward are prominent examples; study their literature for ideas on club member benefits.

In its simplest form, the club concept may only represent an appealing way of justifying frequent communications or payments. Car wash clubs offer their members discounts on weekly washes, for instance, and bank Christmas clubs are simply savings accounts in which individuals deposit a certain amount each week of the year.

Accessories to enhance a product or increase a sale

Adding related accessories to your product offer may make it more unique and appealing. At the same time, the purchase of such accessories may increase your average order size dramatically. What's more, you may be able to achieve a higher mark-up on appealing accessories because of their nature as an add-on to a particular product.

For example, say that one of your bread-and-butter products is a boy's hooded snowsuit in navy blue with bright green trim. If you can develop a stocking cap and mitten set in the same navy blue and green, many customers may pick up the set as an impulse item, increasing your sales. At the same time, offering the hat and mittens makes the snowsuit more appealing because now it is an outfit, not just a generic snowsuit. In such a case, you might push the outfit concept even further by selling the snowsuit plus cap/mitten set together at a savings of a few dollars over the "snowsuit only" price.

Sometimes your accessory sale may be perceived as a helpful service by the customer. For instance, if you sell a product that requires batteries, try selling the proper batteries as a separate item. This increases customer convenience, which may help overcome inertia and make the sale. What's more, if you offer the batteries at a good mark-up, their sale may become a small but helpful source of extra revenue.

The price

Some direct marketers determine their prices solely according to a set of internal parameters. Others look strictly at what the market will bear, as indicated by their competitors' price structure.

The Squire's Choice attracts new customers for its catalog by means of a $^1/_6$ page ad offering a pound of the "largest nuts in the world" for $9.95—a $7.00 savings over the regular price of $16.95 per pound. Reprinted with permission of The Squire's Choice.

Sample the Largest Nuts in the World For Just $9.95

Enjoy your first pound of the largest, most flawless, most carefully prepared nut mix in the world today—at the introductory price of just $9.95! Huge, flavorful Brazilian cashews are combined with whole Hawaiian macadamias and Georgia pecan halves in equal portions, all hand-roasted in healthful peanut oil. So large you'll do a double-take when you see them. For ultimate freshness, they are roasted, packed and shipped daily. The Squire offers you a 100% money back guarantee.

The Connoisseur's Collection: 1 Pound Sampler Size in Gold Gift Box. Reg. $16.95 **Special $9.95** *Add $2.95 Shipping and Handling.*

Call toll-free **800-523-6163** for credit card orders or send check to:

Nuts Shown Actual Size.

The SQUIRE'S CHOICE

2000 West Cabot Blvd., Langhorne, Pa. 19047

Catalog featuring 32 pages of freshly prepared nut, coffee, popcorn, and candy gifts **FREE** with order.   DEPT. 813

The best way to set price is by considering both internal and external factors, and then taking advantage of the direct marketer's considerable ability to test.

Catalog marketers who purchase their products from outside sources often must live with a two-time mark-up—what retailers call a 50 percent mark-up. This means that a product that wholesales for $20.00 will be sold for about $40.00 in a direct-mail catalog. Direct marketers who develop and produce their own products rather than going through a wholesaler may achieve a three- or even a four-time mark-up on their cost of goods.

When considering whether to offer a particular product, first decide how much price flexibility your firm has. Then find out what price level customers consider appropriate for this product. Some inexpensive testing in space ads may show you that your target market is happy to pay $19.99 per pair for polyester slacks, but that they balk at a $24.99 price for the same merchandise.

Even though consumers have their own built-in comfort levels where price is concerned, they may be won over by appeals of exclusivity or outstanding quality. The Squire's Choice, a Pennsylvania-based nut and coffee company, ran an ad in *The*

New Yorker with the headline, "Sample the Largest Nuts in the World For Just $9.95." The ad listed the nuts' regular price at $16.95 per pound, but offered this special sample offer at "just" $9.95. If a group of consumers were asked the question, "How much is too much to pay for a pound of nuts," many of them might be expected to give an answer considerably lower than $9.95. But when the $9.95 price is juxtaposed against the true, regular price of $16.95—and the nuts are characterized with the superlative, "largest in the world"—consumers may begin to see these rather expensive nuts as a bargain.

The choice of a price point for any given product also must be made with the promotion's objectives in mind. In the case of the "largest nuts" ad, the firm was interested in generating a list of gourmet nut buyers. Therefore, The Squire's Choice was willing to sell nuts at a discounted price on a one-time basis to get their product into the hands of consumers they hoped would become regular buyers. Other promotions may be intended to make the biggest possible profit, in which case the highest volume might not meet the stated objective.

A glance at retailers' prices shows that many stores—especially those catering to bargain shoppers—offer prices that end in odd numbers such as $29.99 instead of $30.00. The concept is that at the consumer's first glance, $29.99 appears to be a price in the $20.00 range instead of the $30.00 price it essentially is. Direct marketers must weigh the possible psychological benefits of odd-number pricing against the consumer's perception that this is a bargain-basement pricing system. To combat this perception, consider a price like $29.50 instead of a typical promotional number like $29.99.

Once you determine the best base price for a given product and promotion, further testing may help prove the value of some of the following price strategies or payment terms.

Price strategies

Quantity price

Sometimes you do not even have to offer a comparison along with a "two-for" or "three-for" price: the mere mention of a quantity price may imply a savings to the customer. Catalog marketers sometimes offer items only in quantities of two, three or more when the one-item price is too low to offer cost effectively.

More typically, a quantity price involves a savings comparison, such as "$12.00 each; two for $20.00." Or you might offer even greater savings with a "per-case" price on products like computer disks, photocopier paper, or wine. Another way to offer a volume price is to allow the quantity to accumulate over time, thus encouraging customer loyalty. In this case, you might provide a 10 percent rebate once the customer's total purchases reach a certain level. Or, once they have purchased 10 boxes of typewriter ribbons, for example, they might receive a box of the same ribbons for free.

Discounts for order size

Instead of—or in addition to—offering a "two-for" or "three-for" price, some direct marketers encourage an increase in the customer's order size by offering a discount if the total order reaches a certain level. One way to structure such an offer is to place the target order level for the discount just above the firm's average order size, thereby trading off the discount to achieve a higher average order. For example, if your firm's average order size is $70.00, you might try offering a 10 percent discount for any order over $75.00.

Introductory price

When packaged goods firms introduce a new toothpaste, soap or cereal, they are quick to provide coupons and samples aimed at getting the product into the consumer's hands. In direct marketing, magazines often make introductory offers for new subscribers, while renewers may pay a higher rate. Conventional wisdom in direct marketing is that it is better to offer a coupon for dollars-off the retail price than to offer a discounted price: in this way, the consumer understands what the regular retail price for the merchandise will be.

Refund with initial purchase

Catalog marketers often use this technique to qualify inquiries, asking individuals to pay anything from 50 cents to $10.00 or more to receive the firm's catalog. Then, with the first purchase from the catalog, the initial fee is refunded. Another idea is to offer double the initial catalog price as a discount off the first purchase. This method not only qualifies the prospect, but also provides an added incentive to buy.

Discount based upon a relationship

Sometimes direct marketers will offer a special price on an item only to established customers, and charge the regular price to new customers. For instance, the issue price for a collector plate might be set at $30.00, but those who have already purchased works by the same artist could be offered the plate for $25.00.

Seasonal discount

Some products are ideally suited to seasonal discounts: Christmas merchandise sold in January, for instance, or lawn furniture offered in late winter or at the end of the outdoor season. Another concept is to maximize volume by discounting your product at the height of its season—thereby attracting attention to your firm when the consumer's mind is focused on your type of product. If you try this type of offer, however, be sure that you have sufficient available inventory to fulfill orders immediately: a 15 percent discount on artificial Christmas wreaths offered in November will win you customer loyalty only if you deliver in time for holiday display.

Sale mailings

Sales may be used to clear out overstocked inventory, to level out buying patterns on seasonal goods, or to provide a special opportunity for loyal customers or hot new prospects. Some direct marketers create special sales literature, often becoming a bit more promotional in copy and graphics than they would for a regular mailing. Other firms rely on their standard catalogs or brochures, and modify these materials with inexpensive methods like catalog wrap-arounds, "10% off all merchandise" stickers, new one- or two-color order forms and sale letters, or special price lists.

Loss leaders

Retail stores often draw traffic by promoting a small number of universally appealing items at a deeply discounted price. Direct marketers may do the same, calling such an item an "order starter" because it helps the customer make the decision to order and begin filling out the reply form or dialing the toll-free number. Once the decision to order is made, the customer may then browse around the catalog or mailing to see if there is anything else worth buying. Thus the "order starter" serves the same function as the quart of milk that sends consumers to the grocery store—only to emerge with a sack full of impulse items.

Comparative pricing

Giving customers a point of reference for your pricing may help them decide that your offer makes financial sense. For decades, the Sears catalog has used this comparative technique to show customers how long it has been since prices were this low. For instance, they might headline a featured line of men's underwear with this claim: "Our lowest price for Golden Comfort briefs since 1985." Or they might promote a VCR machine this way: "Our lowest price ever for a VHS-format video cassette recorder." It is important to research such price claims carefully: if you are incorrect, your customers may well take you to task.

Payment terms

What your prospect considers a fair price for a given offer may vary depending on how you ask him or her to pay for the product or service. The more you can reduce the customer's perception of risk and increase ease in payment, the more likely you are to make and keep a sale. On the other hand, it is important to build in protection for your firm to ensure that payments will be made according to agreed-upon terms.

Although it is important to keep the terms of your offer simple and understandable, direct marketing experts agree that a range of payment options often pays off in increased sales. Here are some of the payment plans you may consider or test, from the least to the most restrictive.

Free trial

When a customer visits a retail store, he or she often has the opportunity to try on clothing, listen to stereo equipment, sample food products, and compare colors with swatches of fabric brought from home. Because mail order buyers must take a "leap of faith" and trust that the products they buy will match the description and photos in sales literature, their perception of risk may be lessened with the offer of a free trial period.

When structuring a free trial offer, base the time limit on the type of product you are promoting. It may take only 10 days for a consumer to make a decision about a book or record. But if you are offering a vitamin supplement program that claims to increase vigor and strength over a 30-day period, the free trial needs to encompass that time span. Whatever time period you select, be very clear about the parameters of your offer on the reply device. Does the item have to be returned *within* 10 days, or can the return be postmarked on the 10th day and still be acceptable? Does the 10-day period begin when you ship the item, or when the item is received by the customer?

Some direct marketers offer free trial options only to lists of customers who have been prescreened for credit worthiness. Others do a quick credit check once the free trial request is received, and grant the trial only to those whose credit is good.

If you offer free trial, be sure to promote it strongly in each ad or direct mail package. Some marketers become so used to the free trial concept that they begin to take it for granted and soft-pedal it in their presentations. Since free trial can be a powerful inducement to buy, its availability should figure prominently in your copy.

When the product is shipped according to a free trial offer, you may elect to send the invoice along with the product, calling for payment or return of the product within the free trial period. Or you may send the invoice separately at the time the free trial period ends, along with a letter thanking the customer again for the purchase. If payment is not made and the product is not returned during the free trial period, most direct marketers follow up with a short series of increasingly urgent reminder letters.

Direct marketers who use free trial offers report that although this concept usually yields more orders than a cash-up-front offer would, it also tends to result in more returns. However, in most cases the net result is an improvement in sales, even accounting for the administrative cost of returns and of tracking down late payments. If you cannot make the free trial option work for you, consider polling some of the customers who returned your product to learn why they found fault with it.

Bill me later

Some customers may be intrigued by the opportunity to purchase merchandise now and pay for it at a more convenient time. For instance, you might offer to send Christmas gift merchandise in December, but not bill the customer or his or her charge card until January or February. Or you might sell the customer a complete school wardrobe for a family of children in July, but wait until the school year begins after Labor Day to enter the bill. This option is safest for the seller if the billing is to be done on a major credit card rather than direct bill to the customer. Or you might consider offering this option only to established customers.

Reservation options

The reservation concept offers the prospect ease in responding, and provides increased security for the seller. At the time the purchase decision is made, the buyer only has to return a simple form stating the quantity of the purchase and preferred payment terms. But unlike the free trial option, in which the seller ships the product without any payment up-front from the buyer, reservation customers may be asked to pay for all or part of their merchandise before it is shipped. When the preshipment invoice is received by reservation customers, some of them will change their minds and neglect to pay, thereby cancelling their orders. However, for many marketers the reservation option results in a net increase in sales, even considering its administrative and time costs.

An added benefit of the reservation option is that it can help marketers determine the extent of demand for a product that they are not yet able to ship. By taking reservations instead of up-front payments, they avoid upsetting customers whose money might otherwise be tied up until the product is ready for shipment.

Money-back guarantee

With this offer, the customer pays all or part of the cost of the product before it is shipped. But if the product is unsatisfactory in any way upon receipt, the customer may return it within a specified time period for a full refund or credit. To lower the prospect's fear of risk, such guarantees should be played up to the fullest. In copy, be sure that the guarantee is worded as positively as possible, emphasizing that no questions will be asked if a product is returned. In layout, call attention to the guarantee by boxing it, setting it in large type, and/or surrounding it with a "value border." Mention the guarantee on each piece of selling literature: letter, brochure, order card, and elsewhere if applicable.

Be sure to set out the terms of the guarantee in every detail. For instance, will you refund the customer's original shipping and handling charge as well as the price of the product? Will you reimburse the customer for insurance and shipping the product back

to you? How long does the guarantee period last, 1(
a full year, or forever? Some stalwart direct marketin
L. L. Bean guarantee their merchandise for the life of the p

Split payment

Offer a customer a diamond necklace at $1100.00 and the price may seem staggering. But offer that same customer the opportunity to purchase the necklace for $100.00 a month at no interest, and the proposition suddenly becomes more realistic. Firms with their own credit cards—like American Express and major oil companies—can offer the option of adding one-half, one-twelfth, or some other agreed-upon percentage of an item's cost to an established customer's bill each month. This option has become all the more appealing to consumers now that credit card interest is no longer deductible. With split payments, they can enjoy the immediate gratification of the products they want, without paying interest on their debts.

Many firms handle split payments without their own credit card programs, simply by sending the customer a series of bills. On a four-way payment for a work of art, for instance, the buyer might pay one-fourth before the item is shipped, one-fourth upon shipment, and one-fourth in each of the next two months after the item is received.

"House" charge

Some direct marketing firms establish their own charge-account systems in order to facilitate long-term payments and offer customers a service. To decide whether this is warranted, consider the administrative work and debt collection that may be involved. These costs may outweigh your potential interest income and the goodwill of a house charge option. In general, unless direct marketing firms are already in the credit card business (American Express, Amoco, etc.), relatively few offer their own charge accounts to customers. Instead, they accept major credit cards as well as cash, checks and money orders.

Credit card option

Even very small business ventures today are welcomed by banks to set up MasterCard and Visa charging systems for their customers. Medium-to-large firms usually take American Express as add Diners Club and/or Discover to the mix. ... rcentage of your receipts to the credit card com- ... costs for processing your orders. In turn, the ... pany pays you for each purchase, and your cus- ... e credit card company. Because so many con- ... use credit cards regularly, the credit card option is ... justify its cost. Not only does it increase customer ... it may also contribute to impulse buying and larger ... dition, the risk of dealing with your firm is lessened for ... mers when they know there is a buffer—the credit card ... y—to help them resolve any billing or shipping problems that may arise.

Cash up front

Asking customers to pay the entire amount due by check or money order before product shipment affords maximum security to the direct marketer. Some firms even wait for the check to clear before processing the order and shipping merchandise. Some customers prefer to make their payments up front, but others may need an incentive to do so. You may consider offering free shipping and handling or some other benefit for advance payment.

The place

In marketing terms, "place" is shorthand for distribution system. For retailers, place has to do with store location, ambience and service. Since direct marketers operate through the mail and by phone, their customers' concerns about place have to do with the way buyers are treated in written communications, over the telephone, at the time of shipment, and in dealing with customer service. These factors of place are crucial to the direct-marketing mix, since customers who are poorly treated in the act of purchasing have many other options—including dealing with retailers or other direct marketers. Here are some of the place considerations direct marketers should focus upon.

By mail

In arranging for a purchase by mail, the customer deals with an order form rather than a sales person. In addition to order-form design issues, which are discussed in the chapter on Formats, consumers are concerned with nuts and bolts such as shipping and handling, time of delivery, and sales tax. It is important to make clear how shipping and handling charges are determined. Some firms allocate these charges on an item-by-item basis, determined by weight and method of shipment. Others use a chart to determine shipping charges for a given order based on total price or total weight. Still others expect the customer to determine shipping charges based on geographic zone. Finally, some firms build the shipping and handling charge into the merchandise price. There is no one right way to proceed on this score, except to ensure that the customer considers your shipping and handling charges fair and easy to calculate.

Sales tax is another issue which consumers must deal with in filling out an order form. This is a hot issue for direct marketers, who are lobbying to avoid having to make sales tax payments to states other than those where their facilities are located. Even so, sales tax always must be collected in one or more states, so the direct marketer should strive to make the amount due as easy to determine as possible.

By telephone

There is a set of important decisions for direct marketers to make in arranging to serve customers by telephone. While many firms now employ toll-free 800 numbers, others require the customer to pay for all calls. Still others allow collect calls for out-of-state customers. Some firms provide toll-free customer service lines, while others allow for toll-free ordering but expect the customer to pay for inquiry and complaint calls. While some 800 numbers operate only during business hours, many direct marketers have taken advantage of the fact that their "place" can be available 24 hours a day, with phone lines open at all times.

The level of telephone service is another issue for direct marketers to consider. Some firms hire an outside service to perform a strict order-taking function, while others keep all telephone communications in house, and train their personnel to be customer advocates. Such trained telephone salespeople can assist customers in determining sizes and colors, and find out immediately if an item is in stock or will have to be backordered. They can also be trained to offer customers appropriate add-on items to enhance their purchases—or at the very least to discuss daily specials available at special prices.

Once again, there is no one right answer for all direct marketers offering telephone service. However, it is important to weigh the options available against competitors' services, the wants and needs of your customers, and the size and sophistication of your firm.

Fax and computer communications

Many direct marketers—especially those in business-to-business or high-tech fields—already offer fax ordering as an option. In the years to come, as interactive computer and telephone/television systems are perfected, these communication systems may well become a regular part of the "place" for many direct marketers.

Delivery systems

Another aspect of place for direct marketers has to do with the delivery of goods. Retailers typically deliver goods right into the customer's hands, or ship items locally by U.P.S. or delivery truck. Direct marketers today may offer a number of options aimed at streamlining the customer's purchase, ensuring prompt delivery, and maximizing the customer's ease in receiving merchandise.

Some firms ask the customer what means of shipment is preferred: U.S. mail, U.P.S., or Federal Express (the last at an extra charge). Others offer just one service, such as U.P.S., but will send merchandise using that firm's one or two-day services at an extra charge if requested.

There is considerable competition in today's market to deliver direct response-bought goods as promptly as possible. Firms which keep products readily available and ship reliably and immediately upon receipt of orders have a definite edge over those which barely avoid having to send out notices under the Federal Trade Commission 30-day rule.

The promotion

Offers may be sweetened by many tried-and-true means including premiums and add-ons, sweepstakes and contests, special conditions of sale, and strong guarantees. This section will survey some of the promotional methods which direct marketers have found effective in overcoming customer inertia.

Premiums and add-ons

A free gift may well provide the extra incentive a prospect needs to send for more information, try your product, or purchase it outright. The terms of your premium offer have a great deal to do with its success-and its effect on your bottom line.

At one extreme, you may find it profitable to provide a free gift to everyone who indicates an interest in your product by sending for more information. Other marketing plans call for the shipment of the premium only after the customer has purchased and paid for the item in question. Another concept allows the prospect to keep the premium that is shipped with a product purchase, even if the product is returned for a refund.

In continuity programs, a premium may be offered at the outset, but not shipped until a certain amount of product has been purchased. For instance, a set of figurines might have a custom-designed display case available at no extra charge to series subscribers. If the average series buyer purchases five of eight figurines, the marketer might ship the premium right before this average is reached. This will encourage the buyer to purchase more figurines, with the incentive of filling up the attractive new display device.

There is no one right way to offer a premium: in fact, you may wish to test the structure of your premium offer as well as the premium itself. It is essential in any case, however, to spell out to your customer exactly what he or she must do to earn the premium.

When testing premium offers, some direct marketers opt for the easy course and simply throw in a premium slip describing the free gift and how it may be obtained. For a fair test, however, the premium and terms of its receipt should be a part of each main component of the direct mail package: letter, brochure, and order form. Otherwise you cannot be sure that your prospect is aware of the premium as an integral part of your offer.

Types of premiums

Some direct marketers boast excellent results offering premiums that are directly related to their products: a display stand for a collector plate, for instance, or book ends for a set of illustrated volumes. Other firms—including large publishers who buy their premiums in volume—swear by unrelated products that are perceived to have maximum value. Recent mass magazine premiums, for instance, have included telephones, small stereo systems, and videotapes. Conventional wisdom is that a nonrelated premium brings less committed respondents, so weigh this factor in considering the potential lifetime value of customers attracted by premiums.

Certain premiums are offered continuously—a customer newsletter, for instance, or a regular free gift for every $100.00 of merchandise purchased. If your continuous or regular premium is attractive enough, it will encourage customers to keep up their level of buying with your firm. A prime example of a continuous premium is the airline frequent-flyer club, which strives to build brand loyalty among customers who might otherwise simply choose the airline with the best fare or most convenient flight time.

While many premiums are considered part of advertising cost, others are self-liquidating. This means that they are sold to the customer at your cost. For instance, you might offer a $15.00

The Horchow Collection sends regular newsletters to its best customers, filled with informative articles and special buying opportunities. Others may subscribe to the newsletter for a yearly fee. This issue marked the 20th anniversary of The Horchow Collection. Reprinted with permission of The Horchow Collection.

retail-value book for just $2.99 with any purchase of $50.00 or more.

Ways of using premiums

In addition to a classic premium-with-purchase offer, you might test offering gifts at certain order levels to encourage a larger average order size. For instance, if your average order is $45.00, consider offering a free gift for every order of $50.00 or more in hopes of boosting the average.

Some firms swear by offering several small, free gifts instead of one big one. Other companies have good results with add-on offers such as free gift boxes or gift wrapping.

Books and record clubs are among the marketers who use successful "member-get-a-member" premium plans. They entice members with a certain amount of free merchandise or credit for each new person they can get to commit to a certain level of purchasing.

Sweepstakes and contests

Sweepstakes and other games of chance have become extremely profitable customer incentives for Publisher's Clearing House and many other mailers. Head-to-head tests show that the lure of such contests can substantially increase or even double response for some propositions.

In successful sweepstakes promotions, the fantasy of winning a bright red sports car, a dream house, or $10,000,000 in cash translates into excitement that surrounds your product. And although sweepstakes rules must allow noncustomers to enter on equal terms with customers, prospects tend to believe that they'll have a better chance of winning if they buy something.

When considering a sweepstakes or contest proposition, learn from the masters: study the colorful and complex packages from major magazine sellers for ideas on package design, TV support, and prize selection.

Most important of all, engage the services of a firm that specializes in contest management. The rules, regulations and laws in this area are too specialized to handle safely on your own. For smaller firms with limited budgets, a full-scale sweepstakes may well be too costly and complex to be viable.

More and more direct marketers are testing sweepstakes as a means of stimulating response to subscription drives and product offers. **This self-mailer from *Mother Jones* magazine combines a sweepstakes offer with a subscription solicitation.** Reprinted with permission of the Foundation for National Progress.

Special conditions of sale

By emphasizing the urgency of a prompt response, or by setting special terms for the frequency or conditions of shipment and payment, direct marketers may enhance response and improve their profits. Here are some conditions of sale to consider testing in your direct mail solicitations.

Urgency

Every direct marketing presentation requires a call to action—a message which replaces the personal sales "close" and helps convince the customer to buy right away. There are several typical ways in which the urgency of a prompt response is stressed, encouraging the customer to mail or call in an order immediately instead of putting the sales piece aside.

A *time limit* requires prompt action, but for credibility, it should be accompanied by a reason such as seasonal cut-offs or limited production time. Many direct marketers have excellent success in *remailing* an offer to the better segments of their house or outside lists, reminding the customer that time is running out. The best timing for a remail is approximately two weeks after the original mailing. The simplest form of a remail is the original package, sometimes enhanced by a stamp effect on the outer envelope and order from saying "Last Chance" or similar wording. A pseudo hand-written note on the original letter or a photocopy of the original letter might remind the prospect of the final date for orders, or emphasize urgency in other credible ways. Other marketers create a special "last chance" remail letter with urgency woven into the entire presentation.

When combined with a reduced price, many publications limit their offers to a certain *subscription period.* This same concept—also known as a "subscription block"—has been used to enhance urgency for collectibles, financial services, and other investment-related appeals.

Another way to encourage immediate ordering is to offer a *charter membership* or *subscription* to those who respond by a certain date. The charter designation might afford these customers special offers or privileges in the future. A *limited edition* may feature a cut-off by the number of items made, a time period, or similar limitation. This strategy is widely used in the art, collectibles, and book fields. Finally, the announcement of an *upcoming price increase* may stimulate customers to buy immediately.

Frequency and terms

A wide range of offer structures has been devised and tested by firms selling records, books, collectibles, and other related groups of products that are shipped over a long period of time. Some of these concepts may enhance the attractiveness of other product series you sell.

The *negative-option* concept calls for the customer to agree to take shipment of products as they are made available, unless he or she specifically indicates otherwise. Negative-option plans usually consist of a mailing at monthly or other regular intervals, in which the selection is promoted—often along with a wide range of alternate selections. Unless the customer returns the enclosed card asking for no shipment or an alternate shipment, the regular selection will be sent along with an invoice for payment.

It is important that the wording of the initial negative-option agreement be inclusive enough to be binding: check promotions from long-established record and book clubs for pointers. You will also want to note that the initial incentive for customers to agree to a negative-option program is usually a free or reduced-price offer: i.e. get three books for $1 when you agree to buy three additional books at regular price over the next year.

In a *positive-option* plan, the customer receives regular offerings of product, but must return a card in order to be sent items. Thus no merchandise is shipped unless it is specifically ordered. In general, it will be easier to get a commitment to a positive-option plan than a negative-option plan, but fewer guaranteed, regular sales will result. However, the amount of merchandise returned should be less with this scheme: in a negative-option plan the customer may refuse merchandise on arrival if he or she simply neglected to return the card in time asking that it not be shipped.

To lower shipping costs and get the customer to make a commitment for an entire series of merchandise, many marketers utilize a *load-up* plan. Some firms make the load up a regular feature of their offer, while others make it an option. The marketer must balance the bad-debt potential of shipping merchandise in bulk before it is paid for against the high shipping costs of month-by-month delivery. Once the load up is sent, the customer may be given the option of paying for all the merchandise at once, perhaps with a premium or discount for doing so. Or the customer may take the option of continuing to pay by the month, in which case the firm may send out monthly invoices, or provide a booklet of payment coupons.

When you are selling a product that requires regular replenishment—pantyhose or gourmet coffee, for example—a *ship-'til-forbid* plan may maximize regular sales for you and enhance convenience for your customers. The customer agrees to receive and pay for a regular shipment at intervals, unless and until he or she notifies the marketer to cancel.

Unlike ship-'til-forbid plans that continue indefinitely, a *continuity* plan typically offers the customer a set number of related items to be purchased at monthly or other regular intervals. Some continuity plans obligate the customer to purchase every item, while others allow customers to terminate at any time, or to pick and choose among the items as they are introduced.

If you are designing a club program, charging a *membership fee* helps distinguish those who are eager to affiliate with the group from those who are merely curious. In exchange for the membership fee, the marketer should devise a set of benefits that members perceive as worth their dues. Collectibles clubs offer "members only" purchase options, trips and newsletters, and advance notification of new product introductions or limited editions that are closing. Travel clubs provide a certain amount of free service such as trip planning, as well as discounts on lodging and car rentals, and availability of members-only insurance plans. Some memberships must be renewed yearly, while others require only a one-time fee—or a lifetime membership may be offered for a substantially higher fee than yearly dues.

When setting the parameters for any of these plans, consider encouraging your customer to permit you to charge each new item as it is introduced, using a credit card number. This simplifies payment for the customer, and also helps ensure you of smooth and regular sales. When the customer pays by check, the introduction of each new item constitutes another buying decision that requires you to overcome his or her inertia.

Types of guarantees

Because of the trust inherent in a transaction by mail or phone, it is important for direct marketers to offer a standard guarantee of satisfaction. Typically, such a guarantee allows the customer to return merchandise within a given period of time such as 30 days, and receive a complete refund with no questions asked. Sometimes the refund also includes initial shipping and handling fees and reimbursement for the cost of returning the item. Some firms allow the customer to call a toll-free number and obtain a free U.P.S. pick-up of unsatisfactory merchandise. Whatever the terms of your guarantee, be sure that they are spelled out in detail in your front-end promotion.

For ideas in structuring the wording of your guarantee, gather the promotional materials of seasoned direct marketing firms in your line of business and study their guarantee terms. Just as important is the way the guarantee is emphasized throughout their literature: in the letter, on the order form, in a box as part of the brochure, and perhaps even in the lift letter or other extra selling piece.

Beyond the guarantee of satisfaction, direct marketers may make a wide range of promises to enhance the prospective customer's level of trust in responding. Here are several examples.

Guarantee of acceptance

Insurance marketers use this tool to streamline the prospect's application process and provide a benefit that may not be available with policies purchased direct from agents. Older individuals with a history of medical problems, or people who consider themselves too busy to take an insurance medical exam, may be won over by this simplified application process. The guarantee of acceptance states that, within a given range of age and for a given value of insurance, the prospect cannot be turned down and will not be asked medical questions.

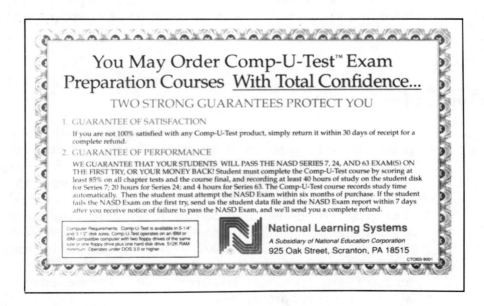

National Learning Systems offers a double guarantee to buyers of its Comp-U-Test™ courses: a Guarantee of Satisfaction and a Guarantee of Performance. The "value border" enhances the official appearance of the guarantee statement. Reprinted with permission of WOL Direct.

Guarantee of performance

Marketers selling educational programs leading to licensing or other testing may use this type of guarantee. The firm sets out minimum standards which the purchaser must meet: so much study time, etc. Then if the customer fails to pass the exam he or she is preparing for, the firm may provide a refund if it is requested within a certain set time period after purchase. A similar guarantee might be devised to cover a do-it-yourself project where the buyer is guaranteed to be able to complete the project by following the instructions and materials provided.

Guarantee of quality

When a prospect has not had the opportunity to examine an item before purchase, a quality guarantee may enhance trust. This guarantee may come from the manufacturer, from the marketer, or from a third-party source like *Good Housekeeping* magazine or Underwriter's Laboratory.

Guarantee of repair or replacement

Some prospective direct mail buyers may hesitate to purchase because they fear they will not have recourse if the product they buy is defective or needs repair. A guarantee that the item will be repaired free of charge within a given time period may help cut down buyer resistance. Likewise, a promise of replacement for defective merchandise reinforces the customer's buying decision.

Attracting qualified sales leads

When a product or service carries a high price, or when the ultimate sale is to be closed in person, the direct marketer's goal may be to generate names of individuals who are interested in the offer and are qualified to purchase.

Such names acquired for a two-step sales process are called inquiries or leads—and even if they do not purchase the initial item that is offered to them, they may well be excellent prospects for later buying opportunities.

Some lead-generation offers may be so attractive that no premium or other incentive is necessary to bring in a large number of names. But in most cases, the offer of a brochure, catalog, premium, or other information will enhance the response of prospects. Here are some of the typical free items that win positive response from prospects:

> Free information/facts
> Free book/catalog/booklet
> Free analysis/estimate/demonstration/sample
> Free meal or trip
> Free evaluation of talent

With all of these offers, be sure to stress that there is no obligation to the prospect. When sending follow-up materials by mail, it is important to overcome mailbox clutter by flagging your materials with wording such as "Here is the Information You Requested." Inside the package, a letter—personalized if possible—would refresh the prospect's memory about his or her request and what is being sent in reply.

Response devices for lead-generation campaigns can serve as a valuable source of data-base information. For instance, automotive firms offer coupons and toll-free numbers in magazines like *Car and Driver* or *Road and Track.* Respondents are asked for their ages, occupations, current vehicle ownership, and time frames for the next automobile purchase. This information helps the company determine the mix of product brochures to send the prospect—and to plan for a contact close to the time of the customer's buying decision. Leads may be followed up by a direct-mail package, telephone call, personal sales call, or staged combination of two or three of these methods.

Tight and loose leads

For some propositions, your goal is to attract as many leads as possible—even if some of them are only mildly interested in your offer. Direct marketers call these "loose leads." In other cases, you may wish to qualify each lead in advance as to eligibility and degree of interest. Such well-qualified leads are called "tight" leads.

To "loosen" the leads you will attract, make it easier to respond. Provide a stamped envelope or a Business Reply Envelope or Business Reply Card. Use bind-in cards in magazine ads. Provide a toll-free number or a pre-labeled card that the prospect can drop in the mail. Some card decks help participants obtain as many leads as possible by enclosing preprinted, pressure-sensitive labels in the deck: the respondent simply attaches one of the labels with his or her name and address to the reply cards representing offers of special interest.

Offering a premium also helps to loosen leads. The less the premium is related to the offer itself, the looser the lead may be. Premiums with high perceived value may also help attract more—albeit marginally qualified—leads. Emphasizing the "no obligation" aspect of your offer should result in more leads. And from the copy perspective, remember the age-old advice to sell the sizzle, not the steak. Tell the customer about all the product's benefits, but save the nuts and bolts—and even the price—for the follow-up contact.

To "tighten" the leads you will attract, be forthright about the price and payment terms of your offer. State that a salesperson will call or will deliver the promised, free materials. Charge money for the information or service rather than making it free. Eliminate post-paid cards and envelopes, and instead require the prospect to use his or her own postage—or even to write a letter or card to request the information. Finally, from the copy perspective, talk about how the product works and why it does what it does. Don't stop with the benefits—delve into the nuts and bolts of the product. Customers who express interest after reading this specific information should be excellent prospects for a sale.

DIRECT MAIL FORMAT DESIGN

8

The format you choose for any direct mail sales presentation should serve as a *visible and active statement of the strategy* put forth in your marketing plan. Like the strategy itself, your format should be based on what you know about your target market and your competitors, the company image you wish to project, and the amount you can safely spend to make a sale or gain an inquiry.

Just as the function of a direct mail offer is to overcome inertia, the job of a direct mail format is to *stimulate action* on the part of the prospect. When designing any piece of your direct mail package, consider how it can be used to help lead the prospect toward the desired action stated in your marketing plan: a purchase, inquiry, or visit to your place of business.

Variety of formats

Selecting a format for a direct mail presentation can be as challenging as choosing an ice cream cone at a store with 33 flavors. While television and radio formats are constrained by time, and print media ads must conform to the parameters of the publisher, direct mail marketers enjoy considerable freedom and control over their packages' dimensions, materials and involvement devices.

Two important constraints, however, must figure into each direct mail design decision: current U.S. Postal rules and budgetary considerations. With these requirements in mind, many direct mailers rely upon standard formats which are cost effective. The basic direct mail format begins with a #10 business envelope or a 6″ × 9″ or 9″ × 12″ outer envelope and includes the following enclosures: a letter, a brochure or flyer, a reply device (which may or may not comprise a separate piece), and a Business Reply Envelope.

While some firms use only these standard formats—and find them very effective in bringing about action—most successful direct marketers continually test a wide range of other formats and supplementary enclosures. This chapter will provide a survey of successful direct mail formats, but it is intended only as an idea starter. Because proven direct mail buyers may receive six or more selling messages in the mail on any given day, the onus is on marketers to continue the search for breakthrough design and copy concepts that cut through the clutter and earn the attention of the prospect.

Sources of format ideas

Direct mail designers do not have to work in a vacuum: sources of format inspiration are readily available.

Sample Files

First, and most basic of all, become an avid direct mail consumer yourself. This need not be costly, if you get into the habit of making as many personal purchases as possible via the mail.

Order products from companies in all price ranges selling clothing, home items, electronics, sporting goods, food, office supplies, and other items frequently sold by mail. Answer inquiry ads for high-ticket items like automobiles, and for intangibles like insurance and mutual funds. Join book and record clubs, and sign up for a continuity series of collectibles. When you do so, mail will roll in from all over the country—not just from the firms you patronize, but from all the companies who rent their mailing lists.

Perhaps your company or agency already cultivates an organized file of competitive materials, commonly called a swipe file. If not, start your own, and categorize it by product type or format—whatever you find most helpful.

Talk with vendors

Involving those who sell you paper, printing, and computer and lettershop services should yield you a constant source of format ideas. As these vendors add new equipment and applications to their plants, they will enthusiastically share the news with you. They should also be eager to show you innovative packages and concepts that they have completed for others, once they are in the mail and in the public domain. Remember also the benefit of showing your vendors your new concepts before the exact size and specifications are set. By shaving a fraction of an inch here and there, or changing the materials slightly, vendors may be able to save you enough money to make a radical idea cost effective.

Read books and trade publications, and attend shows

Books such as this one will give you an overall understanding of the basic direct mail formats, and some ideas for additional sizes, enclosures, and refinements you might consider. Trade publications offer news about production methods and successful packages that may fuel your creativity. Many publications also highlight award-winning packages. And since most direct marketing awards are given for bottom-line performance rather than pure creativity, such noteworthy applications may be well worth considering. Finally, visits to international, national and regional direct marketing shows may help stimulate your creativity as you chat with vendors in their display booths and attend talks on creative and production-related topics.

The outer envelope

Studies show that your prospect may consider your direct mail package for only a second or two before deciding whether to read it immediately, save it for later, or dispose of it. Your choice of size, paper, graphics and message will help the prospect make a decision on whether to open the envelope. Here are some of the factors to consider in designing an outer envelope.

Standard or custom sizing

The most common direct mail envelopes are #10, 6″ × 9″ or 9″ × 12″, but many other sizes are acceptable to the post office: square, oversized, European sized, monarch, invitation-look, etc. Selecting a common-sized envelope generally saves money: always check with your envelope vendor when designing a custom piece to make sure it can be manufactured at an acceptable cost. Odd-sized envelopes may prove to attract more attention than predictable-looking ones, and sometimes an outer envelope is chosen to complement the sizes of pieces that will fit inside. It may well be worth a test, however, to see if a unique envelope with a premium price justifies its cost compared to a standard-sized envelope and package with the same graphics and message.

Materials

Because most direct marketers have their envelopes manufactured from scratch, they have the same wide range of paper and print options that are available for brochures or letters. For last-minute or small-quantity jobs, you may choose to overprint a stock envelope, which will limit your selection of papers and your ability to decorate the envelope. To maximize your options for envelope paper and printing, work with good envelope vendors and plan to order early. Check your sample files for an overview of the types of envelope materials available: everything from simple wove and kraft paper stocks to elegant parchment and laid finishes, and coated papers for four-color printing.

Closed face or window

The traditional direct-mail envelope usually features a window showing through to an address-labeled letter or reply card. This method allows for only one piece in the direct mail package to be labeled or computer addressed. It is also an immediate "tip-off" to consumers that they have received a commercial direct mail offer. With today's many options for computerization of multiple pieces in the same direct mail package, many marketers are opting for closed-face packages that more closely simulate regular typed business correspondence. If you invest in a closed-face package, be sure that the other elements of the envelope maintain this personalized business look: use a stamp or postage meter instead of a printed indicia, and avoid promotional teasers or graphics.

This close-face envelope from American Express features an actual postage stamp and a "typed" address. Top quality textured stock completes the impression of a personal invitation that is well worth opening. Reprinted with permission.

Teasers versus plain outers

While many direct marketers swear by colorful, decorated envelopes and envelope teasers that entice the prospect to look inside, others point to test results that show the same or better performance from packages with plain outer envelopes. A teaser tells the prospect that this is a direct mail offer. It should help lure the prospect inside with the promise of a special offer, free gift, intriguing information, or the answer to a question or group of questions. Sometimes a teaser makes a statement and then trails off, enticing the reader to look inside for the rest of the message. Some marketers have tried beginning the letter on the outside of the envelope, then continuing the story inside. Resist the temptation to disclose too much with your teaser: this may prompt the prospect to make a decision on your offer without even looking inside.

Not all teasers require words. Sometimes it is enough to place a logo or motif on the outer envelope. The prestige of a designer's logo, or that of a European sports car, might be sufficient to entice aficionados inside an envelope. Cat lovers will open an envelope that features a feline. A window that shows through to a picture of the product or a premium may also serve as an envelope teaser.

Involvement devices on envelopes

If your budget permits, you may consider testing yes/no/maybe stickers or other involvement devices on the outside of the envelope instead of inside on the reply form or letter. Another interesting test is to tip the lift letter onto the back of a 9″ × 12″ envelope instead of inserting it inside: this serves to summarize the offer and challenge the reader to look inside, asking "what have you got to lose?"

Stickers and a scratch-off involvement devices show through the window of this sweepstakes offer from Time-Life Books. Stickers may also be affixed to the outside of an envelope. In either case, the intent is to motivate the prospect to open the package and find out more about the offer inside. Reprinted with permission of Time Life Books, Inc.

Corner card

The corner card is the return address that appears at the upper left of the front of your envelope. The return address may also appear at the upper middle of the envelope's back. Usually this will be your own return address, but you might also consider having the corner card list an endorsing organization or an individual. This has been done successfully in fundraising efforts with packages that appear to come directly from Jimmy Carter, Ronald Reagan, or other celebrity or political figures.

Indicia or postage

An easy and cost-effective way to affix bulk-rate postage is to preprint the indicia right on the envelope, but this is a dead give-away of a direct mail solicitation. As an alternative, consider using a postage meter, which gives the look of a regular business mailing even if it displays the bulk rate amount. There are also bulk rate stamps, which may be costly to affix, but provide a personal-letter look. To speed your mailing and provide the ultimate in the appearance of personal mail, consider testing first class mail for some very well-targeted offers.

↓ **INSIDE** ↓

SECRETS

THAT CAN
SAVE YOUR LIFE

Rodale Press tips a lift letter onto the outside of a mailing package to stimulate interest in the book offer inside. Reprinted with permission of Rodale Press, Inc.

PREVENTION
America's Leading Health Magazine

Dear Friend,

Recent scientific studies prove that what you eat has a dramatic effect on your body's ability to fight and prevent illness. In fact, top medical researchers have found that eating certain foods can help you lower your cholesterol level, reduce your risk of heart disease and enable you to enjoy many other health benefits.

Now you can take advantage of these exciting discoveries in a important new book from Prevention magazine. THE HEALING POWER OF NUTRITION is yours free--just for mailing the enclosed card.

You'll learn:

*Four anti-aging nutrients that may help protect you against cataracts, respiratory disease, senility--even cancer! (Page 7)

*How to pump up the iron content of your spaghetti sauce to more than 8 times the RDA. (Page 13)

*How eating more of this versatile entree can help cool the fiery pain of arthritis. (Page 20)

*Delicious foods that "sneak" extra calories out of your body. (Page 27)

*How to lower your cholesterol level up to 30 points in 30 days. (Page 25)

*The detoxifying nutrient you absolutely cannot live without! (Page 36)

*50 top anti-cancer foods you may already have in your kitchen. (Page 18)

To get your free copy of THE HEALING POWER OF NUTRITION, mail the enclosed card today!

Sincerely,

Mark Bricklin
Editor

THE
HEALING
POWER
OF
NUTRITION
from Prevention Magazine

On page 13: A shortage of these two minerals can be life-threatening! Here are delicious ways to make sure you get enough of both.

On page 27: Tired of oat bran? Substitute this tasty dish and enjoy the same cholesterol-lowering benefit.

On page 4: 10 smart tricks to help you get the most nutrition for the least amount of money.

On page 12: How to double your absorption of iron by making this simple dietary addition.

On page 10: The powerhouse vitamin that may help reduce your cholesterol level.

PLUS

- 9 mealtime strategies to help you lower your blood pressure and build stronger bones.
- 12 ways to boost your fiber intake deliciously.
- 14 slimming foods that let you eat well and lose weight.
- And much more!

Printed in U.S.A.

The letter

Because it takes the place of the face-to-face salesperson, the letter is the most essential piece in any direct mail package. Unlike a brochure or reply device, the letter can sometimes stand alone and still make the sale.

So important is the sales letter that Richard S. Hodgson has written an excellent book inspired by *The Greatest Direct Mail Sales Letters of All Time.* Hodgson suggests using this book as an idea source to see how top writers tackle challenging assignments. The book contains some of the most famous and responsive letters in the history of direct marketing, as well as tips from renowned letter writers including Bob Stone, Victor O. Schwab, Ray W. Jutkins, Herschell Gordon Lewis, Don Kanter, and Hodgson himself. The book also contains scores of examples from the "pros" on ways to start and close letters effectively. This volume is highly recommended as a how-to guide for new direct marketing writers and designers, and as a source of reference and inspiration for veterans.

The key to successful letter writing is in creating a personal "me-to-you" communication. Thus the writer and designer of any direct mail letter must immerse themselves not only in product background, but also in knowledge and understanding of the target audience. You must know their hopes, fears and aspirations . . . what kinds of messages stir their emotions and entice them to buy. To get on the right track, study psychographics, material from the database, and letters customers write to your firm. Find out what magazines your target market reads . . . what television shows they watch . . . whom they admire. Walk in the shoes of your target market to prepare yourself for effective communications. Read over past letters that have been the biggest sales winners with the same target audience. Once this careful preparation is done, you will be ready to consider specific elements such as these in the development of your direct mail letter format.

Characteristics of successful direct mail letters

A showcase for benefits

In a typical direct mail solicitation, the selling letter refers to the product features and benefits that are shown in the accompanying brochure. The letter works to persuade the prospect that this product or service will benefit him or her personally. It then creates a sense of urgency that should lead the prospect to respond promptly by mail, phone, or person-to-person visit.

"You" orientation

The word "you" is used frequently in most good direct mail letters, focusing on the prospect's wants, needs, triumphs, home, family, interests and comfort. A good selling letter points out product benefits in a very personalized way, assisting the prospect to visualize having and using this product and thereby enhancing his or her quality of life. Creating these mental pictures helps move the prospect from the awareness stage through interest, desire and finally to action—just as a skillful salesperson does in a retail store or on a showroom floor.

The letter may be lengthy

Some fledgling direct marketers are skeptical about the length of typical direct mail letters: two, four or even eight or more pages in some cases. But an involving and readable four-page letter can be far more appealing to a prospect than a one-page communiqué with long sentences, 20-line paragraphs and no subheads. While some clients and production types like to "button down" the letter length well before it is written—calling for a two-page or four-page letter and asking the writer to oblige—it is usually wiser to let the letter run to the length that is necessary to tell the story effectively.

The letter should be readable

As a rule, direct mail letters feature short sentences, short paragraphs, lots of indentation, and subheads. All of these elements help make letters readable and appealing. Some direct mail letters feature the use of second or even third colors, hand-written "call outs," illustrations and photographs, underlining or highlighting of important points, and headlines before the salutation.

Promotional or straightforward: either may work

Purists and those new to direct marketing may question the wisdom of using promotional ploys like hand-writing, illustrations and headlines in a letter that purports to be a one-to-one communication. The effectiveness of these methods has been proven over the years through extensive testing, however, and they work be-

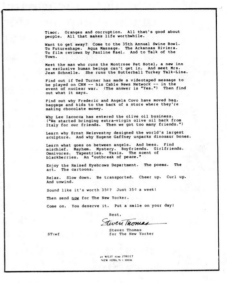

This direct mail letter by Judith Hannah Weiss for *The New Yorker* is highly readable because of its conversational style and short paragraphs. Reprinted with permission of *The New Yorker.*

cause they engage the attention of readers. This is not to say that a more straightforward letter will not pull well: indeed, some effective letters to consumers—especially those making upscale offers or requesting political contributions—may appear as businesslike as correspondence from a Fortune 500 company. As in all direct marketing efforts, the key to success in developing a letter format is to test, test, test.

Elements of a direct mail letter

The Letterhead

The letterhead you select should reflect the image of the product or of the firm that sells it: economical or upscale, modern or traditional, liberal or conservative, sporty or elegant. Some firms add a list of advisors or board members to the letterhead to reflect status, or the historical, religious or authoritative nature of the company and its products. Most direct mail letters are printed on 8½″ × 11″ letterhead, using both sides. Monarch-sized stationery may be used for a more personal look. This smaller size often is used for an endorsement letter or other supplementary note. Sometimes an unusual paper stock is used to attract attention or make a visual point: parchment for an old-time historical look, or lined paper for an informal appearance. For ideas on types of letterheads to try, check the customer service mail for this product. Do these letters from customers arrive on engraved personal stationery, business letterhead, informal notepaper, or a piece of notebook paper? Try testing a similar paper stock for your selling messages.

The Salutation

While many direct mail letters—especially those with a promotional tone—have no salutation at all, others use general wordings such as "Dear Friend," "Dear Collector," or "Dear Preferred Client." In recent years, however, computerization has become cost-effective enough that many letters can be personalized with "Dear Mary Smith" or "Dear Mrs. Smith" as a salutation. Now that the novelty of personalization has worn off—and direct marketers have realized that customers and prospects are not necessarily impressed with letters that have their addresses and names peppered here and there throughout the body—many letters are personalized only in the salutation.

The Signer

In most cases, the letter in a direct mail package comes from the president or other high official of the firm presenting the selling message. Sometimes, when the letter comes from a family-owned firm and the concept is to create a "down home" atmosphere, the letter may be signed by the owner's spouse, mother, or key employee. In other cases, the main selling letter appears over the signature of a third party, someone whose credentials qualify him or her to describe and endorse the product or service being offered.

The typeface

While some direct marketers have their letters typeset, this destroys the illusion that the letter is a personal communication from one person to another, custom-typed especially for its recipient. In general, tests show and conventional wisdom dictates that effective direct mail letters are presented in regular typewriter type. Headlines, subheads and other enhancements may be printed in another typewriter font to add emphasis. Underlining may be done via regular typewriter underlining, or by stimulating hand-underlining. To further the appearance of a personal letter, the second color for hand-underlining, hand-written notes and signatures should be dark blue—the same color as a pen's ink.

The tone

Depending upon the market segment they are intended to reach, effective direct-mail letters may come across as folksy, friendly, high-toned or strictly factual. It is important to create a scenario for the letter: who is writing, who is the recipient, and what are we trying to get across. Envisioning the target market as one typical recipient will help in this process: for instance are you writing to your Aunt Martha the needlepoint hobbyist, or your multi-millionaire boss who is looking for a real-estate tax shelter?

The opening

The beginning of your letter must be an attention-getter, or you will lose the prospect before you even get started. Typical opening gambits include telling a story, asking a question, identifying the prospect as a certain type of individual, or extending an invitation. Become a connoisseur of the direct mail letters you receive, and save those that capture your imagination as idea-starters.

The Johnson box opener

Many direct mail letters begin with a Johnson Box: an indented, boxed introductory copy block that may preview the offer, provide a teaser about the offer, or set the stage for the letter itself. In an interesting twist, some direct marketers use the Johnson Box to offer a short endorsement statement from a third party, commending the offer in the letter to the prospect's attention.

The body

The body of the letter performs the essential job of selling. It refers to the product features and benefits as shown in the accompanying brochure, and explains to the prospect why this product or service will benefit him or her personally. The body of the letter also may include testimonials, evidence to back up sales claims, and other "reasons to buy" copy. In addition, the body of the letter should contain all the nuts and bolts of the offer: price, payment terms, premiums, conditions of sale, and guarantee.

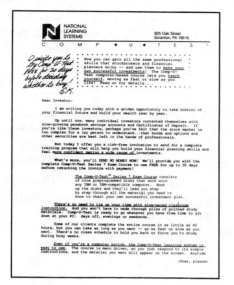
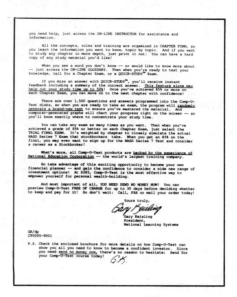

This letter from National Learning Systems illustrates several techniques often used in direct mail: a Johnson Box at the top, a "hand-written" note, and underlining of key points. A second color is used to emphasize the logo, "handwriting," and indented paragraph. Reprinted with permission of WOL Direct.

The close

The end of a direct mail letter serves the function of a sales close. It requires a reinforcement of the "reasons to buy" copy combined with urgency based on time pressure, limited quantities, putting the product's benefits to work right away, or even a subtle version of the old "be the first on your block" pitch.

The P.S.

Studies of direct mail readers tell us that when they pick up a letter, prospects look first at the signature and next at the P.S. Thus the P.S. provides such a vital selling opportunity that most every direct mail letter includes one. The P.S. may be used to restate the prime product benefit; highlight the urgency of the offer; refer the reader to the brochure, order form, testimonials or other component of the package; remind the prospect about the premium; offer a toll-free number for ease in ordering; or emphasize the no-risk nature of the offer due to Free Trial or Money-Back Guarantee.

Letter variations

Letter versions to suit prospect groups

Printing different letter versions is one of the least expensive ways of tailoring a direct mail package to target different market segments. For example, you may use the same brochure for both previous buyers of the product and new prospects, and acknowledge the status of the recipient in the letter. If you rent a list of people who are all travel club members, you might acknowledge this in a special letter and use a different letter for a group of people who are all personal computer owners.

Endorsement letters

If you are able to obtain an endorsement for your product by a respected or authoritative group, or the executives of a club or organization whose members will then be more likely to want to buy, one of the best ways to utilize this endorsement is by means of a special letter to be included along with the main selling letter. Such letters are usually signed by the president of the endorsing organization. In it, the president will mention some of the product's features and benefits from the organization's point of view, and recommend the product to your prospects.

Publisher's letters

In personal sales, one of the most important aspects of closing the deal is overcoming the prospect's objections. In direct mail, many marketers use a "publisher's letter" or "lift letter" to do the same thing. Such a supplementary letter is customarily folded or contained in a separate envelope. On the outside it might say something like "Please do not open this note unless you have already decided not to respond to this offer." Few readers can resist opening such a note, especially when they have been told not to. The note brings up common objections to the product and politely refutes them.

Telegrams, overnight letters, and simulated formats

One way to enhance the urgency of your message is to replace the usual business-type letter with a real Western Union telegram, an Overnight Letter, or a letter in a similar format from one of a number of services. The Western Union services are somewhat costly, but may be justified, especially for "last chance" follow-ups. Western Union does not allow additional inserts, but there are several telegram format services that send computer-printed pieces resembling telegrams via first class mail. These services will allow the insertion of a simple brochure and Business Reply Envelope. Or, you may design your own overnight letter-type piece and have a computer service print your message. Make sure your design is sufficiently different from those of Western Union and overnight delivery services to avoid copyright infringement.

The brochure

The brochure displays the features and calls out the benefits of the product or service being sold. Also called a circular, flyer, folder, or booklet, the brochure illustrates the product, demonstrates its use, and provides interesting background information about it. Just as a good direct mail letter contains all the main sales points about a product or service, so does a good direct mail brochure.

The brochure format

Some direct mail researchers say that the brochure should contain all points of the offer on a single surface, so that the prospect can take it all in at one time without flipping pages or switching from the letter to the brochure. Many successful direct mail brochures, however, have been done in booklet form with various points of the offer explored page by page. Whatever your format, make sure that the brochure copy ends with an urgency statement: don't leave your prospect hanging with a mere recitation of facts.

Consider a range of sizes and folds

Of all the pieces in your direct mail package, the brochure generally provides the copywriter and art director with the greatest range of possibilities where sizes and folds are concerned. One standard brochure is the 8½" × 11" sheet folded twice into a "C-fold" flyer. Many brochures look like booklets and may be stitched or stapled to keep their pages together. If you want your prospect to keep and carry your brochure, consider making it pocket size. If you want to make a big splash, design a broadside brochure that opens up to a flat size of 17" × 22" or more.

Save brochures with sizes and folds you like and consider how they may be adaptable to your products and offers, but don't make a commitment without checking with a trusted printer or two. This will help you avoid paper waste and extra bindery charges. Also remember that any brochure you design for machine insertion into an envelope must have a closed edge for the inserting machine to grab. This will save you costly and time-consuming hand insertion.

Fit the brochure to the product

When their budgets permit, many direct mailers are tempted to create brochures that are pleasing to their own egos—colorful, expensive, splashy, and impressive. For high-ticket, status items this may be the right alternative. But the best way to develop your brochure's look is to consider the target market and characteristics of the product. A brochure selling flower bulbs at 100 for $9.95 does not require an eight-page color brochure on 100-pound coated stock. By the same token, a brochure sent to prospective customers for a $70,000 foreign luxury car cannot convey the proper message if it is printed in black and white on offset paper. Gather the brochures your competitors use or those in similar fields for ideas on paper sizes and stocks, the use of color, and supplementary illustrations. And study brochures used in other fields as well: they may provide fresh ideas on ways to display your product or service.

The brochure must relate to the package

Make sure your brochure fits with the other items in your package. An expensive, slick brochure should be complemented by a tasteful letterhead and a well-designed order form on good-quality stock. By contrast, a two-color flyer on offset stock looks fine with an inexpensive letter and order form.

Color can increase response

Head-to-head tests show that a full-color brochure usually can out-pull the same brochure printed in black and white. This is especially true if color is one of the product's strongest attributes, as is the case with clothing and home furnishings. While few direct mail brochures are done in black and white, some firms use this one-color approach for a homey or small-company look. Other companies use black and white for sale supplements only. Most brochures feature at least two colors, and the majority are done in four colors. However, a black-and-white brochure printed on fine-quality stock can be very dramatic for certain products such as white bisque figurines.

The reply device

Once your customer has made the decision to take advantage of your offer, he or she needs to be eased through the actual buying process. Many firms offer toll-free 800 numbers for this purpose. However, not all customers will use the phone to order—and you may be unable to offer phone ordering for some products and services. In this case, it is essential that your reply device breeze the customer through the act of buying, and reinforce the wisdom of doing so. A reply card that is confusing, complex or intimidating can easily terminate the sale.

A summary of the offer

There should be nothing new included in your reply device, no announcement of a premium, sale price or other terms and conditions that have not been discussed in the letter and/or brochure. The reply device should summarize all the elements of your offer presented elsewhere in the mailing package. At the same time, it should be able to function on its own as a free-standing sales piece. Some customers save only the reply card and put it aside for a later decision: they should be able to use the card to refresh their memories, regain excitement about the offer, and return an order with confidence. Thus the reply card should comfort the buyer with a restatement of the guarantee or other risk-reducing elements of the offer. It is also a good idea to picture the product on the reply card.

Names other than "order form"

Many direct marketers believe that the term "order form" sounds too much like a request for money and a discussion of the mechanics of ordering. They prefer terms that focus more on benefits and less on nuts and bolts. Thus you might name your card an "Invitation," "Preferred Reservation Card," "Free Information Card," or "Membership Application," if these terms are appropriate.

Make it easy to fill out the form

When a reply card is labeled or ink-jet printed with the prospect's name and address, it streamlines the process of responding. If you design the reply card so that the label shows through a window in the outer envelope, it will serve as the means of addressing the piece as well. If you must ask the customer to fill in his or her name and address on the reply form, make sure there is ample space in which to do so. Try it yourself on a photocopy of the boards before you release the form for printing. Make sure that the paper stock you use is easy to write on: get a sample and try this for yourself as well. Some coated stocks do not take well to pens or pencils of any kind. And use a light-colored stock so that any color of pen or pencil will show up. Also, make sure that you specifically request all the information you need to fill the order: name, street address, apartment number, city, state, and zip code.

When to use a BRC versus a BRE

When your prospect is returning only an inquiry or reservation, and no payment is required, you may opt for a postage-paid Business Reply Card (BRC) that the prospect can simply drop in the mail. But if you are asking for any confidential information on the card—a credit card number or the prospect's age, for example—a Business Reply Envelope (BRE) may ease your prospect's mind and make him or her more likely to respond. Of course, if you are asking for a check or money order in payment, or if the offer is one the prospect might want to keep confidential, a BRE is warranted as well.

Tear-off stubs serve a dual purpose

The customer-oriented purpose of a tear-off stub on an order form is to allow the prospect to save a record of his response for future reference. The stub should have your firm's address on it, and allow room for the customer to record what he or she ordered, the date it was ordered, what payment method was used, and when delivery is expected. A statement on this stub of any applicable guarantee is also a good idea, and the stub provides another, more

---

RETURN THE ATTACHED CARD TO GET 3 BOOKS FOR $1 EACH, PLUS A 4th AT THE MEMBERS' PRICE, WITH NO OBLIGATION TO BUY MORE.

Write the titles of the 4 books you have chosen below. Then detach and retain this stub for your records:

Price | Title

$1 _____

$1 _____

$1 _____

Member's $:_____

History unfolds here.

Return this card to get 3 books for $1 each, plus a 4th at the Members' Price, with no obligation to buy more—and to begin your exploration of all that history has to offer.

YES. Please enroll me in History Book Club. Send me the 4 books I've indicated below. Bill me $1 each for the first three, Members' Price for the one on the bottom, plus shipping and handling. I understand that I have no obligation to buy more. However, if I choose not to buy at least one book in any six-month period, you reserve the right to review my membership. A shipping and handling charge is added to each shipment.

Indicate by number the 4 books you want. Then return this portion in the envelope provided.

CAR-RT SORT **CR46
I08-07-0 611006 221046
SUSAN K JONES
251 PLYMOUTH AVE SE
GRAND RPDS MI 49506

0-13 All orders subject to approval. (See other side for facts about membership.)
H790/0

The History Book Club suggests that its prospective members save the tear-off stub as a reminder of the four books they have chosen. With the stub removed, the order form is the right size to fit easily into a standard 6³/₄ Business Reply Envelope. Courtesy History Book Club. © 1990.

---

practical benefit: you may design your card so that removing the stub makes it just the right size for one of the standard Business Reply Envelope sizes. (If the card were sized this small in the first place, it would float around too much in the outer envelope, so that the address label would not show through the window.)

Combining order form and letter facilitates personalization

One widely used format has the order form attached to the sell letter, and perforated for easy removal. In this way, two benefits are achieved. First, the order form and letter can be personalized at the same time. Second, the letter's appeal for urgency is easy to act upon since the prospect does not have to sift through the package looking for the reply device.

Action and involvement devices may help response

To stimulate action with a reply card, many marketers use involvement devices. Here are several variations:

- *Stickers or stamps*—Products, prizes or premiums may be depicted on pressure-sensitive or lick-and-stick stamps. The prospect affixes the appropriate stamps to the reply form.

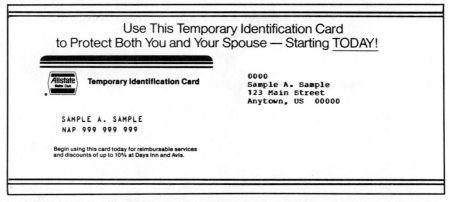

Allstate Motor Club uses a Temporary Identification Card that resembles a regular membership card to interest prospects. The card shows through the envelope window to reinforce the offer of a 30-day free trial membership. Reprinted with permission of Allstate Motor Club.

- *Yes/no/maybe*—To stimulate action, some marketers ask the prospects to respond whether their answer is yes or no. Sometimes a "maybe" option is given, possibly to indicate that the prospect would like to take advantage of a free trial period with no obligation. Stamps with the words YES, NO, and MAYBE are made available on the outer envelope, order form-stub, or letter. The prospect chooses the appropriate one to affix to the reply portion of the form.
- *Membership card*—To give the prospect the feeling of "immediate belonging," some marketers attach a temporary membership card to the reply device, which the prospect can remove and keep before sending in dues or other payment. In its simplest form, such a card could be made of the same stock as the reply form and perforated for removal. However, many marketers have had success using plastic cards similar to credit cards in appearance and weight.
- *Postage stamp*—While the majority of direct mail offers include a prepaid reply envelope or card, the inclusion of a "live" postage stamp adds more urgency to a request for response—especially if it must be transferred from an order form to the proper place on the reply card or envelope. Keep in mind that this method is considerably more expensive than Business Reply Mail, in which you pay postage only for those envelopes that come back to you.

■ *Pressure-sensitive label*—A label may be used to address the letter or outer envelope, and then removed by the prospect and affixed to the order form.

The business reply envelope

Repeated tests show that the cost of providing a Business Reply Envelope is justified in that it encourages a greater level of response. The customer finds it much easier to return an order in a postage-paid, self-addressed envelope than to search around for a plain envelope and stamp.

Business Reply Envelopes also serve an excellent purpose for the recipient: they may be coded by color, size or other means to allow for a quick and dirty way to visually read daily response—even before the orders are input.

To use a Business Reply Envelope, you need a permit from the local post office. To get this you will fill out a form, pay a yearly fee, and receive a reply number to use on your envelopes. You will pay the current first class rate plus a small surcharge for all orders that are returned to you. Provide the post office with money in advance which it may draw against as mail arrives; this will help avoid delays in receiving your mail.

Business Reply Envelopes must be designed and sized in accordance with post office rules. The specifications for Business Reply Envelopes and Cards are available at your post office. Art directors and production specialists need to be very familiar with these rules, as violations waste time and money.

There are standard sizes for Business Reply Envelopes, the most common being sizes 6³/₄ and #9. You may use other sizes within post office guidelines, but they may be more costly if they must be custom ordered from your envelope house. Make sure that the Business Reply Envelope you select fits easily into your outer mailing envelope, and that the reply form fits easily into the reply envelope, preferably without folding.

Other inserts and formats

Mailers have tested and proven the effectiveness of a wide range of additional pieces and special formats that increase response to direct mail offers. For fresh ideas on this score, sift through a wide range of direct mail samples and keep in contact with marketing-oriented printers and other suppliers. Here are a few of the most commonly used inserts and special formats.

Testimonial flyers

If you have or can obtain flattering and believable testimonials from satisfied users of your product, a flyer containing these testimonials may make a good addition to your package. Optionally, you may highlight one or more testimonials in your letter, or put them on a panel of your brochure. Good testimonials offer specific examples of benefits received, performance, or other positive virtues of using your product or service.

Users of established products or services may send you excellent, unsolicited testimonials: keep in touch with your customer service department to make sure you receive them. In the case of new products, you may solicit testimonials from customers who purchase the product as a result of a test mailing. Or you may send the new product to some of your established customers, and ask them to use it and respond with their opinions. Before using any testimonial, you should obtain written permission from the individual who will be quoted.

Premium slips

The customer who barely skims your mailing may not realize that you are offering a premium unless you devote a special piece to it. The premium slip should discuss the features and benefits of the premium, its dollar value if impressive, and what the prospect must do to obtain the premium. Also mention if the prospect is able to keep the premium even if the product is returned for a refund.

Buckslip reminders

These small flyers are most often used to simulate last-minute news. A buckslip might be inserted to tell the prospect that a certain item being offered is now sold out, thus stimulating urgency for buying other items offered. Such a piece might highlight your toll-free 800 number if you have one. Or the buckslip might explain a recent improvement in the product or the offer. It should cover the offer thoroughly enough to make sense to a reader who has not read your promotion package.

The Hamilton Collection uses informative articles like this interview with Gregory Perillo to provide additional background information for prospective customers. The article format provides the appearance of an independent endorsement. © The Hamilton Collection. Reprinted with permission.

Lifelong Love of Horses Inspires Gregory Perillo's "Mustang" Plate

An exclusive interview with Gregory Perillo by Susan K. Jones, Collectibles Investment Advisor

Ever since he first traveled out West at the age of 18, Gregory Perillo has been enthralled by the scenery, the people and the wildlife of the American plains. He began sketching and painting the West as a child on Staten Island, illustrating the cowboy-and-Indians stories told by his Italian immigrant father.

For three decades now, Perillo's masterful paintings and sculptures of Native Americans and wildlife have earned praise from art connoisseurs around the world. His commissions for original paintings now command thousands of dollars, and his one-man shows have appeared in many prestigious international galleries.

Perillo's collector plates are just as well received. In fact, his 1986 "Brave and Free" first issue plate has already risen in value from an issue price of $24.50 to a current quote of $90, with some dealers reporting sales as high as $150. Now for the first time, Perillo has introduced a series of collector plates that will pay tribute to some of North America's most beautiful wild creatures. The occasion for this interview is the introduction of "Mustang," premiere issue in Perillo's North American Wildlife Plate Collection.

S.J. *Greg, most plate collectors associate you with your famous Indian subject works like "Brave and Free." Is wildlife art something new for you?*

G.P. Not at all, Susan. By conservative count, I've completed at least 200 wildlife paintings over the years. Of course most of them have been private commissions.

S.J. *But the introduction of "Mustang" marks the first time you've focused on North American commemorative wildlife for plates?*

G.P. That's right. I wanted to share this aspect of my work with the plate collectors who have been so loyal to me over the years. Frankly, since my original paintings now bring as much as $20,000, I know that only a small percentage of my collectors will be able to own them. That's why it's important to me to paint similar subjects with just as much drama and excitement, and share them with plate collectors at a price we all can afford.

S.J. *There are hundreds of North American wildlife varieties but you selected the "Mustang" as your first*

subject. I wonder, do you have a special affinity for horses?

G.P. I must confess that I do. My earliest recollections of horses are a bittersweet memory from my days as a child on Staten Island. When I was a youngster, my parents couldn't afford to give me an allowance. Many of my friends had spending money, though, and often used it to go horseback riding. I tagged along with them.

S.J. *But what did you do to keep occupied, since you didn't have money to ride?*

G.P. While my friends rode the trails, galloping and resting. Then when I went home I'd show my work to my mother. She'd ask me, "How many horses did you ride today?" I'd pretend that I'd ridden several, and tell her all about them. She always went along with my stories!

S.J. *It sounds as if your parents were very encouraging to you as a child, between your father's vivid stories and your mother's support.*

G.P. Yes, indeed. Once before, Susan, I told you about how my mother used to iron grocery bags for me to use as "canvases" for my paintings. She also used to share a cup of espresso with me at night, long before I was old enough to drink coffee. She'd brew it very strong and that became my paint for artistic experiments.

S.J. *Let's talk some more about your love for horses. When you take your frequent trips out West, do you often see wild horses like the one depicted in "Mustang?"*

G.P. Most often in Nevada. Once you've seen them galloping across the plains, it's a vision that's hard to forget.

S.J. *Then your field research prepared you to paint "Mustang?"*

G.P. That and my favorite place for leisurely research back in New York, the Museum of Natural History. For a major painting like "Mustang," it's important to combine the mind-picture of the horses in action on the range with detailed research on the creature's anatomy. I find the "Mustang" a very romantic subject. I love the freedom . . . the roaming quality of these animals.

S.J. *You've selected a total of eight North American wildlife subjects for this new plate series.*

G.P. That's right, and they're very personal selections. That's why the series is called Perillo's North American Wildlife Plate Collection. These paintings will honor the animals that inspire me the most as an artist. And I hope that the collectors will also find them inspiring.

S.J. *Thanks for telling us all about "Mustang," Greg. What's coming up for you that your collectors might want to know about?*

G.P. I do have some news: the collectors might find interesting. I've been asked to do a one-man show in Korea. It seems that the art of the Southwestern United States is extremely popular there, and I intend to accept the invitation. But if you're hoping for a preview of the upcoming plates in the Perillo's North American Wildlife series, this time I'm **not** telling. I want each new plate to be an exciting surprise for my collectors.

Susan K. Jones has spent more than four years as a writer, observer, collector and investment advisor for the limited-edition collectibles field. She is a founder of and Special Consultant to Collector's Information Bureau, an organization that provides facts and information to collectors in the United States, Canada and Europe.

Article or ad reprints

These pieces add credibility to your offer by including statements from "independent" articles or ads. In many cases such articles are written specifically for the direct mail package and never appear in any publication, but only look as if they had. Where ads are concerned, the marketer might obtain reprints of an ad run in a particular publication and overprint a message such as, "In case you missed our ad in XYZ magazine. . . ."

Questions and answers

A question-and-answer piece gives you the opportunity to restate your offer and the attributes of the product in a new and simple-to-understand form. For example, one question might be, "What makes the new Smith Widget better than the widget I've been buying for years?" The answer would point out the most outstanding and unique benefits of the product.

Samples

If your product is inexpensive and easy enough to send, you might include a sample of it in your mailing. Products frequently sampled in this way include newsletters, stationery, and perfume. Swatches of fabric may be enclosed in clothing offers as well.

Computer disks

Sales of a series of computer disks may be enhanced when an introductory disk is included with a direct mail package or follow-up to an inquiry. The disk might highlight the benefits of the software being sold and allow the prospect to sample some of its applications. Testing such an enclosure may be warranted when the data base of prospects is highly targeted—say, a list of IBM-compatible computer owners who have a demonstrated interest in personal finance.

Live computer disks and VCR tapes now serve as attention-getting enclosures in many direct mail packages. In this instance, National Education Corporation sent along a sample disk to introduce prospects to its Comp-U-Test product. Reprinted with permission of WOL Direct.

*H*ERE IS YOUR FREE
COMP-U-TEST ™ *DEMO DISK*

Simply remove the disk from its protective sleeve and boot it up on your IBM or IBM-compatible computer. Just follow the simple instructions on the disk label.

THIS COMP-U-TEST DEMONSTRATION DISK ALLOWS YOU TO:

- READ THE ON-LINE MANUAL
- STUDY CHAPTER MATERIAL
- TAKE A QUICK-STUDY™ EXAM
- TAKE A SIMULATION OF THE ACTUAL NASD EXAM
- USE THE ON-LINE GLOSSARY TO LOOK UP WORDS
- VIEW A GRAPH SHOWING YOUR TEST SCORES
- PRINT HARD COPIES OF THE MANUAL OR CHAPTER TEXT

You'll enjoy a preview of Comp-U-Test™ — explore its Learning Environment and capabilities to help you master course materials in half the time!

To order your copy of the entire program — Call, FAX or Mail TODAY!

Call 1-800-828-2917 (For FAX ordering, dial 1-717-343-8172)

VCR tapes

Some high-ticket products have been sold effectively with the enclosure of a VCR tape that highlights product benefits. Once again, the potential effectiveness of such a costly promotion depends upon your ability to use the database to prequalify prospects as to their sales potential. VCR tapes are more likely to be used in a fulfillment package sent to qualified inquiries. However, there are now VCR tapes available in cardboard cases that can be used for only a few viewings. They are much less expensive than regular VCR tapes, and may increase the number of cost-effective uses for this type of enclosure.

Gimmicks

To induce a response, some marketers send their prospects actual checks for small amounts of money, which the customer may endorse and cash for responding to or even for simply receiving the mailing. Or the marketer may send a penny or other coin or coins to create interest value, with a line such as, "A penny for your thoughts." Advertising specialties firms can provide a wide range of gimmick items that may be enclosed or tipped onto your promotional pieces. Examples of these might be a packet of instant coffee or aspirin, a lapel button, or a bumper sticker.

Follow-ups

In a series of mailings, varying your formats may inspire fresh interest from your prospects. You might, for example, send an actual photocopy of your original letter, with a handwritten note saying, "In case you missed this special offer the first time around. . . ." Using different outer envelope sizes will encourage prospects to read mailings sent later in a series, as will printing a two-color brochure in a different color combination.

Postcards

Some mailers find that they can sell products via a toll-free 800 number simply by sending a postcard to their prospects. Many magazines use multi-panel postcards for cost-efficient renewal efforts. And a number of firms use postcards as up-front "teaser" mailings, alerting the prospect to a package they will receive soon and including appropriate benefit-oriented language about its contents.

Subscribe to BusinessWeek with this Free Trial Offer

Business Week is written for people who don't have extra time. So it's precise. Concise. On-target. And so skillfully edited you can *use* and *choose* just what *you need* to read.

FOUR ISSUES FREE

You won't waste time with Business Week. And you won't waste money, either. Because with this special offer, you can *prove it to yourself* just how valuable Business Week is.

Just mail the postpaid card and you'll get *four free trial issues*. With no obligation. No commitment, whatsoever.

BIG PLUS

If, after sampling Business Week, you choose to subscribe, you'll receive a savings of 60% off the $2.00 cover price, and you'll also receive a great *FREE gift*. The Business Week Solar Calculator. It doesn't need batteries. It doesn't need cords. It just needs you to push the keys! And backed by a Life-Long Warranty.

THE UPPER MANAGEMENT MAGAZINE

More successful executives — more chairmen, presidents and top managers — read Business Week than any other business magazine. Join them today. And count yourself in on a really good deal.

See reverse side and mail postpaid card now.

BusinessWeek
Post Office Box 506
Highstown, NJ 08520-9970

BUSINESS REPLY MAIL
FIRST CLASS   PERMIT NO. 42   HIGHTSTOWN, NJ

A postcard with several panels may prove to be a cost-effective alternative to a more complex direct mail package. Here, *Business Week* **makes a straightforward free trial offer on a six-panel postcard.** Reprinted with permission of *Business Week*.

Self-Mailers

While the standard direct mailing includes various separate pieces enclosed in an envelope, self-contained mailers come in a number of attractive formats. A self-mailer may be as simple as a mimeographed sheet with an ordering device separated from a letter by a dotted line, or it may be a complex format with ingenious folds, perforations, and combinations of paper stocks to provide a brochure, letter, order form, and pre-formed Business Reply Envelope all in one.

In general, mailers find that they get a better response to envelope mailings than to self-mailers. But people are more likely to pass a self-mailer along to a friend or associate than they are an envelope mailing. So if your offering appeals to a cult audience or special interest group, the self-mailer may work beautifully for you. And because some self-mailers cost less than envelope mailings, the cost per order with the self-mailer may be less, even if you get fewer total orders. Usually the self-mailer concept is worth a test against a successful control direct mail package. Work with an experienced printer to find a cost-efficient format, and try it against your standard envelope mailing.

THE
SCIENCE OF
CREATIVE TESTING
IN
DIRECT MAIL

9

A well-designed, ongoing program of creative testing can reap thousands of dollars in extra profit even for small-volume direct marketers. More impressive yet: a valid test yielding as little as a one-half percent increase in response can mean millions of dollars in extra sales for direct marketers whose roll-out quantities are large. With a firm understanding of the most successful direct mail offers and formats under your belt, you are now ready to learn how to develop your own direct mail creative tests.

This chapter will explain the importance of testing as a way of life in direct mail. You will also learn what elements are worth testing and how to frame a testing program aimed at establishing or beating the control. And you will learn several ways to test creative concepts inexpensively before launching a full-blown mailing program.

Why direct marketers test

The late John Caples explained the value of testing in his book *Tested Advertising Methods* when he said it "enables you to keep your finger on the public pulse . . . to sense trends in advance."

He went on to say, "Regardless of what method of testing you use, the important thing is to have some method of testing. Testing enables you to throw opinions overboard and get down to facts."

Caples continued by explaining what he meant about opinion in advertising. "Testing enables you to guard against an advertising manager whose pet ideas may be hurting your advertising. Testing enables you to guard against an advertising agency whose idea of agency service is merely to turn out pretty layouts and stereotyped copy. Testing enables you to guard against mistaken ideas you yourself may have in regard to advertising."

Indeed, even seasoned creative professionals are often amazed at their own test results. A plain outer envelope may outpull one with a teaser line the copywriter swore was irresistible. The art director's pet 9″ × 12″ four-color envelope may be shown up by a plain #10. On the other hand, the long and involving copy of a four-page letter may more than justify its cost over the simple one-page letter it beats in testing. There have been cases where a simple picture of the product outpulled an elaborate brochure. But in just as many cases, the opposite proved true.

Direct mail testing is not an exact science, because each new product is offered to a constantly changing audience of consumers. The consumers themselves are affected by the season, the weather, the economic news, and the other advertising messages they've seen recently. There are no absolute rules for direct mail testers, except "keep testing."

Copy great Tom Brady calls testing "the R&D of direct marketing." Considering the thousands—even millions—of dollars many firms pour into research and development, the costs of direct mail testing may be easier to justify in this light. Indeed, direct mail experts agree that the test phase of a promotion should not have making money as its goal. Professor Julian Simon calls testing "a way of buying information." It's an investment that can end up saving you a great deal of money—and produce additional profit in later phases of mailing.

The overall purpose of direct mail testing is to determine the desires of the customer or prospect. Do they want your product or service? On what terms will they buy or respond? Which creative approach will attract the most qualified prospects? An understanding of direct mail testing elements will help you frame a test that can answer these questions.

What to test in direct mail

When you begin to market a product or service for the first time, you are testing one very specific thing: its viability, or ultimate profit potential. The first time in the mail, you are testing multiple elements of necessity, simply because you have no control package to use as a benchmark.

You will position your product to be as appealing as possible, based upon any market research, focus groups or other sampling techniques you have used. You will choose the best possible lists, develop the most appealing offer you can, and create the copy and layout that put your product in the most attractive light.

If your initial test fails, you have a choice of abandoning the program or continuing to test, focusing on improving the area or areas you believe are responsible for the test's problematic results. You may choose to leave the creative product alone and test different lists. Or you may elect to test a new positioning, or new copy and/or layout.

If your initial test succeeds by meeting the criteria you have established for viability, then you can focus additional testing efforts on improving the profitability of your program. You do this most effectively by focusing on one element at a time including lists, offer, positioning, copy, and/or layout.

Ensure that your tests make a profitable difference

Some direct marketers become bogged down in testing subtle changes such as light blue versus light grey letterhead, or #6³/₄ versus #9 Business Reply Envelope. Before scheduling such a test, ask yourself "what will I do with the knowledge I gain, and how much money could it save me/make me?" Honest answers to these questions will help you avoid wasting precious test cells with frivolous concepts.

To determine what could be tested in addition to lists and other media, consider these standard creative test ideas.

1. Offer
2. Product Positioning

3. Format (Envelope kit or self-mailer, size, color vs. black and white, number and elaborateness of enclosures)
4. Copy (style, tone, length, density, emphasis on certain features or benefits)
5. Price and Payment Terms
6. Timing/Seasonality
7. Premiums/Bonuses/Discounts

All seven of these test concepts offer the potential for an outstanding increase in sales and profit. Read through the chapters in this book on offers, formats, copy and art direction to spark ideas on how these test concepts might be developed for any given proposition.

How to test in direct mail

There are two main schools of thought about testing creative concepts in direct mail. Although some direct marketers use one method exclusively, both have an important place in an overall testing plan.

Test one new element against the control

Once a mailer has an established control package, the most exacting way to work toward improving the control is to select out one element at a time that could be modified for a possible lift in results. This does not mean that only one test can take place per mailing: your test matrix might include any number of separate element tests, each to be measured against the performance of the control. Your computer house can help you develop viable test cells of names for this purpose. Exhibit 9.1 shows how a simple version of such a testing matrix might look. In this six-way test, the mailer puts half of the 100,000 names in the control cell, using the package which has proven most profitable in the past. This allows the mailer a cushion against which to invest in some carefully thought-out tests, element by element: a more expensive letter, a less expensive brochure, the addition of an extra element, trying a higher price, and experimenting with payment due upon shipment instead of with the order.

The test cells contain 10,000 names each. If the cells are prepared properly, on a random-name basis, test cells of this size are

EXHIBIT 9.1   Direct mail testing matrix

TEST CELL	PACKAGE ELEMENTS	QUANTITY MAILED
A	CONTROL—#10 outer envelope, 2-page letter, 11″ × 17″ four-color brochure, 8½ × 3⅜″ order form, BRE, $40 price	50,000
B	LETTER TEST—Use control package but substitute 4-page letter	10,000
C	BROCHURE TEST—Use control package but substitute 8½″ × 11″ two-color brochure	10,000
D	LIFT LETTER TEST—Use control package but add a short letter answering prospect's objections	10,000
E	PRICE TEST—Use control package but substitute $50 price for $40 price	10,000
F	OFFER TEST—Use control package but substitute ''no money now'' for payment required with order	10,000

large enough to yield a valid test for most direct mail offers. One of the most often-quoted rules of thumb from direct mail guru Bob Stone is that any test cell must have at least 30 responses for a readable result. To obtain this, some mailers are able to work with cells as small as 5,000 names—even less on a responsive house list—while others need larger cells to obtain sufficient orders or inquiries for a readable test.

Element testing works best for mailers who have already established a serviceable control package. This scientific approach seldom results in ''breakthrough'' response increases. Rather, it allows a mailer to steer a good direct mail package toward greatness by fine-tuning one element at a time.

Test a whole new approach

Sometimes called ''breakthrough'' testing, this method is riskier than element testing, but it also stands to yield much greater rewards. It calls for the creative team to put any existing control packages aside and develop a whole new way to sell a product or service from scratch.

Whereas element testing is often executed in-house by staffers who live and breathe the control package, some direct marketers like to open up their breakthrough testing programs to outside creative resources who bring fewer preconceived notions to the project.

On the other hand, a more clinical approach may also lead to a breakthrough positioning or offer. One or more members of the creative team may take the control package apart, paragraph by paragraph, listing the points it makes and considering their relative emphases. This outlining technique allows creative people to consider, point by point, what is good about the control package and what could be improved. They can pull out written points or visual features that could be played up to better advantage.

At the same time, production experts can suggest various formats, personalization methods, printing and paper ideas, and other technical innovations that might help sell the product more effectively.

The negative aspect of testing completely different packages against the control is that when a package emerges as a winner, the mailer never knows precisely why. Another problem is that an untried package is just as likely to result in a costly failure as it is in a profitable breakthrough. Over a period of time, however, direct mailers will do well to mix the exacting, step-by-step science of element testing with some risk-taking breakthrough testing to maximize profit potential.

Tips for profitable testing

From the combined wisdom of successful marketers, here are some points to keep in mind when developing direct mail tests.

- *Make sure that your entire test is mailed at the same time.* If parts of your test mailing are dropped even two days apart, the readability of your results may be compromised by changes caused by news reports, competitive mailings and other uncontrollable factors. If your mailing is so large that it cannot be mailed all in one day from one lettershop, find a lettershop or group of lettershops with more capacity. If any part of the mailing must be dropped earlier, make it the far-flung zip codes—i.e. California and New England if you are in the Midwest. These may require more time for delivery.
- *You need a difference of about 15 percent in results between two test segments to consider the results meaningful.* If, for

instance, you have a 5,000-name control cell that yielded 40 orders and a 5,000-name test cell that yielded 44 orders, the 44-order cell has only 10 percent more orders than the 40-order cell. In this case, you would need at least 46 orders in the test cell to consider it measurably better than the control.

- *When you find a test element that makes a measurable improvement in results, retest it against the control.* Make sure it isn't a fluke before you establish it as part of the new control.

- *Track the long-term profit and loss consequences of any test, not just its short-term results.* It is much easier to produce "loose" leads—people who have indicated a modicum of interest in a product in order to get a free premium—than it is to develop "tight" leads who are expecting a salesperson to call on them. Make sure that your "loose" lead program converts sales at a level high enough to make it more profitable than the "tight" lead program before you pronounce it the winner. The same concept holds true in continuity programs. You may bring in more "starters" with a free book offer, but will they convert into long-term subscribers as well as those who pay $12.95 for their first book?

- *Keep careful records of what you are testing and what results you receive.* The first date you receive orders, and the number of orders received for each test cell on a daily basis, are essential pieces of information. Make sure each test cell is coded on the reply device so that you can track its source.

- *Test each concept for yourself.* Some mailers track the testing of their competitors and then wait to see which kits or ads show up later at the roll-out stage. This knowledge can raise questions to be answered by your own testing plan, but it cannot provide specific answers for your program. You would have to know all of your competitors' objectives and financials to draw absolute conclusions from their testing—and even then, their results would provide specific direction for you only if your situation were identical to theirs.

- *Keep testing.* The marketplace changes constantly due to customers' attitudes, economic factors, and your competitors' offers in the mail. Just because you proved that a two-page letter was better than a four-page letter five years ago doesn't mean that this is still the case. Test some of the same things you tested in the past—and keep looking for new ideas to test. Look beyond your direct competitors for testing ideas—try to adapt the ideas of top direct marketers in many fields to your situation.

■ *It is beyond the scope of this book to discuss further specifics of direct mail mathematics.* Those interested in learning more about planning readable tests and roll-out mailings will find excellent chapters in the following books: *Direct Marketing: Strategy, Planning, Execution* by Edward L. Nash; *Building a Mail Order Business* by William A. Cohen; *Elements of Direct Marketing* by Martin Baier; and *How to Start and Operate a Mail Order Business* by Julian L. Simon.

■ *Many experts say that list testing is even more essential than creative testing to the success of a direct mail program.* Working with a good list broker and computer house, the marketer can develop mailings whereby both lists and creative concepts are tested at the same time, utilizing state-of-the-art database and merge/purge techniques.

Simple pretests for creative ideas

A recent direct marketing research symposium at Northwestern University named the pretesting of creative ideas as the number-one challenge for the burgeoning academic field of direct marketing. Although researchers might frown upon some of the quick and dirty methods employed by direct marketers in search of direction for their creative testing, many successful writers swear by these simple and inexpensive techniques.

Have "the person on the street" read your copy

Show your masterpiece to a disinterested party and ask him or her to read it. Ask the reader to share the main idea with you—what did he or she come to understand from reading the piece of copy? If the idea that is played back does not fit with your strategy, it's back to the word processor. Or perhaps the reader will come up with a new twist you hadn't thought of—a benefit you might be able to amplify by rewording the copy.

Do some unscientific opinion testing

You can get general direction on the viability of various offers, prices and terms by showing your product to groups of people, either in formal focus groups or informal gatherings. Some marketers have remarkable success determining the appeal and perceived value of products just by approaching people in office buildings and shopping malls. Market researchers might scoff at this unscientific methodology, but simply getting the reactions of people who have not seen the product before can spark new creative ideas.

Poll your house list

Your loyal customers may be thrilled to be singled out for their opinions about your new product offerings. Find out from them what they think of your offer, price and terms. Mail them a product description and ask them questions about it. Is it a fair value for money? Is it an appealing product? How likely would they be to buy it? To cut down on "yea-saying," the customers' wish to please you by answering "yes" to most questions, ask them to rate the relative appeal of various products and offers—not just one.

Use the telephone

Some quick calls to a random sample of your house list can provide an even faster reading of a product's viability. This is an inexpensive way to test the waters before putting your offer in print.

Consider a dry test

Perfected by publishers, this technique allows you to make an offer by mail of a product or service that does not yet exist. If the mail response is good enough, continue with further mailings and produce and deliver your product. If the mail response is disappointing, notify respondents that you cannot deliver, sending your apologies and an explanation of technical difficulties. Dry testing is considered allowable by the Federal Trade Commission as long as you adhere to certain disclosure guidelines. For instance, you may not imply that the product already exists, and you must communicate promptly with customers if you cancel the program. It is best to use a "send no money now" offer in dry testing to avoid having to refund money if the program fails.

The importance of a written testing plan

Real estate agents teach their customers that there are three important attributes of a house: location, location and location. Direct marketers have a similar statement when asked for their three basic rules: test, test, test. But it is important that each creative test be a part of a well-conceived, written testing plan. The discipline of such a plan will help direct marketers ensure that each creative test they execute will provide valuable information that can help lead to maximum potential profit.

DIRECT MAIL COPYWRITING AND ART DIRECTION

10

After the rounds of research and meetings, when a direct marketing campaign has reached the concept stage, the copywriter and art director face the acid test. With only a blank computer screen, scratch paper or layout pad before them, these creative people must somehow turn a marketing concept into compelling copy and visuals.

Ask 20 writers and artists how they get from concept to creative product, and you'll receive as many different answers. Some creative people jump right in, writing in stream of consciousness or sketching scores of thumbnail layouts until their creative muse appears. Others do a great deal of restless stirring about, verbalizing their ideas and their midstream creative anguish in equal measure. Still others swear by a step-by-step process they use repeatedly: order card first, then brochure, then letter. Or, first write as many headlines as you can think of for the brochure. Or, first put yourself in the shoes of the target customers and write down all the things they'd want to know about the product or service.

In the midst of their creative fervor, some writers cover their office walls with sticky notes, each of which contains a germ of an idea. To organize their thoughts into a direct mail package or ad, they rearrange the sticky notes again and again before putting words on paper. Art directors have been known to indulge in "folding fits" that look a bit like origami, using layout paper to try out a half-dozen or more brochure formats in various sizes and configurations.

Ideally, the copywriter and art director will spend a good deal of this freewheeling time together, sharing their ideas as they develop and working together toward a harmonious verbal and visual product. Such intense teamwork requires mutual respect, an understanding of the partner's personality and work style, and a willingness to avoid territorial squabbles in the interest of an excellent final product. In the best such copy-and-art teams, neither party remembers nor cares who wrote the winning headline or who chose the cover photo for the brochure. For more on the person-to-person aspects of direct marketing creativity, check Chapter 6 of this book.

There is no one right answer as to how much copy should be included in an ad or brochure, and there is no absolute best visual for any direct marketing presentation. Decisions such as where headings, copy and visuals should appear, what size they should be, and how they should support each other, must be worked out through this respectful interaction of copywriter and artist.

While direct marketing experts assert that such teamwork offers the best chance of success for any creative advertising venture, there are situations in which the copywriter and artist work separately. In this case, one or the other must take the lead. In some instances, the copywriter may prepare rough layouts as an initial guide for the art director's work. In others, the art director may prepare a layout, indicating how much space is available for headings, copy and captions.

Each creative team's style will necessarily be different, but there are some common stages that most creative jobs go through. This chapter will offer an outline for the step-by-step process of copywriting and art direction. It will provide ideas on ways to evaluate and pretest copy and layout without spending undue time or money in the process. Finally, it will provide a few tips on ways to gain inspiration and fight writer's or artist's block.

The creative strategy statement

Before the first word is written or a single line is drawn, the copywriter and art director should accept and understand the Creative Strategy Statement for the job they've undertaken. This format, shown in Exhibit 10.1, is from Ron Jacobs, president of the Chicago-based direct marketing agency Jacobs & Clevenger. It provides good, basic direction for the creation of a direct mail package or ad.

EXHIBIT 10.1   Creative strategy statement

CREATIVE WORK PLAN

Client:

Project title:

Date:

Job no.:

Prepared by:

Key fact
Single most important fact relevant to preparing this advertising.

Consumer problem this advertising must solve
Related to KEY FACT. State in consumer terms. Not what the brand or product needs . . . what the consumer needs.

Advertising objective
How this advertising proposes to solve the problem stated above.

Creative strategy

Prospect Profile: *Portrait of the best prospects, list key demographics, psycho-graphics, product usage facts.*

Competition: *Not a list of brands: what we must replace in order to attract consumers to our offer.*

Promise: *The single most important consumer benefit. The basis upon which this advertising will be built.*

Reason why: *Most important single reason we can give the consumer to believe the promise above.*

LEGAL OR POLICY CONSIDERATIONS/MANDATORY FACTORS

Step-by-step art and copy

While time or monetary considerations sometimes dictate otherwise, the most prudent creative process for the development of art and copy includes at least three main steps.

EXHIBIT 10.2   Step-by-step art and copy

	ART COMPONENT	COPY COMPONENT
STAGE 1: Preliminary	Thumbnail sketches	Headings and subheads
STAGE 2:	Rough layout	Rough copy
STAGE 3: Comprehensive	Comprehensive layout	Final copy

Details of art components

From thumbnail sketches to comprehensive layout, each ad or brochure goes through various stages beginning with tiny sketches and progressing through rough layouts and finally to comprehensives. These final layouts are used for typesetting, keyline and pasteup. As the layout progresses, the creative team selects typefaces, arranges for photography or the creation of drawings to accent the layout, and determines the colors and processes that will be used to produce the work. Once these decisions have been made and type has been set and approved, the keylines will be created, approved, and turned over to the people responsible for separations, film, and printing. These production functions are discussed elsewhere in this volume. Here, the focus is on step-by-step layout creation.

The layout process

There are several distinct layout stages, and in many cases an art director will progress from one to the next without skipping over any. However, it is quite common to proceed directly from thumbnail to comprehensive layouts if the art director, copywriter and client trust each other and the job is fairly straightforward. This is also necessary when timing prohibits an extra step. What's more, with the proliferation of sophisticated desktop publishing systems, art directors find it faster and easier to create complex layouts than in the days when all the work had to be done by hand.

It is never advisable to skip directly from thumbnail sketches to camera-ready art, however, or even from rough layouts to boards. The comprehensive layout is the road map for the typesetter and for the keyliner. What's more, it provides all parties involved with an opportunity to approve or correct a layout before major production expenses are incurred. Thus, the importance of the "comp" should not be underestimated.

Thumbnail sketches

These small sketches indicate the general shape and proportion of the piece being created, and the placement of basic elements such as headlines, photographs, borders, boxes, and so on. Thumbnails are valuable because they give the parties involved something to look at and evaluate beyond a verbal description of how the layout should be done. Because they are small and rough, they allow everyone to explore many different ideas without an undue investment of time.

Rough layouts

Sometimes called "pencil roughs," these layouts are done to actual size, but are not exact as to color, type sizes, photograph and drawing sizes, and so forth. They help everyone involved visualize the finished product, the flow of material, and the impact of an ad or brochure done in that size. They may incorporate actual headings and subheads, if possible, since this again helps in the evaluation of flow and effectiveness. Roughs may be done by the copywriter or by the artist, or as a cooperative effort for presentation to the client.

Comprehensive layouts

Just as its name implies, the comprehensive layout or "comp" covers all the bases. It measures to exact size and reflects all the folds, die cuts and other enhancements of the proposed final product. It indicates color areas and suggests the colors that will be

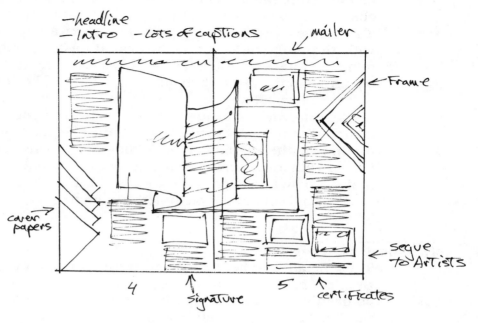

Small thumbnail layouts were the first step in planning art and copy for a 12-page brochure on the A.R.T. Card™, a product of Artagraph Reproduction Technology Incorporated. The finished product shows that numerous changes and refinements were made between thumbnail layouts and final approval. Reprinted with permission of Artagraph Reproduction Technology Incorporated.

used, exact copy areas, the sizes of headings or photos, where borders will appear, and so on. The art director will often attach color and paper samples to such a layout to indicate background hues and texture, and he or she may indicate type sizes and styles right on the layout. When using desktop publishing, the actual copy may be shown in place. The "comp" serves not only to help the client and artist visualize the final product, but also as a blueprint for the creation of camera-ready art.

Details of copy components

Headings and subheads

While the art director works on thumbnails and sketches various format ideas on scratch paper, the copywriter may be considering various headline concepts and secondary points for subheads. Drawing upon the "Key Fact," "Promise," and "Reason Why" from the Creative Work Plan, the writer noodles around with phrases and sentences—and perhaps even has the art director sketch them into the thumbnails to see how they come across on paper. Many direct marketing firms and agencies ask copywriters to provide sets of alternate headings and subheads, along with a short statement of the ad concept and the rationale behind it, before proceeding to rough copy. For an in-depth discussion of how to write headlines for direct marketing sales propositions, see Chapter 14 of this book.

Rough copy

The rough copy stage is one which some copywriters swear by, while others polish their copy to a near-final state before showing it to anyone. Rough copy provides a general indication of copy length, the flow of ideas, tone, sentence and paragraph length, and other copy characteristics. Creative teams who use this stage as part of an approval process may share their rough copy and layouts with each other to touch base and make sure they are still on the same wavelength. Then they may show rough copy and corresponding rough layouts to a creative director or client representative for a general critique before final work is completed.

(a)

(b)

SELF-RENEWAL

Many people become "stuck" in life, confused, unable to move forward. The Programs for Self-Renewal are designed to loosen the cement around your feet and allow you freedom to move again -- toward your unlimited potential.

▼ **115 - Self-Confidence** - One of the greatest gifts you can bestow on yourself is the gift of self-confidence. Develop the confidence to say "No" without feeling guilty. Acquire the self-assurance to feel relaxed and at ease when you meet people. Start on the road to a more confident you with this vital tape.

▼ **110 - Relieve Stress And Anxiety** - Unhappy feelings can really get to you. Learn to tell your feelings how to feel, rather than having them tell you how to feel. Suggestions on this tape can teach you how to feel good all the time.

▼ **106 - Relaxation** - If you would learn to relax, your blood pressure could return to normal, headaches could go away, that uncomfortable, uptight feeling in your stomach could leave. Stress, being uptight in an uptight world, is a major health problem. Use this tape and you could begin to experience peace and calm, joy and relaxation.

▼ **026 - Develop Enthusiasm** - Learn to start an inner fire! Approach everything you do with enthusiasm and you'll always do it better. Shine and the world shines with you!

▼ **023 - Creative Thinking** - Quality ideas and thoughts are all around us. One creative idea can propel you to unlimited prosperity, happiness and fulfillment. Raise the quality of your thoughts, and you will raise the quality of your life.

▼ **011 - Be Positive (Psychic Protection)** - All successful people are able to retreat within themselves when being assaulted by the negativity of others. You can learn this skill and protect your mind. This tape contains simple procedures which can effectively shield you from the negativity of unwanted thoughts and energy.

▼ **101 - Problem Solving** - Unfortunately, most individuals and businesses solve problems by creating bigger problems. Solving problems by patching negative areas is not the answer. The solution is creative problem solving which requires imaginative thinking.

▼ **061 - How To Be Popular** - If you do not have close friends and want to develop this important part of your life, this tape can help.

Buy 3 Programs and get one FREE See Page 3	**MS** 1 Tape Format Music Subliminal	$9.98
	SC-I 1 Tape Format Super Consciousness	$11.98
	SC-II 2 Tape Format Super Consciousness	$14.98

(c)

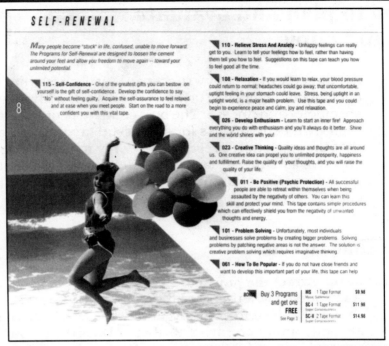

Potentials Unlimited uses a sophisticated, in-house computer system for the creation of its catalog of self-hypnosis tapes and related products. Hand-drawn rough layouts (a) serve as a guide for the creation of computer-generated comprehensive layouts (b) with all art and typeset copy in place. The final, printed catalog spread (c) reflects minor changes from the comprehensive layout. Reprinted with permission of Potentials Unlimited.

Final copy

Corresponding to the art director's comprehensive layout, final copy represents the copywriter's completed and fully polished efforts, ready for approval by the client and then for production. Before releasing copy for the approval and production process, successful writers work and rework their copy to ensure that it presents a compelling sales message in a way that is readable and appealing to the target market of prospects. The way in which writers polish their copy is highly individual: some take a more global view and then work down to the details while others consider their writing sentence by sentence, then in total paragraphs, and then as part of the overall flow of the piece. An essential element of creating final copy is to distance oneself from the work overnight—or at least for a few hours—before taking a final read-through. This cooling off period will allow the writer to spot unclear passages, inconsistencies and even misspellings.

How to plan and evaluate art and copy

Art directors and copywriters can rest assured that their clients or agency managers will critique their work with varying degrees of specificity and finesse. The best creative people, however, build in their own benchmarks for successful layouts and copy to ensure that the work they present is not only fresh and creative, but also effective as a direct marketing sales message. Here are a few basic guidelines for planning and evaluating your own layouts and copy.

Evaluating layouts

Will the layout attract the prospect?

Ask yourself whether the layout presents the personality and tone that will appeal to your target market. Is it casual, sophisticated, elegant, family-oriented, hard-sell? Does the layout reflect the values and tastes of this target market by means of its visual images, typestyle, colors and border treatments?

Is the product the star?

Even experienced art directors occasionally get carried away with typefaces, background colors, or special-effect shots that are gratifying to work on but in fact do very little to enhance a product. When evaluating your layout, ask yourself whether the product is the star or whether you've buried it in "art for art's sake." Ways to "star" the product include showing it as large as possible, depicting it in use, and giving it a flattering background that conjures up positive associations and contrasts in color so that the product will "pop" on the page.

What is the point of the layout?

Try to look at the layout as a customer would. What is it that you are trying to get across? The main focus or point of the ad should be your product's prime features and benefits. What's more, the layout also needs reworking if you cannot quickly discern a point from it. A layout that tries to cover all points equally is destined to confuse or turn off the reader. Remember that your prospect is likely to give your piece only a few seconds' glance before deciding whether to read on. Does this layout have a "grabber" of a point that will encourage the reader's involvement?

Does the layout look inviting and readable?

Some printed pieces are so busy or so poorly typeset that reading them is literally hurtful to the eyes. Others are open, airy, and inviting. To make sure that your layouts are of the latter kind, check to see if your headings and body copy are large enough to be readable (usually 8 on 9 point as a minimum for body copy). Make sure there are no stumbling blocks to the flow of the copy, such as a two-column picture that breaks up a body of related copy for no important reason. Even though long copy is one characteristic of direct mail pieces, make sure that the copy area does not look like a sea of small print. See that the copy is broken up with subheads, small illustrations, and other visual devices.

For space ads: how does the ad look in its editorial environment?

Take your comprehensive layout and place it randomly in the publication where it will run. Does it seem to blend into the background, or does it stand out? Standing out is more desirable, but the ad should shine because of its superiority and freshness—not because it seems incongruous in this publication. Ways to make an ad stand out include:

- Running a long-copy, editorial-format ad in a publication that carries mostly big picture/short copy ads.
- Running a big picture/short copy ad in a publication that normally features editorial ads.
- Running a full-page coupon ad in a publication where most direct response ads are 1/6 page or smaller and appear in the back-of-the-book direct response "ghetto."
- Using a bind-in card that pops up between the pages instead of or in addition to a clip-out coupon.
- Running a full-color ad in a publication where this is a rarity.
- Using emerging technology to personalize your bound-in space ad with the reader's name.
- Running a short ad reversed in white out of black in a publication that has lots of black-on-white ads (be careful with this, as too much reverse copy is difficult to read—and don't reverse out the coupon, or it will be impossible to fill out).

For direct mail pieces: how does it look in a dummy kit?

Evaluating an unfolded layout is one thing, but seeing the piece as it will appear when folded for an envelope—and actually inserting it along with a letter and order form in the envelope—is a very valuable exercise. You can perceive the kit as your recipient will, and you may catch the little problems that could go unnoticed until it's too late: an order form that doesn't fit easily into a Business Reply Envelope, or a brochure that is too bulky when folded down for a #10 envelope.

In this same context, always fold down a brochure layout as it will appear when mailed, to be sure that the recipient's first view of the brochure is an appealing one. You probably wouldn't want the fold to cut your main front cover headline in half, for instance.

Your dummy kit serves two other purposes. First, if you create it with paper of the same weights and sizes that will go into the real kit, you can determine the weight of your kit to make sure it falls within the postal category you seek. Second, the dummy kit helps you to get proper quotes from your printer and lettershop. Your print salesperson and lettershop representative may also be able to point out cost savings on the basis of your dummy—slight modifications that will cut paper and printing costs and make inserting and addressing less expensive.

Is the layout a standard size, or is there a good reason for custom sizing?

Sometimes a product calls for special treatment, an odd-sized outer envelope to give the kit a European look, for instance, or an ad that runs in three parts, diagonally down and across the magazine page, to create reader interest. But unless such a special effect is part of your stated plan, you'll probably want to stick with standard sizes for envelopes, brochures, letters, and ads. This will save you money and time and allow you to take advantage of stock envelopes and standard printing configurations.

Is the use of color and bleeds appropriate for this layout?

Since the first color ad ran in 1937, the conventional wisdom has held that color is superior to black and white when it comes to readership and impact. A 1967 Daniel Starch research report showed that consumers' "noted" scores for half-page color ads in magazines were almost twice as high as those for half-page black-

and-white ads. Yet in some cases, a full-color treatment just isn't necessary. And with the proliferation of color in all media, some art directors now find that black-and-white ads actually gain more attention because of their novelty. Consider as well the impact of the long-running Dewars Scotch ads, in which Dewars drinkers are pictured and profiled. The individuals are shown in black and white, while only the product itself is depicted in full color.

To determine whether color is necessary for your selling proposition, consider what the prospect needs to know and feel in order to making the buying decision. Ladies' dresses in shades of blue, orange and yellow will probably need color depiction, while men's standard white underwear may not. In some instances, a black-and-white presentation may flatter and enhance the product even more than color—in the case of elegant white bisque figurines, for example. In such an instance, you may choose to invest your budget in fine photography and excellent paper instead of color separations.

Some direct mail packages and ads gain the impact they need through the use of two-color printing. By the addition of an accent color to black, or by printing another dark color instead of black on a light-colored stock, you can achieve a multicolored look at a lower cost than with full color.

Bleeds, in which color runs off the page instead of stopping at a white border, can offer a luxury look or a special impact. But because bleeds are more expensive than nonbleeds in printing (they require more paper for trimming), it is worth questioning the need for them when budgets are tight. To be sure of the differential, have your printed piece quoted for bleed and nonbleed prices. For space ads, check the magazine's rate card for bleed versus nonbleed rates.

Other nuts-and-bolts considerations

Are the color combinations pleasing and appropriate for this target market? Does the presentation make your product or service easy to order? In space ads, make sure the coupon is accessible— usually at the lower right of an ad created for placement on the right-hand side of the page. For direct mail packages, be sure the reply form is easy to follow, well spaced, and fits properly into the Business Reply Envelope. Put the layout away for a day if you can afford the time, and then approach it as you would if you were a prospect. Is it pleasing, easy to understand, and effective? If not, go back to the drawing board.

Evaluating copy

There are as many different formulae for direct marketing copy effectiveness as there are copywriters, and some of the big names in the field have become famous for their "ten-point checklists" and "how-to" guides. The following is a distillation of many of these "shoulds." Rather than use a checklist of all the good and bad points of copy that are presented to you from various sources, keep the following hard-won direct marketing concepts in mind when developing and reviewing your copy.

Characteristics of effective copy

The best copy is clean and clear, and presented in language that is simple without being simplistic. Copy great Maxwell C. Ross said that for every 100 words of copy, 70 to 80 should comprise only one syllable. Whenever possible, good copy uses the present tense and the active voice. One teacher of copywriting automatically marks points off students' work every time they use a form of the verb "to be" instead of an active verb. Good copy comes across as friendly—not patronizing or self-important. It flows well and has good transitions. It utilizes connecting phrases such as "what's more," and "in addition." Finally, it draws the reader in from the very first phrase, making reading a pleasure rather than a chore.

The "you" approach

Some copywriters and clients fall into the trap of simply counting how many times the word "you" is used in a direct mail letter or ad. But that is not the point: it's the overall "you" approach that counts. Make sure the copy doesn't talk only of how your product is made and what its features are. First and foremost, customers want to know what's in it for them.

As you prepare your copy, keep product benefits firmly in mind. The copy should address the prospect's wants, needs, hopes, aspirations, lifestyle, and interests. Do your best to evaluate the copy in terms of the market, not your own biases and beliefs. You may be a target for the product you're selling, but as often as not you won't be. Don't make the mistake of slanting your copy toward what pleases you and your own (nontarget) type of person. This is where "infiltrating the market" can become invaluable. Find ways to spend time with typical prospects for the product or service. Learn what magazines they read, what TV programs they watch. Catch on to their speech patterns, slang expressions, and ways of looking at the world. This hands-on research will pay big dividends in your ability to address copy to your prospects that "hits them where they live."

Copy length

There is no reliable rule for copy length. Nothing says that a four-page letter is inherently better than a two-page letter, or vice versa. Nothing says that a 120-second spot is inherently better than a 60-second spot on direct response television: indeed, tests by The Bradford Exchange, Kobs & Draft and other direct marketing firms and agencies show that shorter TV spots may actually out-pull longer direct response messages.

Copy great David Ogilvy states firmly that long copy sells more than short copy, and in general, ads that sell direct carry much more verbiage than general advertising does. But the best advice is to write until the story is told, then revise, edit, and cut the copy until it is clear and strong. Lobby with your account executive and/or client to leave options on copy length open until you work up a rough draft of the copy; then decide whether you need more or less space than originally planned.

Another guideline is that the more complex the proposition, or the higher the price, the more explanation your customer will expect and need before buying. Therefore, for an offer of a free booklet at no obligation, your copy normally would be considerably shorter than what you would need to sell a $3000 photocopy machine via mail or space advertising.

Feature/benefit/value

It isn't enough to point out the features or characteristics of your product. It is more important to make sure the customer perceives the *benefits* of the product, in personal or corporate terms. In other words, you wouldn't say simply that a toaster "has low, medium and high settings." Rather, you would say that the toaster "has low, medium, and high settings" (feature) to toast everything from plain white bread to frozen toaster pastries in seconds" (benefit).

The features and benefits presented should add up to a value that your prospects can perceive and which will lead them to become customers. The best way to make sure you can present meaty, benefit-oriented copy is to make sure you know the product inside and out. As the old saw goes, "sell the sizzle, not the steak.'' Make sure that you get across what the product will add to the customer's life.

It's also vital to make sure that benefits are presented in the order of their magnitude, with the most important given first according to your customer's perceptions and not your own.

Success stories

If possible, provide some success stories of your product in use. One graphic way to do this is via testimonials or endorsements. Testimonials and endorsements should be believable. They should be in the words of real people or representatives of organizations with expertise in your product line. They should be as specific as possible, spelling out results in dollars and cents, pounds lost, compliments received, time saved, or whatever the success story comprises.

Another way to show your success story is to give proof of effectiveness. This may take the form of a notarized statement by an expert, a demonstration on television, or before-and-after shots.

The call to action

The goal of every component of a direct marketing campaign is to induce action: whether ordering by mail, calling, agreeing to buy, or coming into a store. This action must be spurred by the copy, but without coming on too strong. Read the "call to action" copy of some direct advertising you admire, and of your competitors, to learn how they induce a response. Here are some possibilities.

- Limited quantities or limited edition
- Premium for response by x-date
- Charter subscription or membership period
- Seasonal reason, i.e. for delivery before a holiday
- Discount for "early bird" response
- Preseason discount
- Limited-time sale price
- The old "be the first on your block" pitch, presented in a fresh and subtle way that fits your target market
- Urgency based on immediate need—for charity donations

Specificity

Take the copy you've written about a product and read it through, substituting some other, similar product as subject. How much of the copy still works? If much of it works for another products, your copy has failed the specificity test. The cure for copy with this problem is to zero in on your product's *specific* attributes and benefits, making sure that the copy points these out in graphic, descriptive terms. Don't just say "large, economy size;" that could apply to anything from detergent to pancake mix. Say "six pounds of seed and dried vegetable mix—enough to keep two parrots healthy and well fed for three months." Don't simply say, "complements any decor;" that could apply to an air freshener or a sofa. Instead, say "the classic, clean lines of this bleached pine cocktail table complement both traditional and contemporary homes."

Sales sense

The direct response copywriter is first and foremost a personal sales representative. Copy should do everything a personal sales call does—but (with the exception of telephone marketing) in a two-dimensional format. Thus the sales writer must anticipate objections from customers, lead them to positive responses, and then "close" the deal. Compare the copy you've written with a verbal sales presentation on the same type of product, and see how it rates.

Appearance

Work with the art director to learn how your piece will come across visually. Letters should have plenty of margin space to enhance their readability. Brochures should be broken up with subheads. Strive for a paragraph length of little more than six lines whenever possible. The key is readability and appeal. The art director can do a lot with typefaces, leading, illustrations, colors, and so on—but the copy itself must also draw the reader in visually.

Ease of ordering

As a next step, let someone else read your copy—and preferably several people not directly involved in your business. Have them go through the motions to order your product and see if they have any trouble with the reply device and instructions as presented. Can they find the price? Color choices? Size of the product? Expiration date for the offer? Guarantee? Toll-free number? Mailing address to use if coupon or reply card were already used? Ask them what they think the copy is trying to get across, and see if your benefits come back to you in some semblance of your own order of importance. Ask them which parts of the copy they find interesting, dull, easy to understand, and hard to understand.

Some direct marketers request that their "guinea pigs" underline phrases they find remarkable in the copy—and to indicate whether their reaction to each phrase is positive or negative. Then they rework the copy until all the "stoppers" are positive ones.

Getting words and pictures on paper

While there are few jobs in direct marketing as rewarding as creating a successful direct mail package or ad, the birthing process can be long, drawn-out and painful. Most every copywriter and art director can recall a time when the flow of creative solutions to marketing problems stopped cold. But one way or the other, direct marketing "pros" are able to unblock their minds and get back on the track of creativity. Here are some ideas on what to do when writer's or artist's block strikes.

Retrace your steps in the creative process

One of the most common reasons for creative block is that the writer or artist tries to short-circuit the multi-step creative process. While there are any number of step-by-step models for creativity, they all call for an initial period of research and freewheeling "what if" games, an incubation period, a point of discovery when ideas flow fast and furious, and finally an implementation period. Chapter 2 of this book covers the steps to creative discovery in detail. If you have tried to skip from research to implementation, for instance, without taking time for incubation and the "ah-ha" stage of discovery, your creative potential will be sorely limited.

Talk with someone who knows and loves the product

Sometimes even after studying the psychographics of the target market and familiarizing yourself with the product, a lack of excitement will prevent you from getting anything meaningful on paper. In this case, it often helps to spend time with the person who created the product or service, or the individual who currently manages it. Since this person lives and breathes the product, he or she may be able to transmit enough enthusiasm, details and specifics to get you over the hump. In addition, this is a good time to attend a focus group or ask for tapes of recent focus groups or other qualitative research to find out how consumers talk about the product, and what they like about it most.

Switch places with your counterpart

If you're the art director, be the copywriter for a while. If you're the writer, sit down with a layout pad and start sketching. Even the most off-the-wall idea may provide the spark that gets you started, and the unfamiliarity of the other team member's job may force that idea out into the open.

Allow yourself some procrastination time

Whether it's doing the filing that's piled up for six months on your credenza, taking a long lunch with a friend, or working on a completely different project, a bit of procrastination may allow your subconscious mind the necessary time and freedom to produce the germ of a good idea.

Explain the situation to someone who's not involved

Whether you choose to share your problem with your analyst, your spouse, a child or your dog, verbalize the scenario. Oftentimes in stating the problem out loud, a new clarity emerges that allows for creative solutions. If the person you're talking with asks questions, so much the better: you'll be forced to frame your thoughts in an organized way, which may gain you a new perspective on the situation.

Harness the positive power of deadlines

Waiting until the eleventh hour may not be all bad: indeed, creativity expert Roger von Oech says that many of our best ideas come to us under pressure. When the adrenalin's pumping and the clock is ticking, you may find that the perfect (or at least an acceptable) creative solution pops into your head.

Plug into a formula

When you seem paralyzed and unable to get even a few words or lines on paper, pull out a direct mail package or ad from the old swipe file, or reach for your favorite how-to direct marketing formula (see Chapter 2 for several). By matching your current selling challenge to the structured formula at hand, you may be able to get the creative juices flowing.

Ask for help

Call upon your fellow creative direct marketers for a new way of looking at the problem at hand. If you cultivate such relationships, you may well be called upon to do the same for a friend who's reached a dry spell. This kind of creative generosity within an art-and-copy team, an agency or direct marketing company will pay big dividends to the bottom line in the long run—so do your best to develop such a creative network in your workplace.

BUSINESS-TO-BUSINESS DIRECT MAIL

11

Business-to-business is an area of real excitement and challenge for direct marketing creatives. On the one hand, today's business people still receive scores of amateurish mailings in #10 outers, written by the company president and printed on limp stock. There's a challenge inherent in convincing these firms that direct marketing done well can increase results many times over. On the other hand, a number of sophisticated mailers already have made business-to-business direct marketing the most forward-looking area of our field.

The reasons behind this business-to-business revolution are several. First, in recent years there have been remarkable improvements in list segmentation and database management for business-to-business marketers. It is now possible to target business and industrial audiences with precision, and to keep valuable information about customers and prospects accessible on the database.

Second, as business giants discover the power of direct marketing, budgets allocated for mailings have skyrocketed. Selling sophisticated, big-ticket customers by mail calls for an exceptionally creative package. And when the product's pricetag is in four, five or even six figures, the dollars-per-prospect that can be allocated to direct marketing are much more substantial than in most consumer markets.

Third, business mailers have shown a remarkable openness to innovation that goes hand-in-hand with their ability to spend more per prospect than most consumer marketers can. Three-dimensional packages, fulfillment packages complete with VHS videos, and image-building mailings are just a few examples of to-day's typical business-to-business direct mail applications.

Business-to-business direct mail: A growth medium

Today, more dollars are spent on direct marketing than on any other form of business-to-business marketing. The reason for this is simple: as the cost of a personal sales call continues to rise, direct marketing becomes more and more attractive as a pre-approach medium.

Time was, firms believed they could afford to send salespeople on "fishing expeditions," making cold calls on businesses to look for likely customers. But today, as the price of a single personal sales call edges toward $300, firms are looking for ways to cut down their sales costs.

Closing an industrial sale may require an average of four or more calls on the prospect, utilizing the medium of personal sales alone. If direct marketing can be used to eliminate one or more of those $300 sales calls, profits-per-sale to the company may improve substantially. What's more, if direct marketing can help qualify leads for the salesperson, he or she is free to pursue only the best prospects, enhancing efficiency even more.

In addition, many firms have discovered that direct marketing can replace personal sales altogether for certain customer categories. Telemarketing and direct mailings can streamline both initial orders and reorders for small-to-medium-sized customers. Some relatively high-ticket products that used to be marketed via personal sales can now be 100 percent mail sold, for example, smaller photocopiers, fax equipment and office furniture.

How business buyers compare with consumer buyers

An understanding of the business buyer's motivation is an essential starting point for direct marketing creativity. In many ways, the business direct mail buyer is simply a consumer making purchase decisions from an office desk instead of a home easy chair. But there are a number of crucial differences to note—differences that will help shape the most effective creative approach for business-to-business mailings.

Similarities of business and consumer buyers

When making business/industrial purchases, individuals behave the same as they do when making consumer purchases in that:

- *They are regular people* with the same problems, emotions, hopes, dreams and fears that they exhibit on their own time.
- *They are busier than ever before in their work lives*, just as they are in their home lives. They are less disposed to welcome the interruption of cold calls from unknown sources than were previous generations of buyers.
- *They are subject to direct mail clutter at the office*, just as they are at home. In self-defense, they sift out the interesting from the uninteresting with little more than a second's glance.
- *They are part of the "show me" generation*, brought up on ever-present television and newly addicted to the VCR. Pictures, videos and lots of color and action will draw their attention. Long, uninterrupted blocks of black-and-white copy probably will not.

How to attract the consumer within the business buyer

Just because business buyers sit behind desks being paid to make purchase decisions, they do not become emotionless computers. To ensure that your direct mail solicitation will be noticed, read and considered, you must avoid being dull, overly serious or prematurely fact oriented. Although business buyers need the "steak" about a product in order to sell it to management, they must first be attracted by the "sizzle" of enticing packages, easy-to-read copy, premiums, gifts and enhancements.

Understand that business buyers are swamped with demands and don't annoy them. Save them time and money with streamlined approaches: a quick phone call instead of a formal sales call; a postcard instead of a phone call, etc. Consider flashy mailings to cut through the clutter: video, bulky packages, overnight delivery service, etc.

Read over the material in this book's general chapters on offers and formats. There are many ideas to be gleaned from consumer marketing that can be adapted for use in business-to-business mailings in addition to the concepts put forth in this chapter.

Differences between business and consumer buyers

Although many of the business purchaser's personal buying habits carry over to professional buying activities, there are some very specific differences that direct marketers should keep in mind. Here are some points about business/industrial buyers.

- *They are spending someone else's money.* As a private consumer, the buyer is fairly free to purchase items on impulse, without making even a mental list of reasons to justify the expenditure. But when the same buyer makes a purchase for the company—even a purchase as simple as typing paper or replacement parts—he or she must have a rationale for the purchase based on price, service, quality and other factors.
- *They are likely to go through a formal purchasing process.* Although some consumers do extensive comparison shopping, few actually go so far as to evaluate formal bids in a committee. Industrial buyers often are required to use a step-by-step purchasing process of identifying needs, establishing budgets, selecting possible vendors, getting bids, and making a group buying decision.
- *They may be "specialist types" or "purchasing types."* Lumping all business buyers together can be a big mistake.

The engineer, mechanic, or other business person who will actually use the product is likely to be more concerned with quality, ease of use, and such personal concerns as enjoyment and status. The purchasing agent is generally interested in getting acceptable quality and service at the lowest possible price.

- *They may be influenced by company politics.* Business buyers must be prepared to justify their decisions to their superiors, as well as to influencers whose positions make them anti-spending by definition: chief financial officers and rival peers, for example.
- *They may welcome contact with you as part of the job.* Even though many consumers enjoy buying by mail, they often complain about the volume of direct mail they receive at home. That's because buying products for personal use is a leisure activity for them, not their livelihood. But to some extent at least, the mail and phone contacts a purchasing agent receives are a vital part of the job. Your solicitations can help the buyer keep on top of innovations in the field, transmit news about price breaks, and so on. Studies show that business buyers prefer mail contact above all other forms of communication.
- *They may be making complex and costly decisions.* Although some business buying decisions are almost as simple as purchasing toothpaste at the drug store, others are highly technical. Buyers look to the seller for back-up information. They also want to be reassured that the company they are buying from is a solid, stable one to be trusted.
- *They may be insulated by a mail room and a secretary.* Depending upon the title of the person you are reaching and the size of the firm involved, your recipient's mail and phone calls may go through two or more layers of screening before they get to his or her desk.

What is the best approach to the business buyer?

Because of these differences between the business buying mindset and the consumer buying mindset, direct marketers must adjust their strategies and appeals to maximize opportunities for success. Here are some proven ways to do so.

Use lead generation programs that sell the sizzle first—then the steak. Rather than send a complex and expensive mailing package filled with statistics and facts, it is often more effective to qualify prospects first with a preliminary mailing, space ad, or telephone call.

For example, Quest International Corporation sent a series of first class mailings in #10 business envelopes to prospects for their product: a hotel discount service to be used as a marketing premium or member benefit. Only after the prospect responded with a reply card or call to a toll-free number did he or she receive an 11″ × 14″ portfolio mailing including a directory of participating hotels, personalized Quest identification cards to allow the prospect to try the service, several copies of the firm's regular customer newsletter, and other expensive selling pieces. Finally, a salesperson from Quest called the prospect to answer questions and try to arrange a test of the service for the prospect's marketing program.

Lead generation begins by getting prospects to express some level of interest in the product. If leads are to be followed up by mail, you can determine for yourself what makes a good lead, and gear your program to attract "tight" or "loose" leads as you prefer. This book's chapter on offers explains creative approaches to lead generation and follow-up.

If leads are to be followed up by salespeople, ask the sales force what they consider a good lead, and tailor the lead-generation program to suit their requirements. Some sales organizations require little more than a warm body to follow up on, while others want a prospect prequalified right down to the credit check.

One simple way to determine a prospect's level of interest and qualifications to buy is to use check-off boxes on the reply form. (See Exhibit 11.1)

You might also ask the prospect to indicate the size of his or her business, either by number of employees or sales volume. Asking the prospect to confirm his or her title also provides valuable information for the salesperson and the data base.

In consumer markets, major American automakers have used this type of qualification information to stage timed mailings to individuals. For instance, if a consumer indicated on a reply form that he planned to buy a luxury-class car in six months to a year, Ford Motor Company might send him literature on the Lincoln Continental five to six months later, along with some incentive to visit the local dealer. Such a timed mailing, of course,

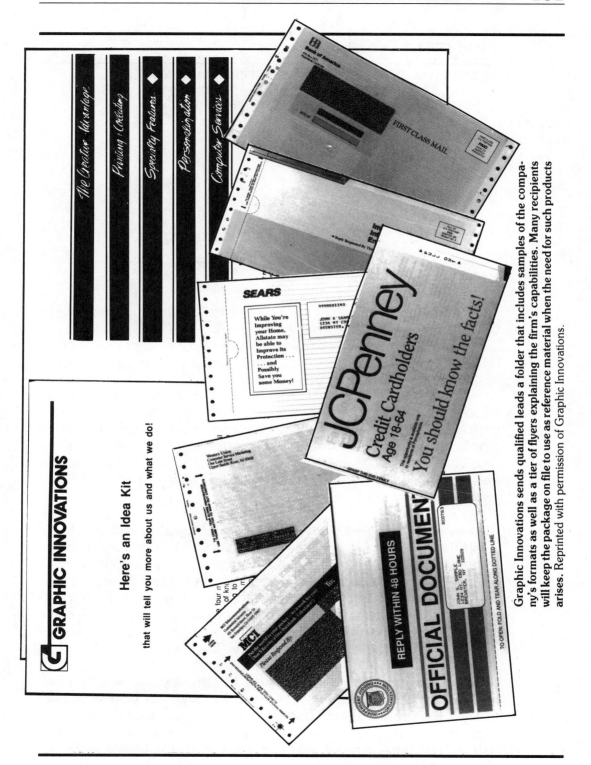

Graphic Innovations sends qualified leads a folder that includes samples of the company's formats as well as a tier of flyers explaining the firm's capabilities. Many recipients will keep the package on file to use as reference material when the need for such products arises. Reprinted with permission of Graphic Innovations.

EXHIBIT 11.1   Check-off boxes

WHEN DO YOU INTEND TO BUY A FACSIMILE MACHINE?

☐ No immediate plans—please send literature for my files

☐ Within six months to one year

☐ Less than six months from now

☐ Immediately
____ Please rush information
____ Please have a salesperson call me at _____
                                                     Telephone Number

---

should be supplementary to an immediate follow-up on the customer's request for information.

Business-to-business marketers should consider customized follow-ups like this, since reaching the business buyer at the time of the purchase decision process is crucial.

For more on the nuts and bolts of operating business-to-business lead-generation programs, several general direct marketing books are very helpful. These include *Successful Direct Marketing Methods* by Bob Stone, *Profitable Direct Marketing* by Jim Kobs, *Direct Marketing Success* by Freeman Gosden, Jr., and *Business-to-Business Direct Marketing* by Bernie Goldberg and Tracy Emerick.

Because your prospects crave plenty of back-up material, give them a fulfillment package worthy to keep on file. Once you have attracted a prospect with the "sizzle" of your initial ad, mailing or phone call, make sure he or she receives a package from you that is substantial enough to encourage its retention. Some mailers offer their fulfillment kits in a file folder format that looks important enough to keep on hand for future reference. Others use presentation folders or binders to achieve that "keep me" look.

Because there may be other vendors bidding against you in a formalized purchase decision, you need to establish your company image. Business buyers must justify their purchase decisions to their bosses, to financial officers, and often even to their peers within the company. All things being equal, the business buyer will probably choose an established firm with a famous name rather than a "no-name" competitor. Even if your price is lower and your product quality is superior, you'll have a hard time making the sale unless you can prove to the buyer that your company is worthy of trust.

Thus building and maintaining a good company image is an important goal for most business-to-business direct marketers. There are several ways in which to do this—and perhaps even break even or turn a profit in the promotional process.

- *The house organ/promotional newsletter.* One method of image building is to develop and mail a handsome newsletter that serves both company employees and customers. The newsletter might contain information about the firm's recent activities and promotions, focus on the functions of a different department each issue, and so forth. The newsletter might also cover the firm's contributions to the community and to charity, fostering its image as a caring corporate citizen. General-interest feature material could also be included, as well as how-to articles related to the firm's field of endeavor.
- *The paid-subscription newsletter.* Service businesses often solicit paid subscriptions for informative newsletters that offer the firm's principals a forum in which to display their expertise. Some companies that began such newsletters as promotional vehicles have been pleasantly surprised that the publications can function as profit centers on their own. Another idea along these lines: the firm's principal might write a regular column in a trade magazine or newspaper in exchange for a free or reduced-cost direct-response ad in the publication.
- *Seminars—for service only or for profit.* Another way to build up your firm's image for expertise in the field is to develop informative seminars and promote them by mail. Some companies offer their seminars free to qualified prospects and customers, while others charge competitive rates, hoping to break even or make money while getting out the word that this is the firm with state-of-the-art expertise.
- *Mail space ads to prospects and customers.* Business-to-business direct marketers can gain extra image mileage from their space advertising programs by mailing clippings of the ads along with a selling letter and a notation on the clipping such as, "In case you missed our ad in XYZ Magazine."

Because your prospects are insulated by mail rooms and secretaries, and because you must cut through the clutter of mail they receive, you need stratagies to get your offer as far as their desks — then get it opened and read. In general, mail rooms and secretaries are unwilling to spare the boss any piece of mail that looks as if it is important, personal, social, or valuable. Here are some ideas on how you can make your mailings secretary-proof.

- *Here is the information you requested.* Every lead fulfillment package should have these magic words—or something very similar—stamped or printed on the front. This wording shows the mail sorter that the boss has solicited the material inside. What's more, this phrase should trigger the recipient's memory about sending or calling for the material. You cannot count on the return address alone to spark recognition. The Popcorn Factory uses a bright red and gold "Information You Requested" sticker affixed to its regular 10" × 13" mailing envelope to alert prospects that it contains the corporate gift catalog they sent for.
- *A plain outer envelope.* A fine quality, closed-faced outer envelope with an address that appears hand-typed may appear important and personal enough to make it directly onto the boss's desk. Don't ruin the illusion by using a label or an addressing mechanism that looks computerized! Another illusion-shattering problem: a bulk mail indicia on a letter that is supposed to appear unique and personal. Use a meter or stamp instead, or mail first class if budgets permit. Some mailers have tried hand addressing closed-faced outers. This appears personal and social, but it can be prohibitively expensive for high-volume mailings. American Express pitched its Platinum Card to executives using a textured, snow-white closed-face envelope with a presorted first class stamp.
- *The invitation look.* Many offers can be developed in an invitation format with a squarish, top-quality outer envelope in white, buff, gray or another neutral tone. Take a look at wedding invitations for size and paper stock ideas. Once again, a promotional look is a tip-off that the contents are not what they seem, so keep the invitation-look outer envelope plain. The mail screener may fear that he/she is tossing out the boss's invitation to an important party, and therefore will pass your mailing on.
- *Appeal to the secretary.* A mailing addressed "To the Secretary of John Doe" meets the problem of mail screening head-

on. Such a package might outline the great advantages of the seller's product *to the secretary*—i.e., time saving, easier to use, more attractive. It could encourage the secretary to suggest the purchase to the boss, even offering a premium geared to the secretary's interests. This should be handled discreetly, however, so that it does not appear to be a bribe. It is best simply to describe the premium, and not state in the promotional copy whom it is meant for or what will be done with it.

■ *Send a product sample.* If your product is something that can be sampled easily, consider sending one or more samples in your mailing package. Something of obvious value—even an item as simple as a pencil, a holiday card or color chart—will probably survive the "mail cut" and also draw the attention of the recipient.

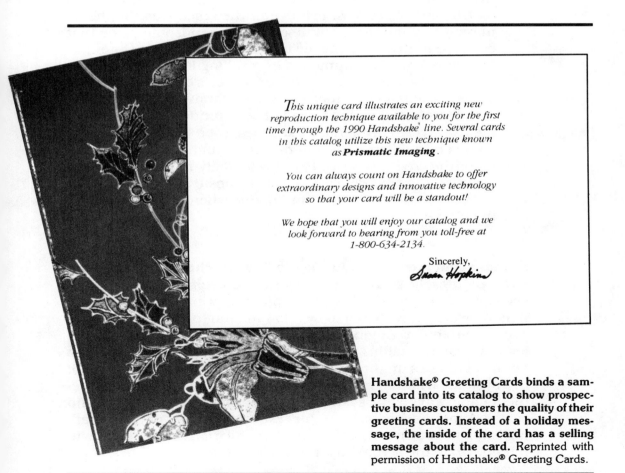

*This unique card illustrates an exciting new reproduction technique available to you for the first time through the 1990 Handshake® line. Several cards in this catalog utilize this new technique known as **Prismatic Imaging**.*

You can always count on Handshake to offer extraordinary designs and innovative technology so that your card will be a standout!

We hope that you will enjoy our catalog and we look forward to hearing from you toll-free at 1-800-634-2134.

Sincerely,

Susan Hopkins

Handshake® Greeting Cards binds a sample card into its catalog to show prospective business customers the quality of their greeting cards. Instead of a holiday message, the inside of the card has a selling message about the card. Reprinted with permission of Handshake® Greeting Cards.

■ *Consider a "lumpy package."* Sometimes called Showmanship, Dimensional, Breakthrough or Spectacular mailings, these three-dimensional packages make it to the prospect's desk because of their novelty value. Even the most jaded executive may be tempted to stop work and open a mysterious package that looks as if it might contain a gift.

A campaign used by *Cuisine* magazine some years ago illustrates this concept. *Cuisine* wanted to reach a relatively small circle of media buyer prospects who might wish to advertise in the magazine. The theme of its campaign was, "If You're Not in *Cuisine*, You're Not in the Kitchen"—meaning that *Cuisine* readers were highly influenced by the magazine's ads when they chose items for their kitchens.

The first of a series of mailings in this campaign was actually a shipment: a box containing a handsome crock filled with wrapped candies. Printed on the crock was the theme message, while the crock itself was a handsome piece that could be used and displayed in the prospect's home or office. Each crock was accompanied by a selling letter.

About a month later, each prospect received another selling letter along with another type of candy to fill the crock, which presumably had already been emptied by the hungry media buyer. Throughout the series, each letter was accompanied by a different food item—in an amount just sufficient to fill the crock. A series like this is likely to have prospects awaiting the next delivery—and in a positive mood to talk to the sales representative from *Cuisine* when he or she calls on the phone.

Because your prospects must justify their purchases and deal with office politics, be sure that you position yourself as a safe bet from every angle. Especially if you are pitching a high-ticket item, it may be worth your while to develop mailing packages aimed at people with different job functions within the firm. For instance, let's say you are selling computer systems. A package mailed to financial officers might emphasize the money-saving qualities of the system, while marketers are told about database enhancements and ways your system gets them information faster and easier. Another idea: put the chief executive officer on your mailing list in hopes that his or her recommendation in your favor will filter down to the actual buyer of your product.

Ways to use direct mail in business-to-business marketing

Some firms can use direct mail to meet a number of different marketing objectives. Here are several possibilities.

As a channel of distribution for certain prospect groups

Customers who are not profitable when serviced mainly by personal sales can become profitable when serviced mainly by mail and phone. Many smart marketers take the time to divide their prospect lists into groups by sales volume and potential. Typical groupings, listed from smallest to largest volume, are:

1. Mail only
2. Mail with occasional phone calls
3. Mail, phone and occasional sales calls
4. Mail, phone and regular sales calls

For promotions to dealers and distributors

The first "sale" many direct marketers must make for a new campaign is to get their dealers and distributors on the bandwagon. Direct mail is an excellent way to communicate a program's goals and tactics so that field representatives know what to expect. Sales contests and incentives can be explained by mail as well.

For promotions to individual salespeople

When a sales contest is underway, it's important to keep salespeople informed. Many direct marketers have had excellent results mailing to salespeople at home to get the spouse and children involved. For a successful contest, try selecting a range of awards that appeal to the family as well as the salesperson. Keep each salesperson posted on individual progress every week or so during the contest to encourage momentum building.

For promotions to specifiers

Often the target of a business-to-business direct mail campaign is not the product's ultimate user. Rather, target audiences such as doctors and architects make recommendations to their patients and customers. The aim of mailings to specifiers is to give them the facts they need to make an informed recommendation. In addition, it is important for you to establish your firm's image, perhaps by creating and mailing a regular newsletter or magazine with articles displaying your knowledge and expertise.

Image mailings

Some direct mailers send regular communications intended strictly as image builders or enhancers. An example is a handsome series from Bradley Printing. Each mailing shows off one or more of the printing firm's specialties. Topics for mailings include holiday greetings, announcement of awards won by Bradley or its clients, and showcasing of customers' artwork and philosophies.

Mailings to schedule sales calls

Sending a letter to ask a prospect for a sales appointment is considerably less costly than an individual phone call, and infinitely less expensive than a cold sales call. Test this pre-approach method to see if it is effective for your sales proposition.

Mailings to open up new markets and approach new customers

Among the least effective direct mail efforts are those made to the sales force's own list of customers and prospects. Rather than limit the firm's horizons to these known quantities, work with a list expert to develop lists of prospects beyond those under the salesperson's nose.

A word about business-to-business formats

The basics of direct mail formats and catalogs are discussed in other chapters of this book. The tips offered here for business-to-business applications will provide additional idea starters.

A letter alone will often suffice

Whereas consumer buyers usually need the reinforcement and "flash" of a brochure and other supplementary mailing inserts, the business buyer may react well to a mailing containing only a letter and a reply card and/or toll-free number to call. This format is especially appropriate for:

1. Asking the prospect for a sales appointment
2. Introducing the sales rep who will then call the prospect by phone
3. Soliciting a lead to be followed up with free information

When a traditional envelope mailing is used, don't try to combine pieces

Often, new business-to-business direct marketers use "logic" to try to save money—with disastrous results. They'll try combining a brochure and letter, or incorporating a reply device as part of a brochure instead of using a separate piece. These tactics are cost saving, but they fly in the face of direct mail experience.

A separate letter serves the personal sales function, while the brochure is the "leave-behind." The reply device closes the sale, so it should be prominent, visible, and valuable looking—not buried somewhere in the brochure.

Keep the elements of your mailing program fresh

Another money-saving ploy of some business-to-business direct marketers is to keep using a standard brochure or mailing package long after it is outdated. Remember that the mailing you send gives the prospect a first impression of your firm—an impression that may be impossible to turn around if it's unfavorable. Update your literature at regular intervals using new product shots, attention-getting graphics and recent staff photos.

Try solo mailings even if catalogs are the backbone of your direct mail business-to-business efforts

Introducing a new product or providing extra support for top selling or high-margin products are two applications to consider for special offers of one item or a line of related items.

Consider self-mailers: they're good for pass-along readership

Many consumer direct marketers say they have a hard time making self-mailers beat the control format of a traditional envelope mailing. But self-mailers carry an extra dividend for business mailers: their pass-along value. Studies show that managers are more likely to drop a self-mailer into the in-box of a peer or subordinate than they are an envelope mailing.

In business-to-business catalogs, be informative, organized and authoritative — but not boring

Don't ignore good promotional language and graphics simply because you are selling a business product. Don't bog yourself down in an explanation of the features at the expense of "sizzle" about the benefits of a product. Avoid using jargon and focusing on technicalities. Nontechnical buyers may be turned off, concluding that your product is way beyond their understanding.

While only the largest consumer catalogs provide a merchandise index, this component is a must for the business customer. In addition, keeping similar products together will help your business customer make direct comparisons of costs, features and benefits.

To emphasize your firm's expertise in the field, provide testimonials and product-in-use information along with the products themselves. Adding how-tos to the copy makes your catalog presentation more lively and helps customers visualize using your products.

Make ordering easy by following these procedures:

1. Provide a phone number the customer can call to expedite matters.
2. Make it clear whether the customer needs a purchase order.
3. Make it clear whether a down payment is necessary or if billing can be done upon shipment.
4. Explain how long shipment takes.

All of these specifics are more important than ever in a business situation, especially when the customer is evaluating you against a competitive catalog or personal-sales representative.

Consider card decks

Card decks may be an inexpensive source of loose leads for business sales propositions—and loose leads can be especially valu-

A business-to-business self-mailer like this bright blue piece from Group 1 Software may well be passed along to the proper party more readily than an envelope mailing. Reprinted with permission of Group 1 Software, Inc.

able for business-to-business operations that can afford follow-up phone calls to qualify the prospect, then personal calls to the best prospects to clinch the sale.

Try offering a product-centered video

More and more lead-generation programs include a VHS-format video presentation as part of the follow-up package. Some firms sell the videos at cost, others request a minimal deposit, and still others send them out free for return on the honor system.

The cost of a video follow-up seems steep until it is compared with a $200 or $300 personal sales call. Watching a video may pre-sell the prospect to the extent that he or she is ready to buy when the salesperson calls by phone or in person. The De-Lite Window Company lends qualified prospects a short video presentation that shows how their windows are made step by step, emphasizing their excellent hard woods and energy-efficient glass. The Progressive Power Tools Corp. follows up space ad leads with a seven-minute video that shows its Linear Link Portable Power Saw in action and features on-camera testimonials from satisfied customers.

Remember the back end

Take advantage of available space in package inserts and invoice stuffers to sell accessories and supplies and help maintain your firm's positive image. Send along your company newsletter, if you have one. Create flyers promoting replacement parts, sales on supplies, service contracts, service check-ups, or free audits of existing systems. Large business and industrial marketers who underwrite television and sports events might stuff their customer correspondence with reminders to watch upcoming shows under their firm's sponsorship. Local businesses that sponsor parades, sports teams, regional television shows, and the like can take advantage of this same stuffer concept.

Copy tips for business-to-business creative people

There are several traps that are all too easy for the business-to-business writer to fall into—especially the in-house copywriter who lives and breathes the same product line for a long period of time. Here are some dos and don'ts designed to help keep your copy fresh.

1. *Don't allow yourself to become production oriented.* Keep the focus of your copy on benefits to your buyer and the ultimate user—not on the latest breakthrough of your research and development department. It may be big news to you and your company president, but that product enhancement means nothing to prospects until you tell them what's in it for them: time savings, money savings, better quality, or whatever.

2. *Don't slow down the sell with product specifications.* Granted, some of your prospects won't make a purchase decision without extensive spec sheets and technical material. But don't bog down your feature-benefit copy with too much detail: if you do, you'll lose the buyer who is strictly results oriented. Put the specifications on a separate page or brochure panel.

3. *Make sure that buying your product looks like a safe bet for someone who believes his or her job is on the line.* Emphasize the safety and security of dealing with your stable and established company. Talk in terms of the satisfaction of the product's ultimate user. For example, tell an architect how pleased the *homeowner* will be with your roofing tiles or greenhouse windows—and why.

4. *Make sure both writer and art director understand the product or service through and through.* Some industrial products are so complex that it's tempting to do a "surface job" of promoting them—pulling out the obvious features and benefits without coming to a full understanding of the product's innermost workings. Resist this temptation. Corner the product manager or the firm's engineer and keep asking questions until you comprehend every aspect of what you are selling. Only then will you be able to write convincingly about the product's most important features and benefits.

5. *Be specific about benefits.* Don't speak in general terms about time or cost savings. Instead, use case histories and examples that put the product's attributes into perspective. Consider how much more effective it is to have a customer say, "A job that used to take me three full days was cut down to just a day and a half the first week I used my XYZ paint spray gun," rather than to have promotional literature say, "The XYZ paint spray gun saves you time and money."

6. *Copy may be long and complex, but keep it easy to read.* In a thorough presentation of a technical product, it is all the more important to use short sentences, short paragraphs, readable typefaces, and subheads.

7. *Use a good art director, and maximize production values.* Don't cut the effectiveness of your carefully prepared copy with a quick and dirty printing job at your local speedy outlet. Invest in the services of an experienced art director and take the time to create a mailing package that positively reflects your firm's image.

8. *Keep reading everything you can about consumer direct marketing.* Many of the action devices, personalization techniques, offers, formats and production methods used first in consumer markets can be adapted to good advantage by business-to-business marketers as well.

DIRECT MAIL FOR RETAILERS

12

In recent years, U.S. sales made via direct marketing methods grew twice as fast as store-based retail sales. What's more, the Direct Marketing Association estimates that direct marketing sales will represent 25 percent of all U.S. business by the year 2000. With these two facts in mind, it comes as no surprise that many retailers and local service organizations are discovering the power of direct marketing. Indeed, whether they use direct marketing methods only to enhance in-store sales, or to establish a direct marketing arm as a separate profit center, retailers have much to gain by learning and applying direct marketing creative techniques.

This chapter will begin with a survey of the reasons why direct marketing provides such excellent opportunities for today's retailers. It will continue with a discussion of the various ways top retailers have integrated direct marketing into their businesses. Finally, a number of specific creative concepts for retailers will be explored, with examples of direct marketing offers and formats from retail firms of various sizes and specialties.

The retailer's growing profit potential in direct mail

Many of the same cultural factors that make shopping by mail so attractive to today's shoppers can hinder the success of a retail sales organization. In addition, typical retail sales and promotion methods carry some inherent limitations that direct marketing can help overcome.

With more dual-career and single-parent households, fewer families are able to make their purchases during the traditional shopping hours of 9 a.m. to 5 p.m. The congestion of 100-store shopping malls is enough to send many consumers home to their catalogs and direct mail offers as well. On top of all this, many customers claim to long for the "good old days" when they could get personal service in stores—not just directions to a central check-out island.

Considering these factors, many retailers find that they can maximize their sales potential by combining the best of retail techniques with the shrewd implementation of direct marketing tactics. In fact, they have learned that if a well-illustrated, well-written direct response solicitation is sent to a customer from a favorite store with a fine reputation, that customer is all the more likely to buy by mail.

Unfortunately, not all retailers and local service firms have discovered how lucrative direct marketing can be for them. They rely on more traditional promotion methods—ones that come to them ready-made like newspaper ads and television spots produced by their ad representatives. They fear that selling by mail will cannibalize their retail sales, even though Sears, J.C. Penney and other top direct marketing firms openly admit that the introduction of a new catalog each season has a positive effect on in-store retail sales.

They criticize direct marketing efforts as "junk mail," even though upscale retailers like Neiman-Marcus, Hermès and Tiffany use the medium regularly and produce stunning mailings with thick, glossy paper and lavish photography. Some retailers try a single mailing that they write themselves, eschewing the advice of direct mail experts. Then when it fails to produce the response rate they anticipated, they write off direct marketing for good, claiming "it doesn't work for us."

Retailers who hold any such concerns may be comforted to consider these reasons why direct marketing can be exceedingly valuable to them.

The persuasive power of direct mail

Some retail customers shop for the pure joy of it. They show up regularly to see what new merchandise has arrived or what special events are scheduled. But such browsers represent only a small fraction of customers. By mail, the retailer can reach the customers who don't have the time or inclination for recreational shopping, and entice them to visit the store for specific reasons and special opportunities.

Steketee's, a Michigan department-store chain, sent out an oversized postcard to let area residents know the store had marked down all gold and silver jewelry by a substantial margin, 54 percent. Such a dramatic mark-down might well be enough to attract even the busiest people to the store.

The customer wants guidance

Direct marketing efforts can help retail customers decide where to shop for unfamiliar items, or build top-of-mind awareness with customers who may need a product or service in the future. And if yours is a specialty business, targeted direct mail can reach your potential customers without the undue waste of advertising in newspapers, on television, or via other mass media.

A local outlet of The Maids International, Inc. sent out a small, four-color flyer to alert homeowners to their cleaning services. In addition to making a pitch for regular cleaning, the flyer lists special projects that prospects might want to have done at some point in the future, encouraging them to keep the piece around for reference.

Direct mail makes you the expert

Economic realities and changing selling methods mean that in many fields the career salesperson is a dying breed. Thus, even though a store may offer state-of-the-art products and services, the customer may not perceive expertise because salespeople are not sufficiently informed about these items. However, the retailer can establish expertise through the mail, by explaining features and benefits of merchandise so that the customer is presold.

Chemlawn sends out colorful mailings to prospective customers before the spring lawncare season begins. In addition to incentives for signing with Chemlawn, the package includes authoritative explanations of typical lawn problems, and how Chemlawn can solve them.

The customer list is a natural

Most every retailer keeps a list of customers' and visitors' names and addresses. Someone's name on that list is your assurance that he or she is interested enough in your products to buy them—

or at least to remain informed about them. Direct marketers without retail outlets would envy the retailer's readily available group of qualified prospects. Using simple database techniques, the retailer can begin keying this list in terms of multiple buyers, big spenders, fur buyers, purchasers of children's items, and other special-interest groups. The list can be broken down for very specific offers to highly targeted audiences.

One warning: Not all retail buyers are direct mail buyers. They may or may not take you up on an opportunity to buy your products by mail instead of visiting the store. But they should be considered your prime prospects for retail traffic-building techniques.

Direct mail allows for a personal slant

Smart retailers take advantage of the personal touch in direct mail to give early announcements of sales and special events to preferred customers. It is much more flattering to a customer to learn of an upcoming sale at her favorite store by means of a private invitation than to read about it in the newspaper. Even more flattering to the customer—and effective for the retailer—are the special in-store, mail and phone buying opportunities developed for preferred customers only. Direct mail allows for an "exclusive invitation" approach that is impossible with mass media such as newspaper or television.

In addition, the personal slant lets retailers develop sales promotion programs especially for certain segments of the community that can be reached by mail or phone. For example, Sears sends mailing packages to working women, explaining in very specific terms how having a Sears Charge can help them save time when they shop in the store, by phone or by catalog.

The retailer's name already carries an image

Imagine sending out the same mailing package—same merchandise, photography, printing, terms and guarantee—under the logo of Neiman-Marcus and under the unknown name of John Doe. Which is more likely to succeed? Direct marketers without a retail affiliation must spend time and money establishing an image with prospective buyers. The customer may resist sending in an order because he or she has no experience with the firm.

By contrast, local retailers carry their images with them into their direct marketing operation—assuming that they tailor their presentations to reflect the style and price level of their existing images. The retailer with a reputation for good service and merchandise has an immediate edge over an unknown firm.

Direct mail helps avoid constraints inherent in other media

In direct mail, the retailer can target the market so specifically that it may pay to send out fabric swatches, offer free samples, print a prospectus costing several dollars a copy, or include several pages of explanatory information enlivened by well-reproduced color photos. Only advertising giants like Apple and IBM can afford to do these things in magazines, but even smaller retailers can come across as lavish "class acts" in direct mail.

Another plus for direct marketing is the ability of even small retailers to test their advertising ideas on a small scale. Retailers can send out a handful of letters making a certain offer to preferred customers, and see how they react before expanding the program to the entire list. Or the retailer can send out one offer to 50 customers and another offer to 50 more, and see which concept performs better.

The combination of retail and direct response is a potent one

Sears research shows that families receiving a Sears catalog are twice as likely as nonrecipients to shop at a Sears store. Even more significant, these catalog recipients spend twice as much at Sears as noncatalog recipients. A smart retailer knows that it is much more profitable to win and keep 10 customers each spending $1000.00 per year than to go after 100 customers each spending $100.00. Direct marketing methods can help the retailer cultivate top-level customers and keep them coming back. What's more, today many firms with retail operations use their direct marketing arms not only as traffic builders, but also to exploit their opportunities in other product lines and beyond their local traffic areas.

Credit cards and installment-credit proliferation.

Now that consumers have widely accepted credit cards and installment buying, retailers may offer high-ticket items via direct marketing, even to customers who do not hold store charge accounts. All the retailer needs to do is offer the charge option of American Express, Visa, MasterCard, Discover and/or Diners

Club. With store charge accounts accepted by customers as a virtual necessity, retailers can launch successful "blanket" mailings to new areas where stores are to be opened, soliciting new charge customers even before the grand opening. Monthly charge statements also become fertile fields for the direct marketer. For the same postage needed to send out the bill, syndicated or co-op offers or the retailer's own direct marketing pieces can ride along in the envelope.

Vendors are often willing to help pay direct marketing costs

Today's retailers are smart to keep their eyes and ears open for opportunities to use a vendor's money for direct marketing promotion. The manufacturer may provide a lush direct mail piece imprinted with the store's name and address, offering a buying opportunity to the store's customers. The many "free with purchase" cosmetics offers sent out by department stores are but one example of this type of co-op arrangement. The customer may order by mail or stop in at the store to participate.

The designer clothing firm of St. John often puts together elegant mailings introducing its spring or fall collections, which are sent to a department store's customers in the store's name. In addition, both Jacobson's and Sakowitz used the same eight-page "Investment Folio of Super Coats"—Jacobson's as a self-mailer, and Sakowitz as an insert in a catalog featuring other merchandise as well.

Direct marketing can expand local horizons

Some retailers are known as the prime source of a local specialty: macadamia nuts in Hawaii, for example, or Navajo rugs and crafts in the Southwest. Other firms are already known by reputation well outside their local areas: Marshall Field of Chicago, for example. In cases like these—or in any case where your business offers something that is not readily available to customers beyond your local area, you may expand your customer base by offering your products by direct mail.

Before you get started, however, you must be sure that your products are unique enough to interest some reachable and sizeable group of customers beyond your local area. The Go Wild Shop, a store catering to the Northwestern University community in Evanston, Illinois, has been able to do just that by mailing its Northwestern University Gift Catalog to alumni of the school all over the United States.

**Direct mail gives retailers the opportunity
to exercise their buying power**

Established retailers already have relationships and lines of credit with vendors, and therefore they command attention with their direct marketing plans. If you wish to play off of success in a certain department or put together a deeper line of merchandise than a department could profitably carry in the retail store, a special mailing package can achieve your objectives.

Lawson Traphagen Hill wrote a book about his experiences in this regard. Beginning as a retailer of shoes, Hill and his wife Marcia realized that there was a large, national market for shoes in a wide range of special sizes. They launched a direct mail program by printing and mailing 5,000 catalogs in 1968. Nine years later, when Hill sold the business, he was mailing 10,000,000 shoe catalogs a year!

Direct mail can help even out seasonal business patterns

The retail store that was bustling with walk-in trade on December 15 can be a pretty empty place on January 15 unless the retailer has given the customer reasons to be there after the holidays. Sales, special events, seminars, continuity offers and many other possibilities spring to mind, and direct marketing techniques can be used to alert customers and prospects to what is taking place.

Mail-in or phone-in ordering are also appealing ideas to the customer who has to battle a foot of snow to take advantage of a January sale in person. Thus, direct mail or phone sales can bring an influx of business even when the weather or other seasonal factors cut down on walk-in trade.

How retailers integrate direct marketing — and vice versa

Once upon a time, the only merchandise a retailer would offer by mail was merchandise that could also be found on the store shelves. But retailers like Neiman-Marcus changed that by using their expertise as buyers to set up separate direct marketing divisions.

"NM by Post" features items available only by mail from Neiman-Marcus. And the regular Neiman-Marcus catalogs carry a disclaimer which says that merchandise contained in the catalog may or may not be carried in Neiman-Marcus stores.

Such nonstore offers allow an established retailer to sell merchandise that is more suited to direct response promotion than to in-store selling. For instance, some of the charming, small gifts offered in NM by Post would be lost on a large retail counter. With proper photography and copy, they can become stars on the catalog page.

The retailer might also consider organizing separate direct-response divisions for catalogs and mailings that offer merchandise in more depth than would be appropriate for most retail stores. Examples of this would be an Orvis or Norm Thompson mailing offering hunting boots in a dozen different varieties, or a department-store flyer promoting several styles of cashmere sweaters in as many as 20 different colors.

Catalog marketers become retailers, too

Neiman-Marcus and Marshall Field began as retailers, and now they have separate direct marketing divisions. But perhaps even more noteworthy today to direct marketers is the trend toward firms beginning as catalog marketers and then branching into retail stores: notably The Sharper Image, Banana Republic and Brookstone. Retailers may learn from the way these firms integrate creative direct marketing methods in their store sales approaches.

The Sharper Image salespeople offer a sharp image—they are clean-cut, and identically dressed in crisp blazers. Once they gain the attention of a customer, they become "talking catalogs," for they understand the intricacies of their high-tech product line and can explain features and benefits to perfection.

The now-defunct Banana Republic catalogs carried out a safari theme—and so do their thriving retail stores. From the "jungle guide" costuming of the salespeople to the testimonial letters that are pinned to the dressing room walls, walking into a Banana Republic store is like stepping into a catalog. More than most boutiques or special-interest stores, Banana Republic exudes a lifestyle—and that's something that fledgling retail direct marketers should take to heart for both their in-store and direct mail efforts.

Brookstone allots a certain amount of space to each product, then places the product in that space with its catalog description tacked beside it. Once again, the store is like walking into the cata-

The Sharper Image builds traffic for its stores and sells by mail and phone using the same monthly catalogs. Stores and catalogs are so well integrated that visiting a Sharper Image store is like stepping into the catalog. Reprinted with permission of The Sharper Image.

log: in this case, a no-nonsense, product-centered atmosphere. Even if the sales clerk doesn't know the product well, there's written material close at hand to help make the sale.

Creative direct mail concepts for retailers

Whether you elect to use direct mail for traffic building only, or to expand your horizons to include actual selling by mail, these ideas from successful retailers will provide food for creative thought. Here's how to use direct mail.

When you open a new store or outlet

If a new store is in an area that may be convenient to some or all of your existing customers, let them know about it and its location. Or send existing customers a special offer to get them to visit the new store: a coupon, announcement of a sweepstakes that must be entered on the store's premises, fashion show, celebrity appearance, or other special event.

Here's an example of a special offer to get customers in the door: Steketee's sent out a postcard announcing a Secret Sale. Each card had a certain percentage off indicated, but not readable unless activated by a "Secret Pen" at the store. Some customers would have 15%, while others would save as much as 100 percent—but they had to visit the store to win.

When you wish to obtain charge customers for a new store

You can rent lists of residents in a new trading area by zip code, and blanket the area with charge-card solicitations. But make sure you take only the most likely zip codes—don't mail to low-income sections of town if yours is an expensive specialty shop, for example. To sweeten the deal, you might offer a free gift with the first use of the new credit card, sending the customer a coupon to redeem on the first visit to the store. Depending upon the store's established reputation and the quality of the promotion, a retailer may yield as much as 5 to 10 percent response with such a "pre-opening" charge card offer.

When a customer has not used the charge card lately

Keep track of your customers' frequency of purchase. If they have not charged an item in the last six months, year, or whatever interval you choose, make them a special offer. You might offer a free premium with any charge purchase or simply ask them to stop into the store for a free gift and to acknowledge that they want to keep their charge account open.

When you wish to attract new customers not familiar with your store

Make a specific, seasonal offer to prospective customers: one that plays into their current wants and needs. For instance, Food-stuffs, a gourmet food shop in a north Chicago suburb, sent out a mailing to residents in the surrounding area offering its fancy boxed picnics just in time for the summer season in Ravinia, an outdoor music festival where many patrons bring their own picnic suppers.

To encourage newcomers to trade with you

Considering that one American in five moves each year, the importance of attracting newcomers to your retail operation comes sharply into focus. Most communities have Newcomers or Welcome Wagon groups that can supply you with lists of new arrivals in the community. For larger retailers, National Change of Address information is available through a number of direct mail computer services designated by the U.S. Postal Service.

A direct mail offer to newcomers, giving them some incentive to stop into your store and perhaps open a charge account, can establish a loyal clientele of people looking for stores and services to rely on. Often the Newcomers and Welcome Wagon groups will deliver your offer for a reasonable fee, bringing with it the positive endorsement of the group.

Montgomery Ward takes the occasion of moving to invite charge applications, with a substantial line of credit offered just in time for redecorating and home repairs. In addition, the Ward offer comes with a certificate good for 10 percent off the first charge purchase.

To establish a continuity program

Burger King, McDonald's, and other fast-food outlets use continuity programs that other retailers can emulate. They have special inserts stuffed into the local Sunday newspapers containing dated coupons for obtaining free or discounted products. This encourages customers to visit the restaurant at least once a week during the continuity program. Dry cleaners might try a mailing to local residents or a newspaper insert with discount coupons or two-for-one offers on suits one week, blouses the next, and coats the next.

Neiman-Marcus works to establish continuity with an elite club approach: the In-Circle® program. With each purchase, charge customers gain points which they may apply toward small premiums like chocolates, or accumulate to earn gourmet luncheons or even exotic, free travel. Only customers who earn 3,000 points or more in a one-year period (representing $3,000 in purchases) are eligible for In-Circle® benefits like a quarterly newsletter, free gift-wrap, and special customer service assistance.

To get the jump on a seasonal event

In the fall, customers start thinking about winterizing their cars or getting the carpet cleaned before Thanksgiving. These and other seasonal concerns offer fertile fields for the direct marketer, who can get a message into the hands of the consumer along with a sweetener to spur action. For instance, a local service station might send out discount coupons for a full winterizing program to past customers, and an occupant mailing to the nearest neighboring zip codes as well.

Many retailers capitalize on customers' gift-giving dilemmas at holiday time by packaging gift ideas in many price ranges in one timely mailing. Herkner Jewelers of Grand Rapids, Michigan, used a handsome pre-Christmas catalog as a traffic builder, featuring jewelry items ranging in price from $15.00 to $32,500.

To offer a personal courtesy touch

The smart retailer knows who his or her most valued customers are, and can use direct mail to reward them with a gift, gain them a private audience with a special visitor, or give them some other thank-you. Last year's fur coat buyers, for instance, might be offered a free cleaning of the coat the following spring just for stopping in at the fur department to see the end-of-season values. Jacobson's offers its fur storage and fur buying customers a special invitation to a fur accessory show, just in time for the fall season.

A bookstore might arrange for top customers to attend a private cocktail reception with an impressive author visitor, announced only to selected people via direct mail. A salesperson with a customer who likes a certain maker's custom suits might drop that customer a note and enclose sample swatches when a new shipment of fabric arrives at the store.

Even veterinarians take advantage of the power of direct mail: many animal hospitals send a personal letter to each patient's master alerting them when it's time for annual shots and enclosing personalized health information pertaining to the dog, cat or other species being served.

To bring established customers in for a sale

Perhaps some of your best customers are people who wouldn't see your sale advertised in a local paper or hear it announced on television. You can mail them a notification of the sale, its dates, and some of the items to be offered, and sweeten the deal by arranging for Customer Courtesy Days before the general sale starts.

Combined store and mail/phone offers

Retailers are most likely to maximize their total revenue during a sale or special event by sending their customers a sale announcement with the option for them to order by mail or phone rather than having to appear in person.

Direct mail support — to keep people informed

Direct mail can help a retailer keep customers aware of new locations, store policies, changes in business hours, or other important facts. What's more, when such an informational mailing is made, stuffers offering merchandise or services can be sent along. For example, a tree surgeon mails his customers a list of recommended services keyed to the customer's own yard, in the spring and summer. Along with the service list come solicitations for products of interest to homeowners, such as fireplace inserts, lawn spraying equipment, etc.

Direct mail support — building image and awareness

More and more retail and professional organizations are developing newsletters today—riding the boom of desktop publishing as well as their understanding that these newsletters add a personal touch in a fast-paced, impersonal world. Along with the informative articles and personal tidbits, newsletters can offer products for sale, highlight new services available from the firm, etc.

Direct mail support — to collect overdue accounts

Before resorting to the expense of a collection agency, many retailers try a series of collection letters to delinquent customers, seeking the response of a prompt payment. Books offering standard formats for business letters give suggestions on effective collection letters.

Direct mail formats for retailers

The main purpose of every direct mail package is to bring about action. Retailers should keep this goal firmly in mind in creating every direct mail piece, from the outer envelope to the Business Reply Envelope.

For retailers, the direct mail package can be understood most easily in terms of the function of each piece.

The outer envelope functions as the store's show window. It should tease the prospect and arouse interest. It should also set the tone for the store: upscale or bargain oriented, trendy or conservative, middle American or wild and exotic.

The letter serves the function of personal sales. It should highlight the features and benefits of the product at hand in words chosen to fit the prospect's needs, wants and desires.

The brochure takes the place of the product itself. It pictures the product, highlighting its features and benefits and demonstrating it in use as specifically as impossible.

The reply device is the close of the sale. It combines the details of payment terms with the sizzle of the offer to usher the customer through the decision-making process with as little pain as possible.

The Business Reply Envelope or the telephone number becomes the medium of sale. Retailers can make this as easy and smooth as possible by paying the return postage or supplying toll-free dialing.

Other inserts and formats to consider are testimonial flyers, premium slips, reminders, articles or ad reprints, questions and answers, samples of the product, etc. All of these are intended to help convince the prospect that his or her purchase decision is a good and reliable one with many positive benefits. See the Chapter 8, Direct Mail Formats, for more information on how to create each of these pieces.

In addition to these general format guidelines, here are some specific format approaches used by successful retailers.

The catalog

Whether it is used strictly for traffic building, for mail and phone orders only, or a combination of all three, catalog marketing bears consideration. For an overview of the creative aspects of catalog marketing, check Chapter 15.

Solo mailings

Retailers with a very special item that has demonstrated, broad appeal to the customer base or a segment of that base may use the standard one-item or solo offer with a letter, brochure, reply card and Business Reply Envelope.

Marshall Field teamed up with Lenox China to present a solo mailing on a Springtime Fragrance Bottle. Such a small porcelain piece could never command as much attention on a retail counter, or even in a catalog. In a one-item offer, its status as a finely crafted work of art can be explored in fitting detail. The package also includes a pitch for customers to send the Fragrance Bottle as a gift, including space for gift card messages for up to four recipients.

Multi-flyer mailings

Rather than print a catalog that will be outdated after one season, some retailers choose to create a modular mailing piece with flyers of the same size for each piece of merchandise. All of the flyers may then be housed in a small portfolio with a flap to keep them together. For the next mailing, the retailer again includes the flyers for merchandise that sold well and is still available, replacing those that are outdated, sold out, or poor sellers. Neiman-Marcus often uses this technique for mailings to its charge customers.

Letters only

A simple letter in an envelope, especially if it is or appears to be hand-typed, can be a very effective way for a retailer to communicate by mail with a customer.

Computer letters

Some oil companies have used computer letters in an interesting way to thank customers and generate increased loyalty and traffic. Checking computerized records, they send the letters to charge customers, thanking them for their x-dollars in charge business last year, with the exact amount filled in by computer. Other retailers might send such a letter to their charge customers and offer them a special gift, or announce the arrival of some specific merchandise. Such computer-generated letters do not have to come from an outside source: smaller retailers might print them out using their own office personal computers and a letter-quality printer.

Handwritten letters or cards

Salesclerks who have been encouraged to keep good customer records will know just who should be sent a note when a new shipment arrives at the store. Service station managers might want to write customers when it is time for another oil change or brake check, and carpet cleaners would write their customers to let them know that a year has passed since the last cleaning job. Be sure your salesclerks are supplied with stationery or cards with the store name, and that they're encouraged to use them to correspond with customers. When appropriate, salespeople may want to contact their best customers by telephone as well.

Another idea for "high roller" customers: have the store's buyer send a postcard from Europe or New York during buying trips, letting the customer know what exotic "goodies" are on their way to the local store. The promise of a sneak preview upon the buyer's return could be an excellent extra enticement.

Self-mailers

To gain immediate attention, try using a self-mailer. This piece may be as simple as a sheet of offset printed paper folded and stapled, or as elaborate as a beautiful four-color piece, with a letter printed on a different paper stock as an insertion. Self-mailers may also serve double duty as free-standing inserts in your local newspaper, as package inserts, etc.

Fake telegrams

Because they suggest urgency, mailings with a telegram look can help a retailer announce a sale or other special, time-limited event quite effectively. Get yourself a real Western Union telegram for inspiration, but don't follow it literally enough to risk infringement. Try a Sale Gram or Back-to-School Gram—whatever name fits your offer best.

The invitation or ticket approach

Retailers can build walk-in traffic with invitations to special events or sales, or with tickets to fashion shows, appearances by celebrities, breakfasts with Santa, etc. One way to do this is to make the invitation look like a formal, personal one by using a squarish outer envelope, fine paper stock and an R.S.V.P. card.

The coupon book

To build traffic for a ongoing product, item or special event, consider offering a book of coupons, or individual coupons, for specific items of merchandise or service. You might also send several free-with-purchase or x-amount-off coupons for your next sale to current customers. Or offer a coupon book or calendar with dated deals to encourage repeat customer visits over time.

An interesting twist on the coupon book is a strip of coupons attached to the parking stub at Pier 39 in San Fransisco. Each coupon offers a free gift or discount when the bearer brings it into a Pier 39 establishment.

Statement stuffers

Why send out a charge account statement or monthly invoice without making one or more offers to go along with it? At the very least, the offers you enclose should cover the cost of mailing the statements. You'll also have the opportunity to keep customers aware of current events at the stores, seasonal reminders, and other service features. Many firms—including utilities such as gas, electric and phone companies—enclose their newsletters along with statements or invoices. Just make sure your pieces are light enough in weight that postage costs do not jump to the next level when they are enclosed.

Package inserts

Once a customer has purchased from you, you will want to bounce back another offer to take advantage of the customer's new allegiance to you. Another copy of your catalog inserted in the package is one idea, or you might supply a coupon for a certain dollar amount or percentage off the next purchase, along with a thank-you letter or a welcome kit. Seasonal bounce-backs are another good idea: Christmas offers in the fall, Easter in early spring, back to school in August, etc.

Co-op mailings or promotions

Work with your shopping center or merchant's group to create a joint mailing highlighting special events, holiday sales, or cross-marketing: i.e., if a customer brings in a movie ticket from the local theater, your restaurant will supply a same-day free dessert with dinner. This can spread mailing costs among a group of retailers and bring in more traffic and good will for all of you.

One additional hint: Whenever you send out a direct mail promotion to customers or prospects, make sure your salespeople know all about it the day it goes in the mail. There is nothing more frustrating to them—or to your customers—than to have people calling or lining up to buy the "featured item from the mailing" only to learn that the salesclerks don't know about it and can't even find it on the floor.

The most important concept for retailers to understand about direct marketing is this: *Target marketing is the wave of the future.* Direct marketing can help you achieve better customer targeting, both for your in-store promotions and for offers soliciting purchases by mail or phone. Each time you consider spending promotional dollars for a retail outlet, think about ways you can offer specific benefits to specific customers, and improve your results using direct marketing techniques!

CREATIVE STRATEGY FOR FUND RAISING AND NONPROFIT MARKETING

13

Each year, Americans contribute nearly $100 billion to charities and nonprofit organizations. That amount is more than double the total donated a decade ago, according to the American Association of Fund-Raising Counsel. And yet as the fund-raising pie grows larger, competition for each dollar becomes more and more intense.

In the early 1980s, the Reagan administration called for increased private-sector funding of social, cultural, and health and human services programs. Soon government cutbacks on domestic spending made many nonprofits face a stark reality: they could either intensify their private fund-raising efforts or sharply curtail their activities.

The power of direct mail in fund raising

During the Reagan years, nonprofit marketers came to a fuller understanding of the potential of direct mail for fund raising. Indeed, fully one-half of the funds generated for nonprofits is solicited by means of mail or mail-assisted campaigns, according to Washington D.C.-based fund-raising consultant Donna Glenn. Only one-third of monies raised were generated by mail as recently as 1979.

213

At that time, the rest of the funds resulted from person-to-person communications.

Although the power of personal persuasion should not be overlooked in fund raising, direct mail has a number of attributes that help nonprofit organizations maximize their resource development efforts.

Direct mail provides:

- A cost-effective, measurable way to target and reach a large number of prospective donors, all at the same time—not when volunteers or staff can get around to it.
- The means to develop a database that is not dependent upon the personal knowledge, special relationships and individual biases of funds solicitors, and which is readily available for use.
- The ability to provide donors and potential donors with "the whole story" about your program in written form—a brochure or other element that can be saved for reference or passed along.
- The chance to highlight appeals for specific groups of prospects and donors based upon age, income, special interests, previous donor history, etc.

The contemporary fund-raising climate

In his book *Marketing for Nonprofit Organizations*, Philip Kotler, a professor at the J. L. Kellogg Graduate School of Management, Northwestern University, explains four steps of fund-raising evolution.

1. *Begging*—Where needy people and groups would implore more fortunate people for money and goods. Beggars perfected many techniques to gain the attention and sympathy of their target audience, such as simulating pain or blindness, or showing their children with bloated stomachs.
2. *Collection*—Where churches, clubs and other organizations would regularly collect contributions from a willing and defined group of supporters.

3. *Campaigning*—Organizations appointing a specific person or group to be responsible for soliciting money from every possible source in a systematic fund-raising campaign.
4. *Development*—The organization systematically builds up different classes of loyal donors who give consistently and receive benefits in the process of giving.

The benefit orientation of stage four—the understanding that each donor needs to receive something in return for his or her donation—keys in to the overall marketing concept. As Kotler says, giving is not a "transfer," but a "transaction." The direct marketers who make sure they are properly repaying their donors—psychologically and/or materially—will be the most successful in fund-raising by mail.

To face the competition for funds in today's nonprofit markets, creative strategists should draw upon the most effective techniques used in general direct mail solicitations. But first, they should use what they know about human nature to position their programs in the most appealing ways possible for potential donors.

Meeting the human needs of direct-mail donors

Daryl Vogel, the Director of Development for Holland Home, an elderly care facility in Grand Rapids, Michigan, says that when the cause is a worthy one, "the donor's need to give is always greater than our program's need to receive." His colleague, Jean Hitchcock of Butterworth Hospital in Grand Rapids, agrees. "I never actually have to ask for money. I just explain the problems that people face in our community, and outline our plans to solve them. If I tell the story truthfully and well, the donors feel the need to ask *me* how they can help, and how much money we require."

As Abraham Maslow explained in his book *Motivation and Personality*, each of us has a never-ending supply of needs to fulfill. As the low-level *survival* needs of food, water, clothing and shelter are satisfied, the human animal begins to crave *safety*, security and avoidance of pain.

Once these basic requirements are covered, people desire *affiliation*—warm social interaction with like-minded people.

Higher yet on Maslow's Hierarchy of Needs is *self-esteem*, developed by means of personal achievement, and the recognition of others. The ultimate need is for *self-actualization*—developing in all areas of life to become an independent, well-rounded person.

Direct mail fund raisers can make use of their own data bases as well as demographic data from list renters and periodicals to determine the "need level" of their most productive target markets, thereby providing attractive benefits to donors.

Fulfilling survival and safety needs

Most desirable donor prospects have the education and money to move beyond the low levels of the Hierarchy of Needs. But even so, "fear" appeals with the theme "there but for the grace of God go I" can sometimes be effective. Prospects may believe that giving to your cause somehow lessens their own chances of family tragedy, losing the power to control their own destinies, or contracting a deadly disease.

Mothers Against Drunk Driving of Hurst, Texas, uses an outer envelope showing a car involved in a fatal traffic accident in which high school students died after a drinking spree. The headline reads, "Don't let this happen to *your* kids." Inside, the grisly facts about highway deaths caused by drunk drivers are juxtaposed with success stories from towns where MADD programs helped save lives during prom and graduation season. The letter asks for a donation of $10.00, $20.00 or $50.00 to set up a similar program in the recipient's own area.

The National Organization for Women, and Planned Parenthood give women scenarios of what life might be like without family planning and pro-choice options.

NOW asks for contributions to a "Campaign to Save Women's Lives," and asserts that anti-abortion forces are also anti-women's equality. To emphasize its points, the NOW direct mail package recounts stories of "intimidation and violence" against doctors and patients in women's medical clinics. Planned Parenthood explains how the U.S. Government's Agency for International Development "extremists" have targeted the group's international family planning program for destruction and asks for help to keep these services available to women everywhere.

The Arthritis Foundation's Michigan Chapter uses the back of its reply form to share the facts about the disease it calls "America's Biggest Pain.'' Copy says that over 36,000,000 Americans have arthritis, and that the chances are that one in seven people will contract it. Copy goes on to warn that arthritis often strikes children, and people between the ages of 21 and 45. Then it suggests a donation of $15.00 to become a member of the Michigan Chapter in the fight against arthritis.

St. Jude Children's Research Hospital uses a similar pitch explaining that 10,000 American children develop cancer each year. To bring this message home, the letter signed by Danny Thomas asks for a donation and ends with a P.S.: ''I hope that your own family never suffers the tragedy of losing a child to an incurable disease. At St. Jude, we're fighting to conquer these killers, and one day someone in your own family may live because we succeeded.''

Fulfilling the need for affiliation

In his book *The Membership Mystique*, fund-raising impresario Richard P. Trenbeth quotes the observation of French philosopher Alexis de Tocqueville that Americans are inveterate ''joiners'' who enjoy associating with like-minded individuals. Trenbeth explains that membership organizations help Americans avoid loneliness, educate themselves, and increase their own perceived status and self-worth.

De Tocqueville believed that Americans are motivated to join together in groups with common goals because in a democracy, all people are theoretically equal. Human nature drives people to affiliate on some basis, just as the various ranks and classes did naturally in Europe's aristocratic societies. Thus fraternal and religious groups as well as organizations based upon specific political, social and cultural goals may fulfill the affiliation needs of Americans.

Trenbeth and other fund-raising executives have called upon this need for affiliation to develop scores of membership organizations whose main purpose is to generate income for an educational, cultural or civic organization. Examples are museum, opera and symphony societies, college and university alumni groups, political action committees, and organizations devoted to animal rights.

The ''transaction'' becomes complete when the organization provides various benefits to its members in exchange for their donations. Here are some examples of benefits which "affiliation seekers" may enjoy—and which may induce them to become members of a group, or upgrade their membership levels with larger contributions.

Social benefits

Conventions

Prison Fellowship Ministries invites its "Friends of the Ministry" and members of its affiliated group, Justice Fellowship, to national conventions such as "Congress on the Bible." The personal appeal of Charles W. Colson, Chairman of Prison Fellowship Ministries and Congress on the Bible, includes the news that "Friends of the Ministry" will receive a $45.00 discount off of the $195.00 convention rate as well as the opportunity to spend four days interacting with as many as 3,000 "Christian leaders like you."

Special rooms for members

Many museums and cultural institutions have set aside rooms for members who reach a certain donation level to use for relaxation and interaction.

Social events

Local and regional organizations often stage dinners, dances, and other special events—either for all members or for those who give at a certain level. Members of the Historical Alliance of the Chicago Historical Society pay a minimum of $500.00 per year and—among other benefits—may attend an annual "members only" dinner party hosted by the Society's President and Board of Trustees.

Volunteer opportunities

As "insiders," members may be afforded special consideration for high-status board and trustee positions as well as places on special-event committees. Such an opportunity may well carry another lucrative "transaction" with it: membership on some high-status nonprofit boards includes the agreement to "give or get" an annual sum of $5000 or more, according to fund-raising expert Jean Hitchcock.

Educational benefits

Newsletters

Sending a regular newsletter to members and donors serves several excellent purposes for fund raisers. First, it helps inform the organization's supporters about how their money is used. Second, it provides the opportunity for "success stories" that affirm the program's effectiveness. Third, it provides a forum for additional fund-raising messages or even sale of cause-related merchandise.

PLAN International USA (formerly Foster Parents Plan) does all of these things in its various messages to Foster Parents. A letter "From the Foster Parents Plan Field Office in Sri Lanka" ex-

The monthly newsletter of Prison Fellowship, *Jubilee*, keeps contributors informed about how Christian prisoners' lives have changed for the better with the organization's help. There are also regular reports on the work of Prison Fellowship's founder, Chuck Colson. Reprinted with permission of Jubilee.®

THE MONTHLY NEWSLETTER OF PRISON FELLOWSHIP   JUNE 1990

JUBILEE

A BRUISED REED HE WILL NOT BREAK ISAIAH 42:3

IMPACT

On His Recent Trip to Moscow, Chuck Colson Saw

SOVIET PRISONS OPEN to the GOSPEL

Ten Soviet officials sat attentively on one side of the mahogany table. Vadim Victorovich Bakatin, minister of Internal Affairs and one of the most powerful men in the Soviet Union, called the meeting to order. Appointed by President Mikhail Gorbachev last year, Bakatin is regarded as a sharp, articulate man, open to new ideas.

Opposite him sat Michael Quinlan, director of the U.S. Federal Bureau of Prisons and head of a U.S. delegation appointed by the Department of Justice, that included Prison Fellowship Chairman Charles Colson, PF board member Jack Eckerd, Associate Deputy Attorney General Margaret Love, and Elizabeth Fine, a subcommittee counsel for the U.S. House of Representatives' Committee on the Judiciary.

Before leaving the U.S. the delegation was briefed on its goals: to suggest ways to make the Soviet prison system more humane and to urge the release of political prisoners.

As the meeting began, Bakatin spoke first, candidly acknowledging that crime in the USSR had increased by 38 percent in 1989. About half of the prisoners under his jurisdiction, 800,000 nonviolent prisoners, had been released through general amnesty. But the country continued to wrestle with a breakdown in order. Did the visitors have any advice to offer?

After Quinlan briefed the Soviets on the U.S. system, he invited Colson to speak. Quoting Feodor Dostoevski and other Russian authors, Colson traced the causes of crime—individuals making wrong moral choices. An endless spiral of lawlessness is inevitable in an atheistic society with no transcen-

Soviet leaders at the Kremlin (above left), once a symbol of repression and persecution for Christians, have opened the nation's prisons for volunteer ministry and welcomed advice on improving their correctional system from a U.S. delegation that included Charles Colson.

dent values, he told the fourth-ranking Soviet leader.

As Colson talked about Prison Fellowship's work—instilling values through a personal relationship with God—Bakatin stopped him. "Explain to me what you do," he said. Leaning forward, Bakatin listened to details about Christian volunteers' devoted ministry to prisoners, former prisoners, and inmates' families.

"That's the answer," Bakatin declared. "That's what we need here. What you're doing, we will approve in the Soviet Union. Whatever you need to get into our prisons, you have my permission."

Colson could hardly believe what he'd heard or what Bakatin, with a twinkle in his smile, said as the men parted, "And God be with you."

Back in the States, Colson reflects, "I never thought I would see that day. But I think within the course of the next year there will be a Prison Fellowship organized in the Soviet Union."

And the process is already underway. Ron Nikkel, president of Prison Fellowship International, traveled to the Soviet Union last October and again in March to meet with Christians who have been ministering in Soviet prisons for the past year. After opening a few prisons to volunteers in February 1989, Bakatin issued a statement in October instructing prison officials across the country to allow churches to come into prisons.

"It's amazing to see how Soviet Christians have responded so quickly to reach out in prisons, especially considering the fear of imprisonment for their beliefs that has existed among Christians," Nikkel says. The goal of his recent trip was to encourage prison volunteers to form a committee to consider a nationwide vision and to interact with and learn from prison ministries in other countries.

CONTINUED ON PAGE 4

P.O. BOX 17500, WASHINGTON, DC 20041-0500, (703) 478-0100

plains how its "health promoters" are working to upgrade the quality of life in the country where one's foster child lives. More personal communications often include letters and cards written by one's foster child or family members, and typewritten reports about how the Foster Parent's regular contributions are improving the child's well-being. From time to time these communications outline problems in other countries and suggest that Foster Parents consider sponsoring an additional child or children.

Magazines

The Smithsonian Institution's handsome monthly *Smithsonian* shows just how effective such a publication can be as a membership benefit. Richly illustrated articles on science, nature, history, art, travel and other subjects follow a monthly letter from the secretary of the Smithsonian Institution. The magazine also includes plugs for Smithsonian Member programs involving study, travel, and events at the various Smithsonian museums.

Perhaps most admirable of all is the status of *Smithsonian* magazine as one of today's premiere direct marketing media for space advertising. In addition, the handsome magazine commands millions of dollars annually in national advertising for furniture, automobiles, cosmetics, investments and other products and services. Thus, the magazine that is positioned as a prime membership benefit is also a source of revenue for this nonprofit organization.

Libraries, reading rooms and reading lists

Membership to many cultural groups and museums carries with it the privilege of entry into research libraries, restricted reading rooms and other research facilities. In addition, for those with scholarly interests, publications of such groups often include lists of suggested reading materials.

Classes, tours and travel

Northwestern University, among many other universities and colleges, offers its alumni numerous opportunities to return to campus for classes, symposia, and special events. Members of the John Evans Club, an organization for alumni and friends of the university which requires a minimum pledge of $25,000, receive even more such invitations—many of which are extended only to

John Evans Club members. Northwestern offers its alumni a series of travel opportunities that benefit both the university and the traveler. The University receives a set amount of the travel fee for each person on the trip. The traveler enjoys the company of an affiliated group—fellow Northwestern alumni—and a stimulating travel opportunity.

Material benefits

For those with the need to affiliate with an organization, a number of material signs of that affiliation can make excellent membership benefits. Here are several examples.

Membership card

Each Smithsonian Associate receives a National Membership Card to be kept in one's wallet. Showing the card at Smithsonian-affiliated museums entitles the bearer to discounts on certain books, records, gifts and magazines, entrance to an Associates' Dining Room in Washington, D.C., and free admission to the Cooper-Hewitt Museum in New York City.

Many other organizations provide membership cards of various colors and designs, each of which signifies a certain level of privilege as indicated by the level of the bearer's donation.

Free admissions/free parking/free coat checking

Even one-time visitors to Colonial Williamsburg in Williamsburg, Virginia, receive a photo identification card which entitles them to admission to the grounds for a full year.

Members of other organizations may be afforded free or privileged parking places, privileged seating in auditoriums, free checking of coats and belongings in cloakrooms, and many other perquisites. Just as important as the time and money savings involved in these benefits is the "affiliation advantage"—being seen as a belonger by virtue of one's admission card, special seating or other visible sign of status.

Merchandise and insurance offers

Affiliated members of organizations may well exhibit similar tastes in art objects, jewelry, clothing and home decor items.

What's more, they may well enjoy wearing and displaying items emblazoned with the name of a favorite cause, school or museum.

The Daughters of the American Revolution offers its members a specially designed Seiko watch bearing the organization's name, motto and Founder's design on the face.

The Winterthur Museum and Gardens in Winterthur, Delaware, creates superb reproductions of items from its extensive collection: bowls, dinnerware and candlesticks of fine porcelain, scarves based upon antique textile patterns, replicas of classic jewelry, and much more. Members of the Winterthur Guild are extended a 10 percent discount on all items offered.

Many insurance companies have special divisions for "sponsored and endorsed" programs whereby a nonprofit organization will suggest a particular carrier and plan in exchange for a payment. The Association of Junior Leagues International offers its members a term life plan "reviewed and approved by the Association" from American Heritage Life Insurance Company and Nationwide Life Insurance Company.

A recent financial services venture for some nonprofits has been involved in credit card accounts that provide a small payment to one's favorite charity with each use. For those who enjoy the affiliation factor, the credit card itself often bears the name and logo of the cause that receives benefits. In addition, Master Card International Inc. has offered its clients the opportunity to vote for their favorite among six popular causes, with at least $2,000,000 in funds divided on a one-time basis according to the votes.

The PLAN International USA MasterCard, promoted through Investors Savings Bank, offers a credit card at competitive interest rate and annual fee levels, with a number of attractive benefits and the potential to raise $100,000 or more yearly for PLAN International USA, by means of small donations to the Plan each time a cardholder uses the account.

Fulfilling the need for self-esteem and self-actualization

If a potential donor has basic physical and safety needs under control, and already feels comfortably affiliated in home and community, he or she may well respond best to fund-raising appeals that feed the need for self-esteem and self-actualization. Benefits proven to motivate such donors by developing self-esteem include those which provide praise and recognition for a job well done. Self-actualization benefits might include opportunities to do specific good toward meeting altruistic goals, and the chance to achieve immortality by leaving something important behind.

Praise and recognition benefits

Publication of givers by name and amount

Mailings, programs and annual reports that list the names of those who have given enough for the "President's Club," "Founders' Society" or other lofty-sounding group encourage givers to increase their donations to a level of higher status and recognition.

Such a plan can feed affiliation needs as well, when members check to see where their friends—or those they would like to be friendly with—fall in the organization's pecking order.

North Shore Country Day School, a private preparatory school in Winnetka, Illinois, solicits annual gifts and awards recognition for givers in the "Hour Society" ($550 to $1,110), "Perry Dunlap Smith Society" ($1,101 to $1,919), and "Headmasters' Society" ($1,920 and up).

Plaques, desk ornaments and plates

Even those donors without a Harvard University diploma or Academy Award to display on their walls or mantels may aspire to receive your recognition award if it is positioned well, built up by mail and word of mouth, and made with quality and enduring good looks in mind.

Northwestern University's John Evans Club gave members a heavy, good-looking pewter collector's plate with a ceramic insert that bears the school colors and the club name. Suitable for hanging in the office or perhaps the den at home, the plate is perhaps less obvious than a plaque would be, but it shows those in the know that its owner has "arrived."

Person of the year awards

Nonprofit organizations may help build group spirit and morale by developing annual awards based partly upon level of giving, but also upon service to the group and community. Built up by means of mailings and word of mouth, such an award might be presented at a gala affair to which members around the country are invited. A weekend of related activities planned by the sponsoring organization would make such an event all the more intriguing.

Altruistic benefits

Many direct mail fund raisers make the mistake of asking donors vaguely to give to an "organization" or "cause" rather than to fulfill a definite need. Asking for funds for a specific person or an immediate need—and perhaps for personal help as well—feeds the altruistic needs of those who seek self-actualization. Here are several examples of organizations which position their requests very specifically and provide a way to involve the donor in producing results.

Plans to aid third-world children

PLAN International USA, Save the Children, Christian Children's Fund and Children, Inc. all ask for $18.00 to $22.00 per month in exchange for the opportunity to "adopt" a specific foster child in the country of one's choice.

Those who choose to "adopt" will receive regular progress reports about "their" child as well as general information about progress in the youngster's country. To help "adoptive parents" feel even more involved, PLAN International USA encourages them to write to the youngsters they are helping, and send periodic pointers about holiday greetings, teaching children about nutrition and safe water, etc. Some adoptive parents actually visit their "foster children," all with help and guidance from the sponsoring agency to ensure that the visit is a positive experience for all concerned.

Common cause

Even before they have pledged money to Common Cause, prospective donors receive a computerized package filled with "urgent senatorial petitions." The "People Against PAC$" mailing, for example, asked for $20.00 regular dues, $30.00 family dues, or other specific amounts for membership in this anti-political action committee division of Common Cause. At the same time it provided the recipient with petitions already computerized with one's name and address, and the names of the senate minority leader and the recipient's two U.S. senators. Additionally, the computerization provided a special message to the senators which varied according to their positions on political action committee legislation then being debated in the U.S. Senate.

Amnesty international

While asking for donations of $25.00 to $100.00 for membership in Amnesty International USA, a space advertisement explains that members will learn how to help free prisoners of conscience all over the world by writing letters to governments and putting pressure on public officials. The unique opportunity to help these prisoners "taste the sweet air of freedom" is available specifically to those who join to make a difference and prove their seriousness with a cash donation. The advertisement contains three case histories told human interest-style to win the prospective donor's attention and emotional involvement.

Effective fund-raising techniques using direct mail

Many of the proven direct marketing methods developed for profit-making ventures are used with great success by fundraisers. Here are some examples, showing how these tried-and-true techniques may be utilized to best effect in the nonprofit arena.

Human interest

Each month, *Jubilee*, the monthly newsletter of Prison Fellowship, arrives in the homes of all Prison Fellowship donors along with a reply form requesting additional funds. Rather than lead off the newsletter with a recounting of Prison Fellowship activities, its editors begin each issue with a Horatio Alger story of an ex-offender who has turned his or her life around with the help of this

Christian organization. Typical is an article on Linda Bowman, "Hooked on Heroin, Healed by Love."

As every journalist knows, the human interest story is a sure-fire grabber, since people love to read about other people. The direct mail fund raiser who can explain the cause or problem at hand in individual, "everyday people" terms stands a good chance of winning the empathy of readers. It's also important to explain the scope of the problem—5,000,000 victims, 12 deaths a day, or whatever the statistics show. But to attract attention initially, telling the story of one person or one family is worth strong consideration.

A warning: make sure the story you are telling is not so hopeless, depressing or shocking that it turns potential donors away. Some direct marketers—especially those dealing with animal issues—paint such a bleak picture (complete with detailed photographs) that the reader feels compelled to turn the page without acting.

Focus on product benefits

In the for-profit world of marketing, there's an oft-quoted poem that contains the lines, "Don't tell me how it came to be, tell me what the damn things does for me." It is aimed at the type of ad that shows the smiling face of the business owner, a picture of his factory, and tells step-by-step how his widgets are made.

Some nonprofit marketers fall into the same trap, telling their donors and potential donors about their wonderful and dedicated staff, newly rehabilitated office building and fool-proof five-year plan. All of this belongs in the organization's annual report, not in its direct marketing pitches. Instead, ads and direct mail packages should focus squarely on the group's action agenda, and the donor's part in it.

The Ms. Foundation for Women, headlines a coupon ad, "We're changing the world from the bottom up. And we need your help." The ad contains nary a word about where they're located or who is on the board. Rather, it combines a recitation of the Foundation's specific accomplishments, an exhortation for women to join in the work, and a menu of current programs outlined with the exact donations necessary to put them into effect.

Use the database and personalization

Developing a good database is sure to stand the fund-raising direct marketer in good stead. This information can be used to segment donors by initial source of the name, frequency and amount of donation, special-interest areas for giving, and much more.

Database information then can be used to position direct mail offers, upgrade donors to new levels, develop special events and opportunities keyed to amount given and interests shown, etc. What's more, the database can be used to create personalized mailings that are flattering to the donor and provide him or her with an incentive to reply.

For example, Alpha Delta Pi Sorority sends its alumnae letters mentioning the chapter to which they belonged as active sorority members. In addition, each letter acknowledges the level of previous contributions and suggests a reasonable increase for the current year's donation. All of this is presented in a personalized letter so flawlessly produced that it appears to be created just for the recipient. The reply card indicates the amount of total gifts to date, and lets the donor know how much more she needs to give to reach the group's next recognition level, be it "Lion Circle," "Violet Circle," "Star Circle," "Adelphean Circle," or the ultimate: "Founders Circle."

Use celebrity endorsements where appropriate

When former president Jimmy Carter decided to join the board of directors of Habitat for Humanity he did much more than attend a few meetings. Mr. Carter began a series of trips to far-flung points across the United States during which he and his wife, Rosalynn, worked with saw, hammer and nails to help build and refurbish homes for the disadvantaged.

Thus a letter from Jimmy Carter asking for funds for Habitat for Humanity comes with a ring of truth to it, especially since most of his work trips for the organization receive extensive publicity.

Actress Victoria Principal explains in her ads for the Arthritis Foundation that she is dedicated to their cause because of close family members who suffer from this affliction. And the long-running, multi-media campaign for "Jerry's Kids" gains immense credibility in the fact that a child of Jerry Lewis' died of muscular dystrophy.

The lesson here is simple: celebrities used for the sake of their celebrity alone may have a marginal effect, if any, on fund-raising programs. But when a well-known person with a demonstrable reason for caring about the cause shows support in your ads and direct mail solicitations, results may increase dramatically.

State your position clearly

Every effective advertising message springs from a sharply defined positioning statement. In fund raising by mail, the positioning statement is essential, because prospective donors need to perceive a clear and specific need before they will be moved to respond.

Thus, fund-raising solicitations can and should be outspoken. They should take a definite stand, even if it may alienate some readers. The readers who agree with this specific, clear-cut position thus can be moved toward whole-hearted support. Campaigns designed to offend no one will be unable to move anyone to action. Political, environmental and women's rights organizations provide excellent examples of stating a case loud and clear to identify passionate supporters.

The People For The American Way Action Fund pulls no punches in its reply form. "Yes, I'll join People For The American Way. I want to help you defend America's spirit of liberty and our Constitutional right to religious freedom against the narrow, intolerant legislative and political aims of the ultrafundamentalist movement." There is no doubt as to what one is endorsing by sending in a donation.

Greenpeace is another organization that spares no pejorative terms in characterizing its mission. "Yes, I want to enlist in Greenpeace's campaign against the slaughter of our marine life and poisoning of our seas. We must protect all of earth's creatures and stop the destruction of our planet. And to support our frontline crews in nonviolent confrontation, I'm enclosing my maximum contribution of $15.00 . . . $25.00 . . . $50.00 . . . other."

Planned Parenthood's Katherine Houghton Hepburn Fund risks offending many—while earning support from many more—with its specific statement of the Fund's three priority areas: keeping abortion safe and legal; teen pregnancy prevention; and preserving family planning for the poor.

Ride the crest of public opinion

Just as smart direct marketers of consumer products "strike while the iron is hot" with seasonal offers, fashion items and fads, fund raisers can take advantage of valuable momentum by requesting money to support causes that are very much in the news.

Presidential campaigns, for instance, give most every political fund-raising organization grist for the mill. Union of Concerned Scientists asked for funds to educate voters about nuclear issues and enclosed a petition to presidential candidates with specific stands on these issues. People For The American Way focused on Pat Robertson's candidacy, asking for funds to "expose Robertson as the extremist that he is." National Organization For Women asked for its supporters' choice for president, as well as opinions on critical women's issues.

Test involvement devices and action techniques

Some fund-raising direct marketers fear that flashy packages and sophisticated techniques will cost them support, since donors may feel that too much money has gone into the marketing effort and not enough toward the cause. But as seasoned for-profit direct marketers will agree, testing a wide range of copy concepts, design elements, and proven direct mail techniques may well increase the efficiency of mailings, even though the package itself may appear more expensive. Here are some ideas from the "for-profit" direct marketer's bag of tricks to consider for fund-raising efforts.

- Yes/No Reply Stickers
- Sweepstakes
- Premium with Donation
- Temporary Membership Card
- Charter Membership
- Free Gift Enclosed
- Action Device—a picture of the product or premium offered to be moved from the letter, outer envelope or reply stub to the return portion of the reply form

- Endorsement Letter from Celebrity or Expert
- Articles or Ad Reprints
- Regular Postage Stamp to Use in Replying
- Invitation-Look Package
- Urgency Formats—telegrams, telegram-like formats and fake telegrams
- Free Information Booklet
- Continuity—in the form of a monthly or quarterly pledge
- Positive Option/Negative Option

Here are several examples of how these direct mail techniques are used by noted fund raisers.

National Audubon Society tested two premiums with membership: a free bird feeder or a free backpack. Each was presented in an identical kit with a peel-off premium token to be placed on the acceptance form. The kit also included a handsome, detachable temporary membership card already personalized with the recipient's name and address.

A number of groups send potential donors sets of personalized name and address labels, asking for a donation in response. The address labels are inexpensive enough to send cost effectively in many cases, yet they may set up a *quid pro quo* relationship in the recipient's mind, encouraging him or her to respond. The address labels often are decorated in such a way as to characterize the recipient's special interest. For example, the Amvets (Lanham, Maryland) labels feature a stars and stripes motif.

The National Society Daughters of the American Revolution sends its members letters setting out specific needs—replacing the pipes in its historic headquarters building, for example. The group uses a negative option approach to offer members a set of note cards for a donation of $10.00 or more. The notecards (with return payment expected) will go to all members who do not return the enclosed card with a negative response.

Ask for specific action

Potential donors need to know exactly what is expected of them, whether the request is for personal action or monetary donation. Successful fund raisers request specific amounts of money on their reply forms, utilizing a database to target groups of donors

National Audubon Society offers premiums such as a free backpack or bird feeder for joining the Society. These direct mail packages include several time-honored direct mail techniques such as premium-related stickers on the outer envelopes, tipped-on trial membership cards, and premium slips describing the backpack or bird feeder in detail. Reprinted with permission of the National Audubon Society, Inc.

who have the demonstrated resources and interest to pay various amounts.

One way to encourage a specific donation amount is to reward the donor with membership in an organization for a $25.00 or $35.00 check—perhaps more if the group is prestigious or the cause is especially worthy. Another method is to explain what a given amount of money can do, for example: "your $50.00 donation will send a child to camp for a week . . . your $100.00 donation will send three children to the state conference."

A number of fund-raising direct mail solicitations call attention to the preferred amount by circling it. The Southern Poverty Law Center suggests donations of $15.00, $25.00, $35.00, $50.00, $100.00 or other amounts. The $25.00 box is circled and highlighted with a hand-written note saying, "Please give this amount, or more if you can."

Use urgency

An urgent call to action is a hallmark of good direct marketing. In the fund-raising arena, urgency often comes quite naturally because of a pressing problem or crying need. It is important to explain why help is needed immediately, to encourage the respondent to act right away instead of putting the reply card aside where it may be forgotten.

In its campaign to save dolphins and other marine life from the threat of driftnet fishing and ocean dumping, Greenpeace makes this urgency statement: "The next six months are a critical 'window' in this campaign, as key legislation and international agreements come up for consideration. We need you now, to help us arouse public attention . . . galvanize the press . . . stir governments around the world to take corrective action."

Eliminate "stoppers"

Once the prospective donor is motivated to act, any number of small interruptions or "stoppers" may impede the process. Make sure your direct mail solicitation makes acting as easy as possible. Ways to do this include enclosing a reply envelope (post-paid if possible), allowing donors to use credit cards to pay, and having a simple, straightforward reply form that is easy to use. Don't forget to insert the reply form into the reply envelope to make sure it fits easily. Even the annoyance of a poorly fitted envelope may become a "stopper" at a critical moment. Some fund raisers provide post-paid envelopes, but ask their donors to help by affixing their own postage if possible. This is likely to be more effective when used for existing donors than in a new-donor solicitation.

The back end for fund raisers

Like any other form of direct marketing, successful fund raising requires a great deal of effort on the back end. It is costly to locate and recruit a donor, and thus it is essential that the marketer use every creative strategy possible to retain and upgrade that donor. Here are a few pointers.

Acknowledge and thank donors promptly

Immediate turnaround when donations are received is essential. If practical, a personal note from the group's president or executive director makes an excellent acknowledgement. Donors to Northwestern University's John Evans Club, who often send checks of $1000 or more at a time, usually receive three separate letters of thanks: from the president of the university, from the dean or development officer whose school will benefit from the money, and from the alumni relations officer.

Grand Rapids-based fund raiser Daryl Vogel says that organizations should "find seven ways to thank donors before asking them for more money." These ways might include thank-you notes, progress updates, newsletter, invitations to events, membership credentials, etc.

Find ways to upgrade donors

The existing donor base is the best source of future money for most fund-raising organizations, and thus these donors should be cultivated carefully to maximize their lifetime values. A good data base will allow the organization to guide donors along a gradual path of increasing involvement and monetary investment by suggesting manageable yearly upgrades and "holding out carrots" involving status, special events, and opportunities.

The Company Of

WOMEN

A MERCHANDISE CATALOG

This portrait entitled "Diane," by Françoise Gilot, symbolizes a woman facing the future with courage and strength. It reminds us of the spirit of the women and children who come to our shelter for help. Please look for the story of one such woman inside, along with information on purchasing this poster (see page 3).

SPRING 1990

TO BENEFIT VICTIMS OF DOMESTIC VIOLENCE AND RAPE

Direct marketers including the people of HDM Muldoon and Catalog Connections helped make possible this *The Company of Women* catalog. Profits from merchandise sales go to benefit victims of domestic violence and rape. Reprinted with permission of The Company of Women, Inc.

book lists symptoms, diagnoses and provides clear and concise instructions so that anyone can safely survive car trouble. Keep it in your Car Kit (see page 3) or in the glove compartment so it's always handy when you need it. Paperback, 176 pages. 4 1/8" x 8 3/4".
FO34 Rand McNally Emergency Car Repair Guide **$5.95**
FO34B Rand McNally Emergency Car Repair Guide 2/**$10.95**

Trashstash™

Starting a fast food chain in your car? Are the empty containers piling up faster than you can throw them away? No ordinary garbage pail, this attractive litterbag hangs behind the passenger seat. Holds up to 3 gallons of garbage (a week's worth of take-out lunch). Closes at the top. Nylon shell with vinyl lining. 9" x 10 1/4" x 6 1/2". Specify red or black. Buy 2 and save!
FO62A Black Trashstash **$13.95**
FO62B Red Trashstash **$13.95**
FO62C Trashstash Set of 2/**$26.00**

Top closes to hide mess

Emergency Fan Belt

Imagine being able to say, "No big deal," when your fan belt breaks. Now you can replace it yourself with this temporary Emergency Fan Belt that keeps you on the road until you reach the next service station. Best of all, you don't have to be a mechanic to use it. Includes easy-to-follow, step-by-step instructions.
FO64 Emergency Fan Belt **$8.95**
FO64B Emergency Fan Belt 2/**$16.95**

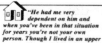

"He had me very dependent on him and when you've been in that situation for years you're not your own person. Though I lived in an upper middle class home, I had no bank account of my own. He was in control of everything. He didn't want me to work...I was penniless."
(continue on page 10)

Lite-A-Lock

Shed a little light on dark parking lots, and unlit doorways, with our Lite-a-Lock. This flashlight adjusts from flood to spot instantly and doubles as a keyring, so it's always on hand. Lite-A-Lock includes a lithium battery with a shelf life of ten years. Plastic case. 2 7/8 oz. Specify blue or black.
FO6A Blue Lite-A-Lock **$18.00**
FO6B Black Lite-A-Lock **$18.00**

If you or somebody you know needs to find a program for victims of family violence in your area, call the National Coalition Against Domestic Violence Hotline at 1-800-333-7233.

Family and Children Sing Alongs For The Car

"Are we there yet?" On your next family excursion keep the gang entertained with the Family and Kids Car Songbooks. Nurture your child's love for music or just have hours of fun on the road. Both sets include an audio cassette tape and songbook of your all-time favorite songs. You and your kids can cruise to classic hits like: Farmer in the Dell, Twinkle, Twinkle Little Star, (Kids Songbook), On Top of Old Smokey, Yellow Rose of Texas, (Family Songbook) and much, much more!
FO97A Family Songbook **$9.95**
FO97B Kids Songbook **$9.95**
FO97C Set of 2 for **$17.95** (one of each)

 To place an order or for information on making a donation call toll-free 1-800-937-1193.
Your purchases will support the work of the Rockland Family Shelter

Executive Auto Notes™

Don't let memory lapses bring you down. Whether you're getting complicated directions or an inspired idea for tomorrow's business presentation, write it down, right now! With Executive Auto Notes you'll have pen and paper in hand at all times. The note pad simply attaches to the inside of your windshield with a suction cup. And its large clip makes it perfect for displaying maps within reading distance and keeping receipts together.
FO96A Executive Auto Notes in Black **$15.00**
FO96B Executive Auto Notes in Burgundy **$15.00**

9

Today, many organizations also spend a good deal of time educating their best donors about matching-grant opportunities, bequests, trusts and other long-term programs.

Consider sales opportunities and catalogs

In recent years, scores of cultural institutions have begun to explore merchandising opportunities aimed at their donors and at a wider range of potential customers. Indeed, there is a large market of individuals who may not care to give an outright gift to a museum or cause, but who may well enjoy buying carefully chosen products offered by that organization.

Museums including The Smithsonian Institution, Museum of Fine Arts/Boston, New York's Metropolitan Museum of Art, The Museum of Modern Art/New York, The Art Institute of Chicago, San Francisco Museum of Modern Art, Winterthur Museum, and many more offer elegant catalogs of merchandise. Products include art reproductions, scarves, children's toys and games, jewelry reproductions, etc.

Minnesota Public Radio offers a catalog called "Wireless" nationwide "for fans and friends of radio." Minnesota Public Television's "Signals" catalog features "unique items related to your favorite public television shows."

Also worth considering are catalogs such as those of Developmental Marketing Group in Oxnard, California. These digest-sized mailings include a wide range of gift merchandise, whose sale benefits various nonprofit causes including Children of the Night, International Wildlife Coalition, and American Lung Association.

Direct mail fund raising is a growing and competitive market. Creative strategists will maximize chances for enduring success by studying the human needs of their target donors, then creating mailing packages and ads that utilize proven direct marketing techniques.

CREATIVE DIRECT MARKETING: BEYOND DIRECT MAIL

III

HOW TO CREATE EFFECTIVE DIRECT RESPONSE PRINT ADS

14

In the years before database management made it possible to pinpoint market segments for targeted mailings, direct marketers looked to magazines and newspapers to attract most of their new customers. Today's legendary mail-order writers—Tom Collins, David Ogilvy and many more—cut their teeth on space advertising.

Back then, segmentation was achieved in the ad itself. A compelling headline and carefully chosen photograph or drawing could grab the right readers and draw them into the body copy. Compact classified ads with one- or two-word headlines did the trick for other firms, with every word carefully chosen to attract prospects and inspire them to action.

With computer technology for direct mail applications advancing day by day, it might appear that the print medium is no longer competitive. On the contrary, many consumer and business-to-business direct marketers still consider magazine and newspaper advertising essential as a primary source of leads, sales, members or subscribers. In some fields, direct mail lists of likely prospects have become saturated over time, so print advertising has evolved into a cost-effective means of soliciting customers.

Other firms use print media to reach groups of customers that cannot be targeted or reached by mail. Since only about half of American adults are considered true direct mail buyers, print media may expand a mailer's reach. Still other companies find print ads an excellent source of incremental business, or a means to support and amplify their efforts in television or mail. Finally, print advertising offers a quick and inexpensive way to test the viability of a product or offer.

Learning from the masters

In his book *A Whack on the Side of the Head,* Roger von Oech states that the surprise value of studying concepts outside of their familiar context can make the ideas more accessible. Thus a look back at some classic direct mail advertisements from decades ago can help clarify the enduring principles they exemplify. Clothing styles, buzz words and status symbols may change, but the appeals that were "grabbers" in decades past can still win a prospect's attention.

Julian Lewis Watkins assembled a priceless archive of ads in his 1959 book, *The 100 Greatest Advertisements—Who Wrote Them and What They Did.* The book includes print ads from the turn of the century through the 1940s, with a supplement of ads that first appeared in the 1950s.

Famed direct mail copywriters whose works Watkins celebrates include Max Sackheim ("Do You Make These Mistakes in English?"); Victor O. Schwab ("How to Win Friends and Influence People"); John Caples ("They Laughed When I Sat Down At the Piano But When I Started to Play!"); and David Ogilvy ("At 60 miles an hour the loudest noise in this new Rolls-Royce comes from the electric clock.").

Today's print ad writers owe a great debt to creative geniuses such as these. For in addition to leaving us the legacy of their ads, they also took the time to share the concepts behind them. The "old masters" of print combined a thorough study of human nature with an understanding of the necessity to "test, test, test"—then record their test results, draw conclusions and build upon them. The general principles they established are as useful today as they were a generation ago.

From the collective wisdom of the direct mail greats of yesterday and today, here are some basic creative concepts behind successful print advertising.

Newspapers as a direct response medium

Because they are published daily or weekly, newspapers offer the most immediate means of testing a proposition in print. Newspapers accept advertising until a few days or even a few hours before publication, while magazines may require up to three months' lead time. Readers consider the offers newspapers contain to be newsy and time-urgent, so if they decide to respond, they are likely to do so quickly.

Newspapers are an excellent medium for local or regional offers. Some direct marketers also use them to heavy-up their coverage of high-potential areas. Such multi-media programs may add newspaper to direct mail and/or television.

The "mass" medium of newspaper may be segmented somewhat by placing ads in specific sections: senior citizens' offers near the obituaries, men's products in the sports section, or propositions of interest to youngsters in the Sunday comics.

Running a national direct marketing campaign via newspaper may prove to be an administrative nightmare, since complete coverage requires securing space in hundreds of publications. On the other hand, national papers such as the *Christian Science Monitor, U.S.A. Today,* and the *Wall Street Journal* offer both immediacy and broad reach. What's more, they can be tested in regional editions before a commitment to national roll-out is necessary.

Also available nationwide, but delivered with the local newspaper, are Sunday supplements like *Parade.* Such ride-along magazines provide better color reproduction than newsprint, a magazine environment for ads, and mass circulation in the tens of millions weekly. Regional test programs and affordable remnant-space buys make *Parade* and its competitors appealing to many direct marketers.

Free-standing newspaper inserts

When they were a novelty back in the 1960s, Free-Standing Inserts (FSIs) represented a very cost-effective way of reaching prospects via newspaper. In recent years, FSIs have suffered from a

Spiegel used this free-standing insert in Sunday newspapers during the summer to attract prospects for the Spiegel Fall Catalog. Spiegel qualified prospects by asking them to send $5.00 by check or credit card, but gave them several incentives to respond: a $5.00 merchandise certificate, crocodile print carry-all, and an extra $5.00 bonus for those who applied for a Spiegel Preferred Charge Account. Reprinted with permission of Spiegel, Inc.

''clutter'' problem similar to that on network television. On television, a two-minute commercial break that once included only two 60-second ads now is routinely splintered into six or more spots, each lasting only 10 to 30 seconds. At one time, the average Sunday newspaper contained only one or two extra inserts, whereas today's weekend edition may be stuffed with retail offers, coupon co-ops, flyers from local aluminum siding companies, and fast-food sales promotion pitches.

At least one FSI format has been successfully copyrighted, making it essential to clear the format you wish to use with a knowledgeable production expert before final plans are made.

Even so, the FSI offers several advantages worth considering by direct marketers of mass-appeal products and services. First, it offers a free-standing, visible advertising medium that does not require page turning for the prospect to find it. Second, it gives the direct marketer control over size, paper selection, color reproduction and format. Third, it allows for a post-paid reply card or envelope, which lets the prospect respond quickly and conveniently.

Fourth, FSIs can offer a total national circulation in the tens of millions. Fifth, advertisers may place ads in co-op FSIs at an exceptionally favorable cost per thousand.

Magazines as a direct response medium

Although there are still a number of "mass" magazines with huge circulations and broad general appeal, in recent years the magazine medium has grown to include many "class" books as well—publications that cater to narrow interest groups such as runners, crafts enthusiasts, or people who keep pet birds. These magazines allow direct marketers to target space ads to specific market segments, much as they do via direct mail lists.

Even among the mass publications, direct marketers may take advantage of segmentation opportunities to help target their ads. These include:

- Regional editions
- Market or metro editions
- Editorial sections providing ad environments for special interests such as
  —Travel
  —Pet owners
  —Decorating
  —Parenting
- Demographic-based editions providing audiences representing groups such as
  —Doctors
  —Students
  —High-income families
  —Women

Although magazines require a longer ad lead time than newspapers, they offer several advantages that newspapers do not. For instance, the life of a magazine ad is considerably longer, since magazines generally are kept in the home for at least a short period—not swept out with the day's trash like newspapers. Magazines offer pass-along value as well: they often are shared with family members, neighbors, friends or co-workers. Color reproduction and paper quality in magazines is generally superior to that of newspapers.

Another important factor is the "implied endorsement" of the magazine when a direct marketer runs an ad there. Since most consumer magazines—and many business publications—are sent mainly to paid subscribers, advertisers can assume that the magazine's readers generally feel somewhat positive toward its editorial material. This positive feeling may carry over to the ads which appear in the magazine as well, bestowing upon them an unstated "seal of approval" from a respected source of information.

Some magazines are considered especially fertile fields for direct response prospecting. While this media list changes frequently, certain publications carry many more coupon ads than others. When ads from the same respected direct marketers appear repeatedly in these magazines, their relative effectiveness is confirmed. Generally accepted good direct response books include but are not limited to:

Smithsonian
TV Guide
Parade
Good Housekeeping
Ladies Home Journal
Family Circle
Woman's Day
Redbook

In addition, various "shelter books"—those dealing with home and decor—are excellent sources of direct mail prospects. Record clubs, book clubs, and major marketers of collectibles run frequent ads in a much broader range of publications. This list should be used only as a general guideline. Indeed, media experts suggest that direct marketers with a new offer begin their print prospecting with the most narrowly targeted publication possible and work "outward" to more general books. Thus a fledgling direct marketer of custom-made dog beds might study the results of an ad in *Dog Fancy* before trying the pet section of a general, family-oriented shelter publication like *Better Homes and Gardens*.

The elements of a direct response ad

Observe people flipping through newspapers and magazines and one thing becomes readily apparent: each article or ad has only a split second in which to engage the prospect's attention. Thus every word and picture must be selected with exceptional care.

There are four main elements of a good direct response advertisement: the headline, illustration, body copy, and response device. Here are some guidelines to use in preparing and combining them in an effective presentation.

Select and entice the audience with headlines

One excellent way to train for direct response headline writing is to spend time on the horseshoe desk of a daily newspaper. Story after story crosses the desk along with the city editor's specifications for exact headline length. Clarity and brevity are essential, for each headline must fulfill two main criteria in just a few words: to summarize the story, and to pique the readers' interest enough to make them read on.

By the same token, a good direct response headline flags down qualified prospects and lures them into the body copy. It is considered the most important element of a print advertisement. Thus, a smart copywriter will invest all the time and care necessary to make each headline irresistible.

Journalists are taught to answer six questions in each news presentation.

WHO	WHEN
WHAT	WHY
WHERE	HOW

These are the questions people want answered immediately about most any situation or opportunity—and thus they are powerful idea-starters for direct response headlines.

Yet because journalists are supposed to remain unbiased, newspaper headlines seldom fall into the "irresistible" category. To make a headline compelling, direct marketers have developed some attractive headline "buzz words" of their own, including these suggested by William A. Cohen in his book, *Building a Mail-Order Business—A Complete Manual for Success:*

advice to	important	remarkable
amazing	improvement	revolutionary
announcing	introducing	secret
at last	it's here	sensational
bargain	just arrived	startling
challenge	last chance	success
compare	magic	suddenly
easy	miracle	wanted
found	new	who else
free	now	why
how	power	which
how to	powerful	when
hurry	quick	

But when we're faced with our own blank piece of paper, how should we put these words together to capture the attention of the prospect? In his brilliant book, *Tested Advertising Methods,* the late John Caples said that irresistible headlines do one or more of the following things:

Appeal to the prospect's self-interest

Example:

"We Guarantee to End Your Foot Pain . . . and We'll Prove It to You . . . Risk-Free!"

Featherspring International selects out readers with foot pain, then promises them something that's in their self-interest, with a bold guarantee statement.

Give news

Example:

"Finally, a waxless, shaveless, creamless, painless method of hair removal. Finally Free."

Mehl International Corp. implies that its products is news, with the powerful lead-off word, "finally."

Arouse curiosity
Example:
"What's this woman doing?"

Green Tree Press asks an intriguing question and accompanies the head with a curiosity-provoking photograph.

Offer a quick, easy way
Example:
"If you can sew on a button you can create a rose."

The DMC Corporation tells how "one simple stitch" can open a world of "thousands of exquisite designs."

An even better headline may result when these key elements are combined.

Example:
"Speak French Like a Diplomat!"

Audio-Forum focuses on self-interest and implies a quick, easy way with its ad for a French course on cassettes.

John Caples stated that of the four main headline appeals, self-interest is by far the most powerful. If we wish to appeal, above all, to the prospect's self-interest, we need to know what people are interested in. We can start by asserting that people are *not* inherently interested in products and services. They are interested in *results*—what products and services can do for them. They are attracted by the *sizzle* not the steak. They want to know about *benefits,* not just product features.

While preparing to write headlines for a product or service, ask yourself what would make *you* want to buy it. If you are not a member of the prime target market for the product, find some people who are, and learn what motivates them. Try to determine their hopes, dreams and aspirations—this can often prove much more helpful than a detailed discussion of their needs for insurance, lawn service or kitchen appliances.

Here are some of the basic human interests, needs and aspirations that well-written headlines may address:

- Money—making it, saving it, investing it for the future, using it to buy possessions, getting it easily (greed).

- Security—health, financial, family.
- Saving Time—ending drudgery, having more leisure, relaxing more, getting more done at work, being more organized.
- Self—improvement, career advancement, better looks, fitting in socially, impressing loved ones and friends, gaining power, increasing pride.
- Enjoyment—travel, escape, excitement, freedom, novelty.

When you sit down to write headlines for an ad, don't stop at one or two. Write all the headlines you can, branching out in different directions. Create some headlines that focus on the main product benefit. Try some others aimed at a different benefit—it just might turn out to be the key to the product's initial appeal. Set the scene for a psychological reward. Work on some testimonial headlines. Keep at it until you have a wide range of options. Then if you think several are equally promising, consider testing them head-to-head to see which ad produces sales or leads most effectively.

Avoid writing headlines that are merely labels such as "New Spring Fashions from Macy's" or "The Prudential Life Insurance Plan." Most effective headlines contain verbs, often vivid ones such as the classic, "How to *Win* Friends and *Influence* People."

In general, it is best to avoid negative headlines, although sometimes a warning not to do something "unless" or "until" may entice the prospect to read on. Cute or funny headlines may amuse their writer, but they seldom gain the attention of the right readers. Above all, make sure your headlines are concise and clear.

Smooth the decision-making process with body copy

If your headline is effective, it has accomplished one of two things: set up a problem to be solved, or teased with an opportunity to be grasped. Now a reader with some interest in your proposition is poised at the brink of the body copy. It is time to continue with a clear, simple and straightforward presentation.

You may opt to begin your body copy in many different ways. Here are several examples:

- Tell a story
- Give a testimonial

- Explain the product's problem-solving or opportunity-grasping potential straight out
- Compare your product favorably with the competition
- Use an editorial format
- Let a spokesman do the talking
- Tell of the marvelous results, then flash back to the problem and how it was solved

Don't use your first paragraph for "warm-up." Jump right in with a strong follow-up to the headline. Many writers find that their strongest lead paragraph is the second or third one they write. By moving the clearest statement of the product's benefits to the forefront, they strengthen their copy.

Once you have shown how your product or service does what you say it does, move on to strike the bargain with the prospect. Explain and justify the price, and emphasize your guarantee to ensure the buyer of no risk.

Create urgency—the need to respond right away. Urgency can be explained in terms of limited quantities, limited edition, or the urgent need of the prospect to put the product's benefits to work.

Ask for the order, and take the prospect by the hand to make sure he or she responds. Tell them to return the coupon, make the telephone call, send in the inquiry.

To maximize response, don't ask the prospect to make choices. The more choices of size, price, color, etc. the prospect has to make, the more difficult it will be to respond.

As for copy length, in general the more you expect the prospect to do or spend, the more copy you need. Break up long copy with action-oriented subheads.

How to design an ad for maximum impact

The way your ad should look depends upon your target market, and the medium in which the ad will appear. A direct response ad in a fashion publication like *Vogue,* aimed at upscale women, might well make use of a full-color bleed presentation with an avant-garde typestyle for headlines. An ad in the *National Enquirer,* aimed at lower-to-middle-income women, would most probably be black and white, set in a newspaper-like typeface that is compatible with that used by the publication itself.

"Here's an Extra $50, Grace
—I'm making *real* money now!"

"Yes, I've been keeping it a secret until pay day came. I've been promoted with an increase of $50 a month. And the first extra money is yours. Just a little reward for urging me to study at home. The boss says my spare time training has made me a valuable man to the firm and there's more money coming soon. We're starting up easy street, Grace, thanks to you and the I. C. S.!"

Today more than ever before, money is what counts. The cost of living is mounting month by month. You can't get along on what you have been making. Somehow, you've simply got to increase your earnings.

Fortunately for you hundreds of thousands of other men have proved there is an unfailing way to do it. Train yourself for bigger work, learn to do some one thing well and employers will be glad to pay you real money for your special knowledge.

You can get the training that will prepare you for the position you want in the work you like best, whatever it may be. You can get it without sacrificing a day or a dollar from your present occupation. You can get it at home, in spare time, through the International Correspondence Schools.

It is the *business* of the I. C. S. to prepare men in just your circumstances for better positions at better pay. They have been doing it for 27 years. They have helped two million other men and women. They are training over 100,000 now. Every day many students write to tell of advancements and increased salaries already won.

You have the same chance they had. What are you going to do with it? Can you afford to let a single priceless hour pass without at least finding out what the I. C. S. can do for you? Here is all we ask—without cost, without obligating yourself in any way, simply mark and mail this coupon.

TEAR OUT HERE

INTERNATIONAL CORRESPONDENCE SCHOOLS
BOX   , SCRANTON, PA.

Explain, without obligating me, how I can qualify for the position, or in the subject, *before* which I mark X.

☐ ELECTRICAL ENGINEER	☐ CHEMICAL ENGINEER
☐ Electrician	☐ SALESMANSHIP
☐ Electric Wiring	☐ ADVERTISING MAN
☐ Electric Lighting	☐ Show Card Writer
☐ Electric Car Running	☐ Outdoor Sign Painter
☐ Heavy Electric Traction	☐ RAILROADER
☐ Electrical Draftsman	☐ ILLUSTRATOR
☐ Electric Machine Designer	☐ DESIGNER
☐ Telegraph Expert	☐ BOOKKEEPER
☐ Practical Telephony	☐ Stenographer and Typist
☐ MECHANICAL ENGINEER	☐ Cert. Public Accountant
☐ Mechanical Draftsman	☐ Traffic Management
☐ Toolmaker	☐ Commercial Law
☐ Machine Shop Practice	☐ GOOD ENGLISH
☐ Gas Engineer	☐ Common School Subjects
☐ CIVIL ENGINEER	☐ CIVIL SERVICE
☐ Surveying and Mapping	☐ Railway Mail Clerk
☐ MINE FOREMAN OR ENGINEER	☐ STATIONARY ENGINEER
☐ ARCHITECT	☐ Textile Overseer or Supt.
☐ Architectural Draftsman	☐ AGRICULTURE
☐ PLUMBING AND HEATING	☐ Navigator
☐ Sheet Metal Worker	☐ Poultry Raising
☐ Ship Draftsman	☐ AUTOMOBILES

☐ Spanish ☐ French ☐ Italian

Name _____

Occupation
& Employer _____

Street
and No. _____

City _____ State _____

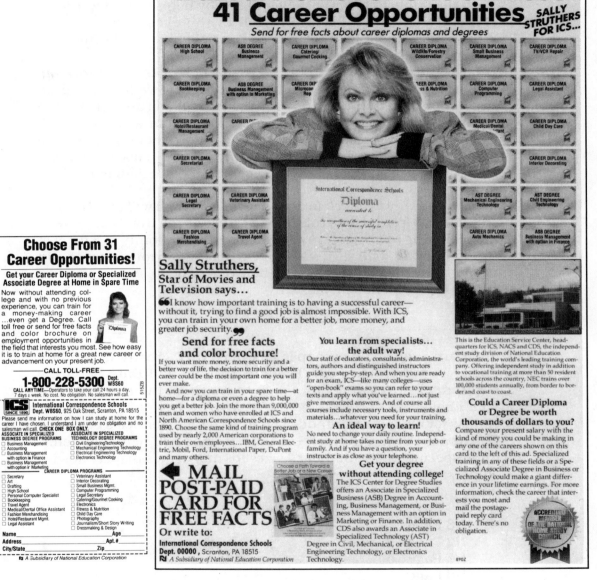

International Correspondence Schools, in business for more than 100 years, has long been a leading force in direct response print advertising. The "Here's an Extra $50, Grace" ad, circa 1918-19, is considered one of the 100 best ads of all time. In that era, most all of I.C.S.'s customers were men. Note the change the years have brought. Now the I.C.S. customer base includes more females than males, and Sally Struthers is an I.C.S. spokesperson. On the other hand, the small magazine ad, "Choose From 31 Career Opportunities!," features a coupon remarkably similar to the one used more than six decades ago. Reprinted with permission from WOL Direct.

Many successful direct marketing ad campaigns have utilized "editorials ads"—pieces crafted to look as much like an article in the publication as possible. This ploy helps capitalize on the credibility of the publication itself in the eyes of its readers. What's more, it implies the unbiased "news value" of the information in the ad.

On the other hand, in his book *Direct Marketing: Strategy, Planning, Execution,* Ed Nash asserts that a well-designed ad stands out from the other ads in its medium. If you are not striving for an editorial look, find some way to make your ad a "stopper" when people are turning pages. Make the product dominate the page . . . emphasize key words in the headline . . . use a color or a readable typeface that's seldom seen in the particular publication.

A good way to check in advance how your ad will appear in its editorial environment is this: make up a dummy that is as close to the real thing as possible, and then insert it randomly in a copy of the magazine where it will appear. Have various people flip through the magazine and test their reactions to learn if your ad stands out or blends in, and why.

Choosing the size of your ad

Standard sizes for newspaper ads may vary greatly depending upon the publication: check Standard Rate and Data Service's *Newspaper Rates and Data* book to check on the newspaper of your choice.

As for magazines, Standard Rate and Data Service's books for Consumer/Farm and Business publications will help you determine specifications. Standard sizes for magazines display ads include:

1   Page
2/3 Page
1/2 Page
1/3 Page
1/6 Page

In addition, you may opt for a double-page spread, one page with bind-in card, or a special insert which you may supply to the magazine.

When testing a new offer, larger direct marketers tend to begin with full-page ads and then test smaller to see if they can gain the same number of sales or inquiries in less space. If a one-page ad works well, many direct marketers also "test up" to a page plus bind-in card, or double-page spread. In his book, *Successful Direct Marketing Methods,* Bob Stone says that the first test "up" from a full page should be to a page plus bind-in card rather than a two-page spread: it is more likely to pay off.

Pros and cons of bind-in cards

Bind-in cards offer several advantages to direct marketers. They add bulk to the magazine and pop up, so it is likely that the book will fall open to the page where your ad appears. They allow for post-paid reply cards on a stock heavy enough to return in the mail, thus making it easier for prospects to reply. For this reason, they often bring anywhere from three to ten times as many replies as an on-page coupon.

CBS Classical Club used a two-page, black-and-white ad with coupon *and* two-color bind-in card to attract readers of *Archaeology* magazine. Having both the card and coupon increases chances of getting more than one order via pass-along readership. Note the attempt to build a database: both card and coupon ask whether the prospect has a credit card and a VCR. Reprinted with permission of CBS Records.

On the other hand, they cost twice to two and a half times as much as a one-page ad, and thus they need to generate many more responses for break-even. In addition, because bind-in cards make it easier for prospects to respond, the names received on bind-ins represent less committed customers than those received on cut-out coupons where the sender pays for the postage.

Color or black and white?

In general, a four-color ad will outpull a black-and-white—but not necessarily enough to justify its extra cost. This can be tested on an A/B split in some publications. Use black and white or full color only: two-color or three-color ads seldom bump the response at all. Bleed ads are generally more attractive than those with white borders, but they are more costly, and not guaranteed to pay out. Test bleed versus nonbleed if you have a product that might benefit by the artistic advantage of a bleed ad.

Choice of typestyle

Direct response ads must be easy to read, and thus serif typefaces are recommended over sans serif. Many art directors try to "sell" the story that sans serif is easier to read: if they pull this on you, ask them to show you a daily newspaper or national magazine with body copy printed in sans serif type—this usually settles the issue. The reason why serif faces make for easy reading has to do with the tiny hooks and squiggles on their letters—they are more soothing to the eyes than the straight lines of sans serif type. Stylish typefaces *may* be used for headlines if this contributes positively to the overall effectiveness of the ad.

When working with an art director who is not a direct response "pro," one other "don't" should be kept in mind. Although reverse type is quite dramatic, it is difficult to read, and should be used sparingly if at all in direct response ads.

Photos and drawings

When a photograph and a drawing are tested head to head, the photograph will almost always win. Using captions under photographs in direct response ads boosts readership, and therefore response.

When choosing photography for your ads, remember to make the product the star. You may be able to borrow attention

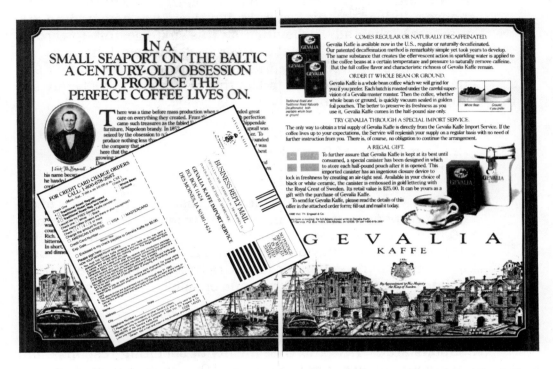

Gevalia Kaffee Import Services goes the bind-in card one better with a bind-in Business Reply Envelope and tear-off reply form. Rather than place a coupon on the face of its handsome, full-color ad, the firm provides an address and toll-free number for prospects to use if the form is missing. Reprinted with permission of General Foods Corporation.

with an intriguing photo that has little to do with your sales pitch, but you won't be able to sustain it long enough to close the sale.

Sure-fire attention getters are pictures of animals and people, so consider using them if they relate directly to your product. Psychologists say that men look more closely at pictures of other men, and women look more closely at pictures of other women. Keep this in mind if your product is being marketed to one sex or the other.

Don't underestimate the power of before-and-after shots. But if you must choose only one photo, make it the "after," never the "before." An upbeat, positive approach is best.

Coupons vs. toll-free numbers

Some fledgling direct marketers rebel against the concept of a coupon. They believe it takes away from the streamlined look of the ad, and they prefer to use only a toll-free 800 number for responses. Indeed, many general advertisers are now adding 800 numbers to their ads, believing that this small gesture toward direct response somehow makes their ad dollars work harder.

The 800 number only may be appropriate for some audiences, but it would be wise to test three different ways before settling for an 800 number only:

1. Coupon only
2. Coupon plus 800 number
3. 800 number only

This way you can determine the most cost-effective means of obtaining responses. It is not necessarily true that the coupon plus 800 number would pull the most responses. The addition of the telephone number may offer only an alternate means of responding. If this occurs, you incur the extra cost of manning 800 number lines without increased revenue or sales.

Designing the coupon

Coupons are a tried and true means of soliciting response, but some coupons are much more effective than others. Here are some tips for creating the best possible coupon:

- Make sure the coupon can stand alone, spelling out the basics of the offer, and including the full address of your company. Many consumers clip only the coupon and put it aside for later action. Don't risk losing a sale by providing them with a less-than-complete means of doing so.
- Put your address and the basics of the offer, including the price, elsewhere in your ad as well. This way, pass-along readers will be able to respond even if the coupon is missing.
- When using a bind-in card, the addition of an on-page coupon provides two means for convenient customer response.
- Resist the temptation to "liven up" your ad with a coupon that is placed sideways, fashioned in an exotic shape, or screened with a color or pattern. A rectangle at the bottom right corner, printed in black on white with readable, serif type, is still your best bet. Some art directors have actually presented coupon layouts indicating type reversed out of black. Unless you plan to provide a pen with white ink to each prospect, beware this mistake!

- Make it as easy as possible for the prospect to fill out the coupon. Provide four lines if possible: Name, Address, City, and State/Zip. Asking prospects to "Please Print" will help eliminate problems in keying names when orders are received.
- Take a photocopy of your keylined coupon and sit down to fill it out for yourself. Make sure the lines are long enough and tall enough to be filled out comfortably.
- Add a friendly note of urgency to the coupon, such as "Clip Here and Mail Today." Dots or dashes to mark the coupon border facilitate easy clipping.
- Make sure to add a source code to every coupon so that each customer's origin can be discerned. Depending upon the sophistication and requirements of your database, you might:
  —add a department number to your address, i.e.
    123 Main Street, Dept. HG-692
    (For *House and Garden*, June, 1992),
  —place a similar code in the corner of the coupon,
  —or assign a number of three or more digits which is coded in your computer system to indicate publication and date.

A word about classified ads

Although many direct marketers today invest millions of dollars in start-up campaigns, there are still many success stories about kitchen-table entrepreneurs who begin their direct mail businesses very small and build up to impressive levels over time.

The least expensive way to start prospecting is by means of classified ads—the short attention-getters that appear in special "shopping sections" at the back of many national magazines.

Yet amateurs fall by the wayside if they underestimate the difficulty of writing an effective classified ad. Every word counts in a piece that may measure only one column inch in length. A classified with a strong headline may bring 10 times the orders received from another ad with a head that does not capture the prospect's attention.

The best way to prepare to write classified ads is to study the best ads in the marketplace. Tear out the ads that appear again and again and keep them to study. Be on the alert for headline tests, and then track to see which headlines show up later, and which are abandoned. If there is competition for your product already in the marketplace, study their ads carefully. Find a way to do a better job in classifieds than they do, perhaps drawing upon the appeals used in other product categories.

When you begin to write your classified ad, don't worry about length right away. Write the best ad you can—even if it's two pages long. Then hone and cut and combine. Eliminate flowery language and extra adjectives. Use action verbs. Pull out the most important product benefit and ruthlessly cut out secondary messages.

Write a number of headlines and be prepared to test them head to head. Consider price and offer tests. Consider testing various lengths for your classifieds. Test using a small coupon versus name and address only.

Investigate opportunities for editorial coverage offered by many shopping sections. If you offer a catalog, consider the many catalog inserts with bingo cards that appear in magazines on a seasonal basis.

Using ads to generate leads

There are a number of situations in which it is more effective for direct marketers to develop a two-step approach to print advertising. Step number one involves the solicitation of a lead, while step number two includes a follow-up by mail and/or telephone to close the sale.

Here are some examples of propositions which may pay out better in the long run with a two-step approach up front.

- For club or continuity offers that involve a long-term commitment—offer the prospect a premium or inexpensive way to sample the product before deciding.
- For catalogs—offer the catalog-only as an alternative to selling a product from the catalog and then following up with a catalog mailing.
- For big-ticket or complex items—sell the "sizzle" in the step one ad. Then send a detailed package that introduces the "steak" only to those prospects who have indicated a certain level of interest.

■ For business-to-business offers—identify quality prospects to be followed up by mail, phone, a sales call, or some combination of the three.

When soliciting leads, it is important to set objectives for the quality and quantity of names you wish to obtain. In some cases, you may wish to maximize the number of loose leads you acquire, and then worry about converting them into buyers later on. In other cases, you may wish to qualify your prospects considerably, obtaining only a limited number of tight leads who are predisposed to buy.

Exhibit 14.1 gives some pointers to use in structuring your offer to obtain tight versus loose leads.

EXHIBIT 14.1   Tight leads vs. loose leads

TO OBTAIN TIGHT LEADS	*TO OBTAIN LOOSE LEADS*
Charge money for information or catalog	*Provide free information*
Do not offer a premium	*Offer a premium*
Offer a product-related premium	*Offer a highly appealing premium unrelated to the product*
Include address only—make the prospect do the work in responding	*Use coupon or bind-in card to minimize work the prospect must do to respond*
No phone number or no toll-free number	*Provide a toll-free 800 number*
Indicate that a salesperson will call	*Indicate that there is no obligation and that no salesperson will call*
Ask questions on the coupon as qualifiers—such as age, phone number, income, when the prospect plans to buy, size of business, number of employees, title and responsibilities	*Simple coupon—asking name and address only*
For business offers—insist that the prospect reply on company letterhead	*Provide coupon or place no restrictions on method of response*
Talk specifically about price	*No talk of price*
Do not participate in bingo card offers—or do participate, but charge for information	*Participate in bingo card offers, and offer information free of charge*

Print ads as a support medium

Some sophisticated direct marketers use print advertising as a means of supporting ads in another medium, or ads elsewhere in the publication.

Supporting ads in another medium

A catalog marketer might insert an FSI in the Sunday newspaper to support a massive catalog drop in the region the newspaper serves. This "frequency" factor adds incremental sales—both from the FSI itself, and from the catalog, as it draws renewed attention to the catalog which should already be in the home.

Television is often used as a support medium for print advertising, inviting prospects to "watch your Sunday paper for this offer." The effectiveness of such television ads may be tested by asking the prospect to circle something on the coupon to obtain a premium or extra merchandise. There is more on television as a support medium in the broadcast chapter of this book.

Supporting ads elsewhere in a publication

Marketers who use this technique caution that it should be considered only as an amplification of primary ads which are already working. It may produce incremental sales by arousing interest for the primary ad. Support ads should have the same graphic look and copy style as the primary ad, so that they all appear to be of a piece. Most often, support ads offer some incentive to turn to the primary ad by highlighting a premium or some interest-arousing information.

Technological advances in print advertising

A number of publications are now pioneering in personalization techniques which may soon be available as standard options for direct response print advertisers.

Farm Journal sends multiple versions of a single issue with different editorial material and ads to suit the needs of hog

Dodge personalized this sweepstakes offer, and bound it into magazines. The object: for prospective customers to visit their Dodge dealers in order to learn if they had won the contest. Such attractive opportunities to personalize print advertising will become more widely available to direct marketers in the years to come. Reprinted with permission of H. Olson & Company.

farmers, cattle ranchers, or farms that produce varied types of crops.

Games magazine paved the way for The Franklin Mint to offer a preprinted name on a Business Reply Card in 1986. The magazine's first use of this technology took place in September, 1985, when *Games* included a puzzle personalized with the subscriber's name.

American Baby offers options to advertisers selling such products as baby food and formula. The magazine can single out mothers with children approaching the age recommended for solid foods. It can also single out which readers have just had their first child, and which have other children at home, and allow advertisers to customize their messages accordingly.

General advertisers are pushing the boundaries of print advertising with pop-up inserts, samples of scent and eyeshadow, and tip-on samples and premiums. All of these advances and more can be considered for tests by direct marketers.

Yet the best advice for direct response print advertisers still echoes from the writings of the "old masters": To write successful ads, learn first about human nature. Then research the product and the market, write your ads with care, and "test, test, test"!

THE CREATIVE APPROACH TO CATALOGS

15

When Montgomery Ward and Sears, Roebuck & Company reigned supreme in the world of American catalogs, their thick "wish books" served the purpose of a general store by mail. Reaching deep into the nation's heartland via Rural Free Delivery, the catalogs of a century ago offered general merchandise to fill the needs of families that might live hundreds of miles from the nearest store.

But as Americans gained mobility and suburbs spilled into what had been remote farmland, many more shoppers were able to visit cities, towns and outlying malls to make their purchases in person. Thus catalog merchandisers were forced to find new reasons for being, based on the needs of a changing culture.

With more than 7,000 catalogs in active circulation today, it is apparent that many catalog marketers have struck a positive chord with consumers through unique selection, ease of shopping from home, and other factors. Yet the swift rise and fall of many shiny new catalogs proves again and again that the market isn't magic: each new book must carve out its own "reason for being" and support its positioning with top-quality, well-targeted merchandise, a crisp creative product, and excellent customer service.

What's more, the days of overnight success for the "kitchen table" catalog entrepreneur are all but over. Fierce competition has driven down the average response rate of both direct mail and space prospecting for new customers. A peek into the mailbox of an inveterate catalog shopper reveals that as many as twenty different books may arrive *daily* between Labor Day and mid-October. This pre-holiday catalog glut rivals even the worst advertising clutter on network television. The situation in space advertising is little better, with catalog shopping guides and small-space ads for catalogs filling the back pages of nearly every likely fall publication.

This chapter will provide a step-by-step guide for direct marketing creative people charged with positioning and creating a catalog. It includes ideas that art directors and copywriters may use to make their creative product as appealing and "user friendly" as possible. It offers proven ways to increase average order size, reader involvement, customer loyalty and impulse purchasing. And it concludes with some hints to help keep the day-to-day output of catalog writers and designers from getting predictable and stale.

Catalog positioning

In the age of "niche marketing," the most exciting aspect of catalog creativity is *positioning.* It is not enough to choose a general merchandise category like women's clothing, food, or children's toys. All of these categories abound with catalogs that have already established an image and a basis of trust with consumers. Rather, the direct marketer must embark on a period of research to identify a unique and viable target market for each new catalog.

The target market

To succeed in the competitive catalog realm, each firm must discover and fulfill one or more *unmet needs* of a target group of consumers. Equally important, the target group must be *reachable* by means of direct mail lists, space advertising or other affordable means. Third, the market must be *sizeable* enough to result in a business with sufficient volume to meet the goals of its sponsoring organization.

Fulfilling an unmet need

Some firms are able to translate their successful retail sales concepts to catalog marketing. For example, the Crate and Barrel catalog echoes the spare, contemporary good looks of the tabletop, cookware and linens stores that preceded it. Other organizations approach the marketplace with only a rough idea of the product category they wish to enter.

In recent years, a number of large firms have recognized the potential of catalog marketing as a new profit center. These wholesalers of products like shoes, meat products or dinnerware miss out on the large percentage of mark-up that retailers enjoy. Thus they may wish to develop catalog concepts around the general merchandise categories they can supply.

One excellent example is Hormel's Austin Street Market, a delicatessen-style catalog built around the Hormel line of hams and other meat products. In the delicatessen context, even Hormel's less glamorous products like salami, Spam and canned stews make sense as part of the product mix. The addition of deli-style products from other sources rounds out the book: smoked

Through its product selection, graphic treatment, colors and copy, the Austin Street Market catalog creates the mood of a neighborhood deli. Reprinted with permission of Catalog Marketing.

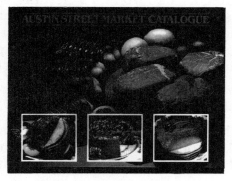

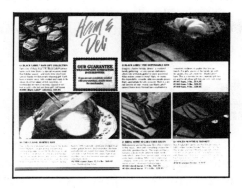

poultry, popcorn, seafood, desserts and candies, exotic coffees, and gourmet kitchen items. The book's copy emphasizes flavors, scents and smells and the color scheme is red, green and white—just like your neighborhood deli.

How to find a "niche"

The discovery of a unique catalog selling proposition begins with two forms of research. The first entails studying the existing catalog competition, while the second involves consumer research to determine the viability of unmet needs you may discover.

Catalog research

To begin the research process, gather as many competitive catalogs as possible. This can be done by answering their ads in publications, or writing or calling the firm to request a catalog. You may obtain publications from the Direct Marketing Association and other publishers that list catalog firms by category. Don't stop with a handful of catalogs: in general categories such as women's clothing or food you should end up with several shopping bags full.

Next, identify the creative team that will be working on developing the catalog positioning. This team might consist of a marketing person, a top-notch copywriter, and an equally experienced art director.

Each member of the creative team should be allowed the time necessary to leaf through all the competitive catalogs for a general impression of the existing market. Then each member may begin conceptualizing in his or her own area.

For instance, the marketing person might create a matrix of some of the best and most sharply-defined catalogs in the product category. Placing orders with a number of these firms is also a good idea, so that their response times and quality of customer service can be noted on the matrix. Exhibit 15.1 shows how a portion of such a matrix for the women's clothing category might look.

While the matrix is under construction, the copywriter and art director can pull examples of distinctive layout, copy, photography, typeface selection and other items of interest from the catalogs they are studying.

EXHIBIT 15.1 Catalog research matrix

CATALOG NAME	MERCHANDISE MIX	COPY/ART "LOOK"	FULFILLMENT
Adam York on the Go	Clothing and accessories chosen for women who travel. Career oriented; midprice range.	Logo looks like a postmark; short copy; serif typeface; ruled-off double columns/page; comments through-out from "Adam."	Ordered 7/15. Order arrived UPS 7/24. One backorder.
Victoria's Secret	Originally all romantic lingerie; now diversifying into casual clothing. We received a summer sale book.	Provocative models and scenes. Heads and subheads to establish each page's story; simple descriptive copy.	Phone order 7/15. They called 7/18 to verify size; order arrived 7/25 via U.S. mail.
The Tog Shop	Classic, middle-American clothes by "name" makers. Great range of sizes and colors. Extensive shoe selection.	Digest size; very simple layout; no headings; descriptive copy in sans serif type. Many pages carry a manufacturer's logo.	No 800#; sent in order 7/15. Arrived by UPS on 7/26.

By sharing what they have found, all members of the creative team begin the process of narrowing down their options, considering the competitive environment and the capabilities of the firm that will publish the catalog.

For example, suppose that a leading textiles firm has determined that it wishes to enter the field with a catalog of women's clothing. This textile company can make most any type of clothing: trendy, classic, inexpensive or more finely crafted and costly. They have no facilities to make undergarments, shoes, purses or other accessories.

Thus the creative team will be looking for an area of unmet need that can be fulfilled with a catalog that is anchored by women's clothing products. These are the items that can be sold at attractive margins, since they will be manufactured by the textile firm with no middleman to cut into profits.

Upon completion of their catalog research, the creative team might agree upon three, four or even ten possible areas of unmet need in the women's clothing realm. They then begin to shape these general ideas into catalog concepts including a working title, merchandising mix, price range, layout and copy concept, and extra factors such as specialized customer service.

In rough form, these catalog concepts might appear as follows:

Unmet Need in the Women's Clothing Catalog Realm— Clothes for career women who want to go right from the office to evening galas or casual events.

Rough Creative Concept—"DAY FOR NIGHT"

A catalog of outfits that can be worn as serious career clothes and then transformed into evening or casual wear. For instance: a black wool dress has turn-back cuffs and collar that can open to reveal black sequins and a low V-neckline. Or with the change of a belt from snakeskin to hand-tooled leather, and the change of a scarf from silk to challis, a tan gabardine shirtwaist goes from work to a casual sporting event in perfect style. Price range would be from $150 to $300 per outfit—for the successful career woman. Layout would be lavish with thick paper stock and copy and photography that amplify the outfits' versatility. Copy would include word-pictures describing the active lifestyle buyers have or would like to achieve.

Unmet Need in the Women's Clothing Catalog Realm— Fashionable yet casual and comfortable clothes for a mother to wear while taking care of her house and children. Something more imaginative than jeans and a sweatshirt, yet affordable and washable.

Rough Creative Concept—"MOM'S WEAR"

A catalog of unique washable clothing with elastic waists and flattering silhouettes—something Mom won't see others wearing in her town. A change from the same old jeans, these clothes might include jumpsuits, easy-to-wear casual dresses, and pants with interesting styling touches. Tops will feature handsome detailing, yet be quick to recover from spilled toddler food, muddy hands and other disasters. Price range would be under $100 per outfit so that they are not out of reach for middle-income families. Layout will be done in primary colors with slice-of-life photos of Mom's busy day, surrounded by adoring kids. Some photos will show a working Mom who does a quick change into her "Mom's Wear" upon arriving home.

Consumer research

After the creative team and the prospective catalog firm come to an initial agreement on some unmet needs it may wish to fill, it is essential to do some groundwork aimed at determining the size and reachability of each prospective "niche."

List and space advertising brokers can be of great help at this stage, assuming that your firm or agency has sufficient clout to command their work on a speculative basis. If not, your own careful research with the Standard Rate and Data books for consumer lists and magazines may suffice.

Look for lists of proven mail order buyers who would be likely prospects for each "niche" you have identified. Can you reach successful career women via list rentals? How about young mothers? Sportswomen? Women who travel? How large is the universe of likely lists in each category you are considering?

Look for space advertising opportunities that will put you in touch with each target market you are considering. Are these magazines known as good mail order books? How large are their circulations?

Next, you need to determine whether the rough creative concepts you have developed have sufficient appeal in the marketplace. Demographic and psychographic research from secondary sources can help identify trends. For instance: a trend toward mothers staying home to raise their children might be a positive indicator for the "Mom's Wear" catalog concept.

Focus-group research can provide consumer reaction to your rough ideas and may well help you eliminate some and add depth to others. You might also consider testing the catalog concept in space advertising—perhaps with a representative product offering that you can fulfill. If you choose to ''dry test'' the catalog concept, do not ask for money. Make it a free catalog offer. Then all you owe responders is an explanation—either that the catalog will be published on x-date and you will send them a copy, or to apologize for the fact that it will not be published after all.

''Niches'' based on factors other than merchandise

Your challenge as the creator of a new catalog is to offer the consumer a range of related products that he or she does not perceive to be as readily available from any source. You may achieve this on the basis of any number of attributes beyond product positioning. For instance:

- *Better selection*—Most consumers know that they can purchase cotton turtleneck tops at a local shopping center. But can they be assured that the colors and sizes they want are available no matter what the season? If you offer reasonably priced cotton turtlenecks in twenty-five different colors and twenty sizes, and keep them in stock for immediate delivery, your catalog may be perceived as having a ''better selection.''
- *Finer quality*—The consumer who buys a jacket off the rack in a midline department store is unlikely to hear about its construction and long-wearing qualities from the clerk. But if you can explain these attributes in copy—and add a testimonial or two from satisfied customers who took the jackets on round-the-world trips—you may well win the customer's admiration as a source with ''finer quality.''
- *More affordable price*—Once again, perception is the key. It may be that a local retailer is more affordable than you are, but if the consumer perceives your product as a value, you may win the sale anyway. You can enhance the value of your product by making it easy for the consumer to obtain it: i.e., toll-free numbers, quick turn-around, returns with no questions asked, etc.
- *Appealing presentation*—The products themselves may not be unique, but if your presentation makes them fun to buy, you may win the sale. Some catalogs win a loyal following with homespun copy and cozy graphics. Others gain the ''snob appeal'' sale with slick presentation on thick paper stock, elegant gift boxes, and other touches of class.

Creating the catalog

Through the multi-faceted research process described above, your creative group and the firm behind your prospective catalog may well be able to define a specific, reachable and sizeable target market. Next the creative group should join forces with merchandisers and catalog operations experts to further develop the catalog concept. A continuous working dialogue among all of these people will help ensure that your sharply defined creative concept shines through in the merchandise, layout, copy, and even the operations of the catalog firm.

Specifically, however, the direct marketing creative team is now charged with defining and developing the copy and layout of the fledgling catalog. They may also become involved with pagination (deciding which merchandise goes on which pages—and how many pages there will be) and space allocation (which products, if any, will dominate a given page or spread).

How to do pagination—the hot selling spots

As you plan and design your catalog, consider the best use of the prime selling spaces in your book.

First is the front cover. Although this can be a prime selling space, many catalog marketers opt to use this first page as a "theme setter." They may show a group of merchandise items that are available for sale inside the catalog, a scene that characterizes the company and its goods, or a seasonal vignette.

The back cover is the second hot spot. It should in most cases be used for selling products with a high sales potential. Be careful that the products you choose for the back cover also characterize what's inside the catalog. If they are too different from the mainstream of merchandise in your book, prospective buyers may never make it past the front and back covers.

The inside front cover spread and the spread after that are next in the prime territory race, along with the center spread and the inside back cover. The spread near the order form also carries high potential. And don't underestimate the power of the order form itself for selling merchandise, especially the add-on or impulse variety. Talk with your printer about bind-in order form designs that give you some extra selling space at an affordable cost.

For these inside hot spots, you will want to choose merchandise with excellent margins and/or top sales potential. But it is also important to consider developing a theme for each spread or section. The copywriter and designer can work together with merchandising people to find pieces that work well together. For example:

- A spread of gift suggestions with all items priced at $25 or less.
- A tabletop spread with dinnerware, glassware, linens and accessories all in blue and white.
- A clothing spread featuring items that work together to create a weekend wardrobe.
- A spread of items especially for children in a general giftware catalog.
- A spread of items that can be personalized.

How to allocate space for each product

Successful catalog firms have widely varied views on this subject. Lands End frequently devotes a cover and inside front spread—or

This Lands' End catalog spread illustrates several of the firm's unique strategies. First, Lands' End has devoted an entire spread to "romancing" one simple product line: knit shirts. Second, the firm offers a much wider range of colors and sizes than one would be likely to find in a retail store. Third, they use real people in action as models, and weave a human interest story in with their selling message. Reprinted with permission of Lands' End, Inc.

even more space—to one staple item like its turtleneck tops or short-sleeved pullover shirts. Austin Street Market, the Hormel delicatessen-in-a-catalog mentioned earlier, squeezes in products with a shoe horn, just as they might appear on colorful, crowded shelves.

The ultimate answer to "how much space does this product deserve?" is this: "whatever amount its sales and profit margin can support." There are exceptions to this rule, of course. Neiman-Marcus and other upscale catalog firms may offer outlandish trips, fantasy adventures and lavish products that require a page or more to describe—and may not sell a single unit. These products are justified because they help to create the catalog's overall aura—and because they are excellent public relations tools.

At the other end of the scale, a cataloger may discover that plain white t-shirts and briefs sell a predictable 500 units each whether they receive full-page treatment or a corner of a buried inside page.

In general, however, the most practical way to assign space is by the numbers. Use your sales history with each item to determine its relative strength. If the item or the whole catalog is new, you will need to do some decision making based on the best information you can gather. Check your competitors' space allocations for general indications. Draw upon your vendors' experience to determine the relative appeal of various products.

Consider the price point and margin of each item: for instance, it only stands to reason that a $500 stereo system has a better chance of justifying a half-page space than a $50 AM-FM portable with earphones. If your house brand of sweater has a three-time mark-up and a designer sweater has only a two-time mark-up, you'd be well served to push the house sweater with a larger space and more lengthy description. Results after your first mailing may well prove that your logical assumptions are wrong, however, and then you can make the necessary adjustments to maximize sales and profits.

If an item did twice as well as you projected, you might try allocating it more space to see if it can do even better. But test this, because some products can do beautifully in a small space while others only "bloom" on a half-or full-page layout.

The layout and copy concept

While the final page line-up is in the works, copywriter and layout artist can be working to develop the catalog's appearance and tone. This stage requires numerous decisions. These include:

- *Catalog size and number of pages*—Consult with merchandisers for number of products—a *very* general average is four to eight products per page. Check with printers to determine cost-efficient formats in the general size range you are considering: subtracting just 1/8" in size can sometimes save many thousands of dollars.
- *Paper stock*—Heavier, coated stocks bespeak an upscale offering. The thinner, grayer and less shiny stocks are less costly and may actually be preferable if you are trying to develop a catalog that looks approachable and affordable. Once again, consult with printers or paper salespeople for ideas on ways to save money and project the image you seek.
- *Illustrations/photography*—Some catalog firms prefer illustrations to photography. Their reasons may include saving money, creating a "down-home" look, or carrying out a theme. Other firms swear by in-studio photography with simple backgrounds that make the product the star. Others try to use existing art from vendors to save money—but this can become costly when transparencies from many sources have to be pieced together at the color separation stage. Still others use more elaborate studio photography or even location shoots in exotic locales. To make the choice for a given catalog, consider budget, the book's current or targeted image, time constraints and product category
- *Layout style*—Choices abound in this area as well. Catalog layouts run the gamut from the simple "square picture with square copy block below" layouts of a Miles Kimball book to the magazine-style looks of the Land's End catalogs, which feature testimonials from satisfied customers who model the items they like best from Land's End. Studying catalogs, magazines, and everything from travel posters to retail store windows may provide inspiration for layouts. Remember in all your work: the products are the stars. They should never be overpowered by "art for art's sake."
- *Copy style*—Once again, there is no clear road to success. Catalogs like L.L. Bean's prosper with long, detailed copy while many other books get by with minimal description and very little copy "personality." Will you have separate copy for each item, or use common-copy lead-ins followed by individual descriptions? Will spreads or pages have headings and/or subheads? Will individual copy blocks have bold-face lead-ins? Will each copy block contain a message of urgency or call to action, or will the selling message be more understated? Once again, the answers to these and other copy questions

Owning the best.

I have a friend in New York who has a 25-year-old Bentley, aluminum bodied, quite fast, and quite beautiful. People driving Mercedes, BMW's, Jaguars, look over their shoulders in despair as he passes by. Where did I go wrong, their faces say.

The thing about his Bentley is that the oil-filler cap, which is spring loaded for quick opening, is identical to, and unchanged from, the oil-filler cap in Bentleys made fifty years ago. In other words, get it right, then don't mess with it. Go on to something else.

This is by way of introducing the best umbrella in the world. How can I be so sure of that? Because the Queen of England bought her umbrella from the same source: Swaine Adeney Brigg & Sons Limited, London.

The Queen of England, I think, could afford a very good umbrella. She can also afford to not get stuck with an experimental model, a provisional model, a see-how-it-goes model of umbrella (or anything else).

Our feeling today, sadly, is that if it's very good, they will stop making it soon. Too bad we feel that way. Too bad there's cause (as lawyers say) for feeling that way.

The Swaine Adeney Brigg umbrella is made from one piece of wood. It's solid and it's thick exactly where other umbrellas snap and fall apart. The runners, caps and ferrules are made of solid brass; the hand spring and top spring is nickel silver. The cover is cut, sewn and tied painstakingly to each rib. The shape (open) is domed (more room to get under it).

Swaine Adeney Brigg also makes riding whips, lunge whips, polo whips, hunting crops, seat sticks, walking sticks, even sword canes. Well, why not? They were established in 1750.

How long will the best umbrella last? I don't know. My Bentley friend told me about a man who bought a Bentley even older than his. It had 250,000 miles on it when he bought it. He's already driven it now an additional 127,000 miles.

The Swaine Adeney Brigg umbrella. Black, of course. Maple handle.

Price: $165. We pay shipping.

(Price upon request: Malacca Crook handle; Whangee Crook handle; Polished Chestnut handle; Furze Crook handle; Solid Hickory handle.)

The road not taken.

(Sleeves shown rolled.)

I always wanted to cross the Sahara, and the Gobi, by foot. But I didn't. I did not swim the Hellespont. Didn't ascend Mont Blanc. Didn't read all the books I had to read. Ached to fly a Ford tri-motor anywhere, even to St. Louis, but didn't. Did not modestly decline the Nobel Prize. Didn't spend even one night at Shepheard's Hotel in Cairo. Not one.

Shepheard's burned to the ground before I could afford to check in. That night, it became my code word for everything unobtained, undone.

In case there are a few things in your life you wanted but won't get, I offer as consolation The Impossibly-Perfect-Night-at-Shepheard's-Hotel-in-Cairo-Bathrobe.

Luxurious, thick, engulfing. Finer than any you have ever seen (as it should be). Discreet Shepheard's logo. All white cotton terry velour.

Sizes: S, M, L, XL, (unisex).

Price: $135. We pay shipping.

To order call toll free 800-231-7341

rush delivery $6.50. see p. 2.

for 606-268-2006 from Kentucky, Hawaii, Alaska, etc.) 8 A.M. to 10 P.M. (EST) weekdays and weekends.

The J. Peterman catalog uses illustrations instead of photographs to sell products whose features and benefits are enlivened by a very readable, narrative copy style. Reprinted with permission of the J. Peterman Company.

can be developed after studying catalogs, space ads, and other writing specimens you wish to emulate. In evaluating alternatives, ask yourself, "which method contributes most to the selling message of this catalog?"

- *Magalogs and advertorials*—Most catalog experts agree that the "magalog" concept seldom works in its purest form: a catalog that appears much like a magazine and just happens to sell products. But well-placed "advertorials"—short blurbs that enhance product appeal or establish the catalog's credibility in the marketplace—can prove well worth the space they require. Subjects of "advertorials" range from menus, party plans and recipes in food and tabletop catalogs to health tips in books aimed at the needs of the over-50 consumer. Some catalogs establish a "voice" who serves as expert spokesperson. For example, Elaine Adler represents Comfortably Yours as buyer and product tester. Copy is written in "me-to-you" style direct from Elaine. She and her staff are pictured in many "product in use" shots. The same is true of Orvis, where a telephone sales representative may show up modeling long underwear or hunting gear, and then appear again—smiling with telephone in hand—on the order form.

- *Type style and type size*—In general, serif type faces are easier to read in copy blocks. Their tiny "tails" and "fillips" are easier on the eyes than sans serif faces that are perfectly plain. Type faces can do a great deal to reinforce the theme and tone of a catalog: nostalgic and warm, contemporary, European or Oriental, classic or avante garde. Save exotic type faces for headings and choose a more recognizable, easy-to-read face for the main copy blocks. Type smaller than 8- point size is nearly impossible for general audiences to read comfortably. If your audience includes children, or if you are appealing to people over 50, try for 10-point type to enhance readability even more.

Producing the catalog

Once the page line-up and the style for the layout and copy have been approved, you may create the final, comprehensive layout. As the catalog design shapes up, make sure that one of your foremost goals is to make the catalog appealing and easy to use. Spreads should flow together in a pleasing whole, and such essentials as the order form, your return address, and your toll-free number should be easy to find.

The copy should expound on the product features and their related benefits. Diagrams, close-up shots, testimonials, and product-in-use ideas will all help "activate" your catalog and make your products seem real and desirable to the prospect.

When direct mail packages—consisting of letter, brochure, order form, etc.—are developed, the copy often is created before the layout. But in most cases, catalog copy is written to fit a completed layout, since space is often at a premium. This does not mean that the copywriter should not have input on copy space; on the contrary, it is best if the writer works directly with the art director to determine which products require more copy and which can be sold effectively with less.

Time was, most direct mail art directors would "spec" copy as a matter of course—telling their writers exactly how many characters would fit a space—or at least providing the number of lines per inch and the number of characters per pica. In many cases today it seems that copywriters must assert themselves to obtain this information. But it is essential that they do so. Good catalog copywriters perfect the skill of writing to the space allowed. Overwriting causes costly, time-wasting resetting of type.

Once the layout is finalized, photography may well be taking place at the same time copy is being written. Copywriters should resist the temptation to write strictly from product description sheets or inferior product shots provided by vendors. If at all possible they should visit the photography site or merchandisers' offices and spend time getting to know the products: trying on clothes, fondling fabrics, taste-testing foods, using electronic items, listening to stereos and finding out if the new VCR is really push-button easy to use.

This personal experience with the product is all the more important when a catalog contains hundreds of items that are extremely similar. Witness the experience of top direct mail consultant Judy Finerty, copywriter for the Nestle chocolate catalog. Judy would be hard-pressed to describe the difference between a semi-sweet Swiss and a semi-sweet French chocolate unless she had tasted them both, one right after the other!

Once photography and copy are complete, and art boards have been created, it is time to proofread and evaluate your work before it goes to the printer. When looking over your creative product, remember the principle of PPIPU: "perfectly plain if previously understood." Often you may become so close to a product and its presentation that you fail to notice essential missing visual or written elements—things a customer needs to know. To avoid this, have unbiased outsiders look over your photos and copy and ask them if anything seems confusing or would turn them off as prospective buyers.

In addition to proofing for typographical errors, make sure your merchandising staff and operations people have a chance for a final "once over." Have them sign off on item numbers, pricing, size ranges, color options and special offers. Make sure that such disclaimers as "battery not included" are made where necessary. Take time to match key letters with photographs one last time: it's amazing how many catalogs have confusing errors where copy "H" actually describes the item keyed "L."

Once you design and typeset your order form, have a number of people—both catalog "regulars" and people who seldom shop by mail—attempt to fill it out and tell you where the glitches are. The order form does not have to be strictly a learn-by-doing proposition: check the competition and some of the more established direct mail marketers to see how they handle such essentials as postage and handling, bill to/ship to arrangements, gift wrapping and enclosure cards, personalization, charge and credit options, etc.

Catalog enhancements

There are a number of ways to amplify the effectiveness of an established catalog. Here are some that have proven profit potential.

Find ways to boost average order size

If your catalog's average order size is $40.00, you are likely to be a great deal more profitable if you can boost that average order to $50.00, $60.00 or more. So why not try some promotional enhancements designed to produce add-on sales and profits? Ideas might include:

- Gift certificates that are good for x-dollars off, but only on purchases of x-dollars or more.
- Clubs for frequent buyers such as the Neiman-Marcus "Inner Circle." Buyers gain points for each Neiman-Marcus charge card purchase and may store them up over a period of a year to receive gifts ranging from a small box of chocolates to exotic trips around the world.
- Free gift with purchase. If you are trying to boost average order size above $50.00 for example, offer a free item of general appeal for orders over $50.00. Add on more free gifts at the $100.00 or $150.00 level as well.
- Discount for volume orders. Offer 10 percent off for orders over $100, for example.

■ Look for order starters and impulse add-on items. Boost average order size with an appealing extra: three monogrammed golf balls for $10.00 in a sporting goods catalog, perhaps, or a set of potholders and mitts for $8.99 in a kitchen and tabletop book.

Use catalog wraps for promotions and sale prices

The life of an expensive color catalog can be extended by adding various four-page outer "wraps." Such a wrap might introduce a new seasonal theme, offer special values, promote certain merchandise, or otherwise freshen and focus the mailing. This is an inexpensive way to make your catalog look new while adding a promotional flair.

Change covers and signatures for seasonal themes

To cut down on production costs yet keep your catalog fresh through repeated remailings to hot buyers, rearrange the signatures (sets of pages) to put seasonal items up front for each mailing. For a Labor Day mailing, a Halloween cover might be followed by Halloween and Thanksgiving merchandise, with general and Christmas items following. For a remail in mid-October, you might try a catalog wrap offering Halloween and Thanksgiving items on sale, followed by a full-color Christmas cover and a rearrangement of pages so that Christmas merchandise is up front.

Consider using a letter

Time was, many catalogs included a letter from the company president on the inside front cover. Nowadays, few firms seem willing to give up this prime space for that theme-setting letter. In recent years, many of these messages have appeared next to the order form. Richard Thalheimer of The Sharper Image has a different compromise—he uses page 4 for his letter and testimonials, thereby saving pages 2 and 3 to highlight the hottest product in the book. Another idea: add a letter to a catalog wrap, or place a separate letter on top of the catalog and shrink-wrap the two together for mailing. Eximious used this approach to attract last-minute holiday shoppers: a catalog mailing arriving around Thanksgiving included a letter listing cut-off dates for Christmas orders and delivery.

Ask for referrals

Use otherwise wasted space on the order form or back of the Business Reply Envelope to ask customers for names and addresses of friends who might enjoy your catalog. A standard wording is as follows:

Do you have a friend who might enjoy the (Name of Catalog) catalog? Please fill in name(s) and address(es) below.

Follow this with no more than three blanks for names and addresses. The first few referrals are usually the best.

How top catalog creative people stay fresh

As mentioned earlier in this chapter, the most stimulating part of the catalog creative person's job is positioning. The workaday job of laying out endless pages of products and writing tightly controlled blocks of formula copy can become deadly dull unless catalog writers and art directors keep themselves stimulated and fresh. Here are some pointers on how to do so.

Keep an eagle eye on the competition

Catalog creative people should become frequent catalog shoppers to ensure that they receive large numbers of catalogs from many product categories. Don't attempt to analyze each catalog the minute it hits your mailbox. Rather, take time once a week or so to sit down with your pile of catalogs and leaf through them just as a consumer would. If something strikes you as particularly unique or interesting, put that catalog in an active file for immediate inspiration. Most all catalogs should be kept for future reference: it's extremely helpful to have a backlog of catalogs filed by product category to make the research job easier when a new catalog project comes along.

Pay attention when ordering from catalogs

See how much you can learn from the experience of ordering and receiving merchandise via catalog. If you order by mail, which order forms seem easiest to use? Which method of collecting money for shipping and handling seems to make the most sense? Do the firms you order from let you know how soon products will be shipped? Do they live up to those promises? If you order by phone, how knowledgeable does the telephone salesperson seem? How pleasant? How efficient? How do various firms handle "specials of the day" by phone? Are there any other creative enhancements you could add to your catalog based on what you hear when ordering over the phone?

Stay in touch with the products

It's tempting to design and write catalogs based on specification sheets alone—after all, you can complete the job much faster that way. But there are features and benefits that can only be discovered when you touch and use the products for yourself. If a good catalog creative person is writing a spread on bath mats, you can bet his or her office is carpeted two or three mats deep with different colors, thicknesses and shapes. Clothing writers gain inspiration by wearing samples so they can better describe soft fabrics and comfortable fit. The hands-on concept is even more important where high-tech items are concerned: you have to understand the product's attributes in use to write about it effectively.

Make friends with the merchandisers

If you're stumped for inspiration, talk with the merchandising people who chose these items for the catalog. Ask them what makes this watch or clock or chenille robe better than all the other ones he or she might have chosen. Better yet, tag along when the merchandiser goes on a buying trip. There you'll have the benefit of sales pitches from the vendors as well.

Think like a consumer

For every single item, imagine the target market and figure out what a member of that target audience would want to see and learn regarding this product. If possible, show the products to target market members and get their reactions. What do they like and dislike? What questions do they have? What reservations?

You can play to their positive reactions and answer their objections in copy and art.

Pay attention to results

The best catalog creators are anxious to know the item-by-item results of each catalog that is mailed. Figuring out why item A lost sales when shown on a pink background instead of a yellow one, or why item B doubled in sales when it was shown in a product-in-use shot, will help keep your job fresh and challenging. Take an active role in space allocation based on previous results.

Don't remain in the "creative box"

It's sometimes tempting to stay in the artist's or copywriter's cubicle, treating the catalog creative function as something akin to assembly line work at an auto plant. But the creative contribution to a good catalog operation can involve much more: ideas to enhance customer service, merchandising, packaging, backorder systems and reminders, etc. Approach the catalog creative function as an overall *marketing* challenge, and it can be much more rewarding for you—and for the catalog's bottom line.

Special note:

The author wishes to thank Herb Krug, President of Herbert Krug & Associates, for his generosity in sharing many of these catalog creative concepts over the years.

BACK-END MARKETING

16

How much does your firm or client have to pay to turn a cold-list prospect into a customer? And what is the lifetime value of that new customer to the company? Most direct marketers expend considerable effort trying to shave the cost of bringing new customers onboard, but that's only part of the challenge. A carefully planned back-end marketing program can greatly improve your average customer's lifetime value to the firm while serving important customer service functions at the same time.

Back-end marketing is the direct marketing term for the important set of tactics used to convert, keep, trade-up, and resell customers once you have their names.

In nearly all direct marketing transactions, the initial customer relationship is expensive to develop. Indeed, sophisticated direct marketers seldom try to break even on the first transaction with a customer. They know that finding a good prospect costs money. Turning that prospect into a customer, and then convincing the customer to buy again and again, are the keys to maximizing ultimate profit. Direct marketers report that their best customer lists respond to offers at a rate five, six, or even ten times higher than that of cold-list prospects.

Many direct marketers have a great deal to learn in the area of back-end creative strategy. They put their greatest marketing minds to work establishing a solid relationship with the customer in their front-end promotions. Then, at the turning point, when the bargain is struck but the product not yet delivered, they make the mistake of turning the customer over to the "efficiency" of an operations department.

These marketers are like a wealthy suitor who wines and dines his lady love for months before proposing. Then, when she says yes, he tips his hat and rides off into the sunset alone, entrusting her to his valet as a stand-in for the wedding and the honeymoon!

In addition to the waste of identifying customers only to lose many of them before a second sale, consider the relatively small pool of potential customers available. The Direct Marketing Association reports that only 45 percent of American householders purchase items by mail. The DMA has launched an ongoing program to lure some of the other 55 percent to become regular direct mail buyers. DMA research shows that the key to converting more Americans to direct mail shopping lies in better treatment of prospects and customers.

The functions of back-end marketing

Considering these facts, the way a prospect or customer is handled on the back end is crucial. Yet in addition to pure customer service functions, back-end promotions can also be used to maximize selling opportunities and effectiveness. Here are some of the objectives of back-end marketing:

- To convert a lead into a buyer.
- To cut returns and reinforce wisdom of original purchases.
- To promote good will for the firm.
- To build long-term customer loyalty.
- To sell products with better profit margins than those sold by front-end marketing.
- To ensure continued sales to the new customer.
- To pay for necessary mailings, such as premium notices, by offering additional merchandise or services for sale.
- To collect funds owed or gain subscription renewals.

This chapter will put forth creative concepts and ideas to assist in fulfilling each of these objectives.

Converting leads into buyers

The objective of many front-end promotions is to obtain a lead for direct mail follow-up. These leads may come to you through space advertising, telephone solicitation, inquiries from publicity stories, unsolicited inquiries, or customer referrals in addition to direct mail.

A quick follow-up is essential, no matter what the source of the lead. The moment the potential customer acknowledges interest in your product or service, he or she begins to "cool off." If you don't answer the lead in good time, the potential customer may not even remember asking about your offer by the time your mailing arrives.

It is therefore imperative that you respond to a lead within a maximum of two weeks. If for some reason your formal conversion package is not ready on time, send your leads a "keep warm" letter. This should thank them and acknowledge their interest, give them a few teasers about the exciting information on the way, and let them know that the information they requested will be forthcoming soon.

Keep following up until a mailing's costs exceed its profits

The extent of your follow-up program should be determined by weighing the product's profit potential against the cost of continuing to promote it. If you are following up on a request for information on a $30.00 video cassette, the cost and effort you'll want to expend will be considerably less than if you are answering leads for a $3000 home entertainment center.

Many marketers try both one- and two-step programs on a given offer, to see which is more profitable in the long run. On the one-step approach, the marketer begins by sending a full-blown direct mail package to prospects, soliciting an immediate sale. On the two-step approach, the marketer might begin with a space ad or simple direct mail package, selling the "sizzle" of the product and inviting people to send for more information at no obligation. Then the full-blown package would be sent only to inquiries, modified slightly to acknowledge their stated interest in the product. These modifications might include:

1. An envelope teaser stating "Here is the information you requested."
2. A revised letter thanking the person for requesting the information before launching the sales pitch.

3. Special wording on other pieces of the mail package that the lead-generation piece may have referred to, such as a premium slip, special-offer order form, and so on.

If you are selling a high-ticket item—like the $3000 home entertainment center or an $800 correspondence school course—by means of a direct mail follow-up, one mailing package is generally not enough to maximize sales potential.

Let's take the example of the $3000 home entertainment center. You may well be able to spend hundreds of advertising dollars to convert just one sale on such an item, especially if you plan to follow up later with offers of accessories, video cassettes and compact discs, and other items with high margins. Thus, to stop after one follow-up package would be foolish. You can balance out the inexpensive sales you make on the first go-round with some harder-won sales generated by later efforts directed at the same qualified leads.

It is not advisable to simply remail the same package time and again to leads, hoping that they will eventually notice your mailing. Instead, come up with a series of mailings with varied appearances, appeals, and premium offers. You may save money through the use of standard components that you can print in quantity for use in several of the mailings. Exhibit 16.1 is an example of a possible campaign to convert leads.

Over a period of time spent selling items in a certain price/margin category, you will learn how many efforts you can make toward a list of qualified leads before the costs outweigh the rewards. Even after all of these mailings, you might follow up again with a telephone call to try to make the sale or at least find out why the customer is not responding. And if the customer does not end up purchasing this item, do not delete the name from your files. This may be a valuable potential customer for another offer you'll make in the near future.

A few additional points should be made about the conversion campaign above. The reason for four-week intervals between mailings is to allow for orders to return in the mail and be noted on your records before the next mailing goes out. Soliciting customers who have already responded is annoying to them, and costly for you. Initial mailings should go first class to make sure they are delivered promptly. To save money, later mailings in the conversion series can be sent third class.

Another way to structure a conversion campaign is the one preferred by many correspondence schools. They make sure that

---

EXHIBIT 16.1   Conversion campaign for home entertainment center

---

Standard Components Checklist

1. 9″ × 12″ decorated outer envelope
2. #10 decorated outer envelope
3. Basic selling letter
4. 8-1/2″ × 11″ color brochure which can be folded down for the #10 outer envelope
5. Premium slip
6. Order form
7. Business Reply Envelope

Extra Components Checklist

A. Testimonial letter
B. Letter from an orchestra conductor who has tested the home entertainment center
C. Extra premium slip
D. Last-chance slip
E. Telegram-format letter

Mailing	Timing	Contents	Mail class
#1	One week after receipt of lead	"Keep warm" letter with "sizzle" about package to come	First Class
#2	Two weeks after receipt of lead	1,3,4,5,6,7 (Outer envelope is stamped: Here is the Information You Requested)	First Class
#3	Six weeks after receipt of lead	2,A,4,5,6,7	Third Class
#4	Ten weeks after receipt of lead	1,B,4,5,6,7 (Outer envelope is stamped: Inside: A Note to You from Famous Conductor (his or her name))	Third Class
#5	Fourteen weeks after receipt of lead	2,3,4,5,6,7,C (Outer envelope is stamped: TWO Free Gifts: See Inside For Details; letter has a handwritten message about the extra premium)	Third Class
#6	Eighteen weeks after receipt of lead	2,E,4,5,6,7,D (Outer envelope is stamped: Last Chance!)	Third Class

---

the initial follow-up kit is loaded with all features and benefits that might appeal to the student: the glamour of the new career, or the chance to learn at home on one's own time schedule, for example. Then, each subsequent mailing highlights one benefit as the theme of its letter, supplemented by a brochure that covers all the positive points about the course.

To learn more about follow-up mailings, send inquiries to a wide range of firms making two-step consumer and business-to-business offers. Save all of the follow-ups you receive, dating them as they arrive. Then you will be able to reconstruct the creative approach and timing of various firms to spark ideas for your own efforts.

Reinforcing the original purchase

Put yourself in the place of your customer for a moment, and imagine that the product you ordered by mail has just been delivered to your home. Better than imagining, make sure that you order products from your own firm or clients on a regular basis, as well as from major competitors. In any case, when a package arrives you open it and find the product inside. There it is: the dress or baseball glove or decor item you ordered several weeks ago, all by itself, without the "sizzle" that was provided on the front end when you made the decision to buy it. This can be a letdown at a crucial moment when the customer needs reinforcement most.

The letdown doesn't have to occur if you, as the direct marketer, provide your customer with some materials to complement the purchase. You can do this for as little as 10 cents per package, although some marketers spend considerably more to reinforce high-ticket purchases. Here are some ideas on what you could include in the package to make customers feel good about their purchases on receipt.

1. *Restate the reasons for buying.* Include a short letter or promotional piece that retells the story of the product and reminds customers of all the features and benefits that convinced them to buy it in the first place.
2. *Restate the guarantee and other terms of the offer.* Remind customers of their opportunity to put the item to use before deciding whether to keep it.

3. *Testimonials.* Include a few quotes from satisfied customers, especially those who have reordered the product many times. Eash testimonial might discuss a different reason why the purchaser has found the product so useful, including ideas on various ways to put it to use.

4. *How-to-information in easy-to-use form.* Even if it seems completely obvious how to put the product to use, remember that your customer is not as familiar with it as you are. A few step-by-step instructions, even on a simple item, will move the customer to start using the product right away. If your item is more complex, how-to information is essential. Before writing these how-tos, of course, you must have a thorough understanding of the product in use. Once you have prepared the material, share the product and instructions with some people who fit your customer profile. See if they find them understandable and useable. If they are confused at any point, your instructions need modification.

5. *Certificates and other documents that customers can save.* This could be a Certificate of Authenticity for a limited-edition collectible, a warranty statement for an appliance, or a small flyer providing an interesting historical background on the product.

Creating goodwill/building long-term loyalty

The Direct Marketing Association has established a set of Recommended Practices for Customer Satisfaction, available through its headquarters at 6 East 43rd Street, New York, NY 10017. This booklet was the result of a four-year (1987–1990) industry-wide Consumer Acceptance program. It covers customers' expectations for order-taking and delivery, returns and cancellations, billing and payment, and customer service. These guidelines were considered necessary, especially in light of the fact that the DMA quotes Simmons research that indicates 37 percent of those Americans who bought by mail in a one-year period experienced customer service problems.

Many of these points fall under the heading of fulfillment and operations. But it is essential that any direct communication with customers carries a marketing orientation. Here are some examples of good-will activities you can carry on to reinforce the customer's positive impression on the back end.

1. *Acknowledge orders.* Unless your firm is one of the minority of direct marketers that can turn around shipments in less than a week, sending an immediate order acknowledgement by first-class mail is a move you should strongly consider. As simple as a postcard or elaborate enough to contain other offers, the acknowledgement eases customers' minds, letting them know that their purchases are on the way. If you can provide them with an estimated shipping time along with the acknowledgement, so much the better.
2. *Let customers know how to reach you.* Provide a specific customer service number and address. Don't make the customer who has a problem hunt too hard to find you. He or she can shop with plenty of other direct marketers who are highly accessible and responsive, and therefore you will also have to be. The ultimate in customer service is a toll-free 800 number for such calls. Land's End touts its 24-hour toll-free number and even suggests that customers call just to say "hi" in the middle of the night if they want to. Many marketers, however, find that it is much less costly to provide an 800 number for ordering only, and a regular, pay-call number for customer-service questions.
3. *Send a letter with each shipment.* The so-called ship letter provides a perfect opportunity to thank the customer for the purchase and avoid post-purchase letdown. If your database allows for it, the ship letter can also welcome brand-new customers, and thank seasoned customers for returning with another order.
4. *Send a welcome package.* In addition to the welcoming ship letter, some firms greet first-time customers with a special package that acquaints them with the product, the firm, and the benefits of buying in this way. The Hamilton Collection, a collectibles marketer, has sent new customers information on how to collect, what is collectible, how to decorate with collectibles, and other pertinent information. To help pay for the mailing, the "welcome kit" has contained buying opportunities for a collectibles book and for display devices.
5. *Give the customer a "thank you" gift, or discount.* With every order over $100.00, you might, as an example, provide a surprise thank-you gift tucked into the package with a note.

In keeping with its gentle, Victorian image, *Victoria* magazine sends new subscribers a welcome letter printed on what appears to be an old-fashioned lace doily. Reprinted with permission of Hearst Magazines D. R. Group.

Or include another offer in the package with a very special discount for preferred customers only. Some firms establish their personalities by providing something special or free with each order. Eximious, a catalog marketer of English products, offers elegant, navy-and-gold gift boxes or wrapping free of charge, all year 'round. A firm in maple syrup country might tuck in a small package of maple sugar candy with every order.

6. *Send a newsletter or other chatty correspondence.* Make the customer feel like a preferred member of your "family" with a newsletter in the product package announcing special offers or discounts for preferred customers only. This may be a great way to clear out small-inventory items and please your customers at the same time. Some firms, notably the Horchow Collection, send newsletters as separate mailings, containing both informative articles and product offers.

7. *Provide "preferred customers only" benefits.* These might include advance mailings when sales or special values are available; a special, extra-helpful telephone salesperson whom only your regular customers know is available; monthly discounts on various items available only to customers who are sent special coupons; quantity discounts; free gift wrapping; or some other "extra" that you offer and deliver only to persons on your present-customer list. Don't make the mistake of offering any of these extra services on the front end—at least not free or at the same discount your preferred people are getting. The service or item must be an exclusive, special-treatment one that makes customers want to continue being considered part of your firm's "inner circle."

8. *Make it simple to return goods.* Because clothing merchants traditionally have very high return rates, you might think they would shy away from telling customers directly how to send back unsatisfactory merchandise. But to get customers to buy something as personal as sized clothing by mail, it is essential that they feel no obligation to keep an unsatisfactory item. Thus, sellers of clothes have learned to make it easy for their customers to make a return or exchange. They may include a return-shipment label in the package or offer a step-by-step guide to returning the item. A simple form for the customer to fill out will also help, and enable you to find out the customer's reason for returning the item, which is valuable market research information.

9. *Send a thank-you note at year's end.* Thanks are appreciated any time of year, but a letter to preferred customers on an annual basis is a nice gesture. If you can computerize the letter so that it mentions items the customer purchased, so much the better. If you're a smaller firm, you might be able to do this without computerization. A thank-you gift for customers at certain purchase levels is a nice gesture, too.

TIME

The Big Picture

Your Personal Guide to TIME Magazine, Subscriber Services and Benefits

"TIME is interested not in how much it includes between its covers but in how much it gets off its pages into the minds of its readers."

—Henry Luce and Briton Hadden
Prospectus for TIME, 1922

Welcome to TIME

While the world has changed since TIME Magazine's founders created the first weekly newsmagazine, the main purpose *behind* the magazine hasn't.

TIME Magazine's mission is to provide its readers with the relevant information, analysis and meaningful insights they need to understand what's happening in our world today. And ultimately our success is measured by our ability to get intelligent people like you thinking about what we print—and then coming to your own conclusions.

Our commitment to you is total. That's why we've created this guide. It will help you get the most satisfaction and enjoyment out of your subscription to TIME Magazine.

I'd like to encourage you to take a few moments right now to familiarize yourself with some of the important features of the world's foremost newsmagazine, as well as the benefits you receive as a TIME subscriber. I also want you to know how delighted we are to count you among our family of TIME subscribers.

Thank you for making time for TIME. We look forward to having you as a reader for many years to come.

Louis A. Weil III
Publisher

The Magazine

The news source that puts it all together for you.

These days, intelligent readers like you need more than the newspaper headlines and sound bites of TV news to make sense of our increasingly complex world. You need TIME Magazine.

Week after week, TIME helps you understand not only what's happening but why—and how it affects your life. Regardless of how much or how little time you spend with our magazine each week, you'll get a perspective on the news no other source can provide. Because no other newsmagazine dedicates more people, energy or resources to bring you the information you need to understand and make sense of the world today.

With TIME's 191 correspondents in 33 news-bureaus throughout the world, you'll enjoy a "you are there" point of view. Pictured below are just a few of the many individuals who contribute to producing our magazine and make sure you get the quality you deserve. No doubt you'll grow to recognize their names and others as they contribute to your weekly enjoyment of lively reading.

It's not enough to report the news. At TIME we are committed to providing you with information in a manageable form and presenting the issues from a meaningful viewpoint. From Indiana to India or New Zealand to New London, TIME connects you worldwide to the important issues of today and the future headlines of tomorrow.

Strobe Talbott
Editor-at-Large

Hugh Sidey
Washington
Contributing Editor

Cathy Booth
Rome Bureau Chief

Jack White
Senior Editor
Nation

Lance Morrow
Senior Writer
Essays

Robert Hughes
Senior Writer
Art

John Kohan
Moscow Bureau Chief

Cover Story

The week's most newsworthy topic—the hottest event of national or international concern and the inside story behind the news.

Information Overload. It's a common complaint of almost everyone today. And TIME Magazine is perfect for people like you who can't take the time to sift through everything you need to know and still be well-informed.

Here's a sample of sections in TIME that shows you the range of exciting and informative coverage.

you'll come to depend upon week after week.

It's more than just the facts. You'll enjoy detailed, easy-to-read graphic representations and breathtaking photographs, as well as insightful commentaries that are critical to your in-depth understanding of the world around you.

Nation

Each week TIME takes you behind major national events and shows you the bigger issues.

Interview

Exclusive one-on-one sessions with the world's most fascinating people. Here's your opportunity to get to know remarkable people in an intimate light.

People

One of our most popular sections that's pure fun. Here's a delightful peek at the rich and famous, hot newcomers and controversial characters in the news.

Medicine/Science/Technology

The latest breakthroughs in these fields and what they mean to your future. Explore the changes, benefits and possible dangers.

Travel

An insider's guide that takes you around the world to exotic retreats, exclusive resorts and heavenly hideaways. Invaluable inspiration for the adventurer in all of us.

New subscribers to *Time* receive this fold-out piece which re-sells the magazine and provides all the information a subscriber needs to know about customer service. Reprinted with permission of *Time* magazine.

The Hamilton Collection sent new customers a welcome by means of this Collector's Information Kit, including *The Successful Collector*© newsletter, customer service facts, information on purchasing collectibles displays and books, and more. Reprinted with permission of The Hamilton Collection.

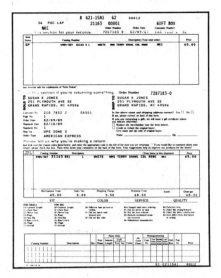

Lands' End makes it easy for customers to return merchandise that is not exactly right by enclosing this envelope and form with purchases. Reprinted with permission of Lands' End, Inc.

Achieving better margins on sales

Because many direct marketers invest money to gain a new customer on the front end, actually going into the red on the first sale, it is essential that their back-end efforts yield a profit from that customer as soon as possible. This can be achieved via back-end efforts in a number of productive ways. Here are several.

1. *Sell an accessory.* Nothing could be more appealing to the proud owner of a new product than something that is custom-made to enhance that prized possession. A personal-sized stereo radio with headphones might come with a "ride-along" offer of small speakers to go with it. A red leather purse might be packaged along with an invitation to acquire a matching wallet and key holder. Or how about a protective cover, custom-made to fit the new fax machine or personal computer? Such items can sell well even at hefty margins, and the profit is all the better since the offer is riding along for free with the shipment of the original purchase.

2. *Sell more, or sell better-quality items.* This tactic works best on items that are in need of quick replacement or replenishment. For instance, when you send the invoice for a magazine subscription, you can offer customers a bargain rate if they will pay for two years right away instead of just one. If you're delivering custom stationery, offer the customer a special deal on a larger quantity reorder, or a better-quality item.

3. *Send along package inserts.* Even if you offer customers something totally unrelated to the item they bought, you stand to do well if this second item is appealing to the same target market. When you have just delivered the main item the customer wanted, the timing and atmosphere for selling a second time are ideal. The customer has a good feeling about your firm, and now trusts you to deliver what you promise. Selling items of your own is one way to take advantage of this opportunity, but you may also consider allowing other direct marketers to buy package insert space in your shipments on a per-thousand or per-sale basis. It is essential, however, that you screen the package inserts that will ride along with your mailings to ensure that they are not competitive with your product line, and that they are in keeping with the image of your firm. If you sell $500 ladies' dresses, for instance, you would not want to allow a package insert for $19.99 lime green polyester slacks.

4. *Ask for referrals.* Getting a referral from a current customer won't help the margin you make on sales to him or her, but it may gain you a new customer very inexpensively. Your customers' friends are likely to be good prospects for you as well, since they probably share the same interests and socioeconomic level. Indeed, you might offer your current customers an incentive for referring potential new customers, the so-called member-get-a-member plan. Record and book clubs give free merchandise to members who deliver friends or relatives as new, paying customers. Frequent flyer programs provide bonus miles to their plan members who do the same. Other firms with unique product lines are able to succeed using a low-key approach, not offering any incentive other than the opportunity to share a good buying source with a like-minded friend.

Ensuring continued sales

After the sale and delivery of a first package to a customer, you'll need a way to keep up communications and sales with the customer. You'll want to set up a schedule of mailings to the customers on your list to keep your name on their minds and—more importantly—to keep bringing in more and bigger sales from them.

The more complete the information you can record on your data base, the better a job you can do at targeting future promotions to individual customers. Send high-ticket offers to high-ticket buyers, for instance, and book offers to previous book buyers. Within these categories, high-ticket jewelry buyers might be broken down into those who prefer sapphires, amethysts, or rubies. Book buyers might be categorized as those who enjoy romance novels, the classics, or history texts.

Ever since Maxwell Sackheim and Harry Schermann started their Little Leather Library and Book-of-the-Month Club, direct marketers have been ensuring continued response by means of a front-end offer that helps win guaranteed sales on a continuing basis. Here are some front-end offers you can make to improve the chances of regular, continuing sales from new customers.

Continuity series

Offer the first of a series of books, records, collector's plates, food items, or how-to lessons on a front-end basis, with the promise of more to come in future mailings. You'll find that obligating customers to buy a number of items later on will probably cut the percentage of your original responses, but will also help avoid attrition as the program continues.

Testing will help you determine whether a tight or loose continuity pitch brings you the most net dollars over the life of the program. A tight continuity offer would explain very specifically to customers that they are expected to purchase x-number of items over a given period of time. A looser pitch would tell them of the existence of the additional items, but give them the option of continuing or not as they please. Loosest of all is the offer that sells the first item only, then approaches the customer with the news that there are more items in a series that they may acquire if they so choose.

If you want to gain the greatest possible number of new customers but still have a continuity series over which to spread your cost of customer acquisition, try a loose front-end sale followed by a load-up offer, or a strong follow-up or "efforting" program on the back end.

The load-up offer

This comes after the customer has received the book, record, or other item he or she originally ordered. You offer the customer the opportunity to receive *all* of the books, records, or whatever you're selling in the series, but to pay for them in convenient monthly installments over a given period of time. This cuts your shipping costs, because you'll send all of the remaining items in a single shipment. If you opt for this system, provide your customers with a coupon book so that they can make their monthly payments easily, or send them a monthly invoice/reminder. Also, test the offer to make sure you aren't stuck with too many uncollectible accounts.

The efforting program

This is another way to bring in additional sales from customers who were offered products on a continuity basis but with no obligation to buy. This is usually a multi-step correspondence plan. Here is how a typical efforting program might work:

1. With the original shipment, send the customer a selling letter, a small brochure with a picture of the next product, and an ordering device.
2. After four weeks, mail again to those who have not ordered the product. Send a different letter, the same or different brochure or picture, and once again an ordering device.
3. After four more weeks, send a more urgent message to those who have not yet responded. A telegram format with a "last chance" order form is one idea.

The number of mailings in your efforting program will depend on their relative effectiveness and the price of the item you are selling. A high-ticket, high mark-up item may still yield acceptable results with a fourth or even a fifth effort, while a low-end product may merit only one or two efforts.

Negative option

Many book and record clubs are run on a negative-option basis: customers agree to receive the monthly selection unless they make the effort to return a card with an alternate purchase, or direct the club to send nothing at all that month. This is a proven way to gain new customers and make them profitable over a given period. Customers are brought in under a "Four Books for $1" type of offer, with the direct marketer making an investment to gain the customer's name and his or her promise to make at least a minimum of future purchases. The customer agrees to buy x-number of books, records, or other merchandise over a given period and also has the option to buy a number of other items via monthly mailings. The key here is to learn by testing how loose or tight the front-end offer must be to yield enough customers, at acceptable sales per customer, in the long run.

Positive option

The positive-option program works exactly the same as negative option, except that the customer will receive no shipment unless he/she returns a card or makes a phone call to initiate it.

Ship 'til forbid

This is the ultimate in a continuity series: the customer gives the direct marketer the right to continue shipping products on a monthly, bimonthly or other basis unless the customer expressly tells the marketer to cease. This can be a smooth way of obtaining nearly guaranteed sales, especially if customers provide their charge-card numbers so that the marketer simply ships the product at regular intervals and puts the charge on the customer's account.

Another option is to ship the item with an invoice enclosed or sent separately, but here the marketer must keep careful records to make sure an acceptable number of items is paid for before additional shipments are made.

In the case of all of these offers for ensuring continued sales, it is important to make sure that the offer and follow-up sales information are worded according to legal requirements as well as sales requirements. The services of an experienced direct mail copywriter, followed by a careful reading by a lawyer with experience in direct mail, will avoid problems later.

Pay for necessary mailings with ride-along offers

Retailers are masters of the ride-along offer, sending stuffers as well as return envelopes with selling messages and tear-off coupons—called "bangtails"—with most every monthly statement to customers. Whenever you send an invoice or other communication to a customer, why not take a cue from the retailers and include some type of offer to help pay for the mailing?

The premium-due notices of insurance companies, for instance, often include stuffers offering information about other policies. An invoice on a continuity program could have a brochure of seasonal merchandise "riding along" with it. Customer-service notices, order acknowledgements, and other correspondence often allow space for a selling message within the one-ounce limit for the lowest rate on first-class mail.

Collection letters for overdue accounts

A well-written series of collection letters is a necessity for many direct marketers who send out merchandise before it is paid for. This back-end function is often neglected, put off, or given half-attention, when it can be taken care of very simply.

Keep in mind that the function of a collection letter is quite different from the function of a selling or efforting letter. In the case of collections, the customer has already committed to the product. You need not sell him or her on the product, but only on the concept of paying for it.

Begin with an invoice and a "thank you for ordering" letter. Restatement of benefits is appropriate here, to reinforce the wisdom of the purchase decision and smooth the way to a payment.

Four weeks later, begin your collection series to those who have not paid. Start with a gentle reminder. Then in subsequent efforts, become a bit more urgent and terse with each letter, using your treasurer or accountant as the signer. Depending upon the dollar amounts involved, your collection series might range from two letters to six or more. In the final letter, take a "last chance" tone and note that you will be forced to turn the matter over to a collection agency if you do not receive payment immediately.

At this point, *do* turn deliquent accounts over to a good collection agency. It is not wise for your firm or client to write harsh or threatening letters to customers who may once again become valued buyers at a later date.

For specific pointers and model letters for a collection series, check one of the standard business-letter reference books.

Gaining renewals for periodicals and clubs

The big money in selling periodicals and club concepts by direct mail is in the renewals. The $12.00 or $25.00 paid the first time around is unlikely to cover both the cost of obtaining the name of a customer and a year's order-fulfillment activities. For each additional year for which the customer can be persuaded to remain a reader or club member, the profit of dealing with him or her improves. Thus it is worthwhile to prepare and implement an aggressive subscription- or membership-renewal program—one with four, six, or even eight steps in all.

Most renewal series begin several months before the renewal date, with a special incentive for renewing early. This might be a discount, a premium, or several free issues of a publication. On the other hand, some marketers hold off on special offers until later in a series because they have found that a good percentage of their customers will respond to a straight offer right away. The marketer can therefore save the more costly offers for the purpose of convincing the less eager segments of their customer lists to respond.

Over the series of mailings, a number of formats may be used. Here are several ideas.

- A simple, double postcard with a tear-off half for the customer to return by business reply mail. All the customer then has to do is check off "Yes," and he or she will be billed for the subscription or membership.
- A telegram-type letter warning that the customer may lose valuable issues or membership benefits unless he or she responds in time.
- A traditional envelope mailing with a feature/benefit letter touting the exciting, specific events and articles coming up for those who renew. This mailing might also include a brochure, premium slip, and reply card.
- A contest offer, giving those who respond either "Yes" or "No" an equal opportunity to win. (Human nature tells the customer that he'll have a better chance of winning if he says "Yes," even though by law that isn't the case.)
- An "action device" tipped onto the letter, such as a sticker that looks like the cover of the magazine, to be transferred to the order form and sent back with the order.
- For membership pitches, a temporary membership card which the customer can keep until the permanent card is sent after the customer sends in the renewal.

A direct marketing creative consultant with a wealth of experience in subscription renewals, Joan Throckmorton, devotes an excellent section of her book, *Winning Direct Response Advertising,* to this topic. It is recommended to those who find themselves planning a subscription campaign for the first time.

Many careers begin in back-end marketing

Because back-end functions can be repetitive and low-budget, most agencies and companies assign their newer and younger creative staffers to these essential support functions. Such an assignment provides a golden opportunity for direct marketers to learn the essential skill of converting prospects into buyers, and nurturing them toward a profitable, long-term relationship with the firm as satisfied repeat customers.

BROADCAST DIRECT MARKETING

17

The star power and the glamour of television and radio sometimes have a seductive effect on direct marketing creative types. We may envy our general advertising counterparts their chances to develop trendy spots for soft drinks—starring the "hot" celebrity of the year and utilizing Top 40 hits for background music. We may compare our stay-put desk jobs to the round-the-world location shoots of American Express TV ads. And if by chance we are recruited to create a direct response TV spot, we may well find ourselves constrained by a low five-figure production budget and a very basic "stand-up announcer" format!

The reality of direct response broadcast advertising is that every spot must pay its own way, just as direct mail packages, catalogs and telemarketing campaigns do. And while general agencies seek awards for their "creative" (read entertaining and/or funny) television spots, direct marketers reap *rewards* for themselves and their clients through the more concrete and enduring measures of sales and profits.

The fact is that today only a small fraction of direct marketing companies utilize broadcast advertising. Television's barriers to entry are enormous: even a minimal test—including production and time buys—costs $100,000 or more. Radio suits the needs of even fewer direct marketers for several reasons: its lack of visual presentation, the limited coverage area of most stations, and the fact that many radio listeners use the medium mainly as background noise.

Even so, there are a number of prominent direct marketers with the right products and enough financial clout to use television cost-effectively. Firms such as Time-Life, Sears, International Correspondence Schools and The Bradford Exchange promote their products for direct sale via television—or solicit leads to be followed up by mail, phone or personal sales call. Other companies, including Publisher's Clearing House, Reader's Digest, and various insurance firms, have used television as a support medium to enhance their direct marketing efforts in print.

In addition, cable television makes direct response broadcast advertising a viable option for more firms each year. Cable beams superstations like WTBS in Atlanta, WOR in New York and WGN in Chicago to homes across the country at reasonable rates. Home shopping channels provide direct marketers with a low-risk way to see their products sold on television. Segmented viewing opportunities increase with every specialty channel that hits the airwaves. And efforts now underway may soon open up buying opportunities via interactive television for every American home with a cable TV hook-up and a touch-tone telephone.

Direct-response radio also holds considerable potential for some products and services, particularly those in the executive and business-to-business realms that can be sold via all-news stations and networks, and through other radio formats that encourage listener involvement.

Thus with present and future prospects in mind, even those direct marketing creative people who have not yet had occasion to do broadcast work will want to soak up as much background knowledge as they can. This chapter provides some basics. For those who want or need to know more, check the books and articles of top direct marketing broadcast "pros" including Alvin Eicoff, John Witek, Shan Ellentuck and James R. Springer. *Eicoff on Broadcast Direct Marketing* is especially valuable for its historical perspective as well as its specific, how-to advice and "firing line" examples. And just as important: take time to watch and evaluate the better direct response spots you discover on TV and radio. In this way, soaking up the techniques of the masters can be enjoyable as well as instructive.

Direct versus general broadcast spots: What is different?

Action versus image

There is one basic difference that sets all direct advertising apart from all general advertising. Like print advertising, TV and radio spots may solicit a purchase, a request for information, or some other measurable action. More often, however, broadcast spots are strictly image builders—designed to create awareness, interest or desire on the part of the consumer, but stopping short of asking for the order. A direct response spot always includes a call to specific action, asking the prospect to respond by mail or phone.

Length

A direct response spot must convince the prospect to act, so in most cases it requires more time than an "image-only" spot. While the length of general ads on TV and radio has shrunk over the years from 60 seconds to 30, 20, 15 or even 10 seconds apiece, the majority of direct response spots still require 60 to 120 seconds to get their message across and close the sale.

Forty years ago, pioneers in direct response television advertising had the luxury of presenting their commercials in the form of 15- or 30-minute "shows." These pitches were written up in the TV listings as regular programming. Today, one of the star attractions at direct marketing seminars is often the showing of one of these early spots, most notably the original Vitamix commercial. Working without a script, a master salesman demonstrates this versatile product while explaining how Americans need the nutrition of fresh vegetables. In those days the TV commercials may well have been more interesting and involving than the programs. Television time was affordable, and there were no restrictions on how much advertising could be shown per hour of programming. Today's costs and program formats make two minutes the longest feasible commercial length with some notable exceptions: full-length infomercials selling sunglasses, anti-cellulite creams and many other products have appeared once again on TV in recent years.

Production values

In the early days of direct-response television, most commercials resembled an in-home version of the carnival pitchman doing his sales presentation from behind a simple table or desk. For decades, most direct response spots were made according to a few predictable formulas because they had been proven to work—and they were inexpensive and risk free. Cooking utensils were presented using hard-sell kitchen counter demonstrations. Ads for records and tapes featured "sound bites" of the various tines combined with an on-screen "roll" that showed the name of every song. Insurance companies invited inquiries by showcasing a celebrity spokesman perched in a book-lined office.

Current research shows that the predictable forms and relatively low production values of direct response commercials hurt their credibility with an important segment of the potential audience. And thus, in order to expand the customer base and add some positive image-building to their direct response ventures, many firms have upgraded the quality of their TV productions in recent years.

It is important, however, to differentiate between higher quality production and adoption of general advertising techniques. Direct response advertisers must remember to focus squarely on the product—to make the product the star. They must guard against using the quick cuts, cluttered backgrounds, humorous asides and flashy techniques that general advertisers consider their stock in trade. These "borrowed attention" devices may be all well and good for image advertisers, but they muddy the waters when a spot is expected to complete a sale in two minutes or less.

In addition, some direct response advertisers may carry their image-building efforts so far that they disqualify their most eligible customers. Middle America does not relate to model-perfect spokespeople wearing designer clothes—especially when they're supposed to be selling a $9.95 kitchen gadget. Real people presented in everyday surroundings can help to maximize the prospect's level of comfort.

What to sell in direct response TV spots

Products that shine in demonstration

Television's prime benefit is that it provides an ideal medium for demonstration. Remember the classic Vegamatic commercials that showed how fruits and vegetables could be sliced, diced, and chopped, all in the wink of an eye? If your product comes alive when shown in use, television may well be a viable medium for you to explore.

Products with wide appeal

Most television advertising time is sold to mass marketers of toothpaste, laundry detergent, soft drinks and other products that almost everyone needs or wants. Kitchen-related products like the Vegamatic or Vitamix appeal to a wide range of people, as do insurance offers, Christmas records, home study courses, and diet plans. If you intend to advertise on the general TV networks, make sure your product is of near universal interest or audience waste will ensure your efforts are not cost effective.

Products appealing to reachable and sizeable market segments

Cable television and syndication now allow for more effective market segmentation than could be achieved in the past. Record clubs, for example, might air ads for country albums on the Nashville Network, or a pitch for a rock album during "Dance Party U.S.A." Sports products and magazines find a natural audience on ESPN, while exercise videos may be pitched effectively during a fitness-related show on Lifetime.

Products already proven in traditional direct response media

Since television is such an expensive medium to test, many direct marketers reserve it for certain exceptional products only. The Franklin Mint, for instance, advertises only a handful of its most successful general-interest collectible products on television— those few that have potential for sales and new customer acquisition that make them worth the up-front cost of television production and time buys. Most of the firm's offerings show up only in magazines and direct mail.

Products with an acceptable price range

You will notice that most products sold directly on television are in the $9.95 to $29.95 range. This is the "comfort level" for most consumers. If you ask more than this for a product on TV you run the risk of eliminating a big part of your audience. You may lose

EXCELSIOR FITNESS EQUIPMENT CO.

SCHWINN AIR—DYNE

EAD-3-60
60 SECONDS

Americans are into fitness -- like never before we realize how vital exercise is to our good health.

And now, Schwinn -- the great American Bicycle Company, proudly presents ...

The Schwinn Air-Dyne ... the state-of-the-art in <u>total</u> body exercise.

It's not just a stationary bicycle ... it's the <u>only</u> exercise bicycle with these <u>exclusive</u> arms that move along with the foot pedals.

Use it for the lower body ... to trim and tone.

The entire body ... for maximum aerobics benefits.

The upper body ... to build and strengthen ...

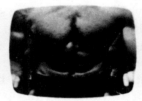
to keep your stomach in shape.

To firm the whole torso.

The Air-Dyne's <u>exclusive</u> wind vane system displaces the air as you exercise -- the faster you pedal, the more you build strength, stamina and vitality.

And, the Air-Dyne has this <u>unique</u> work load indicator ... electronic digital timer ... plus a large, deluxe saddle.

**Available at
ABC Schwinn Cyclery
1234 Main Street
Anywhere, USA
PHONE: 666-6666**

The Air-Dyne is available fully assembled, ready to ride at ABC Schwinn Cyclery 1234 Main Street Anywhere, USA Phone 666-6666

This spot shows how television allows for excellent demonstration of a product, in this case, the Schwinn Air-Dyne exercise bicycle. This storyboard has been set up with still frames from the actual spot, keyed to the appropriate words from the script. Reprinted with permission of Schwinn Bicycle Company.

them for economic reasons, or because their level of trust is such that they won't lay out more than x-dollars for a product they have not yet held in their hands.

However, you may use a two-step process to sell higher-priced items via TV: obtaining leads from your TV ad and then following them up by phone, mail or personal sales call. International Correspondence Schools is one firm using this technique to good effect: their free offer is a thick packet of information on any one of their learn-at-home plans (costing $600 or more) to prospects who call their toll-free number.

Tips for creating direct response TV spots

Get comfortable with the medium

Writers and art directors who have spent most of their careers creating work for the print medium will have to switch gears to be successful in developing television spots. The time constraints of television are difficult to handle at first: it's a real challenge to compact a selling message into 60, 90 or 120 seconds, especially when 20 to 30 seconds of this time must be devoted to ordering instructions. Repetition is a must, both for the call to action and the ordering information, including telephone number and/or address, price of the product, and other essentials.

Just as direct mail creative types often begin the creative process by immersing themselves in their "swipe files," it's an excellent idea to put together your own cassette of top-notch television spots, taped right off the air and spliced together. Watch them over and over to get acquainted with the techniques and rhythms they represent. See how video enhances audio and vice versa. Divide each spot into sections and note how many seconds are spent setting up the situation or problem . . . introducing the product or solution . . . explaining the benefits . . . closing the sale . . . discussing the guarantee . . . giving ordering instructions.

Consider the classic TV direct response formats

Although you are not limited to these typical formats, one may provide the push you need to get some words and pictures onto your blank page.

■ *Problem/solution*—Many general-interest products sold via direct response television solve a common household or personal problem: drudgery of housework, excess weight gain, need to quit smoking, desire to make more money, etc. The TV spot must grab the prospect's attention and hook him or her into the pitch.

A TV ad for International Correspondence Schools did this by setting up the problem of lack of money—and the solution of home study. The ad featured an attractive, young-to-middle-aged woman announcer sitting behind a desk. She began by saying,

> Do you want to make more money? Of course, we all do! And now at home in your spare time, you can train for a rewarding career in . . .

The announcer went on to tell how prospects could use their extra time to earn a certificate in anything from interior decorating to accounting. To find out more, they simply call a free number for more information.

■ *Product demonstration*—Watch the super-sharp knife cut a tomato into 20 perfect slices in a matter of seconds. See the tarnished silverware emerge from the Tarn-X dip looking better than new. Observe as the handy knitting device pops out tubes and circles of yarn in a matter of seconds, ready to make into hats, scarves and art projects. If you have a product that looks like fun to use or makes a hard job seem easy, focus your spot on the product in use, and back up your video with an audio track that reinforces product benefits.

■ *Parallel structure*—To emphasize the superior performance or quickness of your product in use, you may consider using a split-screen technique, or a format in which you switch back and forth between the "old way" and the "new way" of doing something. For instance, an ad might show a homemaker struggling to chop vegetables the old-fashioned way on the left side of the screen, and her counterpart on the right chopping a whole carrot in one motion with your slicer product. This technique can also help showcase a before-and-after scenario that has worked well for decades in selling weight-loss products.

■ *Testimonial*—Also effective for weight-loss products is the on-screen testimonial, where a satisfied customer tells the specific benefits of the product (such as a 50-lb. weight loss) and also the side-benefits (better social life, spouse's renewed interest, better self-image, etc.). Another interesting testimonial technique is that used by *Sports Illustrated* for a preholiday subscription drive. Women explained how buying *SI* subscriptions cut down on the hassle of holiday shopping, and ensured that all the men on their list would be pleased with the magazine as well as the premium, a special video cassette. Using the women personalized the offer, and helped target the pitch to a specialty audience—*SI* gift-givers rather than the sports enthusiasts themselves.

- *Celebrity spokesperson*—If you are selling a parity product, one way to separate it from its competitors in the mind of the television viewer is to associate the product with a respected celebrity. That's why Art Linkletter, Ed McMahon and other well-known pitchmen are called upon to sell everything from sweepstakes entry to insurance via TV direct-response ads. Selecting the right celebrity is crucial, and may well involve intensive market research to determine which individual has the right combination of recognition, comfort level and respect among your target audience.

  A few words of advice on choosing your spokesperson. First, resist the urge to hire the celebrity you and your team admire most: your personal perceptions are irrelevant. Second, insist that the product remains the star in all your efforts. Focus the ad on the product's benefits and use your celebrity as an enhancement to the product. Too many ads expect the product to ride on the coattails of the celebrity's sparkling personality. Third, test your ad concept with and without the celebrity spokesperson if possible. You may well find that the same pitch delivered by a top-notch (and much less expensive) television announcer may yield you just as many sales or inquiries. That's why it's important to negotiate your celebrity contract with staged fees for testing and roll-out: don't obligate yourself to pay high talent fees for your entire campaign until you've had time to read results on your initial test.

- *Slice of life*—Although this technique is used more frequently in general advertising than it is in direct-response TV, there have been successful examples. For instance, a Fingerhut ad selling towels revolved around the interaction of a husband and wife. The premise was that this family never seemed to have matched sets of towels—and the husband, especially, thought that having matching towels would be a

great idea. Presented with gentle humor, the spot showed actors clothed to represent lower-middle to middle-class Americans. It offered a more human approach to selling an inexpensive towel set—as opposed to the traditional method of
stacking up towels on a table with audio saying, "And that's
not all—you get these matching fingertip towels too, all for
the same low price of . . ."

- *Wrap-around*—Magazine and book marketers—notably
Time-Life—have used the wrap-around technique to humanize their ads and grab attention from the audience before the
selling pitch begins. A wrap-around spot begins by showing
an operator who's ready to take calls at the toll-free number.
She says something to this effect:

> Hi, I'm Judy from Time-Life Books. Today we're offering out-
> standing savings on one of our best books, so stay tuned.

Next, a traditional spot for a Time-Life book begins, including
ordering information and an initial close of the sale. Finally,
Judy returns to repeat the offer and its terms, talk about the
premium, and repeat the phone number several times.

    The operator's appearance does several things. First, it
gets the audience's attention by previewing what's coming
up. Second, it makes the concept of ordering by phone more
attractive, since customers know they'll be talking to an appealing and pleasant person like Judy—they can visualize
her. Third, when Judy reappears, she can repeat the offer and
its terms quite naturally. This cuts down the annoyance of
necessary repetition, which would be more noticeable and
objectionable if done by the same announcer twice. Fourth,
the wrap-around technique allows for easy testing of premium offers—and changes of telephone numbers and other
specifics—rather than incorporating them in the more expensive "meat" of the presentation.

- *Romance the benefits*—Some products are difficult to demonstrate on television—but creative people can come up with
exciting ways to bring them across on videotape or film. Holding up a magazine and talking about its feature articles won't
inspire much enthusiasm, for example. But why not try a
fast-paced montage of the best photos in recent issues,
backed up by music that appeals to the magazine's target
market, and enticing audio asking the provocative questions
that these articles answered? A book on the Civil War may

sound dry, but it can come alive on film if a skilled camera-man pans slowly across its illustrated pages and an announcer sets the tone with a dramatic statement about how the war changed the face of America forever. For a travel magazine, a spot with sufficient budget could show readers enjoying what they've learned: eating at an out-of-the-way bistro, shopping in a little-known section of town, getting a first-class airline seat for a coach fare.

Structure the spot to make a sale

With no more than 120 seconds in which to sell your product or service, a highly structured format is essential. Every second should be focused on selling, yet the consumer must not feel pressured or coerced. In his book, *Al Eicoff on Broadcast Direct Marketing,* Al Eicoff suggests a general structure for a direct response TV spot, inspired by the technique of the old-time pitchmen:

The anatomy of a sales presentation
1. Holder
2. Problem
3. Product Presentation
4. Solution
5. Turn
6. Guarantee

What Eicoff terms the "holder" could also be called a promise—either of a free gift, an exciting offer, a miraculous performance, or something new. Many spots are not presented in the strict problem-solution format, and thus the writer may spend more time on the product presentation. Eicoff's "turn" could also be called the move toward the close: the seller tells the price and terms, emphasizes premiums or other incentives, and calls for action. Discussing the guarantee at this point helps eliminate buyer resistance and leads into the final close.

A simpler and more general formula for a direct response spot is this, played out with examples from the International Correspondence Schools (ICS) ad mentioned previously.

1. *Attract the attention of the target group.*
   Example: "Do you want to make more money? Of course, we all do!"

2. *Promise them something they want.*
   Example: "And now at home, in your spare time, you can train for a rewarding career in . . . (various fields)."

3. *Support the promise.*
   Example: The ICS ad tells how thousands of men and women have learned new and valuable skills "without ever setting foot inside a classroom." It goes on to list the various courses of study—everything from TV repair to interior decorating.

4. *Pitch the offer.*
   Example: In this case, the offer is free facts for calling a toll-free number. In the case of a sales pitch, the offer would include premiums, guarantees, price and terms.

5. *Call to action.*
   Example: Give the toll-free telephone number and/or address, and repeat it to ensure prospects have a chance to write it down. Experts say that for a 120-second spot, as much as 30 seconds should be devoted to the "tag," or specific ordering information.

How to turn a concept into a storyboard or script

Start creating your spot by putting ideas down on paper without regard to your 60-to-120-second format. Write down words, phrases and benefits, and then start massaging them into a unified presentation with a central theme. You may begin with an audio concept and then support it with video, or vice versa. Remember to keep your spot as simple as possible, since you need to ensure that your selling message comes across loud and clear. Don't be afraid of repetition—especially in making your offer and closing the sale. Make sure you have supplied all necessary facts a person requires to make a responsible buying decision, including all price and payment terms. Once you are satisfied with your rough copy, then you can begin timing it and adding or subtracting words to fit the 60-, 90- or 120-second format. In doing so, keep in mind the speed and delivery style of your chosen announcer. Listen to tapes of your announcer in action to see how many words he or she can get across in each minute.

Some TV concepts are developed in storyboard form, while others are scripted. A storyboard presents a series of TV-screen images with the corresponding audio typed below each image. A TV script presents a written description of the video portion on the left, and the actual words for the audio portion on the right. Your choice of presentation style will depend on the needs of your client or company as well as your upcoming plans for production.

Using television to support other media

In recent years, major direct marketers such as Reader's Digest and Publisher's Clearing House have begun using television to support their direct response marketing efforts in print media. Support television does not sell directly, but rather takes advantage of the broad reach of television to alert prospects to an offer made elsewhere, such as in the mail, a newspaper, or a national magazine.

Support ads may be as short as 10 seconds or as long as 30 seconds. They should be placed at times when viewers are likely to be attentive, such as during prime-time programming. Support television should be used only in conjunction with campaigns that have already proven themselves independently—as an enhancement, not as a way to salvage a weak offer or a poor direct mail package or ad.

TV support ads are mainly "sizzle," talking about the benefits of a new offer or sweepstakes and telling the prospect where to look for full information. To prove their worth, these ads must pay for themselves in terms of additional sales or qualified leads, as compared to a control campaign run without TV support.

Some advertisers have developed their own action devices to use as part of TV support ads in an effort to determine how many of their customers have seen and remembered these spots. Prospects are told that they will receive a premium or additional product if they make a certain mark or circle a picture on the order form. This instruction is given only in the TV support ads, so people who do not see the ads cannot respond in this special way.

Television home shopping

The phenomenal growth of television home shopping channels is significant for direct marketers, since these call-in shows represent a lucrative opportunity to sell products on TV without the time restrictions of the 120-second commercial.

The creative challenge for most home shopping propositions lies in developing the overall format for presentation. Specific copy is not usually necessary, since part of the format normally involves ad-libs and personal commentary from the announcer.

Direct marketers who are considering expanding their efforts into television can take an intermediate step by working with one or more of the home shopping channels. In this way, marketers can learn which products do best on television, and watch how the home shopping "pros" position and pitch their merchandise.

Direct response radio spots

Because today's radio stations are beautifully segmented by interest area and demographics, direct marketers may be able to utilize radio cost-effectively for special-interest products. But since radio does not offer demonstration possibilities, its applications are limited to those products that may be sold by means of "word pictures."

Two of the longest-running and most effective radio direct response campaigns are those of Earl Nightengale and of *Changing Times* magazine. Both are selling written material in the context of radio shows that establish the speaker as an expert on the topics discussed in the literature.

With the advent of all-news radio stations and other formats that attract business people during drive time, some direct marketers have found radio an ideal medium for reaching affluent executives with pitches for business and personal products. Mobile phones, automobile leases and news publications are just a few of the products that have been pitched successfully via radio. Now that many business people have car phones and even fax machines in their autos, they can complete the direct response transaction even as they inch along the rush-hour freeway!

OTHER CONSUMER DIRECT MARKETING MEDIA

18

Although many direct marketers concentrate their creative efforts on direct mail, space advertising, broadcast spots, and catalogs, there are a number of other media that may be used to stimulate a direct response from the consumer.

Depending upon the client, budget and marketing situation, the direct marketing creative person may be called upon to create copy, layouts or finished art for anything from a matchbook ad to a supermarket "take one."

In most cases, a good understanding of direct marketing techniques will serve the writer and artist well as they produce work for these diverse media. In addition, the creative person should take two essential actions before beginning any assignment in a new medium: obtaining live samples, and calling upon the vendor for advice.

Obtaining Live Samples

Whenever possible, the creative person should decoy the new medium. Ask the vendor to put your name on the mailing list for co-ops and card decks. Order products from firms known to include package inserts in their shipments. Visit the supermarket and pick up samples of the various "take ones" on display. Pull the co-op Free-Standing Inserts of Valassis and Quad from your Sunday newspaper. Save the samples and coupon packs you receive in the mail from Advo and other sources.

Check to see if the alternative delivery service that brings your magazines includes direct response offers in its plastic delivery bags. And don't hang up on the telephone solicitors who call you. Listen to their pitches from beginning to end, absorbing their techniques. You can always decline at the end of the offer, and then see what methods they use to try to overcome your objections.

Study the samples you receive in their own environments. Which card seems to pop out of the card deck? Why? Which package insert in the group of six or eight seems to make the most impact? Of all the telemarketing pitches you listened to, which sold (or came closest to selling) you the product or service? Begin to analyze for yourself what the success factors are in each medium. And watch for the cards and inserts and ads that show up month after month in these media. They may not be barn burners, but they must be effective enough to merit repeat runs. What do you think is the key to their success?

Asking the Vendor for Advice

Sales representatives who make their bread and butter from coops, package inserts or telemarketing can be among your best sources of advice on how to create the most effective creative product. Some vendors are better at this than others, so you should always take their words with a grain of salt. Many vendors offer how-to booklets or reprints of articles that can help you pick up on the appeals and techniques that work best in each new medium.

This chapter will discuss pros and cons of, and creative approaches toward, the following media: telemarketing, co-ops, card decks, co-op Free-Standing Inserts, package inserts and ride alongs, alternative delivery systems, supermarket take ones, and unique ad media.

Telemarketing

Telemarketing is a growing field, with 265,000 firms using this technique in 1990, according to Direct Marketing Association figures. Much of this growth is in business-to-business areas, although consumer direct marketers are discovering effective new uses for the telephone as well.

The boom in database marketing has allowed telemarketers to approach prospects with a great deal more selectivity than they could in the past. On one end of the spectrum is the automatic dialer that calls every number in the phone book with a recorded pitch that begins, ''Congratulations!'' On the other end, more forward-looking and profitable, is the sophisticated telemarketer who calls proven customers or well-qualified prospects with an appealing, well-tailored offer.

Telemarketing is divided into two main segments: inbound and outbound. Inbound telemarketing allows customers to order or make customer service inquiries. This may or may not involve toll-free 800 numbers. Outbound telemarketing takes place when the marketer calls a customer or prospect with an offer, announcement, or request for payment.

Direct marketers are divided on the effectiveness of inbound telemarketing for order taking. Some firms find that their telephone volume merely cannibalizes sales they would have received by mail. Others report a net increase in sales when the toll-free 800 number is offered for ordering. Another plus for inbound ordering is that the operators may offer callers an upgrade on their purchases, a daily special, or a telephone-only sale. This technique can increase average order size and build the relationship with the customer. If the buyer can find out which items are in stock and when they will be delivered, the firm reaps another positive customer relations benefit.

Whether they advocate inbound ordering lines or not, most direct marketing firms now consider a well-staffed telephone customer service operation essential. The best of these operations have customers' ordering histories and current orders on-line so that a status report on back orders and shipments can be made in a matter of seconds. Outbound telemarketing is considerably more expensive than direct mail, yet for firms with offers well suited to the medium, it can be just as profitable if not more so. The key to success lies in targeting the right prospects or customers, and developing a suitable script and approach. Although some firms consider telemarketing a primary medium, others use outbound calling only as a supplementary tool. An example of supplementary use would be calling established continuity customers who have not sent payment for the next book or collector plate after several mail requests.

The creative approach to telemarketing

Effective telemarketing begins with a well-written script. Scripting is important to ensure uniformity of approach as well as split-second timing. The Telemarketing Company, a Chicago-based firm, expects its sales representatives to place between 120 and 140 calls in one four-hour shift. Even allowing for busy signals and prospects that do not answer, this makes a "tight" script essential. Most consumer scripts are written verbatim, while some business-to-business scripts list only the essential points to be covered.

To prepare for scripting, the writer needs the same background material that is necessary for a direct mail package or space ad. Total familiarity with the product or service and its features and benefits is essential. The competitive environment is important, too. Consumers will know whether your offer stacks up, and may compare your offer to others they have seen. A talk with salespeople can be very helpful in clarifying typical consumer reactions and objections to this product or service.

Since telephone prospects may terminate the conversation at any point, it is essential that benefits be presented in order of importance to the consumer. For the same reason, make your script concise. Avoid phrasing and superlatives that might have worked for you in direct mail. Remember that the sales representative and the prospect are having a phone conversation, and eliminate stilted promotional language like "this amazing two-for-one offer."

Telemarketing experts suggest that you load your script with two or even three offers, each keying in to a different product benefit. When framing the offer, draw upon the classic sales approach of "closers"—give the customer an either/or choice rather than a yes/no choice. Examples of this might be a one-year *or* a two-year subscription . . . a wood-grained cabinet *or* a white laminated cabinet.

Every sales pitch draws certain standard objections from prospects. Anticipate these and have standard answers ready for sales representatives to use. For example, if the prospect objects to a product's cost, you might script in an answer that explains that the real cost is only 60¢ a day—the price of a can of soda from a vending machine. Then compare that small cost to the benefits of the product, and restate one or two of them briefly. To avoid wasting time with prospects who will keep objecting rather than saying no, top telemarketers suggest that you terminate the call if the sale can't be closed after you have answered two objections.

The real test of any telemarketing script comes when it is used for practice calls. Have several experienced telephone sales representatives look over your script, suggest changes based on their experience, and then try the script on 10 or 20 prospects apiece. Then meet to determine where the "stoppers" occur in the script, and revise it until you and the sales representatives are satisfied that it is as effective as possible.

The creative person who is interested in telemarketing would be wise to spend some time as a part-time telephone sales representative. There is nothing to compare with the hands-on experience of learning what works and what doesn't when you are in the hot seat, talking to consumers on the phone.

Co-ops

The concept of the co-op mailing is simple: by mailing their offers together, direct marketers can save on postage and test a list of consumers at minimal cost. Many marketers find co-ops profitable, even though the medium is by nature quite cluttered and competitive.

Some firms utilize co-ops as a means of extending the reach of a successful offer—one they are already playing out to the limit in direct mail, space or other media. Others are able to utilize specialty co-ops targeted to specific markets like working women, sports enthusiasts or people interested in learning more about personal finance.

Inherent in the co-op medium are certain limitations. First, other than the narrowly focused co-ops sent mainly to magazine subscriber lists, the co-op is a mass medium. Because your offer comes to the consumer in a package with many others, the private and personal aspects of individual direct mail are lost. Most successful co-op users, therefore, are firms which sell products with broad appeal and affordable price tags: items such as clothing and accessories, books and records, collectibles, home decor accents, family photography, and photo finishing.

The most famous co-op is Donnelley Marketing's "Coupons from Carol Wright." Carol Wright is a mythical lady in the Betty Crocker mold. She sends about 35,000,000 American households her packages of coupons and direct response offers as often as nine times per year. Her target homes are young, medium-income families who are heavy users of coupons. Among the cents-off offers for grocery products, consumers receive a fair number of direct mail buying opportunities. Some of the offers combine sales promotion and direct response: a Yoplait Yogurt insert, for instance, includes both a 30 cents off coupon and a mail-in offer for a recipe booklet.

Another type of direct mail co-op is exemplified by the Advo-System. Advo delivers its "Mailbox Values" through the U.S. mail, combining national cents-off offers for grocery products with local offers from retailers and service organizations. "Mailbox Values" is a fold-over piece with a number of offers nested inside. The piece itself does not carry an address: rather, the postal carrier receives a set of addressed cards and a set of nested "Mailbox Values" pieces. The carrier then delivers the mailing piece along with the card to each addressee. This same system is used for product-sampling campaigns.

Creative considerations for co-ops

Co-op pieces are more like space ads than they are like direct mail packages. In a limited format, amid a great deal of clutter, they must capture attention in a second or two and move the prospect to action. The standard co-op format is four color, and sized at 5-1/2" × 8-1/2" to fit in a 6" × 9" outer envelope. Some pieces are folded in half from a flat size of 8-1/2" × 11", which opens the possibility of modifying a direct mail flyer or a space ad to save production costs. If your piece folds, it should have one closed side on its 8-1/2" dimension to make it machine insertable.

To facilitate ease of mailing and eliminate the need for a reply envelope, some direct marketers print their co-op pieces on high-bulk stock which is heavy enough to meet postal requirements for a Business Reply Card. This type of heavy, uncoated stock is less ideal for color photo reproduction than a coated stock would be, however.

Before creating a design, check with the co-op for its size and weight specifications. For an extra fee, you may be able to include a sample or swatch, use a slightly different size, or insert a heavier piece. Before testing any of these special applications, however, you will do well to test the general viability of the co-op for your product or service.

An effective co-op piece is one that attracts the prospect's attention by means of striking graphics and a "grabber" headline. Use all possible means of streamlining response: post-paid reply card, "send no money now," free trial period, strong guarantee, etc. Check this book's chapter on space advertising for creative ideas that can be applied to co-ops.

For specifics on the types of co-ops available, check the Direct Mail Lists book from Standard Rate and Data Service.

Card decks

Both consumer and business-to-business mailers have discovered the profit potential of one specific type of co-op, the card-deck mailing. This co-op style evolved from a format that was popular more than a decade ago. At that time, postcards were printed together in bound booklets with several postcards to a page. Then the concept was simplified so that a stack of individual 3-1/2″ × 5″ postcards could be mailed in a transparent or decorated plastic outer wrapper. Each mailing typically includes 30 to 100 postcard offers.

Sometimes the card deck comes with an introductory piece from its sponsor. For instance, *Sports Illustrated* magazine sends out a deck with a note explaining that the products and services were carefully chosen to interest its subscribers. Ford Customer Shopping Service includes a welcome card as well as an excellent enhancement designed to increase the ease of response, six pressure-sensitive labels with the prospect's name and address pre-printed and ready to be affixed to the postcards of his or her choice.

Creative tips for card decks

Like other co-op mailings, card decks present a considerable challenge to the writer and artist because of space limitations and surrounding clutter. In addition, studies show that each card receives no more than one or two seconds of attention from prospects. This means that the principles of good space advertising must be observed scrupulously for card decks. For instance:

- The headlines must be short, attention-getting and intriguing.
- The offer must be simple, specific and hard-hitting.
- Choose one to three main benefits only. Flag them for the reader using bold subheads or bullets.
- Strong graphics can grab an eye. Try a four-color card in a deck that has mostly one or two-color pieces. Consider a diagonal design element or other unique "grabber."
- Use urgency and a specific call to action.
- Make your reply device as visible as possible. Try offering a toll-free 800 number to capitalize on impulse buyers or inquirers.

Once you have designed and written your card, make up a dummy and place it in a stack of typical cards from the co-op where you have reserved space. Rifle through the cards and see for yourself: is your piece an attention getter, or just another candidate for the wastebasket?

Co-op free-standing inserts

On Sundays, your local newspaper probably contains one or more colorful, fold-over inserts filled with coupon offers and direct response ads. The best known of these co-op Free-Standing Inserts are those of Valassis, Product Movers, and Quad Marketing. These inserts are primarily known as sales promotion vehicles for grocery products. But direct marketers of clothing and accessories, home decor and tabletop items, giftware, and collectibles are all regular advertisers. Catalog marketers solicit new customers in this medium as well.

The co-op FSIs are the ultimate mass media, reaching as many as 50,000,000 homes via weekly newspaper inserts. Rather than try a full run in either medium, of course, the direct marketer should first schedule a test. Remnant space is readily available, and the sales reps of these firms are quite helpful in devising an effective testing schedule for your proposition.

Creative pointers for co-op free-standing inserts

Valassis, Product Movers and Quad are splashy, colorful media, so you should plan on a four-color ad. When purchasing remnant space, the advertiser must be prepared to run in any configuration, with the coupon appearing left or right, top or bottom. Final art must be provided to fit each of these configurations, as the ads are slotted in at the last minute. A one-half page ad is your best bet for an initial test of a product offer. Catalog marketers soliciting leads may opt for a one-fifth page slot. Ads in co-op FSIs are similar in format to space ads in magazines. Their production specifications differ from those of magazines, however, so be sure to check with the sales rep for details before creating final art.

Package inserts and ride alongs

A package insert is a direct response piece that is inserted along with a shipment of product to a customer. A ride along is a direct-response piece that accompanies a company's regular communications with a customer, such as a mailing to book or record club members.

These inserts may arrive loose, or gathered together in a folder. They may or may not be accompanied by "house offers"—similar pieces that come from the originating company. They may or may not come along with an introductory note from the sender—a piece with the theme, "we have selected these special offers because we thought they would be of interest to you, a preferred customer of the xyz company."

One of the positive points for package inserts is the fact that no competitive offers are allowed. In addition, the advertiser is assured that the recipients are proven direct mail buyers: in fact, since they are just receiving a purchase, they are hotter than the most recent hotline names on the sending firm's list. For this reason, and because a package insert program may be initiated rather inexpensively, some direct marketers use this method to test the viability of a list before renting it for a direct mail test.

Like co-ops, package inserts and ride alongs compete in a rather busy environment. Shipments from the various Horchow companies, for instance, usually contain about seven package inserts, all nestled inside an insert from Horchow itself.

The creative challenge

An insert no larger than 5-1/2" × 8-1/2" is usually acceptable to most companies. Some inserts and ride alongs, however, must fit into a statement-sized envelope, which means they are limited to a folded size of about 3-1/2" × 6".

Within certain constraints, direct marketers may try various enhancements to the basic package insert, incorporating a Business Reply Envelope or Card, for example. Before developing designs, it is wise to obtain specifications, weight limitations and costs from the sales representative. A good deal of this information is also available in Standard Rate and Data Service's Direct Mail Lists book.

Alternative delivery systems

Many of today's direct marketers are disenchanted with the U.S. Postal Service's rate increases as well as reported problems with effective delivery of third class mail. Thus they are more and more likely to test the use of alternative delivery systems for catalogs, magazines, and other offers and products.

Each of these delivery systems brings with it the possibility for inclusion of additional direct marketing offers. For example, in many localities, publishers find it more cost effective and efficient to have their magazines delivered by field service workers in cars rather than via the U.S. mail. Magazines arrive in a protective plastic bag which often contains local or national direct response offers, formatted similar to the co-op and package insert pieces described above.

Supermarket take-ones

In many of the nation's supermarkets, shoppers may choose from a wide array of direct marketing offers displayed on a take-one rack. The rack is usually installed between the store's two exit doors, or just inside the door near the check-out area.

Rodale's Organic Gardening attracts new prospects that might not be available via direct mail lists or space ads by placing this flyer in direct marketing-oriented supermarket displays. Reprinted with permission of Rodale Press.

Supermarket take-ones are a mass medium, but some selectivity is possible. Advertisers may choose the geographic location of their take-one stores to improve their reach in the most likely target areas for a given product or service. Take-ones should be considered a supplementary medium, used in an effort to reach prospects who are not receptive to mail, space or television offers.

Because the standard size for a supermarket take-one is 5-1/2" × 8-1/2" folded, some companies may find that they can use the same format for this purpose and for co-ops and package inserts. In general, however, supermarket pieces are printed on heavier stock than co-ops and package inserts, and almost all of the supermarket take-ones incorporate Business Reply Cards.

Unique ad media for direct response marketers

There are a few other media worth mentioning for consideration by direct marketers. Although they are applicable in only a few selected cases, they may bring incremental sales on some offers.

Paperback book ads

Some publishers allow direct marketers to make coupon offers in the back of their paperback books. As Bob Stone points out in *Successful Direct Marketing Methods*, the book's subject matter provides some selectivity as to male or female, age of prospect, areas of interest, etc.

Matchbook ads

The inside of a matchbook can be used as a coupon. Classic matchbook advertisers are correspondence schools and other self-improvement firms. Contact major match companies like Diamond and Universal—both in New York City—for information.

Comic books and Sunday comics

Remember the Charles Atlas ads in comic books? This medium may be considered for any offer aimed at young people. The Sunday comics also attract a number of adults, so direct response offers attracting all ages may be appropriate.

Understanding the various direct response media in advance of any assignment will stand the creative person in good stead. Increase your file of samples from various media, and familiarize yourself with them. By studying your samples and understanding the marketing concepts that make each medium a good bet for certain types of offers, you may soon find yourself suggesting unique ways for your firm or clients to expand their horizons in direct marketing.

PUBLIC RELATIONS IN DIRECT MARKETING

19

Public relations can make a profitable addition to the direct marketing mix for many products and services. This chapter offers an introduction to public relations for direct marketers. It provides basic information on when and how to implement a public relations plan, how to create a news release and news kit, how to obtain free advertising in shopping sections of magazines, how to develop and communicate with contacts, and some of the essential dos and don'ts for public relations novices.

Publicity is any nonpaid editorial space or broadcast time devoted to your product or service. The word "nonpaid" is the key: with paid advertising, your firm or agency maintains control over the message, but with publicity, you forfeit control. This means that publicity may be either positive or negative.

Public relations involves the overall image your firm communicates, not only to current customers but to prospects and the public at large.

Among your current customers, your public relations image is enhanced by good techniques inside your business: excellent customer service, prompt shipments, products and services that deliver what you have promised, and accurate order processing both by mail and by phone.

An outer-directed public relations campaign—especially one targeted at your best prospective buyers—may help you win them as customers. What's more, a good relationship with the media representatives in your field can gain you a number of opportunities to speak out as an authority when issues come up that affect your industry. If a potentially damaging story starts brewing, those good relationships will mean you're called immediately for the "real story"—not kept in the dark while reporters seek information from your competitors.

Who should do the public relations work?

Knowing the basics of public relations is an excellent skill for direct marketing creative people to add to their "bag of tricks." Having a grasp of public relations "how-tos" is important, since few direct marketing agencies have their own public relations specialists.

If you are assigned to develop a public relations program for a product or service, you have the option to do it yourself or to hire a PR firm or freelancer to take care of the work. The follow-up function—working directly with the media to help encourage "pick up" (utilization) of your news releases and article ideas— may also be done by a freelancer or agency if you choose.

Stability is important here: your best bet in developing relationships with the media is to have the same person contact editors over a long period, so as to build a relationship of trust and reliance. Therefore, if you do not have a good, stable public relations firm to which you can commit for the long haul, the contact function may best be done by you or a member of your staff.

Benefits of a public relations program

Here are some of the specific reasons why direct marketing firms may choose to implement public relations plans as a part of marketing and creative strategy.

1. *To reinforce and improve customer attitudes.* The customer who sees your spokesperson on television or reads an article quoting an expert from your firm gets an extra message that your firm is a leader in its field. Roger Horchow has helped build his catalog firm's reputation as a quality purveyor or tasteful gifts, home decor and clothing items by means of appearances on national talk shows. His consumer-oriented book about the direct-marketing business, *Elephants in Your Mailbox,* also served as a public relations tool.

2. *To expose potential customers to your products or services.* Potential customers may learn of your firm through periodicals or broadcast media and be intrigued enough to watch for your ads or write for your sales literature. For over 15 years, The Bradford Exchange has carried on an international public relations campaign aimed at attracting potential plate collectors. The firm's releases position Bradford as the largest seller of collector's plates, and also explain the fun and excitement this hobby can bring.

3. *Spreading the news about important events and promotions.* An example of this is the way Neiman-Marcus promotes its famous Christmas catalog each year. National television shows, newspapers, and magazines all run simultaneous and often humorous pieces about the latest luxury items Neiman-Marcus has to offer.

4. *Establishing your firm as a leader in its field.* By creating a relationship with local or national media people, or both, your firm will come to mind when they need information about your field. Thus you may find your president or spokesperson quoted as a "leading expert" in a national round-up article in *Money* magazine, *Sports Illustrated* or *The New York Times,* depending on the type of product you sell.

5. *For business-to-business marketers: have the look of an innovator.* Business buyers are sensitive to the research-and-development side of your firm. They want to buy from the company that is forward-looking so that they get the most up-to-date features and technology for their money. Your public relations efforts can help give you that innovative reputation. Indeed, for many trade publications, new product introductions are their bread and butter.

6. *Appearing to be a public-service-oriented firm.* Build good will and prominence for the firm in the minds of present and potential customers by publicizing involvement in programs for the underprivileged, ill, elderly, or for the arts.

What makes good public relations?

Here are some examples of the type of news or feature material you may want to submit to various media sources.

- New product introductions
- New features that make a familiar product better
- Research and development breakthroughs
- Interviews with designers, artists, or creators of products
- How-to ideas for your product and other products in its category
- New ways in which you plan to sell (e.g., a first-time catalog or continuity program)
- Survey of the field (the growth of your product category, reasons behind it)
- Human-interest stories showing your product in use or giving product-related information
- Surveys with results of interest to prospective buyers of your product
- Time and money-saving ideas related to your product, including how to save time buying via direct marketing
- Checklist of hints on buying your type of product or service
- Celebrity stories related to your product or firm
- The history of your product or product category with an angle of current interest such as an anniversary
- Product price decreases or inflation-fighting policies in your firm or industry
- Personnel changes that will have an impact on your field
- Expansion in size and plant capacity

Developing your media list

If you need a national list of newspaper city editors, book review editors or home decor writers, a reference like *Bacon's Publicity Checker* can save you much time. The American and Canadian version of this two-volume reference set covers 7,500 business, trade, farm, and consumer magazines and all 1,750 daily newspapers in the two countries, plus 7,500 weekly newspapers and publisher groups. The books are published annually in October and supplemented quarterly. Along with addresses for the publications it lists, the *Checker* gives current editors' names for general press releases and special-interest subjects. There are also codes to tell you which publications welcome news of new products, trade literature, personnel news, and so on. Beyond this, there is an international version of the *Publicity Checker* that covers over 13,000 publications in fifteen Western European countries.

Both publications are available from Bacon's Publicity Checker, 332 South Michigan Avenue, Chicago, Il 60604. Phone: (312) 922-8419. Bacon's also offers its various lists on mailing labels, as well as other services.

Reporting news to the media

When you have a news story to tell the media, there is no question of exclusivity involved. Information about new store openings, new catalog introductions, new products, and other developments may be sent to all interested editors in general press-release form.

If you send the same news release to several people at the same publication, do them the courtesy of marking the release with the names of the others who receive it. This avoids duplication of effort and potential embarrassment at having two sections of the publication print the same story.

Hints for preparing the news release

News releases should:

- Cover the journalistic basics: Who, What, Where, When, Why, and How.
- Be written in "inverted pyramid" style, with the most important news woven into the first few paragraphs. If your story must be cut, editors will delete the bottom paragraphs. If you bury something important there, it is likely to be lost.

- Reflect the publications you send them to. For best results, get hold of each publication you'll be forwarding the release to and make sure that the angle of the material you send complements its editorial style and readership profile.

You may develop several releases for the same project. For example, a firm that sold "talking watches" prepared releases stressing:

—benefits to sight-impaired people for daily newspapers and senior citizens publications

—the technological breakthrough this watch represented for newspaper and magazine business editors

—the gift/novelty aspect of the watch for trade publications read by giftware buyers

```
Company or Client Name
and Address Here
Contact:  (Your Name)
Day Phone:
Night Phone:

                                        Release Date and Time

THE TITLE GOES HERE, ALL UPPER
CASE AND UNDERLINED LIKE THIS

        The Point of Origin Dateline Goes Here -  The body of the

release should begin one-third of the way down the page so as to

leave enough room for the editor or copy person to write remarks.

The release proper should be all double spaced for ease of reada-

bility and editing.

        Be sure to use normal indents and consistent spacing between

paragraphs.  It is not necessary to triple space between graphs.

All information should be presented in descending order of impor-

tance, ending with the least important items in case last-minute

editing results in the bottom of your release being lopped off.

        Remember to leave at least one-inch margins all around, but

resist the urge to leave huge right-hand margins in order to

stretch your information.  It usually looks like you're writing

in a column.

        When you arrive at the bottom of the first page, leave at

least a one-inch margin and indicate that more information follows

by typing the word "more" with dashes on either side of it.

                            -more-
```

```
                                          RELEASE-- 2


      If more information follows, try not to break paragraphs or

   sentences in the middle.  Never break a work and complete it on

   the next page.

      Slug following pages at the top left with a brief title

   followed by page number.  When you reach the end of your release,

   indicate you are finished by using -30-, -end-, or # # # # #.

                          -30-
```

The news release format. *Source: Handbook for Public Relations Writing,* Thomas Bivins.

- Be as concise as possible. Try for no more than two 8½" × 11" pages, double spaced. Use only one side of plain white paper with generous margins.
- Have an active, factual headline that will catch reader interest. The release should also start far enough down on the page to allow room for the editor to write out his or her own headline.
- List the specific contact person in your organization, plus his or her address and phone number. For best results, list both day and night phone numbers, and make sure to choose a contact person who is regularly accessible by phone.
- Be written in news style, with short sentences and few if any adjectives. Any "sales language" should be presented in the form of an attributed quote.
- Use quotations to humanize the story and lend credibility. Make sure all quotes are properly attributed.
- State "For Immediate Release," or if that is not possible, should say specifically when the material can be released (e.g., "For Release After 12 Noon on Wednesday, January 6").
- Be dated so that an editor who picks it out of a miscellaneous pile knows how long it's been around.
- Carry its city and state of origin at the beginning of the body copy (e.g., "NEW YORK, New York—").
- Have the word "more" at the bottom of each page, and pages numbered in the upper right corner along with an identifying word from the headline. Releases should indicate their completion by means of one of two common signs:

    #####   (or)   –end–   (or)   –30–

■ Be sent infrequently enough so that media representatives perceive them as news—not the firm's latest attempt at self-promotion.

When to use a news kit

When you have a new program or event, or a complex product to introduce to the media, you may choose to develop a news kit to "wrap around" your news release. The basic elements of a news kit include:

■ A cover letter to introduct the kit, list its contents and let the media representative know who will make the follow-up contact, and when it will take place.
■ A folder to contain the other piece of the kit. This can be a plain 11" × 17" folder labeled with a stick-on label, or a more elegant embossed or decorated folder bearing the company logo.
■ The news release itself, prepared according to the guidelines above.
■ A "backgrounder" piece or fact sheet including more detailed historical, biographical, scientific or other information that is too long or complex to be a part of the press release.
■ One or more photographs, prepared as indicated in the photography section below.

How to "pitch" a feature story to the media

A feature story is one that does not necessarily depend on today's news for relevance. It is likely to deal with a "trend" or "angle" on a story.

The classic way for public relations people to place feature stories is to approach editors or reporters with a feature concept. For instance, as a catalog marketer you might approach a magazine editor about doing a feature on shopping for women's clothing by mail. As a business-to-business seller of office furniture, you might approach a trade publication about a feature on the latest trends in open-plan offices.

It is important that you share your specific feature ideas with only one editor or publication at a time. Otherwise, you will lose credibility. The key to good feature writing is a fresh angle. You can't offer the same idea to two different magazines or you will be very unpopular when they come out with similar articles.

When you come up with a feature concept, you should try to interest your first-choice editor or writer in doing a story on it. If he or she turns you down, you may approach another editor in the same way, proceeding until you place the story. Then find another feature angle and work on that one until you locate a publication that is interested.

The most effective way to place a feature story is to write what is called a "pitch letter" to your target editor. Include some "sizzle" about the feature concept you've come up with and an indication of the interviews and background information you can provide.

"Free" advertising in shopping sections

If you have a service-oriented product, a unique "breakthrough" product, a timely offering or one that fills a very specific niche in the marketplace, you may well qualify for free editorial write-ups in major magazines or daily newspapers.

Many magazines offer short blurbs, photographs and ordering information for such products. Sometimes regular advertisers are the only recipients of the "shopping section" space at the back of the book. Other times, publications will run your product information in the hope of enticing you to advertise. In some cases your product will exhibit sufficient news value for the magazine's readers that it will appear as a reader service, with no strings attached.

Although editorial material seldom contains the kind of strong sales-oriented copy found in paid advertising, many firms find that the implied endorsement of an editorial appearance more than makes up for the straight-news tone. Indeed, such free mentions often generate more response than equal-sized paid ads in the same publication.

Products that can attract the attention of newspaper editors need to exhibit even more news or service value than those that appear in magazine shopping sections. The talking watch mentioned earlier in this chapter earned mentions in a number of daily papers when it was "pitched" as a breakthrough product to bene-fit sight-impaired people. It would not have attracted much men-tion in newspapers if positioned as a mere novelty item.

To determine which publications are most likely to use your product information, begin with a list of the media in which you would advertise if budget allowed. For best results, send an indi-vidually word-processed letter to the editor on good-quality letter-head: a "mass mailing" look will kill your chances for attention. In the letter, offer to send the editor a sample of the product if this is feasible. Include a short fact sheet about the product, or a succinct press release covering the basics: who, what, where, when, why, how. A photo of the product suitable for use in the target publica-tion should round out your presentation.

If you have several products to "pitch," prepare a separate mailing for each, to ensure best results. Otherwise the editor may choose only the best of the two or three items in a group mailing. Another hint: find some way of keying the address you give on your fact sheet or release so that when responses come back to you, you'll know which publications they came from. This infor-mation can be invaluable in helping you decide which magazines to use for paid advertising. Be sure to send your information to the magazines way ahead of season: remember that their editorial lead time is as long as three to six months.

This technique works best for lower-priced items. It offers an excellent way to test the waters with new products without mak-ing a commitment to a paid advertising schedule.

A word about photography

The right photograph can help win a place for your story or new product release if it is attractive and of good quality. These guide-lines will enable you to supply the media with the best possible photos.

1. Make sure the photos you send are black-and-white glossies with white borders. Preferred size is 5″ × 7″ or 8″ × 10″. If the publication uses color, have a color transparency on hand to send upon request.
2. Be sure your photos are in focus, and as close-up to the sub-ject as possible.

3. If you are doing a feature story, don't send the publication a "stock" photo. Do special ones if at all possible, and talk with the editor about what he or she would prefer.
4. Never send the same photos you are using for your ads, even on product information releases. Use a fresh angle and background.
5. Provide a caption for each photo and attach it at the bottom of the photograph so that it can be removed without ruining the photo. Don't clip, staple or fold the photo. Use cardboard in the mailing envelope as a stiffener to avoid photo damage.
6. Do not ask to have photos returned to you unless the editor has made a special request.

Following up your release or pitch letter

Many firms just send out their news releases and hope that publications will pick them up. But with news releases and pitch letters alike, the chances for placement increase if you follow up by phone.

Except for hot, timely stories, allow the editor or writer a few days after its probable receipt to read over your release or letter. Then call him or her to see if you can provide more information, photographs, or other help. Here are some guidelines for media relations.

1. Respect the writer's deadlines. This is especially crucial when calling a daily newspaper. Generally, the last deadline for morning papers is early evening of the night before, so it is best to call morning-paper writers in the morning. Afternoon papers "go to bed" at mid-morning, so try these people after lunch.
2. Do not start out by asking if the writer or editor is going to use your story. It is better to inquire if he or she has received your information, and to ask if you can provide more background or answer any questions. Be cooperative and helpful, and don't press.
3. Don't make a pest of yourself by calling back after that first contact. If the editor or writer is undecided when you first

speak with him or her, ask when you should call back and wait until then for a second contact.

4. Never use your firm's advertising power as "bait" to obtain editorial space. Some periodicals, especially trade publications, may come after you with this "one hand washes the other" pitch, and you may end up making such an arrangement. But don't suggest it yourself or you risk losing a good media contact by compromising someone's journalistic standards. Another hint: never send or follow-up a release with the advertising sales rep: always work directly with the editor.

5. Use each contact as an opportunity to build a good rapport and working relationship with the publication. Even if they don't pick up this particular piece of news or this feature idea, they will make a mental note that you are a helpful and available source of information in your field. Make sure that they have your phone number for future reference, and before long you may be receiving calls soliciting your help with ideas they have.

6. Don't ask to see any story before publication. Don't ask to edit your quotations. Don't ask for tear sheets. These are three of the most aggravating questions you can ask an editor or writer. You must trust them to write your story fairly and well. And it's your responsibility to buy a copy of the publication, just like everyone else.

Media interviews

If you or another representative of your firm is called upon for quotations or an interview, make sure you are prepared. Here are some tips:

1. Never bluff. Be honest. If you don't have an answer, say that you don't know but that you will try to find out. If the question regards something that you are not authorized to discuss, just say so. Never come out with the deadly answer, "no comment." Never give an answer "off the record." In making such statements, you put the reporter in the dangerous position of knowing something he or she can't use. This often backfires.

2. Don't try to make the interview a commercial for your company or product. Credits for you and your firm will develop in the context of the article. You are only too obvious if you try to work every question around to an answer that promotes your interests alone.
3. On the other hand, when given the opportunity to state your case, don't be afraid to reemphasize your main points. The reporter may not catch them the first time around.
4. Be calm, friendly and helpful. If you promise the reporter some additional facts, literature or photos, deliver them promptly. Remember that the reporter's deadline is firm.

Amplifying the public relations plan

As your public relations plan develops, you may want to develop some additional ways to build and improve your firm's image. A newsletter sent regularly to customers, prospects and media representatives is one idea to consider. An unbiased fact book about your field of endeavor could spark media interest in approaching you for quotes as an "industry leader." It could also become a lead-generation piece for your commercial direct marketing efforts. Sponsorship of a popular nonprofit fund-raising event or cause is another way to gain positive media attention.

To summarize: public relations is an underused and undervalued tool for direct marketers. It offers a relatively inexpensive way to amplify paid advertising efforts, to obtain publicity, and to enhance the firm's public image in the eyes of present and potential customers. Direct marketing creative people should consider some form of public relations as a facet of every marketing plan.

DIRECT
MARKETING
PRODUCTION

IV

PREPARING ARTWORK FOR PRINTING

20

A typescript of copy and a comprehensive layout may be enough to sell a direct marketing concept to a client, but there are many more vital production steps that must take place before the direct mail package or ad is printed and distributed to the target audience. And although many copywriters and art directors complete their formal involvement at the copy and layout stage, learning the basics of production will serve any direct marketer well for several reasons.

First, a knowledge of production helps writers and art directors understand the possibilities—and the limits—of the medium they are creating for. Second, creative types can make their plans more cost-effective when they know the timing and process involved in producing their work. The third reason has to do with self-interest: individuals who wish to move out of the "creative box" into overall management must fully understand the big picture—and be able to work with and supervise production operations. Fourth and final is the matter of mutual respect: the writer or art director who takes the time to understand production jobs will earn more cooperation and help from artists and technicians in achieving a top-notch creative product.

This chapter picks up where Chapter 9 left off: once the copy and layout have been created and approved, and it's time to prepare artwork for printing. This process includes typography, photography and illustrations, keyline/paste-up, separations, and space ad preparation.

Typography

Good direct marketing typography is unobtrusive. It contributes to the visual message about the product or service without calling attention to itself. Good typography catches the reader's eye with headlines, leads smoothly to the subheads, and provides easy readability in body copy.

Copywriters may contribute to the appearance and readability of their typeset copy by keeping sentences and paragraphs short, writing sufficient lead-ins and subheads to keep copy interesting, and dividing the copy story into sections. Another important function for the copywriter is writing to size: ensuring that each head, subhead and body copy section fills the space allotted to it without running over.

In general, the layout artist or art director specifies typefaces when the comprehensive layout is created. This job includes not only the selection of the face and its size, but also the width of columns, use of space between lines of type (leading), and technicalities such as setting type flush left or flush right, or to wrap around an illustration or photograph. Here are some considerations for typeface selection and typesetting.

Type styles

Serif typefaces are those that have fine lines at the top, bottom and corners, while sans serif faces are plain and modern in appearance. Serif faces are easier to read in long copy blocks, and give a more traditional appearance. Some studies also show that serif faces lend more credibility to a presentation. Sans serif faces give a contemporary look and are easy enough to read in all but long-copy, small-type situations. Some art directors do insist on using sans serif type for long copy, mainly because they prefer its appearance. A glance at the main body copy of newspapers and books, however, shows that the more readable serif typefaces are used almost without exception.

There are hundreds of different type styles, some used with great frequency and others reserved for special applications. Use the specialty typefaces with care: they are not familiar to your reader and may draw attention away from the selling message. A good rule is to use that Oriental-look typeface or the circus-style one for headings or perhaps for subheads, but to select a more traditional face for body copy. Another good rule is not to use a specialty typeface unless there is a good reason for it, such as an Old English typeface for headings about a new line of traditional British wool clothing.

You may wish to select a typeface that fits your corporate identity, and then use that same face in almost all of your ads and mailings. Or you may choose a new typeface for each promotion— one that reflects the specific product or service being sold. Although it is not necessary to stick with the same typeface in different sizes for all headings, subheads and body copy, it's wise to limit your selection to one or two type styles on any one printed piece unless you're an experienced typographer. Otherwise the results may be confusing and distracting to the reader.

With a given typeface, you have a number of options. Most faces feature a regular type, a bold (darker and thicker) version, and a light version. There are also condensed, extended and italic versions of most faces. In addition, you may opt to use all capital letters in certain headings or subheads, although this inhibits readership to some extent.

Type sizes

Type sizes are expressed in "points" for height and "picas" for width. There are 72 points to an inch of height, and six picas to an inch of width. Another measure of height—most frequently used by newspapers—is the "agate line." There are 14 agate lines to an inch.

Generally, it is considered difficult to read any type smaller than 8 points, although in a publication that uses small type for its body copy, like *TV Guide,* you might be able to succeed with 6- or 7-point type. The type sizes for promotional body copy range from 6 points to about 14 points, depending on the overall size of the piece and the impression you wish to make. Headings and subheads generally range from about 12-point up to 48-point or even 72-point type.

When your target market focuses on children or senior citizens, it is wise to use larger type for body copy. Another aspect of type size that enhances readability for prospects of all ages is leading, the amount of white space between lines of type. The larger the type, the more leading is necessary for good appearance and

SERIF TYPE:

abcdefghijklmnopqrstuvwxyz

SAN SERIF TYPE:

abcdefghijklmnopqrstuvwxyz

1 POINT LEADING:

Language is a systematic means of communicating ideas or feelings by the use of conventionalized signs, sounds, gestures, or marks having understood meanings.

2 POINTS LEADING:

Language is a systematic means of communicating ideas or feelings by the use of conventionalized signs, sounds, gestures, or marks having understood meanings.

6 POINT:

abcdefghijklmnopqrstuvwxyz

9 POINT:

abcdefghijklmnopqrstuvwxyz

12 POINT:

abcdefghijklmnopqrstuvwxyz

20 POINT:

abcdefghijklmnopqrstuvwxyz

30 POINT:

abcdefghijklmnopqrs

48 POINT:

abcdefghijklm

72 POINT:

abcdefgh

readability. When one point of leading is added, an 8-point type format would be expressed as "8 on 9" or "9 on 10," where the second number refers to the addition of the leading. If type is set "solid," with no leading, this is expressed as "8 on 8" or "9 on 9." Several points of leading might be added to 14-point copy for optimum readability.

It is important to note that not all 8-point type takes up the same amount of space. For instance, an 8-point typeface called Souvenir Demi Bold gets 2.68 characters to the pica, while 8-point Helvetica Condensed Bold gets 3.74 characters to the pica. This fact impacts both copywriters and art directors. To create the right amount of copy, writers need to know more than just that their work will be set in 8-point type. It is sometimes more helpful to ask the art director to figure out how many characters will fit in a block of body copy. Art directors may want to have a small amount of the copy typeset in various typefaces and sizes (including condensed, extended, etc.) to determine which is most readable and effective for the space available.

Working with the typesetter

Many art directors today are able to see their layouts come alive in print right away by means of desktop publishing. A new typeface may be chosen in a matter of seconds, and sizes may be modified with just a few key strokes. Other firms and agencies deal with outside typesetters, and need to communicate their requirements effectively.

It is important to send the layout or a good copy of the layout to the typesetter, with copy areas keyed to the typescript itself. Generally, you can save money and time by providing a computer disk that already contains final copy: this saves rekeying the copy at the typesetter's. Or you may be able to link your computer to the typesetter by means of a modem. In any case, to complete your job the typesetter needs to know typeface, type size, and other specifics such as flush left or flush right, justified or not justified, centering, and spacing of lettering and words.

Reading typeset proofs

The first question when the typeset proof is presented is the simplest: "Does it fit?" To check, lay each portion of typeset copy over its corresponding area of the layout to confirm that it fits. Typesetters provide a see-through tissue copy for this purpose. If the copy does not fit, the layout may be revised, the copy may be cut, the type size may be reduced, or some combination of these actions may take place. Any such changes should reflect cooperation between the layout artist and copywriter so that the final product does not suffer.

Assuming that the copy fits, the next step is to check the proof for technical aspects such as broken or fuzzy type, proper spelling, "breaks" from line to line, word spacing, and proper leading. Avoid having type extend over illustrations: it inhibits readability. It is also important to consider the readability of body copy. Make sure that any columns of type are narrow enough for easy reading: some experts say that columns should be no more than about 40 characters in width—similar to newspaper columns. Also check to see if any paragraphs are too long and need to be broken up. Last but most important of all, proofread to ensure that the typeset version matches the approved copy, word for word.

Saving money on typesetting

Because the cost of typesetting varies widely within a given metropolitan area, it is worth the time to get quotes from several sources. In addition, careful preparation of copy and layout will save the typesetter's time and your money. In-house typesetting via desktop publishing is a viable cost-saving option for some firms and agencies, and it also allows for more flexibility and timeliness in production.

Another way to economize, and enhance your presentation at the same time, is to use regular typewriter type for sales letters. Such letters are more credible than typeset letters, and can be typed up on your own word processor, then keylined into position on an art board. Another cost-saving move is to have the publication in which you're advertising set your space ads, assuming the copy and layout are simple enough that you can trust their staff's judgment.

Photography and illustrations

Studies show that in general, photography gets more positive attention from prospects than illustrations. If you can afford it, and if photography fits into your selling message, it is a good idea to add one or more photographs to your layout plan. Generally these photos will feature the product itself or the product in use, but they may also help create an image or identify the target market.

To find a suitable photographer, ask for referrals from business associates or trade organizations. Be sure to make it clear that you are looking for an experienced product photographer, not a portraitist who specializes in family or individual "people shots." Check the work of the photographers you are referred to, and interview them to see what experience they have that qualifies them to work with your product line. Make sure the photographer has a feel for your merchandise and what you are trying to achieve.

In addition to a photographer, you may need to hire a photo stylist. Certain stylists specialize in working with food, clothing, or other product lines. Their expertise can be well worth the cost to ensure that hard-to-photograph products are portrayed to best advantage.

Set-ups for photography

Experts agree that lighting is the single most important factor in successful product photography. Good lighting impacts your product's appearance in regard to color, tone, dimension and detail, so be sure that yours is a photographer who takes proper care in this area.

Backgrounds for product shots should not be chosen for their artistic quality or uniqueness, but rather for the way they complement the product. In general, a background color that contrasts with the product will enhance it best. Simple, plain-colored backgrounds often are the most effective since they do not compete for attention with the product itself.

Props can be important in that they help set the tone, give lifestyle cues to prospects, and provide size relationships to the product. If a human hand is shown holding the product, for example, its relative size is easy to determine at a glance. If you need unusual props, consider working with a prop rental house. Such firms are available in most major cities.

Don't reject the concept of a product-in-use shot if you happen to be marketing an intangible service. Your in-use shot for an insurance policy, for example, could show a person receiving a benefit check in the mail while recuperating from illness in the hospital.

If you choose to do photography on location, you may wish to utilize the services of a freelance location finder to line up proper interiors or exteriors for your application. Depending on the setting you require, you may be able to make a deal with a furniture store, hotel, or private homeowner for the use of their property and furnishings. The going rate for use of in-home spaces for photography is $200.00 per day and up. Use of well-known public spaces like big-city libraries and museums can be extremely expensive, so check on the cost before committing to the photography concept.

It is often a good idea to take an instant camera shot of any photography set-up before starting the actual photo shoot. The camera "sees" things you may have missed—and even an inexpensive shot like this can tell you if you and the photographer are on the right track with lighting, props and positioning.

Evaluating photography

When photography is presented to you, make sure that the shots will work effectively in the size they will appear in your printed piece. An 8″ × 10″ print, for example, comes across very differently than a two-column product shot in an ad. If cropping is necessary, check it carefully to make sure the composition of the photo is not destroyed.

Check all product shots at every stage for fidelity to your product. Remember that this photograph will provide your customer's entire perception of your product, and that if it's kelly green in the picture, buyers will expect it to be that exact kelly green shade when it is delivered.

Sources of free or inexpensive photos

If the cost of professional, custom photography is beyond your budget, consider sources of free photography that has already been done. If your firm is not the manufacturer of the product you are selling, check with the manufacturers to see if they can supply product or product-in-use shots. The U.S. Government provides a wide variety of good, general mood-setting shots free of charge. Try trade organizations, Chambers of Commerce, and other sources of free photos that may suit your needs.

There are many stock photography services listed in the Yellow Pages of good-sized cities, and they offer a wide range of photographs on many subjects. These organizations supply good-quality photos at fees that should be considerably less than for comparable custom photography.

When to use illustrations

If photography does not suit your purpose, you may wish to commission the creation of line drawings or illustrations to enhance your layout. Most art directors should be acquainted with artists who create various types of illustrations. Some firms which use illustrations often may even keep one or more illustrators on staff.

In addition, you may want to subscribe to a ''clip art'' service—a firm that supplies you with a steady stream of non-copyrighted artwork that you can use to illustrate your brochures and ads as required. As in the case of stock photography, clip art can save a good deal of time and effort—assuming you avoid choosing illustrations that appear too generic or dated.

Keyline/paste-up

Keylines—also known as mechanicals, boards, or camera-ready art—are the final step of preparation for offset printing. Paste-up is the process of affixing art and type on a keyline prior to platemaking and printing. The keyline itself begins with a white art board upon which the exact flat size of the brochure, letter, ad, order form or other piece is drawn. The keyline artist uses a light blue pencil for this purpose, since its color will not be picked up in the offset reproduction process. These ruled blue lines provide the framework within which all photos, art, borders and type must be arranged using a T-square or ruler.

Whatever appears on the final keylines will show up in the printed product, so it is essential that everything be perfectly squared up and clean—without fingerprints or dirt. Some paste-up artists use rubber cement to affix art and type, while others prefer wax. Rubber cement holds better than wax, but wax is less messy to use.

Once the original keyline is complete, the paste-up artist may add acetate overlays which indicate versions of the main piece to accommodate price tests, different logos or addresses, etc. To ensure that each overlay lines up properly, the paste-up artist adds registration marks on both the overlay and the main keyline. Then the layout artist places a good-quality vellum tissue over the entire keyline on which screen percentages and other instructions to the printer may be added. Colors to be printed other than black are indicated by means of a colored felt-tip marker that outlines the affected type areas, and a numbered color chip taped to the tissue.

If the keylined piece is to be printed using a four-color process, the boards are sent to the separator along with color transparencies of the photos that will be separated.

All of these steps for keyline and paste-up may be handled via computer if you have access to sophisticated desktop publishing equipment. In this case, the keyline is created on the computer screen, a color copy is generated for proofing purposes, and the art and instructions are sent to the separator or printer by means of a computer disk or modem.

Check carefully for errors at keyline stage

Exceptional care should be taken in proofreading at the keyline stage. Changes after this point are very costly. When a keyline is presented, first compare it to the comprehensive layout and the typescript to ensure that it is accurate, line by line and word for word. Use a ruler to check each dimension of the piece. Compare the position of the panels to the comprehensive layout, remembering that the flat keyline may necessarily show certain panels upside down or out of sequence because of the way they will appear when printed and folded.

If the piece is to include elements of computerization, make sure that the correct space has been left to accommodate the computer fill-ins. Check that the label area—or area for computerized addressing—is sized correctly and positioned to correspond with any windows it must show through. Compare the layout to the boards to ensure that any perforations, die cuts, or other special processes are indicated.

Take time to check for all necessary key codes, stock numbers and other identifying marks, and make sure that they are correct. Look carefully at the order form. Recompute amounts, shipping charges, and tax to make sure the figures are correct. Photocopy the order form board and fill it out as if you were the customer, making sure that each step is understandable and simple to complete. If at all possible, have a neutral party read over the boards for typographical errors and spelling. Those close to the job may read over the same error time and again and not recognize it—until it shows up in the printed piece.

Separations

Color separation technology continues to advance day by day. New computerization techniques have made the preparation process of four-color printing faster, more versatile, and more efficient. Many of these high-tech applications, however, are still the province of large and sophisticated direct marketers only. Thus it behooves direct marketing creative people to understand the color separation process and to engage in dialogue with prospective suppliers. This will enable them to choose the most cost-effective and time-saving separation method for a given job.

The color separation process involves photography through filters that isolate four colors: red, yellow, blue and black. Every color may be achieved in some combination of the three primary colors. Black provides depth, detail and gray tones which add realism to the picture. To create separations, red is photographed through a green filter; yellow through a violet filter; and blue through an orange filter. A specialized filter for black is added for a total of four separate negatives—the "color separations."

After corrections to ensure fidelity to the original color transparency, the separations are photographed through a halftone screen. This produces four halftone plates made up of myriad tiny dots: one plate each for red, yellow, blue and black.

When the separations are photographed, each of these four color plates is rotated slightly away from the others so that when the four plates are superimposed in printing, the dots generated in the halftone process do not completely overlap. In this way, instead of "mud," you obtain a good reproduction of the original colors. The plates are printed one by one using transparent inks, usually in the sequence of yellow, red, blue, and then black.

How to work effectively
with color separators

There are many things that can be done to save money and time in the creation of separations, and to ensure the best possible final product. First, good and sharp photography is essential. Color fidelity in photography is the first key to color fidelity in separations and printing. What's more, color corrections at the separation stage are almost always more costly than quality color photography.

Second, make sure the color transparencies you supply are clean and without scratches or glitches. Although your separator may offer to clean them up for you as part of the process, it is often cheaper to reshoot than to take advantage of the (expensive) wonders of modern technology.

Third, when several product shots are involved in a single job, you can save considerable money and time by having your art department or studio create the pages of your materials with everything in position. This requires that your photography all be shot in the same focus, so that the separator can scan them all together. Costly problems may arise when a marketer tries to use a supplier's "canned" product shot instead of getting a product sample and shooting it to fit the parameters of the job.

Fourth, make sure your color separator knows what you are expecting in terms of color fidelity. Some customers will settle for "pleasing color" in order to save money, while others insist on absolute color fidelity at any cost. These decisions about color quality have to do with the nature of the product, its price point, and company image, among other factors.

Fifth, agree upon what type of proofs you expect: chromalins or press proofs. Chromalin proofs are less costly than press proofs, but their colors will be slightly "off" from those in an actual press run. These proofs are not printed on paper, but merely indicate what the color-on-color appearance of a printed piece will be. Chromalins usually show colors more vividly and with sharper detail than what you will obtain in a press run. If your color work is very exacting, you may require press proofs that are created on a proofing press at the color separator's plant. A cost-saving note: if you are printing a small quantity of high-quality pieces, you may save by having the entire run done on the proofing press rather than moving the job to another print shop. Ask your separator for a price quote.

Evaluating color separations

It takes a trained eye to critique and correct color separations well, but even the novice can learn to tell a good separation from a poor one. Basic questions to ask include:

- Are the flesh tones natural?
- Is the grass green?
- Are the red roses red and the violets purple?
- Is the detail of dark-toned objects discernible, or do they disappear into mud?
- Do the whites appear white without too much yellow, pink or blue?
- Are the details crisp?

Unless you have been trained to order specific, technical corrections on separations, it is safer to comment on what appears incorrect than to instruct the separator on how to fix it. In other words, you might point out that the skin tones appear too red or yellow—then let the separator make adjustments until the desired result is achieved.

Space ad preparation

Since publications have varied requirements for ad production, it is wise to communicate with their advertising representatives to make sure that your ads are sized and prepared correctly. Standard Rate and Data Service's newspaper and consumer magazine books list considerable information on publications' column widths, number of columns, page dimensions, trim size, binding method, printing process, and color availability.

Line drawings may be supplied as part of your camera-ready art, but photographs, and drawings with shades and tones must be photographed through a screen to achieve a dot pattern. This process is known as screening. There are various types of screens, so check with each publication's advertising representative for details.

PRINTING AND PERSONALIZATION

21

By following the steps outlined in the previous chapter, direct marketers will complete their camera-ready art and separations in preparation for printing. This chapter continues the step-by-step production process with information about printing methods and options, paper selection, press start-ups, and personalization.

Printing methods and options

Production personnel facing any printing challenge must consider three interdependent factors: time, quality and cost efficiency. When sufficient time is allowed for completion of a printing job, cost efficiency and quality generally can be improved. There are many other variables that affect quality, including choice of printing method, pre-press preparations, and paper selection. Cost efficiency is also a function of the suitability of the printing equipment chosen for a given project. This section provides information that will allow creative direct marketers to optimize the time/quality/cost factors in each printing job.

Selecting a method of printing

Although most direct mail printing jobs today are completed using the offset lithography method, direct marketers should also be familiar with two other methods that may be used for some applications: letterpress and rotogravure.

Offset Lithography

In this method of printing, art is photographed and reproduced on film. The image and non-image areas are separated by means of an on-press process. The image to be printed is treated to accept ink, while the non-print area is treated to accept water. Although this method is not as well adapted for producing highlights and shadows as are letterpress and rotogravure, it has two important virtues. Preparation for offset printing is relatively fast and inexpensive, and it is well adapted to today's methods of desktop publishing.

There are two main types of offset printing presses: sheet-fed and web. The sheet-fed press prints on individual sheets of paper, one by one. It is slower than web printing, but can allow for better quality printing and color fidelity. However, sheet-fed printing is not cost effective in higher quantity ranges (50,000 and up, generally), and you should therefore look into web printing if your quantities are this large. The web press is fed its paper from a continuous roll. There are small web presses meant for one- and two-color work (such as letters) and large presses that are as long as a railroad car. Generally, a printer prices the work done on these presses by the hours of press time used, so be sure to check what kind of press the printer's quote is based on.

Letterpress

Although new letterpress machines are no longer being made, some publishers and printers still keep them in use because this method provides a very sharp and clear image. Although high quality is achieved, letterpress is relatively costly and time consuming. It involves the mechanical separation of image from non-image. The print area is raised above the non-print area so that ink rollers only touch the portion that becomes the printed image.

Rotogravure

Although experts agree that rotogravure provides a superior printed product, it is cost effective only in very large quantities, usually several million at a minimum. Rotogravure allows for sharp detail and printing even on very light and inexpensive newsprint paper stock. It also involves the mechanical separation of image from non-image, but the process is different from letterpress. In this case, the image is sunken by etching into a copper cylinder or plate. Rotogravure is most commonly used in direct marketing by major catalog firms.

What the printer needs to know

To obtain an accurate quote from a printer, it is wise to supply as much detailed information as possible. Make sure that each bidder gets the same information, so that you are comparing apples to apples when all quotes are in.

This list of specifications will provide an outline for the type of information your printer will require. It is wise to develop your own quote sheet that you can use to fill out this information whenever you need to get quotes. This worksheet then can become the basis for a comprehensive purchase order once you award the job.

Print quote specifications

- *Quantity*—Total quantity, plus breakdowns for any versions within the main quantity for price tests, different dates, etc. Also indicate how many overrun copies you will accept and pay for. This may range from 3 to 10 percent depending on your policy.
- *Size*—Indicate both flat size and final folded size as well as the number and type of folds necessary. Create a diagram if folds are unusual or easy to misinterpret.
- *Paper stock*—Weight, finish, color, brand name if known. If you cannot describe the paper by its specifications, attach a sample. If you plan to supply your own paper, indicate this and attach a sample.
- *Colors*—Number of colors per side (expressed as 4 over 4 for four colors on both sides of a single sheet; 4 over 2 for a four-color front and two-color back; 2 over 2, 1 over 1, etc.). Also indicate whether separations are being supplied.
- *Specified colors*—Indicate Pantone Matching System (PMS) color(s) if known.
- *Halftones*—If any halftones are to be used, indicate how many and what size they will be.
- *Bleed or nonbleed*—Or mixed bleed and nonbleed, if applicable.

- *Proofs*—Type of proof you require, such as bluelines, chroma-lins, on-site press approval, etc.
- *Finishing*—Type of binding, die cuts, perforations, glues, varnish, or embossing, if applicable. You will also want to discuss with the printer whether these operations will be conducted on-line or done separately once printing is complete.
- *Packing*—How to pack and label printed material.
- *Delivery*—Where to deliver materials, when they should arrive, and to whose attention.

Paper selection

While most direct marketers do not purchase their own paper for printing, this can be the most cost-effective way to proceed in three main instances: when you plan to use an unusual paper stock, when you use the same paper stock again and again, or when you print an extremely large volume of material.

Even if you plan to have your printer purchase paper for you, it is important to become involved in the process of paper evaluation and selection. Because paper accounts for 30 to 50 percent of total production costs, and an average of 50 percent of printing costs, an effective selection can positively impact your budget and enhance the appearance of your printed piece.

Before selecting paper, consider the purpose of each piece you are printing, as well as the market segment it will reach. If you are creating a throw-away flyer, an inexpensive stock will probably suit your purposes. But if you are developing a reference catalog for expensive products, you may well want to invest in a heavy, coated stock with exceptional whiteness, brightness and opacity.

When developing an entire direct mail package, be sure to coordinate your paper choices. Just as colors should be coordinated, so should paper textures, weights and types.

The following attributes of paper will impact your decision-making process.

Weight. Paper weights are expressed in pounds, with each figure indicating the weight of a 500-sheet ream of paper. There are two sets of designations, one for "bond" stock and one for "book" stock. The standard bond paper stock is 17" × 22" and the standard book paper stock is 25″ × 38″. Thus, a 20-pound bond paper is one in which 500 sheets of 17″ × 22″ paper weigh 20 pounds (common bond papers are 16, 20 and 24 pounds). A 50-pound book paper is one in which 500 sheets of 25″ × 38″ paper weigh 50 pounds (common book papers range from 30 to 120 pounds, with those in the 50-to-100-pound range the most widely used).

Strength. The web-offset process requires especially strong paper that will not burst, tear or break under stress. Another measure is surface strength, which evaluates whether bits of the paper are likely to shed onto the printing blanket, resulting in hickeys (blemishes) on other printed pieces.

Smoothness. In general, the smoother the paper, the better its printability. Smooth sheets allow for flatness under printing pressure, which results in better dot formation and greater fidelity to the original image.

Brightness. The brighter the paper, the more expensive it will be. Brightness is a measure of how much light the paper reflects in combination with the transparent inks printed upon it.

Gloss. Another function of light reflection. The higher the gloss, the more costly the paper.

Opacity. The more opaque the paper, the more costly it will be. Opacity is measured on a scale of 1 to 100, with 100 being completely opaque. Opacity is important because "show through" from the other side of a printed piece is distracting to the selling message, and detracts from a quality image.

Bulk. This measure of thickness is established by measuring how high a pile of given paper stock is. High-bulk stock may increase opacity without adding weight. It is often used for business reply cards that must be sturdy enough to meet U.S. Postal Service standards.

Whiteness. Some papers tend toward pink, blue or grey, while others approach pure whiteness. A very white stock enhances color reproduction and fidelity.

Grain. This is a function of the alignment of paper fibers in a paper stock. Paper should be folded with the grain for best results.

Finish. Stocks may be coated with clay and rolled to a matte, dull, gloss, or ultragloss finish. Coated papers are good for color reproduction and fidelity, but extremely glossy papers may be hard to read under fluorescent lights. Uncoated stocks are called vellum, antique, wove and smooth. Their finishes are determined by the way in which they are run through the finishing rollers.

Press start-ups

For simple, one- and two-color jobs, you may choose not to attend the press start-up, relying instead on blueline proofs. Such proofs allow you to check one more time for typographical errors, to see that all halftones and art are in the right places, and that there are no specks or broken type to compromise the final print job.

The importance, complexity, and quality of the job you are printing will impact your decision on whether to attend the press start-up in person. When color fidelity is essential, your presence at the printing plant may help ensure the quality standards you require. However, some clients put so much trust in their printing sales representatives that they allow these individuals to give press approval for millions of color brochures.

If you or your representative decide to attend the press start-up, be aware that these events seldom take place during "bankers' hours." Most color presses run 24 hours a day, and when it is time for a new job to go on press, that is when the press approval must take place. You will need to be on call for a possible middle-of-the-night summons to the printing plant to see your important, full-color job go on press.

At the press start-up, the pressman will begin to run your job and bring you samples to check against your chromalins or press proofs for fidelity. You will also want to make sure the printing is in register. Use a jeweler's magnifying glass to see if the dot pattern is crisply in line, or "hanging" over the edge. Take time to make a folding dummy from one of the proofs—it's better to catch an error in panel configuration now than after all 5,000,000 pieces have been run. Once the color is approved, make sure that the material that has been run up to that point is destroyed—not salvaged after you leave as part of the press run.

Personalization

The first computer letters were produced in 1952, but it has only been in the past 20 years that methods of personalization have been widely used by direct marketers. Four decades ago, very few firms could take advantage of computer letters because of limitations of the technology and—just as important— because so few computerized lists were available on magnetic tape.

During the 1960s and 1970s, impact printing was introduced, followed swiftly by ink-jet and laser processes. Yet even today, the more sophisticated personalization techniques only can be used cost effectively by larger mailers. However, with the range of options now available for personalization, most mailers can find a way to communicate more personally with their customers. The following personalization methods are presented in order from the simplest to the most sophisticated, costly and complex.

Labels. Generated from a magnetic tape containing names of customers or prospects, labels are prepared so that they can be affixed one by one to an order form, outer envelope, or catalog. Labels commonly bear a key code in addition to the recipient's name and address. Pressure-sensitive labels allow for the buyer to transfer the label from the addressing device to the reply device, thus assuring that the direct marketing company knows the original source of the name.

Word processing. Today even the most inexpensive personal computers can be outfitted with software that allows for the creation of personalized letters. When used in tandem with a letter-quality or near letter-quality printer, such personalized letters— prepared using impact printing just as an individual letter would be—give the recipient the impression of a one-to-one message. The applications of word processing are usually limited to smaller lists for two main reasons. First, word processing is a comparatively time-consuming process. Second, while word processing goes on, the personal computer and printer are tied up, thereby limiting other business functions.

Impact printing. Similar to a word processor, impact printing combines the look of an individually typewritten letter with the opportunity to do fill-ins of names, addresses, and other information relevant to the recipient. Impact printing usually is done by an outside service, and is considered best for short runs with limited personalization. There is no type variation possible with impact printing.

Ink-jet printing. This computerized process for personalization improves on flexibility, but is also more costly to set up than impact printing. In this method, ink is sprayed onto a bar with a series of holes determined by a magnetic tape. Ink-jet printing is used mainly for mailing-address labels and letters. It is well adapted for long runs and extensive personalization, and can accommodate varied typefaces.

Laser printing. Laser printing is more versatile and considerably faster than the personalization methods that came before it. It allows for personalization in various parts of a direct mail package—order forms, letters, brochures, and action devices all may be personalized using laser printing. This electromagnetic process allows a computer to cue charged particles as to where they should adhere, thereby producing the printed message. Laser printing allows for considerable typeface variety, including capabilities for a typeface that looks handwritten.

Who will do your personalization?

Some firms that do extensive personalization may purchase their own impact printers, or perhaps even ink-jet or laser printing capabilities if they use them continually. Many direct marketing companies, however, will seek an outside source for completion of their personalization work, be it a computer service bureau, printer, or full-service lettershop.

To select the best vendor for your job, first decide which method of personalization you prefer. Then, in dealing with prospective vendors, compare not only their prices—but also their time frames for completion of the work. A careful look at the vendor's equipment list will also help you perform a "reality check" on the firm's capabilities for quick-turnaround projects.

PRODUCTION PLANNING/WORKING WITH SUPPLIERS

22

Producing direct mail is an art akin to juggling: you must keep several balls in the air at once. A day's work on a single mailing might require monitoring the arrival of lists at the service bureau, ordering outer envelopes, finalizing copy, choosing a brochure type style, and supervising photography. Considering that most production managers coordinate at least two or three mailings at once, the importance of communication and careful scheduling is obvious. This chapter will explain how buyers of direct mail services can work best with the various suppliers who will bring their ideas to life. It will also discuss the best ways to schedule mailings, as well as the importance of a detailed production time line.

Working with direct mail suppliers

All too often, direct marketing creative people wait until their ideas are cast in cement before involving the vendors who will provide printing and production services to complete a job. It is a much better policy to invite vendor participation from the earliest stages of creative planning. Interaction among copywriter, art director, production manager and vendors will ensure the most cost-effective creative solution to the problem at hand. What's more, vendors with state-of-the-art formats and processes to

369

share may provide ideas that increase the number of creative options to consider.

The help of knowledgeable vendors can be especially crucial if you are new to the production process—and therefore vulnerable to mistakes that may cost time and money. Many fledgling direct marketers cleverly seek out a group of dependable, experienced suppliers to rely on until they learn enough about production to proceed on their own.

Direct mail is a very complex medium for production. Lists of names must be rented from outside sources, or selected from house files. The lists must be prepared for mailing—a process that may involve merge/purge, preparation for zip code sequencing or carrier route presort, and production of labels or of magnetic tapes for personalization. The preparation of pieces for mailing includes typography, art and photography, keyline and paste-up, separations, paper selection and purchase, and printing. Lettershop services might include personalization as well as insertion—or personalization might take place "on line" as pieces are printed and assembled.

In some cases, each of these functions is completed by a different organization—each with its own strengths and weaknesses. The more "cooks in the broth," the more opportunities there are for vendors to point the finger in blame at others along the production line. But when vendors are included as part of a team—invited to attend everything from the initial brainstorming session to the final evaluation meeting—the chances increase for smooth and harmonious transfers from one production stage to another.

Considerations in selecting vendors

There are several important factors to consider in selecting vendors for direct mail applications. These include price, service, flexibility, creativity, quality, suitability and timeliness.

Price

This is an important consideration in any direct mail venture. The lower the cost per thousand of your package, the lower your break-even figure. But selecting the lowest bidder without evaluating other factors can be a mistake. Make sure that each bidder has quoted the job using the exact same specifications. Then compare each bidder's qualifications using the other criteria listed here. You may be better off using a supplier whose price is a bit higher, but who can deliver better service, more creative ideas, or more timely delivery. Another hint: when you ask for prices, don't stop with a quotation on your original quantity for mailing. Also have each vendor bid on your projected roll-out quantities. A small vendor may be able to deliver a bargain price on a test quantity of 100,000 but may be unable to compete on roll-outs of a million or more. A large vendor whose test-quantity price seems high may be much more cost-efficient for the roll-out. In that case, you might want to negotiate with the larger vendor for a better price on the test quantity. Or consider switching vendors between test and roll-out—although this can be a dangerous proposition fraught with potential problems in the transition.

Service

A good direct mail vendor is available to answer any question and to hold your hand throughout the production process. In addition to these obvious qualifications, the direct mail purchaser will want to look for subtle signs to select the right vendor for the job. Does the vendor have a good understanding of your business and its particular challenges? Do you feel mutual trust with the vendor? Does the vendor speak in layman's terms to you, or is your head spinning with technical language the vendor seems to think will impress you? If you believe that a particular vendor will fit in well with your way of doing business, you can facilitate the service function by helping the vendor to understand your company and your needs. Allow the vendor to see the big picture. Take him or her on a company tour . . . provide examples of past successes and failures . . . introduce the vendor to all major decision makers whose opinions will impact production decisions. A good vendor will relish this opportunity to gain knowledge that will help him or her serve you better. If a vendor seems too busy to soak up this vital background information, look elsewhere for the service you need.

Flexibility

Some separators, printers and lettershops are so tightly booked that they will schedule your job to begin at a particular hour of a particular day. If you miss that date for any reason, you may be bumped back days or even weeks in the schedule. Other vendors are more flexible—able to juggle their schedules and work your job in even if your production timetable falls behind. Still other firms can accommodate your late job—but only if you are willing to pay overtime costs for night, weekend and holiday work. Discuss scheduling with your vendors as soon as you become serious about using their services. Ask them what will happen if your job arrives an hour . . . a day . . . two days late or even later at their shop. Hold them to the promises they make. And a word to the wise: to avoid problems, set a production timetable that allows for a margin of error. There is nothing more unfair than to present a lettershop with a job that is supposed to be in the mail "tomorrow," when they were expecting materials in time to allow two weeks for insertion, labeling and mailing.

Creativity

Some direct marketers don't allow their vendors to be creative. Instead, they present them with a set of very rigid specifications—right down to the weight and finish of the paper stock, or the exact positioning for personalization. Some vendors are perfectly content to function as order takers, and would not have many creative suggestions even if they were invited to provide them. On the other hand, the best vendors offer their ideas whether they are solicited or not, suggesting everything from formats and printing press configurations to ways of streamlining the color separation process. Look for vendors who are full of ideas designed to save you money and time, or to add an extra flourish to the package you are designing. Their enthusiasm adds to the creative environment much more than a vendor who is strictly interested in writing down nuts and bolts like quantity, number of inserts and mail date. For your part, be sure to ask your vendors' advice about the creative challenges you face: there may be an easy solution that can be accomplished during the process of production, printing or lettershop activities.

Quality

Measurements of quality in direct marketing must always consider the objectives of the mailing piece. Some simple pieces selling items that do not require color photography may be fine printed on plain offset paper, and utilizing stock envelopes overprinted with one-color type. Even so, there are good one-color printing jobs and poor ones. Talk to your vendor about your objectives for quality in two regards. First, discuss your needs in terms of color fidelity, quality of paper stock, uniqueness of format, extent of personalization, etc. Then discuss quality control in relation to the production of the job itself. Look at your vendors' samples of previous jobs done in your price and quality range. How crisp is the type? How clean is the printing? Are there "hickeys" and other imperfections to mar the appearance of the job? A good vendor will understand your parameters of quality and not insist that every job be a jumbo spectacular extravaganza. At the same time, a good vendor will be just as vigilant about the quality control of a two-color, two-fold brochure on offset paper as he or she is about a glossy, four-color mailing with 12 inserts.

Suitability

When a new vendor comes to call, find out all you can about the company's suitability for your needs. Ask for an equipment list, and find out how much capacity the vendor has available for you. A lettershop may list 10 six-station inserting machines, for example, but neglect to tell you that half of them are reserved much of the time for a regular client. Ask the vendor about his or her experience with firms in your business. Find out if this particular sales rep has experience with your type of business—perhaps the company has another rep that would be better suited to consult with you. Ask for references from firms of comparable size and sophistication, and check them carefully. Find out about the stability of the vendor: does his or her firm pay their bills on time? There are few things more frustrating than learning that your printer or lettershop has gone bankrupt and shut its doors—with your job half done and inaccessible.

It is also important to find out if the vendor ever does subcontracting, and under what circumstances. Ask if you will be informed when a job requires subcontracting, and who will take responsibility for problems that may arise. Ask the vendor what his or her firm's invoices are like. Do the invoices conform to the language used on quotations? Some firm's invoices are so complex that this factor alone is enough to lose them business to companies with "user-friendly" invoices. What about up-charges? Will you be alerted in advance if additional money is needed? Explain to your vendors in no uncertain terms that additional charges should be discussed as soon as they become necessary. You should not accept unexplained upcharges that appear for the first time on an invoice. Ask the vendor what his or her firm's payment terms are: they may vary considerably. Some companies expect money up front from new customers, while others routinely extend Net 30 Day terms. You may be asked to submit references for a credit check: find out if this will be necessary and how long the credit check may take.

Timeliness

Part of every estimate or quote should include a statement of the time necessary to complete the job. Once again, some vendors are more flexible on time than others. Ask the vendor if the "two weeks" figure holds only if you deliver materials on a specifically scheduled date. How long would it take to complete the job if it came into the vendor's shop unannounced? What if time were of the essence and you were willing to pay for overtime and weekend work—how short could the time frame then become? The answers to these questions will help you determine how helpful this vendor will be when you are in a time crunch, or when rush jobs come up unexpectedly.

Your responsibilities as a buyer

Vendors have expectations for a good working relationship, just as direct mail buyers do. There are several things that you can do to ensure that you will be a preferred customer with the vendors of your choice. These include paying fairly and on time, creating a team atmosphere, limiting the number of vendors you use, giving vendors one source for authoritative information, showing appreciation for a job well done, and fostering good communication.

Payment terms

In most cases, sales representatives are not paid commission on the jobs they expedite for you until your firm pays its bills. That means that unless you make sure your bills are paid according to agreed-upon terms, you may be compromising your sales rep's livelihood. It only stands to reason, then, that customers who pay on time will receive preferred treatment from vendors. If your vendor asks for payment terms that are more stringent than you are used to—say, Net 10 Days instead of Net 30 Days—the time to discuss other arrangements is up front rather than after the job has been billed. As a direct mail buyer, make it your business to know your firm's policy on paying bills. You may have to become an advocate for your best vendors to ensure that they are paid on time. If you abdicate this responsibility, you risk diluting your vendors' loyalty to you.

Another point about payments: some buyers pride themselves on squeezing the last dime out of their vendors on every single job. All vendors expect that there will be times when they need to "sharpen their pencils," even to the point of eliminating profit for their firms and commissions for themselves. But if this unprofitable situation is the case every time they deal with you, the vendor will soon move on to more fertile fields. The moral: expect your vendors to make a fair profit from your business, and you will encourage their loyalty.

Team atmosphere

It will be in your best interest to foster a team atmosphere among your vendors and your co-workers. In addition, it may take some of the burden away from you if separators, printers and letter-shops can communicate among themselves without having to go through you with every question. Cultivate vendors that you can trust, and share with them the information they need to do their jobs well. If it seems to you that a vendor is probing for proprietary information, ask why he or she needs to know. There may be a good reason. For instance, list brokers cannot do the best possible job for you without knowing what lists have worked in the past. Printers may ask when you expect to roll out with a mailing so that they may pencil it onto their schedules. On the other hand, if you ever feel that your sales rep is acting as a spy, discuss it with him or her, and consider dropping the vendor. An atmosphere of mutual trust is essential for smooth direct mail production.

Limit your vendors

Having only one vendor for each type of application can be a mistake, but having too many vendors can be just as grave an error. Your best bet is to cultivate a manageable group of excellent vendors. Each vendor should receive enough business to make you an important client, but not so much that he or she becomes complacent or considers your account a monopoly. When impressive new vendors come onto the scene, invite them to bid competitively with your existing roster of vendors. Don't make the mistake of "jumping ship" for an untried vendor whose quote is a few cents lower on a per-thousand basis. Try new vendors cautiously, and consider other factors such as their service, timeliness and quality before adding them to your active roster of suppliers.

Provide one central information source

Vendors need one final authority who gives them their orders and deals with their concerns—not a roomful of people providing conflicting ideas with no clarification. Be sure that you—or someone in your firm—has both the responsibility and the authority to serve as the vendors' central source of information.

Show appreciation for a job well done

Buyers often assume that vendors should get all their gratification from the money they earn. Some buyers treat vendors as a Santa Claus for grown-ups—they expect the vendors to give and give without ever receiving anything in return. This may extend beyond professional service: indeed some direct mail buyers expect lavish lunches, baseball tickets, and other "freebies" from their vendors at regular intervals. One production buyer enlisted his sales representatives to show up one Saturday morning to sod his front lawn! Vendors expect to render professional service—and to pick up the tab for lunches—but they all too seldom receive a simple thank-you when they go out of their way to do an exceptional job.

Smart buyers will provide praise where it is due—just as readily as they complain when there is a problem. Some firms go so far as to arrange vendor recognition parties where they thank their best suppliers for a job well done. Other buyers are thoughtful enough to write detailed letters of thanks when a sales representative provides exceptional service. These letters may become valuable testimonials which are greatly appreciated by the vendor—and help to build loyalty in the process.

Foster good communication

Just as you quiz prospective vendors on their records for price, service, capacity and other factors, you should be willing to let your sales representative know what is important to your firm. Will you be buying primarily on the basis of price, or is top-notch quality the goal? Does your firm run on a predictable timetable, or should the vendor expect late materials and last-minute changes? Spend time going over previous jobs with new vendors, telling them about the challenges you have faced, and inviting them to provide ideas for improvements. After a vendor completes a job, take time to sit down and go over the finished product. Discuss how it could be improved next time around—and how your working relationship could be enhanced.

When to let an advertising agency do your production

A quick read through this section should convince most readers that direct mail production is a complex process. In most instances, firms that produce mailing quantities in the millions each year will reap savings of both time and money by developing their own in-house production departments to expedite this work. On the other hand, there are several reasons why you may prefer to allow an advertising agency to handle your production chores.

If your mailings are small or infrequent, you will not have much opportunity to develop clout with vendors. You may be much better off dealing with an agency or production firm that has developed the relationships necessary to carry out your job smoothly and on time.

If you don't have trained personnel on staff, it will be false economy to try to save an agency mark up by keeping the work in house. People who are untrained in production can innocently make mistakes that cost you huge amounts of time and money. Until you can recruit a top-notch production staff, you will be safer using outside services for expediting.

If price is not your number-one object, you can save yourself and your staff the hassles of production by paying an agency or production firm on either a fee basis or a mark up of services (usually 17.65 percent).

Scheduling and critical dates

Success in direct marketing has much to do with proper timing. Seasonal and competitive factors are important, as is the phasing of tests and roll-outs within your own program.

Sometimes the optimum promotional schedule is fairly straightforward, as in the case of a holiday-theme product or an item tied to the Summer Olympics or the World Series. And even when there is no obvious "season" for your product or service, the dynamics of the marketplace may make it better for you to mail or promote during some weeks or months than during others.

Seasonality

General rules of thumb for the best and worst direct mail months are a helpful starting point for your efforts. But you must test for yourself to determine whether January is truly the best month for you.

In his book, *Successful Direct Marketing Methods,* Bob Stone offers the following information generated by a three-year test program for a nonseasonal item. Here is what happened in the test that Stone ran, where a rating of 100 is the top score:

MONTH	RATING
January	100.0
February	96.3
March	71.0
April	71.5
May	71.5
June	67.0
July	73.3
August	87.0
September	79.0
October	89.9
November	81.0
December	79.0

You might try the same technique if you have a nonseasonal offer: mail the same number of direct mail kits to random groups from a homogeneous list at the beginning of each month of the year.

According to this study, June is the worst month for mailings, yielding only two-thirds as well as the "top" month of January. But if your offer is for merchandise that is especially appealing in June—a sale on swimsuits and lightweight summer shirts, for instance—June might be a fine month for you despite the rule of thumb. And obviously, if your offer is related to Christmas, you won't let the 79.0 in September or the 81.0 in November scare you away. Your firm's scores naturally will differ dramatically from the average for nonseasonal items.

If you are entering the test phase of a campaign, experts agree that you should run your first test in the strongest season for your product. You can then factor in the seasonality component for later tests simply by considering your best month's results as 100 percent and multiplying the new test-month rating by the number of orders in your best month's figure. This will let you estimate the number of orders you may expect in the new month. Here is an example, assuming the same number of pieces mailed to equal portions of a homogeneous list:

January rating:	100.0	January results:	90 orders
June rating:	67.0	Anticipated June results: $(90 \times .67 =)$	60 orders

As for business and industrial mailings, factors like the Christmas holidays and other vacation periods have some effect on marketing schedules. However, the seasonality factor here depends mostly on the industry in question. School supplies sold to school districts have a demand based on the school calendar. And if you are mailing to landscapers, your prime time will differ dramatically from that of snowmobile parts suppliers. But if your seasonality factor isn't so obvious, some testing to determine what months spark better lead and sales responses with the same offer could provide you with profit-building information—or at least some explanation of what may be disturbing slides in response from time to time.

If you are planning to advertise in magazines and newspapers, competitive factors should be taken into consideration. Nonseasonal propositions do best when not pitted against heavy ad schedules that ordinarily exist at holiday time. In addition, advertising readership is down in the summer, or at least attention levels suffer at this time, because many people are on vacation. So the best times for direct response space advertising are generally January through the beginning of spring, and Labor Day through Thanksgiving.

If you are selling summer products, of course, you musn't take this warning too seriously. You can begin testing in the early spring to determine your own response curve by month or week. And if your product is Christmas-related, you may safely promote up until the time when you cannot promise delivery by Christmas (or—and perhaps more importantly—until the time when your consumer no longer *believes* you can deliver, even if you know you can). This time frame is widening yearly with today's low-cost shipments via Federal Express and other courier services.

The critical date schedule

The first step in establishing a schedule for any direct response medium is to *determine the optimum date for the message to reach the prospect.* In direct mail, for instance, it is not enough to schedule only up to the date your message is mailed. If you are doing a bulk mailing, it may take 10 days or more before all of your prospects receive the piece you've mailed. And in space advertising, don't take the cover date of the publication as a given for its arrival at the prospect's door: check out the delivery date specifically, and then choose the proper issue for the impact you seek. Then work back from the optimum delivery date to determine a schedule that will accomplish your goal. You may still be able to make a date that seems uncomfortably close, but only with a firm schedule and much vigilance. Following are some of the checklist factors in critical-date schedules for direct mail and space advertising.

Direct mail

There are as many direct mail critical date schedules as there are firms in the business, and very little agreement about how long it takes to get certain things done. Where there are many parties involved, and a computerized letter operation is being used, a direct mail program may require a six-month schedule. On the other hand, firms whose approval processes are swift and whose suppliers are accommodating may be able to take a mailing campaign from the concept stage to the prospect's hands in a matter of a few weeks.

Naturally, each link in the chain of such an operation considers his or her timing to be paramount. A prototype schedule from a printer, for example, allows a month for printing but only three days for copywriting. You can imagine that the writer's optimum schedule would be quite different. We will therefore list the factors important in a mail-campaign schedule, in the basic order in which they are done. You can adjust these as needed to determine a workable schedule for your own campaign.

Critical date factors

1. Approve marketing plan.
2. Create rough layouts and copy (this is often necessary for list owners to approve rentals to you).
3. Select and order lists (obtaining the lists for a campaign takes several weeks, and a merge/purge may take a week or longer to complete).
4. Obtain price quotes for color separations, printing, lettershop work, and other necessary production services; award jobs to vendors; make vendors aware of time schedules so they can make available the proper amount of time for your job.
5. Approve rough layouts and copy, and proceed to comprehensive layouts and final copy.
6. Order envelopes; in most cases manufactured envelopes take longer to produce than other printed materials (three weeks or more).
7. Arrange for photography and have product shots and other necessary photography completed.
8. Approve final layouts and copy and proceed to typesetting, keylining and paste-up.
9. Receive lists from broker and expedite merge/purge operation so that it can be completed in time for lettershop work.
10. Approve keylined boards and send four-color work to separator.
11. Approve color separations by means of chromalin or press proofs.

12. Send boards and separations to printer(s).
13. Approve blueline proofs from printer(s).
14. Supervise press approvals at printer(s).
15. Send mailing instructions to lettershop, including list of all materials that will be delivered there.
16. Expedite folding and binding of printed pieces.
17. Coordinate arrival of envelopes, printed pieces, and labels (product of list merge/purge operation) at lettershop.
18. Expedite lettershop work (labeling, materials insertion and mailing).
19. Ascertain exact mail date (national penetration will be approximately 10 days later).

Once you have developed a critical date schedule that works for you, it is an excellent idea to set up a computer program that plugs in the optimum dates for you, based on the drop date for mailing. In addition, your computer program can help you develop a master calender that helps keep track of all the projects you have going, all on one spread sheet or bulletin board.

Space Advertising

The critical date schedule for a space advertising campaign is simpler than for a direct mail campaign in that there is no involvement with printers, lettershops or lists. However, a space advertising campaign has the added factor of having to meet the publication's closing dates for space reservations and materials. These dates vary by publication. Check the consumer or business *Standard Rate and Data Services (SRDS)* books for magazines to determine these dates for publications in which you wish to place ads. There you will also find the specifications for the types of boards or film each publication needs, so that you can direct your production people accordingly. For newspaper ads, *SRDS* has a newspaper rate and data book that provides the same helpful information.

23

LISTS, SERVICE BUREAUS, THE POST OFFICE AND LETTERSHOPS

For most creative people, responsibility for a direct mail package ends once they proof their copy on keylined boards or approve color on a press check. And although many creative types know at least the basics of list selection, merge/purge and mailing, they may not have occasion to learn the nuts and bolts of these operations. The more the creative person knows and understands, however, the more valuable he or she can be to the direct marketing team at large.

This chapter will explain the basics of list selection, database marketing and list brokerage, merge/purge and other functions of a computer service bureau, postal regulations and relations with the post office, and lettershop functions.

List selection, databases and list brokerage

No matter how excellent your product and how outstanding your creative execution, your direct mail package is destined to fail if it is sent to the wrong list of prospects. In recent years, marketers have begun to take fuller advantage of computer applications to hone in on the best target markets and list segments for their offers.

There are three basic types of lists a direct mailer may use. These are customer lists, lists of proven mail-order buyers, and compiled lists.

Customer lists

Sometimes called "house lists," these files belong to the firm because they contain names and addresses of individuals who have purchased merchandise in the past. Customer names are the most responsive lists of all because these individuals have established a relationship with the direct marketing firm. A franchise has been established: these individuals want or need the company's goods or services, they are satisfied with prices and payment terms offered, and they know and trust the company.

Many direct marketing firms also keep lists of inquiries ands referrals. The prospects on this list are those who have not yet purchased a product or service. They have expressed interest through a mail or phone response, or have been referred to the firm by an active customer. These names may prove to be more responsive than names rented from other firms, but they are generally less responsive than customer lists.

Mail-order buyers

Direct marketing firms may choose to offer the names of their buyers or inquiries for one-time rental at a "per thousand" fee. When you rent such lists, you may test an "nth name" sample of as few as 5000 names initially, and then rent larger quantities from the list if the original test proves successful. Rental fees generally range from $50.00 per thousand and up, depending upon the "list selects" you make. Many lists are offered with selections based on age, sex, income, purchase history, geography, or zip code.

The three main criteria for list evaluation are recency, frequency and monetary. You should expect to pay more for recent, or "hotline" names—individuals who have purchased from the renting firm within the past three months or six months. Customers who buy often (frequency) are also especially attractive. The monetary criterion helps you zero in on customers who can afford your price range, be it $25.00 for a monogrammed turtleneck top or $600 for a compact disc system.

In addition to general mail responsiveness, a list's affinity for your type of product is very important. For example, if you plan to market a line of limited-edition collector plates, you might rent lists of individuals who buy collector prints, jewelry, and home accessories by mail. A point to keep in mind: in this case, you would probably not be successful in trying to rent lists of collector plate buyers from other companies: they would turn down your rental request as being too competitive. Once you have built up your own list of collector plate buyers, however, you might well be able to exchange names with some direct competitors.

Lists of proven mail-order buyers are next on the hierarchy, after customer lists and inquiries/referrals. The *Standard Rate and Data Service (SRDS)* book of lists available for rental is the size of a metropolitan telephone book, attesting to the variety of mail-responsive lists that are available.

Compiled lists

These are usually created from a data base of information put together for purposes other than promotion. Examples might be membership lists, automobile or boat registrations, telephone directory lists, or standard industrial codes. Such lists are considerably less desirable for direct mailers than are lists of proven mail-order buyers, since the names they contain are not prequalified in any way.

Compiled lists may be used with success if they are specific enough in content. For instance, a compiled list of college marketing professors is a worthwhile possibility for a firm selling marketing textbooks. Another possibility is to use computer techniques such as regression analysis to identify the most likely segments of a compiled list. Techniques of this type, however, are often too expensive to be cost effective for small- and medium-sized firms.

How to develop and use a database

The most important concept to remember in establishing and building a database is to keep the customer as the focus. Don't become so fascinated by statistics that you forget to look at things from the motivational side. Strive to understand why consumers do what they do.

To return to the corner store analogy, a database is little more than a sophisticated version of the old-fashioned retailer's "data retrieval system." The corner grocer probably kept all of his data in his head. And he had few enough customers that he could keep it all straight. But today's successful personal sales executive is likely to have a file or at least a rolodex with cards about each customer.

The insurance salesperson knows size of family, ages, disabilities and health problems, whether any family members smoke or indulge in dangerous hobbies, who travels extensively, and even whether his customers exercise regularly. The real estate star knows when each customer last changed houses, how much they spent for that house, what kind of financing they arranged, and when they're likely to be in the market again. Real estate agents also keep track of family size and changes in status—i.e., when the last child goes off to college—because these factors have a great deal to do with when a customer might be in the market to buy or sell.

The designer clothing salesperson knows her customer's size, her favorite designers, and her preference for suits, separates, dresses, evening wear, etc. She makes it her business to know whether this customer goes South for the winter or stays in the North—this has to do with the weights of clothing the customer will wish to own, and whether she'll be in the market for resort wear.

The idea is this: as direct marketers develop their lists or databases, they should think about what they'd like to have on rolodex cards or in file folders about each of their customers. The database is basically the same thing—the only difference is that since it's captured in an automated form, it's much easier to call upon in volume. Instead of going after one customer at a time, you can go after *all* your tennis buffs, *all* your new empty-nesters, or *all* the ladies who head South for the winter right after Christmas.

This information may be captured in several ways. For example, it may come as a result of inferences made based on products or services purchased, and the timing of such purchases. It may be recorded on the basis of customer questionnaires. Or it could come from lifestyle data based on customer zip code or other key information.

Essentially, database marketing allows direct mailers to move beyond quantitative measures such as age, sex and geographic area. Now they can draw knowledge about subtler differences of customers' attitudes and lifestyles. Ultimately, both demographic and psychographic information helps marketers target their audiences and refine their selling messages better than ever before.

List brokerage

Some direct marketers choose to rent their lists directly from the owner or list maintainer, bypassing the function of list broker. But there are good reasons to retain the services of a knowledgeable list broker, especially if your list rental volume is substantial.

List brokers serve as advisors on list selection, and as expeditors for list rental arrangements and list delivery. The advice of a list broker is free to prospective list renters. The broker is paid a commission (in the range of 10 to 20 percent) by the list owner whose lists are rented through the broker.

To establish a relationship with a list broker, the direct marketer needs to share information about the products and services being sold, present and projected volume, selling methods, and past list results. This requires a measure of trust on the part of the direct marketer, but the list broker's recommendations will only be as good as the background data he or she has received.

The list broker provides recommendations for rentals in the form of data cards carrying recent information on prospective lists. Data card information includes the list universe, average order size in dollars, and available "selects" by sex, geography, dollar amount, purchase type, etc. The broker may also supply a rationale for each list: why it makes sense for your firm to test it for a given product or promotion.

Smaller direct marketers, or those who mail infrequently, may bypass the list-brokerage function since brokers prefer to work with major mailers with frequent roll-out mailings in six- or seven-figure volume. If you fall into this group, you will find the SRDS book on direct mail lists an invaluable source of information on lists and how to rent them.

Computer service bureaus

Most direct marketers know the computer service bureau as a company that completes the merge/purge function. Although merge/purge is an important aspect of the service bureau's work, these firms may perform a number of other jobs for a direct marketing company, including database management, list analysis, and personalization.

Merge/purge is a shorthand term representing the function of combining lists (merge) and removing duplications (purge). If mailings are small, or if they are being made to only a few lists that may not include many duplications, it is not practical to perform a merge/purge function costing $1000 and up. However, if mail volume is large, and if a number of lists are being tested, it becomes cost effective to eliminate duplicates.

When using merge/purge, it is not unusual for a mailer to eliminate 12 to 15 percent of the total names rented for a given promotion. At a mailing cost of $400 per thousand, you save yourself up to $6000 on each 100,000 names rented. In addition, you eliminate the prospect's aggravation at receiving two or more of the same mailing piece.

Merge/purge instructions to the service bureau should include prioritization of lists. The most expensive lists should receive low priority. Less expensive lists should come next, and finally the highest priority should go to the house list—names the mailer already owns and for which no rental fee should be paid.

In the merge/purge process, the computer scans high-priority names first. The computer credits each name and address to the list on which it first appears. If a name and address appears on two, three, four or more of the rented lists, the computer makes a note for its analysis report, but "purges" the output of those names. Thus the output for expensive, low-priority lists might be 80 percent or less of the input names. If the mailer or list broker has negotiated a "net down" agreement, only the names actually mailed will require a rental payment.

The merge/purge process also may include several other important functions. *Address standardization* ensures that addresses and zip codes are corrected if necessary, or removed from the output if they cannot be mailed. The "nixies," or invalid names, should not have to be rented by the mailer. *Internal duplications* within each list are eliminated to avoid renting and mailing the same name twice. *DMA pander names* are also eliminated: these are individuals who have written to the Direct Marketing Association asking that they not be sent unsolicited direct mail offers. *Key coding* of each name and address can be done according to the mailer's orders. Finally, the *net name output* can be prepared to meet postal specifications: in zip-code sequence, third class presort, or carrier-route presort. In addition, the output names can be presented in the form of labels to be affixed to envelopes or order cards, or on magnetic tape for use in laser, impact or ink-jet techniques.

Database management

Good list maintenance helps ensure the cost effectiveness of mailing to a house list. It also increases the list's value as a rental property to other firms. As new buyer names come onto the file, a service bureau can be charged with the responsibility of recording information such as name, address, category (such as buyer, inquiry, referral), original order history (source, date, dollar amounts), and other variables. In addition, the service bureau can check for duplication against the current file, correct zip codes, standardize street addresses, and carrier-route code each name. When house list names are mailed, the service bureau can also be charged with updating order history.

List analysis

At the discretion of the mailer, service bureaus can create a wide range of analysis reports that direct marketers may use to draw conclusions about rental lists—especially in comparison with their own house lists. For instance, a *multi-buyer* report contains all records identified as duplications by a merge purge. *Statistical reports* profile each merge/purge, providing such information as gross input, percentage of customer names eliminated, percentage of duplicates eliminated, list prioritization, number of pander names eliminated, single versus multi-buyers, net output, percentage of internal duplicates, state-by-state totals, and other information. *Sales by state/sales by carrier route reports* let mailers find out which regions, states and carrier routes perform best for certain products and offers. *Sales by sex, method of payment and average order size* can also be tracked.

Personalization

Some service bureaus offer various personalization services in house, using their own laser and impact printers. Using the service bureau to create computer letters may save time if the firm's capacity is high enough for your application. It may also eliminate some of the expediting work necessary to transfer the merge/purge output to a printer. Mailers may prefer to have the service bureau stop short of this step, preparing the magnetic tape of names to be transferred to a printer or lettershop for completion.

Postal regulations

The United States Postal Service (USPS) recognizes direct mail as a huge market, one whose volume helps keep first class rates down for consumers. USPS regulations allow for a wide variety of acceptable formats and mailing rates. However, direct mailers must observe a very specific set of postal rules and regulations.

One of the most valuable relationships for any direct mailer is an ongoing communication process with the local post office or bulk mail center. Postmasters can provide "how to" materials that will save considerable time in creating mailable pieces. In addition, it is essential that you understand exactly how your local postmaster enforces certain regulations that may be open to various interpretations. Indeed, a cordial relationship with the postmaster can be very helpful if a critical matter ever comes up.

Most experienced direct marketers can tell at least one horror story about a postal problem. Perhaps it was a Business Reply Card that was not quite thick enough to be sent through the mail, resulting in lost orders. Or maybe it was a first class piece with an outer envelope just a shade over 11-1/2" wide, resulting in a surcharge for "nonstandard first class mail." One marketer prepared a direct mail package that, according to his scale, weighed a shade under the basic maximum weight for a bulk-rate mailing (currently 3.3667 ounces). More than a million kits were printed and prepared at the lettershop before it was discovered that according to the post office scale, the kit weighed a shade *over* the maximum bulk-rate weight. With many thousands of dollars in extra postage due, the marketer decided to have the envelopes opened, and each piece inside the kit trimmed down. All of this could have been avoided if a dummy kit had been carefully prepared and weighed on the post office scale in the first place.

The bottom line is this: if in doubt, ask your postmaster. A few minutes spent on the phone or in a face-to-face visit may save you a great deal of time and money.

Mailing classes

Postage rates and regulations change frequently, and therefore the most specific advice this book can provide is that you obtain current rate charts and regulatory materials from your post office.

There are several frequently used direct-mail classes: first class, second class, postcards, third class, and nonprofit bulk rate.

First class mail

The easiest to use but most expensive, first class theoretically provides mail "penetration" to all parts of the continental United States within three days. There are no special sorting requirements, although mailers may obtain a discount for barcoded first class mail, or mail sorted in zip-code or carrier-route order. This is only practical when large quantities of mail are involved, since the cost of presorting by zip code may outweigh the savings for small to medium quantities. The presort option is often used by local department stores, banks, and other firms that have large numbers of customers in only a few zip codes.

Most direct marketers consider first class mail too expensive for mass mailings. In the testing phase they may use first class mail because of its fast penetration, to obtain quick answers about the viability of their offer. In addition, first class mail carries more immediacy than bulk-rate mail, and appears less like advertising to most consumers. First class mail may well be used for mailings to existing customers, both for a prompt turnaround and because the volume of these customers' orders makes the more expensive mailing rate cost effective.

Another reason for mailing first class, at least periodically, is to take advantage of automatic mail forwarding and the return of undeliverable mail to the sender. This is an inexpensive means of helping to keep your list clean.

Second class mail

This category of service is available only to newspaper and magazine publishers who issue their periodicals at least four times yearly. To be eligible, a publication must have a paid or controlled circulation, and feature editorial material—not just advertising. Less expensive than first class mail, this service nonetheless provides relatively fast delivery. This form of mailing is government subsidized to make mailing of publications a viable and affordable venture.

Postcards

Currently, postcards not smaller than $3\text{-}1/2'' \times 5''$ and not larger than $4\text{-}1/2'' \times 6''$ are eligible for the special postcard rate. The cards must also be at least 0.007 inches thick. Because there are color regulations and maximum-thickness regulations as well, it is advisable to check with the post office if you plan to use a non-standard postcard format.

Third class mail

Most direct mail is third class mail. Indeed, in one 10-year span, the annual volume of third class mail more than doubled. This category includes mailings at single-piece rates and bulk mailings. Single-piece rates apply to mailings of less than 200 pieces or of less than 50 pounds. The real savings for mailers are to be had in third class bulk-rate mailings, in which a piece weighing up to 3.3667 ounces can be mailed for approximately two-thirds the first class rate for a one-ounce piece of mail.

A bulk mailing requires the mailer to acquire a bulk-rate permit at the post office where he or she will drop the mail. There is a fee involved. In addition, the mailer must present the mail in zip-code sequence, bundled or bagged according to post office regulations. There are facing (labeling) requirements and other regulations to be followed in order to obtain the substantial bulk rate savings. Your post office and your lettershop will be able to help you conform to proper bulk mailing procedures and your postmaster can give you current rates and application information.

Even greater savings may be obtained by additional computer coding, which saves the post office time in sorting and distributing mail. The barcoding and nine-digit zip code (carrier-route code) system allows mailers to sort and bundle their mail down to the level of the individual mail carrier's route. Large mailers often save money at the post office in this way, since their mail quantities are large enough, and their computer programs sophisticated enough even to computer-generate mailbag tags for carrier-route coding. Smaller mailers may well find the basic third class bulk rate to be the most cost effective, since additional sorting is most likely to involve considerable computer time and cost.

A further point about the bulk-mail permit is that firms need a separate permit for each town from which they mail, unless they qualify for and obtain a "universal indicia." Such an indicia can save money and time, and it also allows for the preprinting of outer envelopes for use at any location. An additional benefit of the universal indicia is that its wording includes the name of the direct mail firm rather than the city of origin. Some mailers obtain the universal indicia strictly for this small promotional benefit.

Nonprofit bulk rate

Nonprofit organizations may take advantage of additional savings when they prepare mail according to third class bulk-rate regulations. A post office bulk rate fee must be paid. Your postmaster can provide information and details about qualifications.

Business reply envelopes and cards

Most tests show that mailers who pay return postage for their customers get a higher level of response than those who require the customer to pay his or her own postage. For this reason, most front-end mailings are accompanied by Business Reply Envelopes or Cards. Bind-in cards in magazines and Free-Standing Inserts provide the same opportunity for prepaid postage.

To qualify for this service, the mailer must obtain a First Class Permit from the post office that will be receiving the incoming mail from customers. In addition, the mailer must provide postage money in the permit account to pay for incoming mail at first class rates plus a service fee. It is essential to keep sufficient funds in this account; otherwise the mailer's incoming mail will be held until he or she has properly funded the account. Besides holding up the receipt of orders, having mail held in this manner destroys the mailer's ability to forecast on the basis of number of orders received each day.

Business Reply Envelopes and Cards must be prepared according to a special set of regulations. This information is readily available at your local post office.

Alternative delivery

Rising postal rates and continued concerns about nondelivery of third class mail have prompted many direct marketers to consider alternative methods of delivery. Many magazine publishers have discovered that they can beat the price of second class mail by using private delivery services. The giant direct marketing firms as well as strong trade groups like the Direct Marketing Association continue to study ways to make alternative methods of delivery efficient, cost effective, and readily acceptable to consumers.

Lettershops

Time was, the lettershop was little more than an envelope-stuffing service, with row upon row of individuals inserting materials into envelopes by hand. In recent years, the science of preparing mail has advanced at an astonishing rate. Today most mailings are prepared so that all of the pieces may be inserted by machine and the envelopes labeled in zip-code sequence by machine, sealed, and bundled for mailing, all with a minimum of human intervention.

Some lettershops still provide hand-insertion services for mailings that are not machine insertable, and there are still cost-effective services available for smaller mailers who do not need six-station inserters and other sophisticated equipment. On the other hand, the range of lettershop services available to today's larger mailers is quite broad, and includes folding, collating, trimming, autotyping, laser printing, and many more.

What to look for in a lettershop

To select a good lettershop, do a bit of detective work. Ask for the recommendations of other mailers whose volume and type of mailings are similar to your own. Visit the booths of lettershop services at trade shows and read their literature to learn about their capacity, specialties, and extra services. Then select several lettershops and visit their premises personally. Consider the following in evaluating each shop.

Neatness and organization. The work of a lettershop is meticulous and detail oriented. Did the lettershop seem to run smoothly?

Equipment. Compare the shop's printed equipment list against your own visual check. Does the firm's capacity match its promotional materials? How many machines were "down" during your visit? How many employees were standing around idle? Did the machines appear to run smoothly? Were there service people available to fix any breakdowns promptly?

Capabilities. If you have need of special services, make sure this lettershop can fulfill them. For instance, most mailings have six inserts or fewer: if yours have more, the lettershop will need multi-station machines to handle them. Do you need a shop with polybag inserters, bursters or folding machines? Will you be using oversized outer envelopes? Do you need to have the lettershop affix seals, labels or plastic cards?

Warehouse. It is essential that the warehouse be clean, dry and well organized. Are inventories stacked neatly? Would your materials stay in mint condition there until they are inserted? Ask to see how materials are recorded when they are received to ensure that your valuable printed matter is placed in inventory with care.

Post office arrangements. Does the lettershop have a good relationship with the post office? Is there a postal official on site? If not, how far is the lettershop from the post office?

Customer relations. Did the lettershop provide you with a list of the things they need to know to make your mailing run smoothly: source of materials, insertion order, codes, etc.?

Timing. Find out how many shifts the lettershop runs each day. They can double or triple their available capacity for you if they are able to run evening and midnight shifts.

Working with the lettershop

There are three things a mailer must do to ensure good service from a lettershop. First, provide materials that are in good condition, packed according to the lettershop's specifications. Second, provide a complete record of what will arrive at the lettershop and how it is to be prepared. Third, keep in communication with the lettershop to make sure things proceed in a timely manner.

Provide materials in good condition

Your printer and computer house will probably provide materials directly to the lettershop according to your orders. Check with the lettershop for instructions about how they prefer to receive materials: how boxes should be labeled, the preferred sizes for cartons, how materials should be stacked, and so on. Improperly boxed and shipped materials may become curled, damp, or otherwise uninsertable while in storage at the shop, and this extra care may therefore yield you savings in time and money.

The service bureau may provide labels, tapes, or other materials to the lettershop. Since labels may be generated in rows of one, four, or any number of other configurations, you have to know the configuration your lettershop needs for smooth machine operation. Also make sure the service bureau knows whether you want Cheshire labels, pressure-sensitive labels, or some other type of label to fit the lettershop's needs.

Provide proper documentation

If you give your lettershop a letter or form which tells what they will be receiving, how it will be marked, where it will come from, and what to do with it, your mailing will be off to a good start. The lettershop also needs the order of insertion you prefer. The following order of insertion is preferred by most mailers, because it allows the reader to see the letter first, while the reply form shows through the die-cut outer envelope.

With outer envelope face down:

1. Letter
2. Brochure
3. Other pieces (premium slip, publisher's note, etc.)
4. Business Reply Envelope
5. Reply form facing backwards so label shows through outer envelope

Keep communicating

It is up to you to follow up on a daily basis and check with the lettershop to make sure things are proceeding smoothly. If they are not, you will have to prompt the printer, envelope supplier, service bureau or other source of the problem to get things back on schedule. This is especially important because mail dates, for the most part, must remain firm. List rentals are protected only for a certain mail date, and you cannot make a casual decision to delay a mailing.

More hints for dealing with lettershops

- Ask the lettershop for a hand-inserted sample of each mailing configuration in your project *before* machine inserting begins. Misunderstandings are much easier to correct at this point. These packages should also be weighed to make sure they meet postal regulations for first or third class mail.
- Get proper documentation for everything you mail through a lettershop. Postal form 3062 tells you the date your material was mailed, postage cost, number mailed, and how mailed: carrier route, five-digit presort, carrier-route presort, etc.
- Supply postage money to the post office or lettershop in plenty of time. The lettershop will not advance postage money. Make out the postage check to the U. S. Postmaster.
- Book your lettershop well in advance when big mailings are coming so that they can alert the proper authorities at the post office. This is especially important in smaller cities where million-piece mailings are rare.
- Design outer envelopes with enough tolerance left to right and top to bottom to ensure that inside pieces will be machine insertable. General guidelines: outer envelope should be at least 1/2" wider and 1/4" taller than the largest inserted piece.
- Art directors should work closely with lettershops when designing unique packages. To make sure pieces are machine insertable, certain rules must be followed. For instance, all pieces must be a minimum thickness and weight. If the outer envelope flap is deeper than 1-1/2" to 1-3/4", it may cause problems in inserting. Also important: each inserted piece must have a closed side for the inserting machine to grab.

BROADCAST PRODUCTION 24

Most direct response radio spots are simple enough to record in a local studio with voice-over talent and perhaps a few sound effects. But from storyboards or script to the finished product, television production may require a more specialized set of creative skills.

Forty years ago, a direct response "pitchman" would stand before a single camera and deliver his sales message from beginning to end. But even many of today's low-budget spots involve multiple cameras, computer graphics and other tricks of the trade.

This chapter will explain the basics of television production for direct response marketers, as well as some tips on selecting and working with a television production house.

Start with the script and storyboard

In the early stages of the creative process, the function of the TV script or storyboard is to sell the commercial's concept. For production purposes, the script and storyboard become the control documents that ensure the creation of a spot that fulfills the client's expectations and stays on budget.

Your storyboard renderings can help pin down such variables as background, costume, number of different shots, lighting, and camera positioning as well as details related to the presenter and other actors. At this stage you should also be able to specify musical backgrounds, sound effects and other needs for the audio portion of the spot.

Remember that simplicity is the key to success for most direct response spots: keeping the backgrounds spare and the number of actors or presenters to a minimum helps retain the focus on the product you're selling.

Since production time is very expensive, having a script that details every shot including camera placement can save on costly experimentation. On the other hand, some directors prefer to leave the specifics a bit looser. What works best for you will depend on your budget and relationship with the director. Here are some of the terms commonly used as abbreviations in television scripts:

Video terms

CUT—Move immediately to the next shot without detlay

DISS—Dissolve: a slower change of scenes in which the old shot "dissolves" into the new

INT—Interior

EXT—Exterior

ECU—Extreme close-up

CU—Close-up

MS or MED—Medium shot

LS—Long Shot

2-SHOT—Shot including two people

BKGRND—Background

FRGRND—Foreground

PAN—Camera moves across

TRACK—Camera moves with action

ZOOM—Shot moves in or out

FADE IN/FADE OUT—Move slowly from black to the scene, or from the scene to black

Audio terms

VO—Voice-over

ANNCR—Announcer

SFX—Sound effect

MUSIC UP—Music dominates

MUSIC UNDER—Background music

MUSIC OUT—Music stops

Take advantage of the visual TV medium

Television is an action medium, and direct marketers will be wise to take advantage of its visual possibilities. Just as a feature film director can open up his production much more than the director of a stage play, the direct marketer should use motion on film to help call the prospect to action.

Adding action to a television spot need not be expensive. Even still photographs can take on a vivid effect when the camera pans across them, or when they are dissolved, one into the other. Affordable computer graphics can bring your logo alive and move your price and phone number onto the screen in interesting and unique ways. When using actors, add some movement to the script: let the actors walk from one part of the set to the other, show the product in use, or change scenes for a before-and-after effect.

In all that you do, make sure that your video and audio work together: if you are saying one thing and doing another, the prospect's confusion may well cause him or her to tune out.

To sharpen your video skills, watch commercials, television shows and feature films from the director's point of view. Watching classic films can be most helpful because the incongruity of styles, manners and dress will help keep you on your toes to notice the director's techniques. In addition, the directors of 50 years ago did not have as many expensive technical tricks of the trade at their disposal as filmmakers do today. From them, you can learn how to get a point across effectively and inexpensively.

Get bids for your television production

Most direct marketing broadcast experts suggest that you obtain several competitive bids for any spot you plan to produce. In addition to comparing prices, it is important to check each production house's samples—in this case their reels of film. Ask each prospective producer to show you a reel of work that is comparable to the job you're planning in terms of budget, product type, generating sales versus leads, production values, etc. Make sure each firm you consider is well grounded in direct marketing—don't be swayed by an impressive set of flashy general advertising spots.

To be sure that your bids are exactly comparable, give each production house the same script or storyboard, and the same instructions. Firms may offer you a guaranteed price or a cost-plus price. With the guaranteed price, you warrant that the commercial you wish to produce is exactly what is presented on your script or storyboard. The production house gives you a firm price for creating that spot, and agrees not to charge you more if they incure overtime or added expenses. The cost-plus price allows for more flexibility if your script or storyboards are not completely firm, or if you want the producer and director to try some different possibilities in the studio. In this case, you should ask for an overall "ball park" price, as well as a breakdown of what hourly or daily charges you will incur during production.

Experts say that the pre- and postproduction periods are crucial to the success of your spot—both in terms of its quality and keeping it on budget. Careful planning on your end is the best way to keep costs to a minimum. During the "shoot" itself, indecision is very expensive, since charges for everyone from the make-up person to the high-priced talent will keep adding up while you decide what to do.

Preproduction includes the selection of costumes, props, location or studio space, music, dancing or other special talents if applicable, and personnel for everything from the on-air talent to the costumer, make-up person, camera operators, sound and lighting specialists, script person and set designer. Postproduction focuses on the editing function, which once again may be simple or complex depending upon how tightly you plan your production.

Variables to consider in planning a TV spot

If your budget is substantial, you may be able to plan on a celebrity presenter, original music, location shoots and other extras for your direct marketing spot. But if you funds are limited, each of these factors needs to be considered very carefully.

Casting

Your producer may do your casting for you, or you may negotiate for the talent yourself. Some direct marketers try for a shortcut, or even massage their own egos by casting themselves or employees in the role of the TV salesperson. However, this is seldom a good idea: to make a sale or obtain a qualified lead in 60 to 120 seconds requires the services of a trained actor or actress—preferably one with substantial direct marketing experience.

Music

Many direct marketers do not require any music at all in their spots—especially those with a straightforward, "me-to-you" pitch. If music is required, you may be able to use stock tunes that your production studio can make available to you. A custom score may be less costly than you think, however: consider contracting with a local source to develop what you need so that the music can complement the spot.

Few direct marketers have gone so far as to commission the creation of their own jingles, but the idea is worth considering. As direct marketing TV spots move toward image-building as well as selling, having your own catchy jingle rolling around in consumers' heads may be a very powerful marketing idea.

Studio versus location

In general, location shooting is more expensive than using a studio. However, if you need a standard location like a homey kitchen or family room, money can be saved by renting a suitable home from its owner rather than building a set for one-time use. Direct marketers selling exotic travel services and other such concepts will need to strongly consider budgeting funds for the location shots that set their products apart. On the other hand, many products to be sold direct via TV can be displayed most effectively in a simple, in-studio demonstration.

Film versus tape

Both film and videotape have their proponents for direct marketing TV spots. Your own time factors, budget and preference will help you make this decision, but here are some pros and cons to consider.

Film adds depth and subtlety to a presentation because of its softness. It is considered a quality medium, and thus it is used extensively for TV spots by general advertisers of packaged goods. Editing film is simpler and less expensive than editing videotape, but film permits slightly less time for sound: 58 seconds out of a 60 second spot. Although 35mm film looks better and is easier to edit than 16mm film, the less expensive 16mm version may offer a compromise for some direct marketers.

Videotape gives the impression of immediacy and reality. It provides sharp focus and good color. With good-quality lighting it can approximate the depth of a film presentation. It is faster and less expensive to shoot than film, and may be viewed immediately, without a time lag for processing. Although some directors are able to edit in the camera with videotape, editing in this medium is a time-consuming and costly proposition. Unlike film, videotape offers a full 60 seconds of sound for each 60 seconds of tape.

A GLOSSARY OF TERMS FOR CREATIVE DIRECT MARKETERS

This glossary provides an overview of the terms and buzzwords used by writers, art directors and production people in direct marketing. It is by no means complete. Several more comprehensive glossaries include those in Richard S. Hodgson's *Direct Mail and Mail Order Handbook*, Bob Stone's *Successful Direct Marketing*, and Robert F. Scott's "Glossary of Copy Preparation and the Graphic Arts" in *Who's Who in Direct Marketing Creative Services*.

ACETATE—The transparent material used to produce overlays on art boards (keylines, mechanicals). These overlays of type or art provide the printer with information regarding various versions of a promotional piece, or material to be printed over the main message.

ACTION DEVICE—A tab, sticker, or other item in or on a mailing package which makes the prospective customer "do something" that leads toward a sale. Example: stickers representing both magazines available for subscriptions and prizes available for winning, within sweepstakes packages from Publishers Clearing House and American Family Publishers.

AIDA—Attention, Interest, Desire, Action: the standard formula for the steps through which direct mail copy should take the prospect in order to induce a response.

ALTERATIONS—Changes which a customer or author makes on a typeset manuscript and which are not due to typographer's error, and therefore are chargeable to the customer.

ART—The general term used for illustrations and photography used in promotional literature; also the material from which printing plates are made.

BACK END—As opposed to front-end activities, back-end activities are those that take place after an initial order is received. This term may also indicate the customer's buying activities with the firm after an initial order.

BANGTAIL ENVELOPE—An envelope which serves a promotional purpose via an extra flap that holds product information, an order form, or both. Often used in credit-card statements, premium notices, and the like, where the "bangtail" promotion rides along free.

BARCODING—Vertical bars and half-bars printed in a proscribed format on the outside of a mail piece to facilitate automated processing. The barcode represents the zip code and, perhaps, the carrier-route to which the piece is addressed. This saves postage for the mailer when done according to post office specifications.

BASTARD SIZE—A nonstandard size of promotional piece which requires special handling and may well cost more than an item of more usual size or configuration.

BOARD—See keyline.

BINDERY—The facility that binds together books, magazines, or pamphlets. "Binding" means wiring with staples, sewing, or plasticizing, depending on the thickness and desired appearance of the bound piece.

BINGO CARD—Deriving its name from its resemblance to this type of game card, the bingo card is a tear-out business reply device inserted in a magazine. The reader simply circles the appropriate numbers on the card to request promotional literature or sales follow-up from advertisers in the publication.

BLACK AND WHITE—Another term for one-color printing, where black type or art on white paper is utilized.

BLEED—Where the printing on a piece goes all the way to the edge of the paper. This is accomplished by printing beyond the margins of the piece and then trimming to the margins.

BLUELINE—A proof taken from the negative from which a printing plate is to be made—the customer's last opportunity to check for errors before printing.

BODY COPY—The main blocks of copy in a printed piece, as opposed to headings and subheads.

BOLDFACE—A heavy-faced type.

BOUNCE BACK—An offer to a customer which comes to him or her along with the fulfillment of an order. Also a name for an offer to an "affinity" buyer, e.g., one to whom you would "bounce back" an offer on a second set of child-subject collector plates after the first purchase of a set on that topic.

BROADSIDE—The name for a brochure that folds out to a flat size of 11″ × 17″ or larger. The "broadside" format lends itself to a dramatic product presentation whereby all elements of the offer may be presented on a single reading surface.

BROCHURE—Also called a circular, pamphlet, or flyer, this is the general term for a descriptive piece of literature used for promotional purposes.

BULLETS—Dots or asterisks used to introduce short, declarative selling statements about a product. Also a term for the statements themselves.

BULK MAIL—Third class mail which comprises a large quantity of identical pieces, sorted and batched by zip code before they reach the post office. They may also be carrier-route coded if the quantity and savings warrant. Bulk-mail privileges require a permit from the post office.

BUSINESS REPLY MAIL—A card or envelope with the indicia of the company receiving the order or inquiry. It allows the inquirer or buyer to mail the card or envelope back postage-free. The user must obtain a permit from the post office to utilize business reply.

CALL OUT—Information used to describe or bring attention to a photograph, diagram or illustration in a promotional piece, usually connected to the applicable part of the visual by a line.

CAMERA-READY ART—See keyline.

CAPTION—Typeset description of an illustration or photograph.

CARD DECK MAILING—A group of postcards that contain promotional information and business reply capabilities, sent to a group of people with certain characteristics (e.g. attorneys, marketing executives, physicians, etc.).

CARRIER ROUTE PRE-SORT—Sorting mail into a nine-digit zipcode sequence so that it is ready to be distributed to individual U.S. Postal Service carriers. This saves additional postage over five-digit zipcode sequencing.

CASH WITH ORDER—A request for payment in full when the order is placed.

CATALOG—A book or booklet whose purpose is to show merchandise and descriptions, and offer the said merchandise for sale via an order form, telephone, or retail outlets.

CENTER SPREAD—The middle two pages of a bound catalog, magazine, or book.

CHARACTER COUNT—The number of letters and spaces that will fill a specific area in a printed piece.

CHESHIRE LABELS—Mailing labels prepared for use with automatic labeling machines. The machines affix the labels individually to the mailing envelope, letter, catalog or order form.

CLIP ART—Illustrations, borders, and other graphics available for artists to use in design and pasteup. The cost of the clip art book itself is usually the only fee, as these designs are not copyrighted.

COATED PAPER—A smooth-finished paper that provides good photographic and printing reproduction. The paper is coated with a thin layer of clay and may be finished to a dull, matte or glossy appearance.

CODE—Also known as a key code or source code, this is a number, series of letters, or other identifying device used to determine the source of an order or inquiry. It may appear on the order form or label, or within the return address or coupon on a space ad.

COLLATERAL MATERIALS—Printed materials used to support a sale or prospective sale, such as instruction manuals, certificates of authenticity, or warranty information.

COLOR KEY PROOF—Also called a chromalin, this is a proof provided by the color separator that shows the approximate expected result of four-color printing.

COLOR SEPARATION—The translation of an original photograph or other piece of artwork into separate plates for four-color printing.

COLOR TRANSPARENCY—A positive photographic image protected by a transparent cover.

COMPILED LIST—As opposed to a list of buyers of a specific product or service, a compiled list does not promise any sort of past buying activity. Rather, it is a group of names gathered from directories, public records, registrations, and other sources which share something in common (such as being marketing professors).

COMPREHENSIVE LAYOUT—Also called a "comp," this is a layout for a prospective printed piece that is complete enough to permit the ordering of finished illustrations, photography, and typesetting.

COMPUTER HOUSE—A firm that offers various computer services, including list computerization and maintenance, merge/purge operations, and computer letters.

COMPUTER LETTER—A letter generated by a computer for the purpose of personalizing a name, address, previous buying record, or something else.

CONDENSED TYPE—A narrowed version of a typeface used to conserve horizontal space.

CONTINUITY PROGRAM—A program that has multiple parts, such as a series of books, records, collector plates, or recipe cards shipped on a monthly, semimonthly, or quarterly basis. The items are unified by a common theme and often by a common price per shipment.

CONTROL—A promotion package or ad that has been proven to perform at a certain level and that is used as the benchmark for future testing.

CONVERSION—Turning a prospect into a lead or buyer, or making a lead into a buyer.

CO-OP MAILING—Two or more (usually noncompetitive) offers combined in one envelope and sent to prospects to cut down the individual mailing, postage, and other costs. See the *Standard Rate and Data Service Consumer Lists Book* for a list of organized co-op mailings.

COPY—A manuscript, typescript, or other written material to be used in preparing a printed piece such as a letter or brochure.

COPYRIGHT—An exclusive right that the law grants to authors and artists, or to the owners of other works.

COPYWRITER'S ROUGHS—Rough layouts prepared in pencil by a copywriter to indicate the relative sizes and positions of elements in an ad, brochure, or other piece of selling literature.

CORNER CARD—The imprint of the sender or the return address on an outer envelope or catalog, which may include the logo or slogan of the mailing firm.

COUPON—The return portion of an ad, which may involve a purchase or a request for more information.

CREATIVE DIRECTOR—The individual responsible for an agency or company's creative product. The creative director may begin as a copywriter, art director, or a combination of both.

CROP—To trim off a portion of a photograph or illustration to eliminate extraneous background and/or make it fit available space.

CUSTOMER LIST—The names owned by a particular firm. These names may be collected through outside solicitation, purchase, or compilation. Also known as a "house list."

DATABASE MARKETING—An automated system used to identify customers and prospects by name, and to use quantifiable information about these people to define the best possible purchasers and prospects for a given offer at a given point in time.

DECOY—To inquire or purchase from a company with the intention of learning about its products and methods of promotion.

DECOY NAME—A "tipoff" name (a false name at your address, perhaps) inserted in a mailing list. Also known as a "seed name," or "salting the list." This assures that the mailer knows when his or her list is being used and how, and helps prevents its unauthorized use.

DEMOGRAPHICS—Social and economic information about people or groups of people, including age, income, educational level, and other data.

DIE CUT—Special cut-out shapes on printed pieces created by using sharp steel dies to cut paper.

DIRECT MAIL—The use of the postal service to send a common message to persons selected by list, zip code, or other means.

DIRECT MARKETING—Obtaining leads or selling by means of a specific message to a specific prospective buyer or inquirer.

DOUBLE-TRUCK SPREAD—A two-page spread.

DUMMY—Any "mock-up" of a printed piece used to test its appearance, weight, readability, or other properties.

DUOTONE—Two plates are combined to create a piece of art with a darker and a lighter shade of ink.

ENAMEL PAPER—A coated stock.

EYEBROW—Also called "overline." A lead-in to the main heading which appears above the heading on a printed piece.

FIRST CLASS MAIL—Mail that may or may not contain individual messages, but which is afforded priority treatment because of the amount of postage it bears.

FLUSH LEFT/FLUSH RIGHT—Typesetting done so that copy lines up on the left side or the right side, with the other side ragged edged.

FOUR-COLOR PROCESS—Also called the full-color process, it indicates the four color plates commonly used in color printing. Their colors are yellow, magenta (red), cyan (blue), and black.

FREELANCER—An independent writer, consultant, artist, or other service provider who is not employed by any one firm, but who works with various firms or agencies.

FREE-STANDING INSERT (FSI)—A promotional piece that is not constrained by the specifications of a publication, but which is inserted loosely into that publication. It allows an advertiser to "ride along" with the daily newspaper, for instance, while still printing full-color material on a good-quality paper stock.

FRONT END—The marketing activities that take place before the entering of an initial sale or lead from a prospect.

GANG RUN—Running several same or similar print jobs together to save money and time.

GIMMICK—A small device that may be tipped onto a direct mail letter, order form, or brochure, to call attention to the piece or dramatize the offer.

GRAPHIC ARTS—The general term for the field of printing, and for creative work on promotional materials (including art, layouts, and photography).

GUARANTEE—The marketer's promise regarding the prospective buyer's satisfaction, and the specific terms of that promise (e.g., replacement guarantee, money-back guarantee, buy-back guarantee, etc.).

HALFTONE—A plate, printed piece, or process involving the shooting of artwork through a lined screen which breaks up the art into a dot pattern.

HEADS/HEADINGS/HEADLINES—A short phrase designed to attract attention to the offer at hand and lead the reader through the body copy and subheads that follow.

HICKIES—Marks on printed material caused by dirt or foreign material during the printing process. They may appear on all pieces or only on a few samples.

HOTLINE NAMES—The most recent buyers on a direct mail list.

HOUSE LIST—See customer list.

INDICIA—Envelope markings substituted for stamps or other regular cancellations in bulk mailings.

INQUIRY—A person who has not yet purchased anything from a firm, but who has been identified via a response to an ad or other solicitation in which he/she asked for (usually free) information.

JOHNSON BOX—Named after Frank Johnson, the copywriter who first used it, this is a boxed-in headline or short lead-in paragraph that appears at the top of a direct mail letter.

KEY CODE—See code.

KEYING—The practice of coding blocks of copy to the pictures they describe by means of a letter or number.

KEYLINE—Also called a mechanical, camera-ready art, or boards. This diagram of copy and art for reproduction is the guide used in making plates and printing a piece.

KILL—Eliminate or delete certain copy, illustration, or whatever is so marked.

KROMECOTE—A very glossy, coated paper stock.

LABEL—A piece of paper (it may be pressure-sensitive or not) that carries the name and address (and possibly an identification code) of a prospect or previous buyer. It is affixed to an order form, letter, or outer envelope for mailing purposes.

LAID PAPER STOCK—A paper, often used for letterhead printing, which is not woven but appears to be.

LAYOUT—A rendering of a proposed printed piece, indicating positions for headings, copy, art, and borders. The term may also indicate color treatments.

LEADING—The space that appears between printed lines. Some leading is necessary for readability.

LETTERHEAD—The stationery used by a particular business, printed to identify that firm via a logo, name, and address.

LETTERPRESS—A traditional printing method in which the print area is raised above the nonprint area so that ink rollers touch the portion that becomes the printed image.

LETTERSHOP—The firm that handles the labeling of order cards and envelopes and the insertion and mailing of direct mail solicitations.

LIGHT TABLE—A frosted glass table with lights underneath that makes it easy to view transparencies.

LINE DRAWINGS—Solid-black-line artwork that does not require halftone reproduction.

LIST—The names and addresses of prospects, customers, or both who have something in common, whether it be previous buying habits, occupation, or other attributes. Also known as a file.

LIST BROKER—A professional counselor to renters of direct mail lists. The broker provides recommendations on list rental for specific propositions, and may be made privy to the results so that he or she can help plan future testing and roll-outs. The broker also helps expedite the receipt of lists, merge/purge operations, and other list-related matters.

LITHOGRAPHY—A printing process that involves the use of plates made from photographs. Offset lithography is simply called "offset" in most cases.

LOAD-UP—On continuity propositions, a system whereby the customer is sent the bulk of product at once, to save on postage and packaging costs. Generally, the customer is then asked to remit the monthly or semimonthly fee using payment coupons from a booklet until the entire set is paid for.

LOGOTYPE—Also called logo. The trademark or signature of a company, which may simply be indicated by a certain typeface, or by artwork.

MAIL DATE—The day agreed upon between a list renter and list owner as the "drop date" for a specific mailing at the post office.

MAILER—A firm which does direct mailing (lettershop), or a carton in which products are shipped. Also a term for a direct mail piece.

MAIL-ORDER BUYER—A person with a history of frequent and recent purchases by mail, and thus a good prospect for a new mail-order proposition.

MECHANICAL—See keyline.

MERGE/PURGE—A computer process whereby lists may be merged together to facilitate zip-code sequencing and the testing of segments, and can be "purged" of duplicate names, pander names, and other undesirable names, or names that are to be saved for later mailing.

MOONLIGHTER—A freelancer who is also employed regularly by a single firm.

MULTIPLE BUYER—Also called a multi-buyer or repeat buyer. A person who has purchased more than once from a firm, on different occasions.

NEGATIVE OPTION—Used by many book and record clubs, this calls for the customer to send back a response if he or she does not want to purchase a monthly selection. The terms must be spelled out carefully and agreed to by the customer, under Federal Trade Commission regulations.

NESTING—A procedure designed to cut costs and save time in the mailing/insertion process. One piece of literature is placed inside another before insertion into an envelope, thus cutting the number of positions necessary on the inserting machine. The procedure may also be used to nest an appropriate order form with selling or other literature.

NET DOWN—The quantity of names left after a merge/purge eliminates duplicates.

NEWSPRINT—A low grade of paper used chiefly for newspapers. Made from groundwood pulp and sulphite pulp and finished by machine.

NEWS RELEASE—An announcement sent to newspapers, magazines, television and radio stations, or other media with news about a person, event, product or service.

OFFER—The specified buying terms presented to the prospect, including price, payment options, delivery terms, and premiums.

OFFSET PAPER—A type of paper suited to offset lithography. It usually refers to a lower grade of offset lithography paper, as opposed to a more expensive or coated stock that might also be used for offset printing.

ONE UP—Printing one impression of a printing job at a time. Also two up, three up, four up, etc.

OUT OF REGISTER—Lack of alignment of colors that are to be printed one right over the other, resulting in "hanging" dot patterns.

OVERLINE—A phrase or heading which appears above the main headline on a brochure or other promotional piece. Also called a "kicker."

PACKAGE—The entire direct mail solicitation, typically including the outer envelope, letter, brochure, order card, Business Reply Envelope, and whatever other elements may be included.

PACKAGE INSERT—A promotional offer that is included in the shipment of a product. It may be from the firm shipping the product or from a different firm, via a fee or royalty arrangement. See the *Standard Rate and Data Service Consumer Lists Book* for available package insert arrangements.

PACKAGE TEST—A test of a direct mail element or elements within a given package, against the control package.

PAGINATION—Determining how type will break from page to page, or how catalog products will appear from page to page.

PANTONE MATCHING SYSTEM (PMS) COLORS—Standard, numbered shades and colors that are available to printers in premixed form and may be selected when a specific background or accent color is desired.

PASS-ALONG—The factor of additional readers for a direct mail piece or ad, obtained when the recipient passes the piece along to others. Self-mailers are considered best adapted among the direct mail formats for obtaining pass-along readers.

PASTE-UP—The gluing or waxing down of art and type on a keyline in preparation for platemaking.

PERSONALIZATION—The addition of the name or other individual information about a prospect or buyer to a promotion. Often done by computer.

PHOTOSTAT—Also called a stat. A high-quality reproduction of camera-ready art which may be used for offset printing.

PICA—A measurement of lines of type. There are six picas to an inch.

PICK UP—An indication that a designated piece of copy or art will be reused without modifications.

PIGGYBACK—An offer that "rides along free" with another offer.

PLATES—Short for printing plates, which are used to separate image from nonimage material during the printing process.

POINT—A unit of measurement for type, with 72 points to an inch of height.

POSITIVE OPTION—A system whereby, unlike a negative option, the customer must send back a reply if he or she *does* want merchandise. It is used for some club appeals.

PREMIUM—An offer of a free item to the buyer as an incentive to purchase or try a product.

PRESS PROOF—A proof made on a regular press after color separations are complete, and used to check color before the full run is made.

PRESS RELEASE—See news release.

PRESSURE-SENSITIVE LABELS—Also called peel-off labels. These are address labels often used where one label needs to serve both the addressing and return function. They may be removed from the outside of a catalog or envelope and placed on the ordering device.

PROGRESSIVES—Also called progs. A set of proofs that can be separated to show each color on its own, and put back together to see how the four colors combine.

PROOF—A reproduction of art and/or type used for proofreading, editing, and checking for layout errors.

PROSPECT—The name of a person who is seen as a potential buyer for a product, but who has not yet inquired or purchased from a firm.

PSYCHOGRAPHICS—Lifestyle or attitude characteristics, as opposed to the merely statistical indicators of demographics.

PUBLICITY—Any form of nonpaid promotion in the media.

PUBLISHER'S LETTER—Also called a "lift letter." An auxiliary letter in a mailing that keys in on a specific selling point and/or answers objections to help close the sale.

RECENCY/FREQUENCY/MONETARY—The three criteria by which a name on a rental list is evaluated. How recent was the last purchase, how often has the individual purchased, and how large is the average order.

REFERRAL—Also called "friend of a friend" or "the buddy system." This is a plan whereby the seller asks customers or prospects to identify friends who are likely to be interested in the same kind of merchandise or offer. The customer may be offered a premium for doing so.

REPLY CARD—Also called "Business Reply Card" or "BRC." An order card or inquiry card which may be dropped into the mail post-paid, since it bears the sender's address and postal indicia.

RESPONSE RATE—The percentage of orders per thousand mailed that results from a mailing or ad insertion in a publication.

ROLLOUT—A scheduled mailing of the remaining names in a list universe, if a list test is successful and a possible subsequent, larger test validates the initial results.

ROP—Run of paper or run of press. A newspaper space placement that is within the regular editorial sections of the newspaper, as opposed to a free-standing insert.

ROUGH—The first draft of a copy or layout.

SCREEN—A grid used in a special camera to create halftone prints.

SELF-MAILER—A one-piece, direct mail item that is not a catalog, but which does not come in an envelope.

SERIF—A typeface featuring lines or strokes that project from each character. SANS SERIF type does not have these flourishes.

SHEET-FED PRESS—An offset press that prints on sheets of paper which are fed into the press one at a time. Usually used for smaller quantity and/or higher quality printing.

SIGNATURE—A section of a catalog or book which may be eight or more pages in length. Catalogs may be repositioned by signature to simulate a new look for remailing.

SILVERPRINT—See blueline.

SOLO MAILING—A solicitation for a single product or product line.

SOURCE CODE—See code.

SPLIT RUN—Two versions of an ad run in the same publication via a system whereby every other copy of the publication carries one ad and the next in line carries the other. This allows for statistically accurate testing.

STANDARD RATE AND DATA SERVICE (SRDS)—Chicago-area firm that publishes periodical guides to the users of Business Publications, Canadian Ad Rates, Card Deck Rates and Data, Community Publications, Consumer/Agri-Media, Direct Mail Lists, TV Network Rates, Newspaper Rates, Print Media, Spot Radio, Spot TV, and other data.

STET—A proofreader's word which, when applied to a word or phrase of copy that has been marked out, means "leave it as it was."

STORYBOARDS—A series of drawings created to provide a rough idea of the visuals planned for a television spot. The corresponding audio is displayed below each drawing.

STUFFER—An enclosure in a package, statement, newspaper or other medium for the purpose of selling a product.

SWIPE FILE—The direct mail packages, space ads and other samples of competitive advertising literature saved by a copywriter or art director for inspiration in developing new ideas.

TEASER—Also called an envelope teaser. The copy on the outside of an envelope whose purpose is to move the reader to open it and read the offer inside. Also refers to a teaser ad: an enticing ad that encourages the reader to watch for further developments in later-running ads.

TESTING—A preliminary mailing or ad insertion that determines the relative chances of success of a given proposition in a given medium.

THUMBNAILS—Miniature layout sketches used to give a general idea of what a direct mail piece will look like.

TIP-ON—Something glued to a direct mail letter, order card, or other printed piece. It may be a gimmick or an action device.

TRADE PUBLICATION—A magazine intended for those involved in a specific trade or profession.

TRAFFIC BUILDER—A direct mail piece that does not have the solicitation of a direct order as its main goal, but rather is meant to bring customers into a retail store.

UNIVERSE—The total number of people who fit a certain set of characteristics. Also, the total number of people on a specific mailing list.

UPCHARGE—A vendor's additions to the price initially quoted. Should be discussed with the customer before they are added to the bill.

UP FRONT—Getting the payment for a product or service before it is shipped.

VALIDATION—A mailing that takes place after an initial test, to verify the results before a rollout.

VELOX—A reproduction of an original piece of art or photo. It may be line art, a halftone, or a combination of the two.

WEB PRESS—An offset printing press that has a rotary action and uses large rolls of paper. It is used for larger quantity printing (usually 50,000 pieces and up).

WINDOW ENVELOPE—An envelope with a see-through area that allows for a labeled reply device and which may also serve as the address mechanism. The window is die cut, and may remain open or be covered with a see-through material.

ZIP-CODE SEQUENCE—The arrangement of names and addresses on a list, beginning with 00000 and progressing through 99999. This provides proper sorting for the third class postal bulk-rate mail. It may go further, to a nine-digit number, for carrier-route coding and even greater savings at mailing time.

PERIODICALS AND BOOKS

Periodicals

The following periodicals will be of interest to the creative direct marketer. Their addresses and phone numbers are subject to change.

Advertising Age—Published by Crain Communications, 740 Rush Street, Chicago, IL 60611. Weekly. (312) 649-5200

ADWEEK—Published by ASM Communications, 49 East 21st St., New York, NY 10010. Weekly; in regional editions for New England, East, Southeast, Midwest, Southwest, and West. (212) 529-5500

American Demographics—Published by American Demographics, Inc., P.O. Box 68, Ithaca, NY 14851. Monthly. (607) 273-6343

Business Publications Rates and Data—Published by Standard Rate and Data Service, Inc., 3004 Glenview Road, Wilmette, IL 60091. Monthly. (708) 256-6067

Card Deck Rates and Data—Published by Standard Rate and Data Service, 3004 Glenview Road, Wilmette, IL 60091. Semiannually. (708) 256-6067

Catalog Age—Published by Hanson Publishing Group, Inc., P.O. Box 4949, 911 Hope Street, Six River Bend Center, Stamford, CT 06907. Monthly. (203) 358-9900

Catalog Business—Published by Mill Hollow Corporation, 19 W. 21st Street, New York, NY 10010. Monthly. (212) 741-2095

Consumer Magazine Rates and Data—Published by Standard Rate and Data Service, Inc., 3004 Glenview Road, Wilmette, IL 60091. Monthly. (708) 256-6067

Direct—Published by Hanson Publishing Group, Inc., P.O. Box 4949, 911 Hope Street, Six River Bend Center, Stamford, CT 06907. Monthly. (203) 358-9900

Direct Mail Lists Rates and Data—Published by Standard Rate and Data Service, Inc., 3004 Glenview Road, Wilmette, IL 60091. Bi-monthly. (708) 256-6067

Direct Marketing—Published by Hoke Communications, Inc., 224 Seventh Street, Garden City, NY 11530. Monthly. (516) 746-6700

DM News—Published by Mill Hollow Corporation, 19 W. 21st Street, New York, NY 10010. Twice Monthly. (212) 741-2095

Fund Raising Management—Published by Hoke Communications, Inc., 224 Seventh Street, Garden City, NY 11530. Monthly. (516) 746-6700

Graphic Design: USA—Published by Kaye Publishing Corp., 120 E. 56th Street, New York, NY 10022. (212) 759-8813

Newspaper Rates and Data—Published by Standard Rate and Data Service, Inc., 3004 Glenview Road, Wilmette, IL 60091. Monthly. (708) 256-6067

Print Media Production Data—Published by Standard Rate and Data Service, Inc., 3004 Glenview Road, Wilmette, IL 60091. Quarterly. (708) 256-6067

Who's Mailing What—Published by Who's Mailing What! Inc., P.O. Box 8180, Stamford, CT 06905. Monthly. (203) 329-1996

Books and Tapes

The following is a short list of some of the books and cassette tapes this author has found especially helpful in formulating direct marketing creative strategies. It is by no means complete. For a good survey of the direct marketing books and monographs currently available, contact the Direct Marketing Association, Inc., 11 West 42nd Street, New York, NY 10036. (212) 768-7277. Ask for "The Source: For Books, Reports & Directories for Direct Marketers." DMA offers books at special prices for its members; at retail for nonmembers.

Building A Mail Order Business: A Complete Manual For Success by William A. Cohen. 2nd Edition. Published by John Wiley & Sons, New York.

Business-to-Business Direct Marketing by Tracy Emerick and Bernard Goldberg. Published by the Direct Marketing Institute, Hampton, NH.

Catalog Marketing: The Complete Guide to Profitability in the Catalog Business by Katie Muldoon. 2nd Edition. Published by American Management Association, New York.

Class: A Guide Through the American Status System by Paul Fussell. Published by Summit Books, New York.

Confessions of an Advertising Man by David Ogilvy. Published by Atheneum, New York.

The Creative Organization, edited with an introduction by Gary A. Steiner. Published by The University of Chicago Press, Chicago.

Direct Mail and Mail Order Handbook by Richard S. Hodgson. 3rd Edition. Published by Dartnell Corp., Chicago.

Direct Mail Copy That Sells! by Herschell Gordon Lewis. Published by Prentice-Hall, Inc., Englewood Cliffs, New Jersey.

Direct Marketing Design: The Graphics of Direct Mail & Direct Response Marketing by the Direct Marketing Creative Guild. Published by the Direct Marketing Creative Guild, New York.

The Direct Marketing Handbook, edited by Edward L. Nash. Published by McGraw-Hill, Inc., New York.

The Direct Marketing Market Place by Edward Stern. Published by Hilary House Publishers, Hewlett Harbor, NY.

Direct Marketing: Strategy, Planning, Execution by Edward L. Nash. Published by McGraw-Hill, Inc., New York.

Direct Marketing Success by Freeman F. Gosden, Jr. Published by John Wiley & Sons, New York.

DMA Statistical Fact Book. Published by the Direct Marketing Association, Inc., New York.

Eicoff on Broadcast Direct Marketing by Al Eicoff. Published by NTC Business Books, Lincolnwood, IL.

Elements of Direct Mail by Martin Baier. Published by McGraw-Hill, Inc., New York.

Fundamentals of Copy and Layout by Albert C. Book and C. Dennis Schick. 2nd Edition. Published by NTC Business Books, Lincolnwood, IL.

Getting Back to the Basics of Public Relations and Publicity by Matthew J. Culligan and Dolph Greene. Published by Crown Publishers, New York.

The Greatest Direct Mail Sales Letters of All Time by Richard Hodgson. Published by Dartnell Corp., Chicago.

Growing A Business by Paul Hawken. Published by Simon and Schuster, New York.

Handbook for Public Relations Writing by Thomas Bivins. Published by NTC Business Books, Lincolnwood, IL.

Herschell Gordon Lewis on the Art of Writing Copy by Herschell Gordon Lewis. Published by Prentice-Hall, Englewood Cliffs, NJ.

How to Build a Multi-million Dollar Catalog Mail-order Business by Someone Who Did by Lawson Traphagen Hill. Published by Prentice-Hall, Englewood Cliffs, NJ.

How to Create Successful Catalogs by Maxwell Sroge. Published by NTC Business Books, Lincolnwood, IL.

How to Start and Operate a Mail-order Business by Julian L. Simon. 4th Edition. Published by McGraw-Hill, Inc., New York.

John Caples, Adman by Gordon White. Published by NTC Business Books, Lincolnwood, IL. (Out of print).

Marketing for Nonprofit Organizations by Philip Kotler. Published by Prentice-Hall, Inc., Englewood Cliffs, NJ.

The Membership Mystique by Richard P. Trenbeth. Published by the Fund-Raising Institute, Ambler, PA.

My Life In Advertising & Scientific Advertising by Claude C. Hopkins. Published by NTC Business Books, Lincolnwood, IL.

Ogilvy on Advertising by David Ogilvy. Published by Crown Publishers, Inc., New York.

The 100 Greatest Advertisements—Who Wrote Them and What They Did by Julian Lewis Watkins. Published by NTC Business Books, Lincolnwood, IL. (Out of print).

The Practical Handbook and Guide to Focus Group Research by Thomas L. Greenbaum. Published by Lexington Books, Lexington, MA.

Profitable Direct Marketing by Jim Kobs. 2nd Edition. Published by NTC Business Books, Lincolnwood, IL.

Response Television: Combat Advertising of the 1980s by John Witek. Published by NTC Business Books, Lincolnwood, IL.

Secrets of Successful Direct Mail by Richard Benson. Published by NTC Business Books, Lincolnwood, IL.

Selling by Mail by John W. Graham and Susan K. Jones. Published by Charles Scribner's Sons, New York.

Successful Direct Marketing Methods by Bob Stone. 4th Edition. Published by NTC Business Books, Lincolnwood, IL.

Systematic Approach to Advertising Creativity by Stephen Baker. Published by McGraw-Hill, Inc., New York.

A Technique for Producing Ideas by James Webb Young. Published by NTC Business Books, Lincolnwood, IL.

Tested Advertising Methods by John Caples. Published by Prentice-Hall, Inc., Englewood Cliffs, NJ.

A Whack on the Side of the Head by Roger von Oech, Ph.D. Published by Warner Books, New York.

Who's Who in Direct Marketing Creative Services. Published by WMW! Books, Stamford, CT.

Winning Direct Response Advertising by John Throckmorton. Published by Prentice-Hall, Inc., Englewood Cliffs, NJ.

Cassette Tapes

NEWSTRACK® Advertising Classics with highlights from the writings of Leo Burnett, Rosser Reeves, Albert D. Lasker, Claude C. Hopkins, Maxwell Sackheim, Alvin Eicoff, Fairfax M. Cone, and David Ogilvy. Published by Newstrack®, Englewood, CO.

A Whack a Kick and a Poke: How to be More Creative by Roger von Oech. Published by Nightingale-Conant Corporation, Chicago, IL.

ASSOCIATIONS AND CLUBS

By joining one or more direct marketing associations, creative people come in contact with experienced professionals, and individuals who are breaking new ground in creative strategy. Seminars by experts will yield new ideas. Networking with people from other agencies and firms will keep you up to date with advances they are making. Informal talks with vendors, freelancers and consultants may make you aware of new sources of help.

As a member of one or more of these associations, you will be on mailing lists that will enable you to receive information about services, seminars, publications, books, and other opportunities pertaining to the direct marketing field.

This list includes some of the most prominent direct marketing associations that will be of interest to creative people. There are also local and regional clubs located in San Diego and Orange County, California; Denver Colorado; six regions of Florida; Atlanta, Georgia; Honolulu, Hawaii; Indianapolis, Indiana; Louisville, Kentucky; Baltimore, Maryland; Detroit, Michigan; Lincoln/Omaha, Nebraska; New York, Hudson Valley, Upstate, and Long Island, New York; Cincinnati, Dayton and Cleveland, Ohio; Tulsa, Oklahoma; Portland, Oregon; Memphis, Tennessee; North and Houston, Texas; Vermont/New Hampshire; Seattle and Spokane, Washington; and Ontario, Canada. In addition, there are Women's Direct Response Groups in New York, Chicago, and Washington, D.C.; and the Direct Marketing Creative Guild is located in New York City. Contact addresses and phone numbers for all of these clubs are subject to change as their yearly officers begin new terms; phone the Direct Marketing Association's Clubs/Associations Network for current information.

The following clubs and associations have permanent contact addresses.

INTERNATIONAL

Direct Marketing Association, Inc.
6 East 43rd Street
New York, New York, 10017
(212) 689-4977

DMA is the largest and oldest international trade organization in the direct marketing field. It represents users, creators, and suppliers of direct mail advertising and other direct marketing techniques. It has nearly 7,000 individual members representing more than 3500 companies in the United States and 45 other countries. The organization's dues levels are dependent upon the size of the firm and the number of members who will join DMA.

ARIZONA

Phoenix Direct Marketing Club
c/o Mrs. Ruth L. Shea, Administrator
P.O. Box 8756
Phoenix, Arizona 85066
(602) 268-5237

CALIFORNIA

Direct Marketing Club of Southern California
c/o Ms. Jan Nathan, Executive Director
2401 Pacific Coast Highway, #109
Hermosa Beach, California 90254
(213) 374-7499

San Francisco Ad Club
c/o Ms. Mary Arnold, Executive Director
150 Post Street #325
San Francisco, California 94108
(415) 986-3878

DISTRICT OF COLUMBIA

Direct Marketing Association of Washington
Suite 300, 655 15th Street, N.W.
Washington, DC 20005
(202) 347-MAIL

ILLINOIS

Chicago Association of Direct Marketing
c/o Natalie Holmes, Executive Director
600 S. Federal, Suite 400
Chicago, Illinois 60605
(312) 922-6222

MASSACHUSETTS

New England Direct Marketing Association
c/o Ms. Pam Jennings, Administrative Coordinator
1357 Washington Street
West Newton, MA 02165

MINNESOTA

Midwest Direct Marketing Association
9925 Lyndale Avenue South, Suite 657
Minneapolis, Minnesota 55420

MISSOURI

Direct Marketing Association of St. Louis
c/o Ms. Pauline R. Battiste, Executive Director
12686 Lonsdale Drive
St. Louis, Missouri 63044
(314) 291-7405

Kansas City Direct Marketing Association
c/o Miss Gail Field, Administrator
P.O. Box 1133
Kansas City, Missouri 64141
(816) 472-0880

NEW YORK

Direct Marketing Idea Exchange, Inc.
c/o Mr. Nat Ross
50 East 10th Street
New York, New York 10003

PENNSYLVANIA

Philadelphia Direct Marketing Association
c/o Ms. Arlene Claffee, Staff Assistant
190 S. Warner Road, Suite 100
Wayne, PA 19087
(215) 688-5040

WISCONSIN

Wisconsin Direct Marketing Club
c/o Ms. Ann Wells, Executive Director
1404 South 89th Street
Milwaukee, Wisconsin 53214
(414) 453-9004

CODE OF ETHICS
FOR DIRECT MARKETERS

Although there are some unethical operators in the direct response field, firms that are in the business for the "long haul" adhere to the rules of the Federal Trade Commission and their individual industries, such as state regulations on the selling of insurance. To provide guidance for their members, direct marketing organizations have established their own sets of ethics and self-regulatory rules.

For a very complete list of regulations and ethics, consult the Direct Marketing Association's *Fact Book on Direct Response Marketing.* For an overview of what is considered accepted business practice, here is the Code of Ethics of the Chicago Association of Direct Marketing (CADM):

We hold that a responsibility of the CADM to its members and to all individuals and firms who use, create, produce or supply material and lists for direct response marketing is to be a constructive and useful force in business and the economy in general.

We further hold that, to discharge this responsibility, they should recognize their obligation to the public, the medium they represent, and to each other.

To this end, CADM requires the observance of this Code of Ethics as being in the best interests of the public, all advertising and of direct response marketing users, creators, producers and suppliers.

This code is intended to serve as a benchmark for the kind of business conduct which experience has shown to be wise, foresighted, and constructive.

Because we believe dishonest, misleading, immoral, salacious or offensive communications make enemies for all advertising/marketing including direct response marketing, we require observance of the Code and its standards, by all members of CADM.

1. Direct response marketers should make their offers clear and honest. They should not misrepresent a product, service, publication or program and should not use misleading, partially true or exaggerated statements. All descriptions and promises should be in accordance with actual conditions, situations and circumstances existing at the time a promotion is made. Direct response marketers should operate in accordance with the Better Business Bureau's Basic Principles contained in the BBB Code of Advertising and be cognizant of and adhere to the postal laws and regulations, and all other laws governing advertising and transaction of business by mail, telephone, and the print and broadcast media.

2. Direct response marketers should not disparage any person or group on grounds of sex, race, color, creed, age or nationality.

3. Solicitations, regardless of medium used, should not contain vulgar, immoral, profane or offensive matter nor promote the sale of pornographic material or other matter not acceptable for advertising on moral grounds.

4. Photographs and art work representing or implying representation of a product or service or fund raising program for nonprofit organizations should be faithful reproductions of the product, service or aid offered by the fund raising program. All should be current and truly representative. All descriptions and promises should be in accordance with actual conditions, situations and circumstances existing at the time of the promotion. Photographs and art work representing or implying situations related to a product, service or program should be in accord with the facts. If models are used, clear disclosure of that fact should be made in immediate conjunction with the portrayal.

5. If laboratory test data are used in advertising, they should be competent as to source and methodology. Reference to laboratory test data should not be used in support of claims which distort or fail to disclose the true test results.

6. Direct response marketers should not use unsupported or inaccurate statistical data or testimonials originally given for products or services other than those offered, or testimonials making statements or conclusions known to be incorrect. If testimonials are used, they should contain no misstatement of facts or misleading implications and should reflect the current opinion of the author.

7. Direct response marketers should not make exaggerated

price comparisons, exaggerated claims on discounts or savings, or employ fictitious prices.

8. Direct response marketers should sufficiently identify themselves in every solicitation to enable the consumer to contact them.

9. Solicitations that are likely to be mistaken for bills or invoices should not be used.

10. Products should be distributed only in a manner that will provide reasonable safeguards against possibilities of injury.

11. Direct response marketers should be prepared to make prompt delivery of orders. Any delay should be promptly reported to the customer informing him of his right to consent to the delay or obtain a refund.

12. The terms and conditions of guarantee should be clearly and specifically set forth in immediate conjunction with the guarantee offer. Performance guarantees should be limited to the reasonable capabilities and qualities of the product or service advertised.

13. When products or services are offered on a satisfaction guaranteed or money-back basis, any refunds requested should be made promptly. In an unqualified offer of refund or replacement, the customer's preference shall prevail.

14. Direct response marketers should not make offers which purport to require a person to return a notice that he does not wish to receive further merchandise in order to avoid liability for the purchase price, unless all the conditions are first made clear in the initial offer that is accepted by the purchaser by means of a bona fide purchase order. (For detailed specifications regarding Negative Option Plans, see Federal Trade Commission regulations.)

15. Unordered merchandise should not be sent unless such merchandise is clearly and conspicuously represented to be "free" and the recipient clearly informed of his unqualified right to treat it as a gift, and to do with it as he sees fit, at no cost or obligation to him.

16. A product or service which is offered without cost or obligation to the recipient may be unqualifiedly described as "free." "Free" may also be used conditionally where the offer requires the recipient to purchase some other product or service, provided all terms and conditions are accurately and conspicuously disclosed in immediate conjunction with the use of the term "free" and the product or service required to

be purchased is not increased in price or decreased in quality or quantity.

17. Direct response marketers should not use or permit to be used unfair, misleading, deceptive or abusive methods for collecting money owed by delinquent accounts.

18. Direct response marketers who use the telephone to solicit sales or donations should not tape conversations without a beeping device or consent.

19. All telephone contacts should be made during reasonable hours.

20. Direct response marketers should not make telephone calls in the guise of research or a survey when the intent is to sell.

21. Direct response marketers using the telephone should make every effort not to accept orders from minors without the consent of parents.

22. Conscientious efforts should be made not to call telephone subscribers who have unlisted or unpublished telephone numbers unless a prior relationship exists, and telemarketers should remove that person's name from their contact lists when requested to do so.

23. Direct response marketers should make no percentage or commission arrangements whereby any person or firm assisting or participating in a fund-raising activity is paid a fee proportionate to the funds raised, nor should they solicit for nonexistent or nonfunctioning organizations.

24. Direct response marketers who sell instruction, catalogs, or merchandise-for-resale or sell or rent lists should not use misleading or deceptive statements with respect to the earning possibilities, lack of risk, or ease of operation.

25. Those who rent, exchange or purchase lists should make every effort to ascertain the origin, current ownership and market profile of such lists in the interests of directing their promotions only to those segments of the public most likely to be interested in their causes or to have a use for their product or services.

26. Those who permit the outside use of their lists should at all times be aware it is not in the best interests of the public or of themselves to allow their lists to be used by organizations that do not observe the CADM Code of Ethics.

27. Direct response marketers who rent or exchange their lists should offer to all those whose names appear on such lists the option to have their names not included when rental or ex-

changes are made. They should also make conscientious efforts to remove names from their customer or donor lists when requested either directly or in accordance with the DMA Mail Preference Service.

28. No lists should be used in violation of the lawful rights of the list owner; and any such misuse should be brought to the attention of the lawful owner.

INDEX